Medieval Europe
A Short History

Medieval Europe
A Short History

SIXTH EDITION

C. Warren Hollister
University of California
Santa Barbara

McGraw-Hill Publishing Company
New York St. Louis San Francisco Auckland Bogotá Caracas
Hamburg Lisbon London Madrid Mexico Milan Montreal New Delhi
Oklahoma City Paris San Juan São Paulo Singapore Sydney Tokyo Toronto

This book was set in Palatino by the College Composition Unit
in cooperation with Monotype Composition Company.
The editors were Christopher J. Rogers and Peggy C. Rehberger;
the production supervisor was Leroy A. Young.
The cover was designed by Amy Becker.
Maps by Russell H. Lenz and John V. Morris.
R. R. Donnelley & Sons Company was printer and binder.

Cover Photo: Giraudon/Art Resource, N.Y.

Illustration credits appear on page 361.
Copyrights are included on this page by reference.

MEDIEVAL EUROPE

A Short History

2 3 4 5 6 7 8 9 0   DOC   DOC   9 5 4 3 2 1 0

ISBN   0-07-557141-2

Library of Congress Cataloging-in-Publication Data

Hollister, C. Warren (Charles Warren), (date).
    Medieval Europe: a short history/C. Warren Hollister.—6th ed.

      p.   cm.
    Includes bibliographical references.
    ISBN 0-07-557141-2
    I. Europe —History—476—1492.   2. Middle Ages—History.
    I. Title
    D 117.H6   1990
    940.1—dc20   89-28323

About the Author

C. Warren Hollister, Professor of History and Chair of Medieval Studies at the University of California, Santa Barbara, received his B.A. from Harvard and his M.A. and Ph.D. from UCLA. A Fellow of the Medieval Academy of America, the Royal Historical Society (London), and the Medieval Academy of Ireland, he served as Vice-President for Teaching and 1984 Program Chair of the American Historical Association, President of the Pacific Coast Conference on British Studies, Fellow of Merton College, Oxford, and of the Australian National University, Co-Chair of the University of California Press Editorial Board, and Chair of the National Development Committee for the College Board Advanced Placement Test in European History. He is currently President of the International Charles Homer Haskins Society, Immediate Past President of the North American Conference on British Studies, President-Elect of the Medieval Association of the Pacific, and Vice-President/President-Elect of the American Historical Association, Pacific Coast Branch.

Professor Hollister's twelve books have run through more than thirty editions and have been translated into a number of languages. He is also the author of more than forty scholarly articles on medieval history and co-author of a children's fantasy. He serves or has served on the editorial boards of *Albion*, the *American Historical Review*, the *Journal of British Studies*, the *Journal of Medieval History*, *Medieval Prosopography*, and *Viator*. He has been honored with Guggenheim, NEH, Fulbright, ACLS, SSRC, and American Philosophical Society Fellowships. He has lectured at numerous colleges and universities across America and at such overseas universities as Oxford, Cambridge, Ghent, Leyden, Utrecht, London, Manchester, Newcastle-upon-Tyne, Exeter, Sydney, Auckland, Tasmania, Melbourne, Western Australia, Bologna, and Moscow.

Among Professor Hollister's other honors are the UC Santa Barbara Faculty Research Lectureship, the campuswide UCSB Faculty Teaching Prize for 1983, the 1987 Denis Bethell Memorial Lectureship of the Medieval Academy of Ireland (Dublin), the 1988 Wilkinson Memorial Lectureship of the University

v

of Toronto, the Triennial Book Prize of the Conference on British Studies, the E. Harris Harbison National Award for Distinguished Teaching (Princeton), and the Walter D. Love Memorial Prize for the best scholarly article of 1980 in the field of British history or literature.

To My Father
and in Memory of My Mother

Contents

PART 3
The Late Middle Ages:
The Ordeal of Transition

List of Maps

List of Illustrations

Preface

During the summer vacation between my sophomore and junior years of college, as I was reading the abridgement of Toynbee's *A Study of History* (amidst more sophomoric activities), it struck me that the culture that surrounds and shapes us is a product of its medieval past. My friends responded to this thrilling discovery with a most depressing apathy. One of them remarked that he thought it was weird to spend one's time studying dead people. Nevertheless, I took the eminently sensible step of changing my major from Political Science to History and enrolled in every medieval history course that Harvard University offered. Apart from a short and unpleasant term in the armed forces, and an even shorter exposure to the deadly tedium of law school, I have been absorbed in medieval history ever since. I have tried in this textbook not only to present medieval civilization clearly and briefly but also to convey something of the excitement that drew me to the subject originally and that captivates me still.

The sixth edition of *Medieval Europe*, like its earlier incarnations, is designed to be used as a core book around which supplementary readings of the instructor's choice can be assigned or recommended. The text has been reexamined word by word and revised throughout to incorporate new research and achieve greater clarity. Revisions for this new edition cover the gamut from barbarian invaders to female mystics.

McGraw-Hill and I would like to thank the following reviewers for their many helpful comments and suggestions: Bernard S. Bachrach, University of Minnesota, Robert Gottfried, Rutgers University, Carla L. Klausner, University of Missouri–Kansas City, Joe W. Leedom, Hollins College, and Harry Rosenberg, Colorado State University. I am also grateful to Brian Tierney, Richard Dales, Robert Brentano, Barbara Hanawalt, Michael Doles, and the late Donald Sutherland for their helpful suggestions on earlier editions of this book, to instructors and students from far and near who have sent me their suggestions and impressions, and to my research assistants, Alberto Ferreiro, Stephanie Mooers Christelow, Miriam Davis, Angus MacDonald, and Penny Adair. For all mistakes and infelicities in this new edition I cheerfully take full responsibility. Don't blame Alberto, Stephanie, Miriam, Angus, or Penny!

My good friend the late Robert S. Hoyt used to offer his students one dollar for each error they could spot in his textbook on medieval Europe. I would never be so rash. But to every reader who calls my attention to passages in this book that are murky, misleading, muddled, or just plain wrong I promise a grateful reply and future amendment. As the twelfth-century historian Henry of Huntingdon so artfully put it,

"What I have well performed in grace approve,
Where I have erred, correct me in your love."

C. Warren Hollister

Introduction

There is an old-fashioned notion, long discredited yet still popularly accepted, that medieval Europe was an historical disaster. Today, the very word "medieval" brings to mind such deplorable things as midnight curfews, foreign governments we dislike, and tangled graduation requirements. The Middle Ages, stretching across a thousand years from the fifth century to the fifteenth, are still viewed by some as a long, aimless detour in the march of human progress—a thousand years of poverty, superstition, and gloom that divided the old golden age of the Roman Empire from the new golden age of the Italian Renaissance. During these thousand years, as a famous historian once said (in 1860), human consciousness "lay dreaming or half awake." The Middle Ages were condemned as "a thousand years without a bath" by one well-scrubbed nineteenth-century writer. To others they were simply "the Dark Ages"—recently described (facetiously) as the "one enormous hiccup in human progress." At length, sometime in the fifteenth century the darkness is supposed to have lifted. Europe awakened, bathed, and began thinking and creating again. After a long medieval intermission, the Grand March resumed.

Historians today no longer believe in this Rip Van Winkle theory. Generations of research have shown that during the Middle Ages society was constantly changing, so much so that the Europe of 1300 was vastly different from the Europe of 600. Historians now realize that medieval Europe was very creative, intensely so during the centuries following A.D. 1000. By the close of the Middle Ages—by about 1500—Europe's technology and political and economic organization had given it a decisive edge over all other civilizations of the earth. Columbus had discovered America; the Portuguese had sailed around Africa to India; Europe had developed the cannon, the printing press, the mechanical clock, eyeglasses, distilled liquor, and numerous other ingredients of modern civilization.

During the "modern" centuries that followed, from about 1500 to 1945, European fleets, armies, and ideas spread across the globe and transformed it. Even today, independent non-European countries remain deeply influenced by European ideas about science, medicine, economics, politics, and social justice. The legislative bodies that govern the United States, Mexico, Canada,

1

Israel, Japan, India, and many other non-European states are descendants of the parliaments and assemblies of medieval Europe. And the Communist systems of China, Russia, Cuba, and elsewhere are similarly based on Western European ideas, some of which can be traced back before the time of Karl Marx to the Christian radicalism of the Middle Ages. In 1381, for example, rebellious English peasants attacked the established social order with the slogan of a classless society: "When Adam dug and Eve span, who was then the gentleman?"

In short, anyone who wonders how Europe was able to transform the world, for good or ill, into the global civilization that envelops us today must look to the medieval centuries for an important part of the answer. For during the Middle Ages, Europe grew from a primitive rural society, thinly settled and impoverished, into a powerful and distinctive civilization. It is this story that our book will tell.

PART ONE

The Early Middle Ages
The Birth of Europe

THE EARLY MIDDLE AGES: AN OVERVIEW

This book is divided into three sections. The first, "The Early Middle Ages," spans the troubled, formative centuries between the collapse of the Roman Empire in the West and the emergence of Western Europe as a major civilization—growing in population, wealth, territory, and cultural creativity. By the end of the fifth century the Western Roman Empire had disintegrated; by the mid-eleventh century the revival of Western Europe was well underway. Accordingly, the term "Early Middle Ages" refers here to the period between about A.D. 500 and 1050, though such dividing lines are of course arbitrary and would have passed unnoticed at the time.

Rather than descending suddenly from the sky onto Europe in A.D. 500, we will approach it on foot from out of the Roman past. Looking briefly at the Roman Empire at its height, in the first and second centuries A.D., we will then explore the ways in which Roman civilization was transformed during the third, fourth, and fifth centuries. The Christianization of the Roman Empire will receive particular attention because Rome's conversion to Christianity was of decisive importance to the future of Europe, both western and eastern. We will trace the collapse of Roman imperial authority in the West, the Germanic invasions, and the establishment of Germanic kingdoms across the regions of Western Europe and North Africa once ruled by Rome. With this running start we will have arrived at A.D. 500.

Roman civilization gave way to three successor civilizations, three heirs: Byzantine, Islamic, and Western European. Since the subject of this book is medieval Western Europe, the other two inheriting civilizations will receive only a chapter each. These chapters will stress the influence of Byzantine and Islamic civilization on the emerging culture of Western Christendom.

The Early Middle Ages witnessed repeated invasions of the West, accompanied by political and economic turmoil. Illiterate, hard-bitten landholders led their retinues in battle, often in losing causes, against Muslim armies of the expanding Islamic empire. More often, the warrior-landholders of Western Christendom fought among themselves. Western cities became underpopulated and ruinous, while the countryside suffered periodic famines and plagues along with the ravages of war. Nevertheless, Christianity gradually expanded as monks carried their missionary work into pagan Germany, the Netherlands, and Anglo-Saxon England. Monasteries, planted in the wilderness, became centers of prayer, agricultural production, and learning—outposts of civilization where the Latin literary heritage of ancient Rome was kept alive through the copying and study of old manuscripts.

Around A.D. 700 a new Christian dynasty, the Carolingian, began to extend its authority over France, western Germany, and, later, northern Italy. Working closely with the Church, the Carolingians built an empire that eventually stretched across most of Western Christendom. Charlemagne, the greatest of the Carolingians, assumed the title "Roman Emperor" in A.D. 800. But lacking large cities and an educated bureaucracy, Charlemagne's empire was fragile. It collapsed during the 800s amidst a new wave of invaders: Vikings, Muslims, and Hungarians. In the course of these invasions, and partly in response to them, strong kingdoms emerged in England and Germany. In France where the monarchy long remained feeble, the burden of defense fell to dukes and counts, who fortified their lands with castles and gradually tightened their control over lesser landholders.

By about 1050 the invasions had run their course. The Muslims were in retreat. The Vikings and Hungarians had adopted Christianity and become participants in Western civilization rather than predators of it. Cities were growing once again in the west European heartlands and commerce was increasing. The Church was entering a period of reform and spiritual renewal, and literacy was spreading.

This revitalization can be described (crudely but conveniently) as the coming of a new era. The Early Middle Ages began with the decaying of an old and powerful civilization and ended with the maturing of a new one, radically different from ancient Rome yet, in a sense, its child.

1

Rome Becomes Christian

THE "GOLDEN AGE" OF ROME

During the first and second centuries A.D. Rome was at the height of its power. Roman emperors ruled in relative peace over an immense realm that encircled the Mediterranean Sea and bulged northward across present-day France and England. Not all of them ruled wisely; several of Rome's "golden-age" emperors were decidedly dull-witted and a couple of them were (to put it charitably) mentally ill. The first-century emperor Caligula used to have his favorite horse wined and dined at imperial banquets and made plans to have the beast raised to the office of Roman Consul. (The project was cut short by Caligula's assassination.) And the less said about the emperor Nero, the better. But a number of the emperors were able and far-sighted, and even under the worst of them the imperial government continued to function. Roman legions guarded the far-flung frontiers, paved roads tied the provinces to Rome, and Roman ships sailed the Mediterranean and Black Seas, rarely troubled by pirates or enemy fleets. Scattered across the Empire were cities built in the classical Roman style with temples, public buildings, baths, schools, amphitheaters, and triumphal arches. Their ruins are still to be seen all around the Mediterranean and beyond—in Italy, France, Spain, England, North Africa, the Balkans, and the Near East—bearing witness even now to the tremendous scope of Roman political authority and the tasteful uniformity of Roman architecture.

The Empire extended about 3000 miles from east to west (the approximate length of the United States). According to the best scholarly guesses, its inhabitants numbered something like 50 million, heavily concentrated in the eastern provinces where commerce and civilization had flourished for thousands of years. Egypt, Israel, Mesopotamia, and Greece had all fallen by now under Roman authority, although Greece exerted such a dominating influence on Roman culture that Romans could express some doubt as to who had conquered whom.

To the east Rome shared a boundary with the Parthian Empire, which gave way during the third century to a new and aggressive Persian Empire.

6

But elsewhere Rome's expansion from the Mediterranean Basin was halted only by the Arabian and Sahara Deserts, the Caucasus Mountains, the dense forests of Central Europe beyond the Rhine and Danube Rivers, the barren highlands of Scotland, and the Atlantic Ocean. In short, the Roman frontiers encompassed virtually all the lands that could be reached by Roman armies and cultivated profitably by Roman landowners.

Economic and Social Conditions

Notwithstanding the elegance of Roman cities, the imperial economy was based primarily on agriculture. By the first and second centuries A.D. the small family farms of the Roman past were giving way across much of the Empire to large estates owned by wealthy aristocrats and tilled by slaves or half-free peasants. Although the products of Roman farming varied considerably from region to region, the principal crops of the Roman Empire were grain, grapes, and olives—the so-called Mediterranean triad that had dominated agriculture in the Mediterranean Basin for countless generations. Grain (chiefly wheat and barley) and grape vines were cultivated throughout most of the Empire. From these the Romans produced two of the basic staples of their diet: bread and wine. Olive trees were also grown in abundance, though their vulnerability to cold restricted their cultivation to the frost-free lowlands around the Mediterranean Sea. The inhabitants of the Mediterranean Basin used olive oil in the place of butter, which was favored by the Germanic tribes to the north but turned rancid in the southern heat.

Through much of Italy grain production had been giving way to the raising of sheep and cattle, and the fertile wheat-growing provinces of Egypt and North Africa had by now become the primary suppliers of bread for the teeming populace of Rome (perhaps 700,000). Such specialization in agriculture was made possible by the Roman Peace—the *Pax Romana*—that linked distant provinces into a single political-economic unit and safeguarded the Mediterranean sea lanes.

The culture of Rome's "golden age" captivated the historians of past centuries. Never, they wrote, was the human race so happy as in the great days of the Empire—the first and second centuries A.D. They viewed Rome's decline and fall as the supreme historical catastrophe, the triumph of barbarism and religion. Today historians see the matter quite differently. Roman classical culture was impressive, but it was also narrowly limited, shared only by the Empire's upper-crust. And although all inhabitants benefited from the Roman Peace, the great majority of them were impoverished and undernourished, and vast numbers were enslaved.

Such conditions persisted throughout the "golden age" and beyond, not as economic misfortunes that might be remedied by antipoverty programs but as the means necessary for the functioning of great estates, mines, and wealthy households. The leisured lives of the Empire's elite, and the very survival of the imperial economy, depended on the muscles

of slaves and poor laborers, who constituted eighty to ninety percent of the total population.

Nor was the Roman Peace as peaceful as one might think. Germanic tribes hammered repeatedly at Rome's frontiers and often penetrated them, while deep within the Empire towns and countryside suffered a degree of local violence and mayhem unimaginable today. The Roman provinces of the "golden age" were

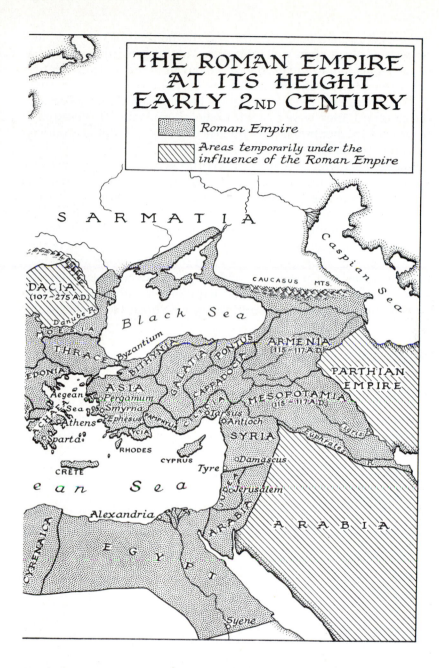

drastically underpoliced and undergoverned. The professional administrative class of the entire Empire numbered less than a thousand.

Roman women, even the wealthiest, were forbidden to hold any political office. By long tradition they were expected to stay home and obey their husbands, but many Roman wives declined to meet these expectations. Indeed, in the Empire's later centuries women acquired considerable independence with respect to marriage, divorce, and the holding of property, and upper-class women were often well educated. The Roman father, however, was the master of his family and exercised the power of life or death over his newborn children. If he liked their looks, he let them live; if they seemed scrawny or deformed, or if the father already had enough children (particularly female children), they were cast out to die of exposure. This custom of infanticide was yet another brutal consequence of Rome's marginal economy: the Empire could not afford excess mouths.

The imperial economic system provoked no general rebellion because the lower classes knew no better way of managing an empire. Virtually all ancient civilizations were afflicted by mass enslavement, impoverishment, malnutrition, internal violence, the suppression of women, and the killing of unwanted infants (although the religion of the Hebrews prohibited infanticide). In these respects Roman imperial civilization was no worse than the others, and in the larger cities, where public baths and free bread were available, it was significantly better. Life in Rome's "golden age" could be pleasant enough if one were male, adult, very wealthy, and naturally immune to various epidemic diseases. But if this was humanity's happiest time, God help us all.

THE THIRD AND FOURTH CENTURIES

Anarchy and Recovery

During the third century conditions grew still worse. Invading tribes broke through the frontiers again and again, forcing cities to construct protective

Chronology of the Later Empire

All Dates A.D.

205–270:	Plotinus
235–284:	Height of the third-century anarchy
306–337:	Reign of Constantine
325:	Council of Nicaea
330:	Founding of Constantinople
354–430:	St. Augustine of Hippo
376:	Visigoths cross Danube
378:	Battle of Adrianople
378–395:	Reign of Theodosius I
395:	Final division of Eastern and Western Empires
410:	Alaric sacks Rome
430:	Vandals capture Hippo
451–452:	Huns invade Western Europe
440–461:	Pontificate of Leo I
476:	Last Western emperor deposed by Odovacar
481–511:	Clovis rules Franks, conquers Gaul
493–526:	Theodoric the Ostrogoth rules Italy

walls and threatening for a time to tear the Empire to pieces. Imperial survival depended increasingly on military defense, and the Roman legions, well aware of that fact, made and unmade emperors. Roman armies repeatedly battled one another for control of the imperial office until (to exaggerate only slightly) a man might be a general one day, emperor the next, and dead the third. No less than nineteen emperors reigned during the calamitous half-century between 235 and 285, and all but one were murdered or killed in combat. With political anarchy came social and economic breakdown. The cost of living soared 1000 percent between A.D. 256 and 280, and growing numbers of soldiers and administrators obliged the government to levy higher and higher taxes on its peasants and townspeople. Many fled their homes and jobs to escape the tax collector. The "golden age" had given way to what one third-century writer described as an "age of iron and rust."

The Empire was saved, though just barely, by a series of warrior-emperors of the late third and early fourth centuries. By tremendous military effort they threw back Germanic and Persian armies, recovered the lost provinces, and restored the old frontiers. They also took measures to arrest the social and economic decay and to reconstruct the Roman administration on authoritarian lines. These measures have often been criticized, and with some justice. But they enabled the faltering Empire to survive for nearly two more centuries in the West and for over a thousand years in the East.

The two chief architects of the new policy were the emperors Diocletian (284–305) and Constantine (306–337). Under their regimes the loosely governed Empire of earlier days was rebuilt into an autocracy supported by a huge army and bureaucracy. Workers and peasants were tied by law to their jobs and frozen into a hereditary caste system. The status of the emperor himself assumed godlike proportions. Borrowing from Greek and Persian court ceremonial, the new emperors employed all the known arts of costume, makeup, and drama to make themselves appear majestic. Everyone had to fall prostrate in the emperor's presence, and Constantine added the touch of wearing a diadem on his head. Back in the first and second centuries, emperors had striven to work harmoniously with the political institutions of the former Roman Republic—the Senate, the civic magistrates—which during the "golden age" continued to enjoy much prestige but little independent power. Under the new regimes of Diocletian and Constantine, the Senate was drained of authority while the emperor became *dominus et deus*—"lord and god." The imperial dignity, so debased during the third-century anarchy, was now exalted in every possible way.

The New Religious Mood

Amidst the invasions and economic crises of the third century and the rigid autocracy of the fourth, the upper-crust civilization of classical Rome began giving way to styles and hopes that had long been percolating among the Empire's masses. As these subterranean ideas floated to the surface, the elegant, worldly culture of the "golden age" became more mystical and impressionistic. Fundamental changes occurred not only in court ceremonial but also in such areas as literature, philosophy, and art.* Underlying them all was a basic shift in religious outlook that shaped the intellectual world of the late Empire and the civilizations that would later succeed it.

Tormented by growing economic hardship and insecurity, the urban poor of the third- and fourth-century Empire turned more and more from the boisterous and unlikely gods of the Greco-Roman Olympic cult—Jupiter, Juno, Apollo, Minerva and the rest—to compelling new religions that offered release from individual guilt and the promise of personal salvation and eternal life. These new "mystery religions" originated in the older, eastern cultures that Rome had absorbed into its empire. From Egypt came the cult of the goddess Isis, from Persia came the cult of the savior Mithras, from Asia Minor came the worship of the Great Earth Mother, and from Palestine came Christianity.

The gods and goddesses of Olympus survived for a time but in profoundly altered form. During the third century, all that was vital in the pagan cults was incorporated into a new philosophical scheme called "Neoplatonism" (based loosely on the much earlier thought of the Greek philosopher Plato). Neoplatonism was the creation of the third-century philosopher Plotinus, one of the most influential minds of the Roman imperial era. Plotinus taught the doctrine of one god, who was infinite, unknowable, and unapproachable, except through a mystical experience. This god was the ultimate source of everything, spiritual and physical. All existence was conceived of as a series of circles radiating outward from him, like concentric ripples in a pond, diminishing in excellence and significance as they grew more distant from their divine source. Human reason, which the Greeks had earlier exalted, now lost its fascination, for at the core of reality was a god that lay beyond reason's scope.

Plotinus and his followers regarded the multitudes of pagan gods and goddesses as crude but useful symbols of the true Neoplatonic god. Though poorly suited to the deepening mood of otherworldliness, the pagan cults were given new life by the overarching structure of Neoplatonic philosophy. They were themselves brought into line with the trend toward mysticism and monotheism. The distinction between Jupiter and the new eastern deities was steadily blurring.

CHRISTIANITY

It was in this supernatural atmosphere that the Christians converted the Roman Empire. Some of their beliefs and practices resembled those of older and

---

*Late Roman art is discussed on pp. 36–40 and illustrated on pp. 37–41. Art lovers are welcome to look ahead; others can be patient and read on.

competing religions: baptism, eternal salvation, the death and resurrection of a savior-god, the sacramental meal, human brotherhood under a divine father—none of these was new. Yet Christianity was more than a recombination of old beliefs, more than simply another of the mystery religions. It differed from them above all in two fundamental ways: (1) its founder and savior was an actual historical personage: compared with Jesus such mythical idealizations as Isis and Mithras would have seemed faint and unreal; and (2) its god was not merely the best of many gods but the One God, the God of the Hebrews, unique in all antiquity in his claims to exclusiveness and omnipotence, and now detached by Christianity from his association with a chosen people to become the God of all peoples.

Jesus had lived and died a Jew. He announced that he had come not to abolish Judaism but to fulfill it. In his earliest biographies, the four Gospels, he is pictured as a warm, magnetic leader who miraculously healed the sick, raised the dead, and stilled the winds. His miracles were seen as credentials of the divine authority with which he claimed to speak. His ministry was chiefly to the poor and outcast, and in Christianity's early decades it was they who accepted the new faith most readily. He preached a doctrine of love, compassion, and humility; like the earlier Hebrew prophets, he scorned empty formalism in religion and favored a simple life of generosity toward both friend and enemy and devotion to God. He did not object to ritual as such, but only to ritual infected with pride and divorced from love of God and neighbor. In the end he was crucified (a common form of execution at the time) for criticizing the complacency of the established Jewish priesthood and claiming to speak with divine authority. The enthusiasm of his following seems to have alarmed Roman provincial officials, who may have feared a national Jewish uprising.

According to the Gospels, Jesus' greatest miracle was his resurrection—his return to life on the third day after his death on the cross. He is said to have remained on earth for a short period thereafter, giving solace and instruction to his disciples, and then to have ascended into heaven with the promise that he would return in glory to judge all souls and bring the world to an end. The early generations of Christians expected this second coming to occur quickly, which may be one of the reasons why formal organization was not stressed in the primitive Church.

From the beginning, Christians not only accepted Jesus' ethical teachings but also worshiped him as the Christ, the incarnation of God. In the Gospels, Jesus distinguishes repeatedly between himself—"the Son of Man"—and God—"the Father"—but he also makes the statement, "I and the Father are one." And in one account he instructs his followers to baptize all persons "in the name of the Father and the Son and the Holy Spirit." Hence, Christianity became committed to the difficult and sophisticated notion of a single divinity with three aspects. Christ was the "Son" or "Second Person" in a Holy Trinity that was nevertheless one God. The doctrine of the Trinity produced a great deal of theological controversy over the centuries. But it also gave Christians the unique advantage of a single, infinite, philosophically respectable God who could be worshiped and adored in the person of the charismatic, lovable, tragic Jesus.

The Early Church

The first generation of Christianity witnessed the beginning of a deeply significant process whereby the Judeo-Christian heritage was modified and enriched through contact with Greco-Roman culture. Jesus' own apostles were little influenced by Greek thought, and some of them sought to keep Christianity strictly within the ritualistic framework of Judaism. But St. Paul, an early convert who was both a Jew and a Roman citizen, succeeded in steering the Church toward a more encompassing goal. Christians were not to be bound by the strict Jewish dietary laws or the requirement of circumcision (which would have severely diminished Christianity's attraction to adult, non-Jewish males). The new faith would be open to all people everywhere who would accept Jesus as God and Savior—and open to the bracing winds of Greco-Roman thought.

St. Paul traveled far and wide across the Empire, winning converts and establishing Christian communities in many towns and cities of the Mediterranean Basin. Other Christian missionaries, among them St. Peter and Jesus' other apostles, devoted their lives as St. Paul did to traveling, preaching, and organizing—often at the cost of ridicule and martyrdom. Their work was tremendously effective, for by the end of the apostolic generation Christianity had become a ponderable force among the impoverished townspeople of Italy and the East. Within another century it had spread through most of the Roman Empire. The urban poor found it easy to accept a savior who had worked as a carpenter; had surrounded himself with fishermen, ex-prostitutes, and similar riffraff; had been crucified by the imperial authorities; and had promised salvation to all who followed him—free or slave, man or woman.

From the first, Christians engaged regularly in a sacramental meal of bread and wine that came to be called the "eucharist" (the Greek word for thanksgiving) or "holy communion." It was viewed as an indispensable channel of divine grace through which the Christian was infused with the spirit of Christ. By means of another sacrament, baptism, one was initiated into the fellowship of the Church, had all sins forgiven, and received the grace (moral strength) of the Holy Spirit.

As Christian historical documents become more common, in the second and third centuries, the organization of the Church begins to emerge more sharply than before. These documents disclose an important distinction between the clergy, who govern the Church and administer the sacraments, and the laity whom they serve. The clergy, initiated into the Christian priesthood through the ceremony of ordination, were divided into several ranks: the most important were the bishops, who served as spiritual leaders of

Christian urban communities, and the ordinary priests, who conducted religious services and administered the eucharist under a bishop's jurisdiction.* The most powerful of the bishops were the metropolitans or archbishops of the more important cities, who supervised the bishops of their districts. Atop the hierarchy were the bishops of the three or four greatest cities of the Empire: Rome, Alexandria, Antioch, and later Constantinople. These leaders, known as patriarchs, governed the Church across vast areas of the Mediterranean world.

In time the bishop of Rome came to be regarded more and more as the highest of the patriarchs. His preeminence was based on the tradition that St. Peter, foremost among Jesus' twelve apostles, had spent his last years in Rome and suffered martyrdom there. St. Peter was held to have been the first bishop of Rome—the first pope—and later popes regarded themselves as his direct successors. Nevertheless, the establishment of effective papal authority over even the Western part of the Church was to require the efforts of many centuries.

Christianity and Classical Culture

Medieval and modern Christian theology is a product of both the Jewish and the Greek traditions. The synthesis began not among Christians but among Jews, especially those who had migrated in large numbers to the Greco-Egyptian metropolis of Alexandria. Here Jewish scholars—in particular a religious philosopher of the early first century A.D. named Philo Judaeus—worked toward the reconciliation of Jewish Biblical revelation and Greek philosophy that was to influence both Jewish and Christian thought across the centuries.

Following the lead of Philo Judaeus, Christian theologians strove to demonstrate that their religion was more than merely an appealing myth—that it could hold its own in the highest intellectual circles. Plato and the Bible agreed, so they argued, on the existence of a single God and the importance of living an ethical life. But as Christians explored their faith more analytically, they began to differ among themselves on such difficult issues as the nature of Christ (how could he be both God and man?) and the Trinity (how can three be one?). Some opinions were so inconsistent with the majority view that they were condemned as "heresies." As questions were raised and orthodox solutions agreed on, Christian doctrine became increasingly specific and elaborate.

The early heresies sought to simplify the nature of Christ and the Trinity. One group, the Gnostics, insisted that Christ was not truly human but only a divine phantom—that God could not have degraded himself by as-

---

*The Latin word for bishop is *episcopus,* from which is derived such English words as "episcopal" (having to do with a bishop or bishops) and "Episcopalian" (a member of the Anglican communion in America, belonging to a church governed by bishops). One medieval writer referred slightingly to a bishop's concubine as an *episcopissa,* but since medieval bishops were supposed to be chaste, the term was very seldom used.

suming a flesh-and-blood body. Others maintained that Christ was not fully divine, not an equal member of the Trinity. This last position was taken up in the fourth century by a group of Christians known as Arians (after their leader, Arius), who spread their view throughout the Empire and beyond.

The orthodox position lay midway between Gnosticism and Arianism: Christ was fully human and fully divine. He was a coequal member of the Holy Trinity who had always existed and always would, but who had assumed human form and flesh at a particular moment in time and had walked the earth, taught, suffered, and died as the man Jesus.

Christianity and the Empire

From the first the Christians of the Empire had been a people apart, convinced that they alone possessed the truth and that the truth would one day triumph. They were eager to win new converts and uncompromising in their rejection of all other religions. They were willing to learn from the pagan world but unwilling ever to submit to it. Consequently, Christians were often objects of suspicion and hatred. Their refusal to offer sacrifices to the state gods resulted in imperial persecution, but only intermittently. Violent purges alternated with long periods of official inaction. The persecutions could be cruel and terrifying, but they were neither sufficiently ruthless nor sufficiently sustained to exterminate the whole Christian community, and martyrdoms only strengthened the resolve of those who survived. (The pagan emperors might have learned much from Christian inquisitors of sixteenth-century Spain on the sub-

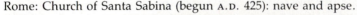

Rome: Church of Santa Sabina (begun A.D. 425): nave and apse.

ject of liquidating troublesome religious minorities.) The most severe imperial persecution, and the last, occurred at the beginning of the fourth century
under Emperor Diocletian. By then Christianity was too well entrenched to
be destroyed, and the failure of Diocletian's persecution made it evident that
the Empire had little choice but to accommodate itself to the Church.

A decade thereafter Emperor Constantine undertook a momentous reversal of imperial religious policy. He himself became a Christian convert,
and in 313 he granted the Church official toleration and protection. In the
generations that followed, Christianity enjoyed the active support of a line of
Christian emperors. Great aisled churches were built at imperial expense. The
combats of gladiators, which had traditionally provided savage amusement
for the urban masses, gave way under Christian influence to the less bloodthirsty sport of chariot racing. The practice of crucifixion was brought to an
end. And infanticide was prohibited by imperial law. It was repugnant to
Christians, as it had always been to Jews, and it was losing much of its social
utility in an era of declining population. Slavery continued, for the imperial
economy could not survive without it. The Church urged its members to free
their slaves, but few were willing to comply and suffer the resulting economic
ruin.

The gratitude of some churchmen toward the Christian emperors rose to
the point of adulation. Constantine could no longer claim to be a god, but he
was lauded as the thirteenth apostle, the master of all churches, the divinely chosen ruler of the Roman people. The first empire-wide council of the Church, the
Council of Nicaea in 325, was dominated by his regal presence.

Rich and poor alike now flocked into the Christian faith. Although paganism long survived, particularly in the countryside, Christianity had grown
by the end of the fourth century to become the dominant religion of the
Mediterranean world. No longer persecuted and disreputable, it was now official, conventional, respectable. And of course it lost some of its former spiritual intensity in the process. Bishops and patriarchs now tended to come from
wealthy aristocratic families. And as so often occurs in human institutions,
victory was accompanied by an intensification of internal disputes. Fourth-
century Christianity was marked by bitter doctrinal struggles, and here too
the Christian emperors played a commanding role. Arianism, the most powerful of the fourth-century heresies, was condemned by Constantine and the
majority of churchmen at the Council of Nicaea. But thereafter the imperial
government fluctuated: some emperors opposed Arianism while others supported it, and orthodox and Arian leaders shuffled in and out of exile at the
imperial whim. At length the sternly orthodox Emperor Theodosius I (378–
395) banned the teachings of the Arians and broke their power, making orthodox Christianity the official religion of the Roman state. Theodosius out-
lawed paganism as well, and the old gods of Rome, deprived of imperial
sanction, gradually passed into memory.

Although Arianism was now prohibited in the Empire, it survived among
some of the Germanic tribes along the frontiers. These peoples had been con-

Colossal Head of the Emperor Constantine, Rome,
early fourth century.

verted by Arian missionaries around the middle of the fourth century, at a
time when Arianism was still strong in the Empire, and the persecutions of
Theodosius had no effect on the faith of Germanic tribes. Consequently, when
in time these tribes poured into the Western Empire and established successor states on its ruins, they found themselves divided from their Roman subjects not only by culture but by bitter religious antagonisms as well.

The Latin Doctors

Constantine's conversion hastened the process of fusion between Christianity
and Greco-Roman culture. During the generations following his death, the
process was brought to completion by three Christian scholars—St. Ambrose,
St. Jerome, and St. Augustine—honored in later years as "Doctors of the La-

tin Church." Working at a time when the Empire was swiftly becoming Christianized, yet before the intellectual vigor of classical antiquity had faded, they used their mastery of Greco-Roman thought to interpret the Christian faith. Nearly seven centuries were to pass before Western Europe regained the intellectual level of late antiquity, and the writings of these three Latin Doctors therefore exerted a commanding influence on succeeding generations.

Although Ambrose, Jerome, and Augustine made their chief impact in the realm of thought, all three were immersed in the political and ecclesiastical affairs of their day. St. Ambrose (*c.* 340–397) was bishop of Milan, a great city of northern Italy that in the later fourth century replaced Rome as the imperial capital in the West. Ambrose was a superb administrator, a powerful orator, and a vigorous opponent of Arianism. Thoroughly grounded in the literary and philosophical traditions of Greco-Roman civilization, he enriched his Christian writings by drawing heavily from Plato, Cicero, Virgil, and other giants of the pagan past. And as one of the first champions of ecclesiastical independence from the authority of the Empire, he stood at the source of the church-state controversy that was to affect the medieval West so deeply in later generations. When Emperor Theodosius I massacred the rebellious inhabitants of Thessalonica, St. Ambrose excommunicated him from the church of Milan until he should beg forgiveness. The emperor's public repentance set a long-remembered precedent for the principle of ecclesiastical supremacy in matters of faith and morals.

St. Jerome (*c.* 340–420) was the most celebrated Biblical scholar of his time. A restless, troubled man, he wandered throughout the Empire, living in Rome for a time, then fleeing the worldly city to found a monastery in Bethlehem. Jerome's monks devoted themselves to the copying of manuscripts, a task that was to be taken up by countless monks in centuries to come and which, in the long run, resulted in the preservation of important works of Greco-Roman antiquity that would otherwise have perished. The modern world owes a great debt to Jerome and his successors for performing this essential labor.

St. Jerome himself was torn by doubts as to the propriety of a Christian immersing himself in the works of pagan literary figures such as Homer and Virgil, Horace and Cicero. He was terrified by a dream in which Jesus denied him salvation with the words, "You are a Ciceronian, not a Christian." For a time Jerome renounced all pagan writings, but he was much too devoted to the charms of classical literature to persevere. In the end he concluded that Greco-Roman letters might properly be used in the service of the Christian faith.

Jerome's supreme achievement lay in the field of scriptural commentary and translation. It was he who produced the definitive translation of the Bible from its original Hebrew and Greek into Latin—the language of the Western Roman Empire and of medieval Western Europe. The result of Jerome's efforts was the Latin Vulgate Bible, which Catholics have used up to the present century. By preparing a trustworthy Latin version of the fundamental Christian text, he made a decisive contribution to Western civilization.

St. Augustine of Hippo (354–430) was the foremost philosopher of Roman antiquity. As bishop of Hippo, an important city in North Africa, he was deeply involved in the political-religious problems of his age, and his writings were produced in response to vital contemporary issues. In his *Confessions* he described his own intellectual and moral journey along a twisting path from youthful hedonism to Christian piety. He wrote in the hope that others, lost as he once was, might be led by God into the spiritual haven of the Church.

Augustine wrote voluminously against various pagan and heretical doctrines that threatened Christian orthodoxy in his age. In the course of these disputes, he examined many of the central problems that have occupied theologians ever since: the nature of the Trinity, the existence of evil in a world created by a good and all-powerful God, the authority of the priesthood, the compatibility of free will and predestination. Out of his diverse writings emerges a body of speculative thought that served as the intellectual foundation for medieval philosophy and theology.

Augustine was disturbed, as Jerome had been, by the danger of pagan thought to the Christian soul. But, like Jerome, he concluded that although a good Christian ought not to *enjoy* pagan writings, he might properly *employ* them for Christian ends. Accordingly, Augustine used the philosophy of Plato and the Neoplatonists as a basis for a new and thoroughly Christian philosophical scheme. As St. Thomas Aquinas observed, looking back from the thirteenth century, "Whenever Augustine, who was expert in the philosophy of the Platonists, found in their teaching anything consistent with faith, he adopted it; those things which he found contrary to faith, he amended."

Plato had taught that abstract ideas were more important than tangible things. He believed that we acquire true knowledge not by observing things and events in the world of nature but by reflecting on the fundamental ideas that underlie the physical universe, just as a mathematician operates in the abstract world of pure numbers. Elaborating on Plato, the Neoplatonists viewed God as the center and source of reality and saw the natural world as merely a dim reflection of its divine source—a faint outer ripple in the concentric circles of existence, scarcely worth considering.

Augustine used Christianity to reshape the insights of Plato and Plotinus. Like the Neoplatonists, he believed that the material world was less important than the spiritual world, but it was nevertheless the creation of a good and loving God who remained actively at work in it. God had created the first man and woman with the intention that they and all their descendants should attain salvation—should live forever in God's loving presence. But rather than creating mere human puppets, God gave humanity freedom to choose between good (accepting his love) and evil (rejecting it). As a consequence of Adam and Eve's choosing wrongly, humanity fell from its original state of innocence, became incorrigibly self-centered, and thus severed its relationship with God. But God reknit the relationship by himself assuming human form in the person of Jesus—suffering, dying, and rising again. The original sin of the first man, Adam, was redeemed by the crucifixion of the sinless God-man, Christ, and the possibility of human salvation was thereby restored.

Accordingly, the central goal of the Christian life is to attain the salvation that Christ has made possible. One can achieve this goal only by becoming a loving, unselfish person, and Augustine insisted that we are powerless to overcome our self-centeredness except through divine grace. He saw us as incapable of earning our own way into heaven. This being so, nobody deserves salvation, yet some achieve it because their moral characters are shaped and strengthened by God's grace.

The necessity of divine grace to human salvation is a central theme in the greatest of Augustine's works, the *City of God.* Here he set forth a comprehensive Christian philosophy of history that was radically new and deeply influential. Rejecting the Greco-Roman notion that history repeats itself in endless meaningless cycles, he viewed it as a purposeful process of human-divine interaction beginning with the creation and continuing through Christ's incarnation to the end of the world. Augustine interpreted history not in economic or political terms but in moral terms. To him, the single determining force in history was human moral character; the single goal, human salvation. God was not interested in the fate of kingdoms or empires, except insofar as they affected the spiritual destiny of individuals. And individual salvation depended not on the victories of imperial legions but on the cleansing of human moral character by divine grace. True history, therefore, had less to do with the struggles between states than with the war between good and evil that rages within each state and within each soul.

Augustine divided humanity into two opposing groups: not Romans and barbarians as the pagan writers would have it, but those who live in God's grace and those who do not. The former are members of the "City of God," the latter belong to the "Earthly City." The two cities are hopelessly intertwined in this life, but their members will be separated at death by eternal salvation or damnation. Human history, therefore, has as its purpose the growth and welfare of the City of God.

The writings of St. Augustine have shaped Western thought in fundamental ways. His theory of the two cities, although often reinterpreted in later generations, influenced political ideas over the next thousand years. His Christian Platonism dominated medieval philosophy until the mid-twelfth century and remains a significant theme in religious thought to this day. His distinction between the ordained priesthood and the laity has always been basic to Catholic theology. And his emphasis on divine grace was to be a crucial source of inspiration to the Protestant leaders of the sixteenth century.

As a consequence of Augustine's work, together with that of his contemporaries, Ambrose and Jerome, Christian culture was firmly established on classical foundations. At Augustine's death in 430 the Western Empire was tottering, but the Classical-Christian fusion was now essentially complete. The strength of the Greco-Roman tradition that underlies medieval Christianity and Western civilization owes much to the fact that these three Latin Doctors, and others like them, found it possible to be both Christians and Ciceronians.

2

The Waning of the Western Empire

"DECLINE AND FALL"

The Splitting of East and West

In the year 330, a century before Augustine's death, Constantine founded a new, eastern imperial capital on a strategic waterway connecting the Black Sea with the Mediterranean. This city, a second Rome, was built in grand style on the site of a Greek town called Byzantium, which Constantine immodestly renamed Constantinople—"Constantine's City." When in later centuries the western half of the Empire had fallen to Germanic invaders and the eastern half survived alone, Constantinople became Europe's greatest metropolis. The lands that its emperors ruled are commonly called the "Byzantine Empire," after old Byzantium.

Ever since the late third century, the Roman imperial office had been split from time to time between a western emperor and an eastern emperor, and by the end of the fourth century the split had become permanent. Thenceforth, although the Roman Empire continued to be regarded as a whole, one emperor ruled the eastern half from Constantinople, while another ruled the western half—no longer from Rome but from some more strategically situated capital, first Milan, then Ravenna.

This political split reflected a cultural and linguistic division of long standing. The Latin tongue of the early Romans had spread across the western provinces, but Greek remained the major language in the East. (The educated elite throughout the Empire tended to be bilingual.) The eastern half of the Empire—Greece, Egypt, and the eastern Mediterranean provinces—had been civilized far longer than the western lands of North Africa and Western Europe, far longer than Rome itself. The East contained the bulk of the population; much of Western Europe would have had the appearance of occasional islands of cultivation in an otherwise unbroken wilderness. The eastern cities were larger, more numerous, and more commercially active than the newer cities of the West. Indeed, the western cities—including Rome—were chiefly military, administrative, and cultural centers rather than centers of commerce. Supported by taxes of the country folk, they were economic parasites living off the labor and productivity of the agrarian regions around them. Under the circumstances, the West was bound to suffer from an unfavorable balance of trade with the East. In exchange for eastern silks, spices, jewels, and grain, the West had little to offer except slaves and hunting dogs—and a diminishing supply of gold coins. Thus, with the coming of large-scale Germanic invasions in the fifth century, the Eastern Empire managed to survive while the political superstructure of the western provinces disintegrated.

Reasons for the Fall of the Western Empire

Many reasons have been proposed for Rome's decline and fall—no less than 210 different reasons according to a recent survey. They include such factors as sexual orgies, climatic changes, bad ecological habits, and Christianity. None of them makes much sense. The Eastern Empire was more thoroughly Christianized than the Western, yet it survived for another thousand years. The most spectacular Roman orgies occurred in the pagan "golden age"; Christian conversion made them unstylish, and the invasions occurred long after the age of orgies had passed. More significant was the failure of the Roman economy to change or expand and the parasitical character of the western cities. Then too, the fifth-century western emperors tended to be less competent than their eastern colleagues, and more open to the hazardous policy of filling their armies with Germanic troops under Germanic generals.

The riddle of Rome's "decline and fall" will probably never be completely solved, and even the question itself is misleading. For Rome did not literally fall. Instead, it underwent an immense strategic withdrawal from the less productive West to the wealthy and long-civilized provinces of the eastern Mediterranean. Some historians have found it puzzling that the Western Empire endured as long as it did.

Back when the Empire was expanding, its economy had been nourished by a constant influx of booty and slaves. But once expansion ceased, the West was unable to compensate by more intensive internal development. There was no large-scale industry, no mass production. Instead of importing manufactured goods from major urban centers, the various regions of the Empire tended more and more to produce them locally, and therefore less efficiently. Industrial production was held in low esteem by the Roman aristocracy, who considered it unrefined to engage in commerce or industry. They preferred to draw their wealth from their great plantations, their status from high public office, and their pleasure from the good company of fellow aristocrats. The Henry Fords and Thomas Edisons would never have been invited to their parties.

The Roman economy remained agrarian to the end, and basic farming techniques advanced very little during the imperial centuries. The Roman plow was adequate but rudimentary, and windmills were unknown. There were some water mills, but nowhere near as many as in, say, eleventh-century England; Roman landowners continued to rely on their slaves and seemed little interested in labor-saving devices. The horse could not be used as a draught animal on Roman plantations because the Roman harness crossed the horse's windpipe and strangled him under a heavy load. Consequently, Roman agriculture was powered by oxen, slaves, and peasants.

The economic exhaustion of the Western Empire was accompanied by population decline, runaway inflation, and deepening poverty. And at the very time that the labor shortage was becoming acute, the army and bureaucracy were growing ever larger. Higher and higher taxes on fewer and fewer taxpayers resulted in the impoverishment of the urban middle classes, and by the fifth century the western cities were declining in wealth and population. Only the small, exclusive class of great landowners managed to prosper. As early as the third century they were withdrawing from civic affairs, abandoning their town houses, and retiring to their estates in the country. They warded off marauders and imperial tax collectors alike by assembling armies of their own and fortifying their villas. Having deserted the cities, the aristocracy would remain an agrarian class for the next thousand years.

The decline of the city was damaging to the urbanized administrative structure of the Western Empire. More than that, it crippled the civic culture of Greco-Roman antiquity. The civilization of Athens, Alexandria, and Rome could not survive in the fields. It is in the decay of urban society that we find the crucial connecting link between political collapse and cultural transformation. In a very real sense Greco-Roman culture was dying long before the final demise of the Western Empire; the deposition of the last Western emperor in 476 was merely a delayed entombment. By then the cities were shrinking. The rational outlook of Greco-Roman classicism was transformed. The army and even the civil government had become Germanized as the desperate emperors, faced with a growing shortage of people and resources, turned more and more to non-Romans to defend their frontiers and keep order in their state. In the end, Germans abounded in the army, entire tribes were hired to defend the frontiers, and Germanic military leaders came to hold positions of high authority in the Western Empire. Survival had come to depend on the success of Germanic defenders against Germanic invaders.

The Roman Legacy

In another sense, however, Greco-Roman culture never died in the West. It exerted a profound influence, as we have seen, on the Doctors of the Latin Church and, through them, on the thought of the Middle Ages. It was the basis of repeated cultural revivals, great and small, down through the centuries—in the era of Charlemagne, in the High Middle Ages, in the Italian Renaissance, and in the neoclassical movements of the eighteenth and nineteenth centuries. Roman law endured to influence Western jurisprudence. The Latin tongue remained the language of educated Europeans for well over a thousand years, while evolving in the lower levels of society into the Romance languages: Italian, French, Spanish, Portuguese, and Rumanian. And the dream of Rome inspired empire builders from Charlemagne to Napoleon.

Even though dismembered by the Germanic invasions of the West, the Roman political administration survived through the Middle Ages in the organizational structure of the Church. The ecclesiastical "dioceses" and "provinces," presided over by bishops and archbishops, were patterned on Roman administrative units that had borne identical names. The bishops of the late Empire had become increasingly involved in imperial governance, participating in numerous civic functions and checking on the activities of Roman officials. When the imperial government collapsed in the West, bishops tended to fill the vacuum by assuming political control over their dioceses, seeing to the maintenance of the food supply, and supervising the repair of walls and fortifications. Since most bishops were now drawn from office-holding families of the old Roman aristocracy, such duties came easily to them.

In these ways and many more, the legacy of classical antiquity was passed on to the medieval West. Europeans for centuries to come would be nourished by Greco-Roman culture and haunted by the memory of Rome.

THE GERMANIC IMPACT ON ROMAN EUROPE

The civilization of medieval Europe emerged as a synthesis of three cultures: Classical, Christian, and Germanic. The age of the Latin Doctors witnessed the virtual completion of the Classical-Christian synthesis, but the impact of Germanic culture had only begun to be felt. It was not until the eighth century or thereabouts that a fusion of Classical-Christian culture with Germanic culture was achieved, and only then can it be said that Western civilization was born. The intervening era—the sixth and seventh centuries—provides a fascinating view of a new civilization in the process of formation. Throughout these turbulent years the Classical-Christian tradition was preserved and fostered by the Church, while the Germanic tradition governed the organization of the successor states that rose on the carcass of the Western Empire. The Germanic invaders soon became at least nominal Christians, and some of them were much influenced by Rome. But for centuries a cultural gulf remained between the Church with its Greco-Roman–Christian heritage and the Germanic kingdoms. The Church of the early Middle Ages was able to preserve ancient culture only in a simplified form, for ecclesiastical leaders and lay aristocrats rose from the same social milieu. Still, it remained the great task of the early medieval Church to civilize and Christianize the Germanic peoples.

Germanic Customs and Institutions

In the later fourth century, Germanic peoples from central and southeastern Europe began to press harder against the imperial frontiers. It is hazardous to make broad generalizations regarding their culture and institutions, for customs varied from tribe to tribe, and tribes themselves were unstable, taking form around successful war leaders, then disintegrating when their military fortunes declined. The Franks, the Angles, and the Saxons were agrarian peoples whose movements were slow, but who, once settled, were difficult to displace. Little influenced by Roman civilization, they came into the empire as non-Christians. The Visigoths, Ostrogoths, and Vandals, on the other hand, were more mobile. All three had absorbed Roman culture to a considerable degree before they crossed the frontiers, and all had been converted in the fourth century to Arian Christianity. But such differences notwithstanding, the political and social structures of the various Germanic tribes disclose important similarities.

A contemporary account of early Germanic institutions is to be found in a short book entitled *Germania,* written by the Roman historian Tacitus in A.D. 98. This work is not altogether trustworthy; it is a morality piece written with the intention of criticizing the "degeneracy" of the Romans by comparing them unfavorably with the simple, upright Germans. And one should always bear in mind that the fourth-century Germanic settlers had fallen much more deeply under Roman influence than the Germans whom Tacitus described. Nevertheless, if used cautiously, Tacitus' *Germania* is a valuable source of information on the early Germanic peoples. We can accept his description of tall, blue-eyed people with reddish-blond hair, living in simple villages. And he correctly points out that Germanic women enjoyed considerable independence and respect. They were valued members of Germanic communities because they performed much of the agricultural labor. German men specialized in hunting and warfare, though women occasionally joined in even these pursuits. But Tacitus' picture of Germanic sexual equality is contradicted by the evidence from early Germanic law codes, which regard women as lifelong minors under the legal guardianship of their father, their husband, or, if the husband died, his nearest kinsman. Tacitus likewise exaggerates when he praises the Germans for their chastity and generally virtuous behavior. On the whole their vices seem to have been no less numerous than those of the Romans, but simply cruder. Their standards of personal hygiene are suggested by the observation of a fifth-century Roman gentleman: "Happy the nose that cannot smell a barbarian."

Like the Romans, the Germans used iron tools and weapons. Their chief activities were tending crops or herds and fighting wars. Violence was common, not only between tribes but within them as well. When someone was killed, all close relatives were bound to avenge the death by conducting a feud—declaring war, as it were—against the killer's family. In the boisterous milieu of the tribe, killings were all too common, and in order to keep the social fabric from being torn apart by blood feuds, it became customary for the tribe to establish a *wergeld,* a sum of money that the killer might pay to the relatives of the victim to appease their vengeance. Wergelds varied in size depending on the victim's sex, age, and social status (they were highest for aristocratic adult males and women of childbearing age). Smaller payments were established for lesser injuries such as the cutting off of a victim's arm, leg, thumb, or finger, until in time every imaginable injury was covered, down to the little toe. There was no guarantee, however, that the assaulter would agree to make the payment or that the offended kin-group would agree to accept it. Despite all efforts to control them, blood feuds continued far into the Middle Ages.

Ties of kinship were strong among the early Germans, but they were rivaled by those of the war band, or *comitatus,* a group of warriors bound together by their loyalty to a chief or king. The comitatus was a kind of military brotherhood based on honor, fidelity, courage, and mutual respect between the leader and his men. In warfare the leader was expected to excel his men in courage and prowess, and should the leader be killed, his men were honor-bound to fight to the death even if their cause should appear hopeless. The heroic virtues of the comitatus persisted throughout the early Middle Ages as the characteristic ideology of the European warrior aristocracy.

The comitatus was a subdivision of a larger unit, the tribe, whose members were bound together by their allegiance to a chieftain or king and by their recognition of a common body of customary law. The laws of the Germanic tribes were radically different from those of the Roman Empire, dealing not with broad, systematic concepts but with wergeld schedules and similar devices for controlling violence and private feuding. Legal decisions often depended on whether the parties were able to adhere precisely to complex procedural formalities. Innocence or guilt was determined by requiring the accused to submit to a process known as the "ordeal." One might, for example, be required to grasp a bar of red-hot iron and carry it some specified distance or take a stone from a boiling cauldron. If, after several days, the hand was healing properly, the accused was judged innocent. If not, the verdict was guilty. Similarly, the accused might be lowered into a pond by rope to sink or float. Sinking was a proof of innocence and floating a proof of guilt: the pure water would not "accept" the guilty.

Through such appeals to divine judgment, the Germanic peoples sought to achieve community consensus—to heal the breaches in interfamily relationships created by acts of violence. Throughout the early Middle Ages it was chiefly these Germanic customs, rather than the sophisticated, impersonal concepts of Roman law, that governed jurisprudence in Western Europe. For Roman law depended not on local consensus but on the enforcement authority of a powerful state, and no such authority emerged in Western Europe until the twelfth century. Roman law survived the fall of the Western Empire in fragmentary or bastardized form, but only in the twelfth century did it undergo a fundamental revival in the West. Even then its victory over Germanic law was gradual and incomplete.

The centuries just preceding the invasions witnessed the development, under Roman influence, of relatively stable royal dynasties among many Germanic tribes. Perhaps an unusually gifted warrior and his kindred would gather military followers around him to form a new tribe—rather like the formation of a new criminal gang in urban America. But if the new tribe was successful in war, its leader or leaders might claim royal status and even, in time, descent from some divine ancestor. When a king died, the assembly of the tribe chose as his successor the ablest member of his family. This might or might not be his eldest son, for the tribal assembly was given considerable latitude in its power to elect. The custom of election persisted in most Germanic kingdoms far into the Middle Ages. Its chief consequence during the fifth-century invasions was to ensure that the tribes were normally led by clever, battle-worthy kings or chieftains at a time when the Western Empire was ruled by weaklings and nincompoops.

The Germanic Migrations

The Germanic peoples had long been a threat to the Empire. They had defeated a Roman army in the first century; they had probed deeply into the Empire in the second century and again in the mid-third. But until the late fourth century the Romans had always managed eventually to drive the invaders out or absorb them into the Roman political structure. Beginning in the 370s, however, an overtaxed, exhausted Empire was confronted by renewed Germanic pressures of great magnitude. Lured by the relative wealth, the productive agriculture, and the sunny climate of the Mediterranean world, the Germanic tribes tended to regard the Empire as something to enjoy, not destroy. Their age-long yearning for the fair lands across the Roman frontier was suddenly made urgent by the westward thrust of a tribe of Asiatic nomads known as Huns. These mounted warriors conquered one Germanic tribe after another and turned them into satellites. They subdued the Ostrogoths and made them a subject people. Another Gothic tribe, the Visigoths, sought to preserve their independence by appealing for sanctuary behind the Roman Empire's Danube frontier. The eastern emperor Valens, an Arian, sympathized with the Arian Visigoths, and in 376 he took the unprecedented step of permitting the entire Visigothic people to cross peacefully into the Empire.

There was trouble almost immediately. Corrupt imperial officials cheated and abused the Visigoths, who retaliated by going on a rampage. At length, Emperor Valens himself took the field against them, but the emperor's military incapacity cost him his army and his life at the battle of Adrianople in 378. Adrianople was a military debacle of the first order. Valens' successor, Theodosius I, managed to pacify the Visigoths, but he could not expel them.

When Theodosius died in 395, imperial authority was split between his two youthful sons. Arcadius, barely eighteen, became emperor in the East; Honorius, a child of eleven, assumed authority in the West. As it happened, the two halves were never again rejoined under a single ruler. Not long after Theodosius' death, a vigorous new Visigothic leader named Alaric led his people on a second pillaging campaign that threatened Italy itself. In 406 the desperate Western Empire recalled most of its troops from the Rhine frontier to block Alaric's advance, with the disastrous result that the Vandals and a number of other Germanic peoples crossed the ill-guarded Rhine into Gaul. Shortly thereafter, the Roman legions abandoned distant Britain, and the island was gradually overrun by Angles, Saxons, and other Germanic war bands.

In 408 Emperor Honorius engineered the murder of his ablest general, a man of Vandal ancestry named Stilicho. Honorius was by now an adult in his mid-twenties, but the evidence suggests that he was mentally retarded. He apparently suspected, perhaps with reason, that Stilicho's devotion to the imperial cause was less than fervent. But without Stilicho Italy was virtually defenseless. Honorius and his court barricaded themselves behind the impregnable marshes of Ravenna, leaving Rome to the mercies of Alaric. In 410 the Visigoths entered the city unopposed, and Alaric permitted them to plunder it for three days.

The sack of Rome had a devastating impact on imperial morale. "My tongue sticks to the roof of my mouth," wrote St. Jerome on hearing of the catastrophe, "and sobs choke my speech." But in historical perspective, the event was merely a single incident in the disintegration of the Western Empire. The Visigoths soon left Rome to its witless emperor and turned northward into southern Gaul and Spain. There they established a Visigothic kingdom that endured until the Muslim conquests of the eighth century.

Meanwhile other Germanic peoples were carving out kingdoms of their own. The Vandals swept through Gaul and Spain and across the Straits of Gibraltar into Africa. In 430, the year of St. Augustine's death, they captured his episcopal city of Hippo. They established a North African kingdom centering on ancient Carthage and took to the sea as buccaneers, devastating Mediterranean shipping and sacking coastal cities—including Rome itself.* The Vandal conquest of North Africa cost Rome much of its grain supply, while Vandal piracy shattered the peace of the Mediterranean and dealt a crippling blow to the waning commerce of the Western Empire.

Midway through the fifth century the Huns themselves moved against the West, led by Attila, the "Scourge of God." Defeated by a Roman-Visigothic army in Gaul in 451, the Huns returned the following year, hurling themselves toward Rome and leaving a path of devastation behind them. The west-

---

*Historians have had few good things to say about the Vandals, but of course they are no longer here to defend their reputation. We are indebted to them for providing our language with such colorful words as "vandal," "vandalize," and "vandalism."

ern emperor left Rome undefended, but the Roman bishop, Pope Leo I, some-how persuaded Attila to withdraw from Italy—and he died shortly afterward. His empire collapsed, and the Huns themselves vanished from history. They were not mourned.

In its final years the Western Empire, whose jurisdiction now scarcely extended beyond Italy, fell under the control of hard-bitten military adventurers of Germanic birth. Emperors continued to reign for a time, but their Germanic generals were the powers behind the throne. In 476 the general Odovacar, who saw no point in perpetuating the farce, deposed the last emperor—a boy named Romulus Augustulus ("little Augustus"). Odovacar sent the imperial trappings to Constantinople and asserted his sovereignty over Italy by diverting a third of the agrarian tax revenues to his Germanic troops. Odovacar claimed to rule as an agent of the Eastern Empire, but in fact he was on his own. A few years later the Ostrogoths, now free of Hunnish control and led by an astute king named Theodoric, advanced into Italy, conquered Odovacar, and established a strong state of their own.

Theodoric and Clovis

Theodoric ruled Italy from 493 to 526. Although apparently illiterate, he respected Roman culture: Arian Ostrogoths and orthodox Romans worked together harmoniously under his governance, repairing aqueducts, erecting new buildings, and bringing a degree of prosperity to the long-troubled peninsula. The improving political and economic climate gave rise to a modest intellectual revival that contributed to the transmission of Greco-Roman culture into the Middle Ages. At a time when the knowledge of Greek was dying out in the West, the philosopher Boethius, a high official in Theodoric's regime, produced a series of Latin translations of Greek philosophical works that served as fundamental texts in Western schools for the next 500 years. Boethius wrote his masterpiece, *The Consolation of Philosophy*, at the end of his life when he had fallen from official favor and was imprisoned. The book's central theme is that earthly misfortunes cannot affect the inner life of a virtuous individual. Although such a notion is consistent with Christianity, Boethius drew his ideas primarily from the thought of Plato and the Stoics. Boethius was himself a Christian, yet he never mentioned Christianity explicitly in his *Consolation of Philosophy*. Nevertheless, this work remained immensely popular throughout the Middle Ages.

Theodoric's secretary, Cassiodorus, was another scholar of considerable distinction (though incorrigibly long-winded). A wealthy Roman aristocrat, Cassiodorus spent his later years as abbot of a monastery that he had erected on his own lands in southern Italy. Like Jerome, he set his monks to the task of copying and preserving the literary works of antiquity, both Christian and pagan.

During the years of Theodoric's rule in Ostrogothic Italy, another Germanic king, Clovis (481/2–511), was creating a Frankish kingdom in the former

Roman province of Gaul. Although far less Romanized than Theodoric, Clovis possessed a keen instinct for political survival. He adopted the straightforward policy of murdering all possible rivals. Gregory of Tours, a sixth-century bishop and historian, quotes him as saying, "Oh woe, for I travel among strangers and have none of my kinfolk to help me!" But Gregory adds, "He did not refer to their deaths out of grief, but craftily, to see if he could bring to light some new relative to kill."

It will perhaps seem odd that Bishop Gregory approved wholeheartedly of Clovis's rule. That savage monarch—who lacked even the family loyalty of a mobster—is pictured in Gregory's *History of the Franks* as one who "walked before God with an upright heart and did what was pleasing in his sight." The explanation is that Clovis, having been untouched by Arianism, was converted directly from Germanic paganism to orthodox Christianity. He respected and favored the churches, whereas other Germanic rulers were handing them over to the Arians. Clovis himself regarded Christianity as a kind of magic to help him win battles, but the Church supported him as a hero of Christian orthodoxy.

Another reason for Clovis's good press was that he maintained relatively warm relations with the old landholding aristocracy (to which Bishop Gregory of Tours belonged). Because of the depopulated condition of the countryside, there were adequate lands for all—Frank and Gallo-Roman alike. The great land-owning families of Roman times were for the most part left in place—to enjoy their fields and their bishoprics and to serve as high officials in the Frankish regime. From their point of view, Clovis's victory was not so much a conquest as a *coup d'état*.

In succeeding generations, Frankish and Gallo-Roman landowners, sharing a common religion, fused through intermarriage into a single aristocratic order. As centuries passed, the royal name "Clovis" was softened to "Louis," and the "Franks" became the "French." And the friendship between the Frankish monarchy and the Church developed into one of the determining elements in European politics.

Europe in A.D. 500

As the sixth century dawned, the Western Empire was only a memory. In its place was a group of Germanic successor states that vaguely prefigured the nations of modern Western Europe. Theodoric headed a relatively tolerant Ostrogothic-Arian regime in Italy. The orthodox Clovis was completing the Frankish conquest of Gaul. The Arian Vandals lorded it over a restive orthodox population in North Africa, seizing the wheat plantations and introducing former aristocrats to the joys of field work. The Arian Visigoths were being driven out of southern Gaul by the Franks, but their regime continued to dominate Spain for the next two centuries. And the Angles and Saxons were in the process of establishing a group of small, non-Christian kingdoms in Britain that would one day coalesce into "Angle-land," or England.

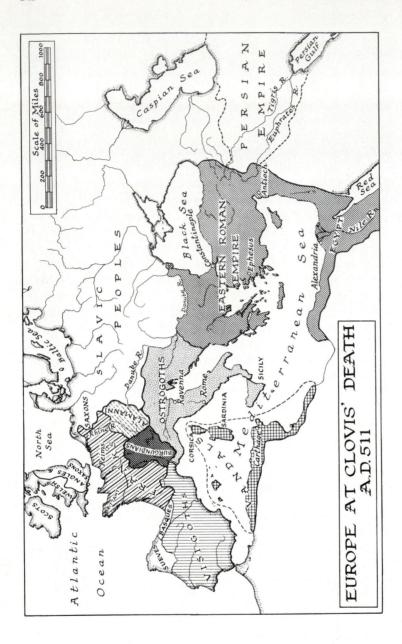

EUROPE AT CLOVIS' DEATH
A.D. 511

While Germanic kingdoms were establishing themselves in the West, the Roman papacy was beginning to play an important independent role in European society. We have seen how Pope Leo I (440–461) assumed the task of protecting the city of Rome from the Huns, thereby winning for himself the moral leadership of Italy. Leo and his successors declared that the bishops of Rome—the popes—constituted the highest authority in the Church, and following the example of St. Ambrose, they insisted on the supremacy of Church over state in spiritual matters. In proclaiming its doctrines of papal supremacy in the Church and ecclesiastical independence from state control, the papacy was wisely disengaging itself from the faltering western emperors. In the fifth century these papal doctrines remained little more than words, but they were to result in an ever-widening gulf between the Eastern and Western Church. More than that, they constituted the opening phase of the prolonged medieval struggle between the rival claims of popes and monarchs. The mighty papacy of the High Middle Ages was yet far off, but it was already foreshadowed in the boldly independent stance of Leo I. The Western Empire was crumbling, but eternal Rome still claimed the allegiance of the world.

3

Byzantium Endures

THE SURVIVAL OF THE EAST ROMAN EMPIRE

By the opening of the sixth century, the Western Empire had decomposed
into a group of Germanic successor states. But the eastern emperors, with
their capital at Constantinople, retained control of an immense, crescent-
shaped realm girdling the eastern Mediterranean from the Balkans through
Asia Minor, Syria, and Palestine to Egypt. As we have seen, the East had
always been more populous than the West. Its civilization was far older and
more deeply rooted; its cities were larger and more numerous. The class of
free landowning peasants, which had diminished so drastically in the West,
was larger and more prosperous in the East. Commerce and industry had
always been livelier there, and the resulting balance of trade caused gold coins
to flow constantly eastward. Understandably, when invaders poured across
the imperial frontiers in unprecedented numbers, the East proved far more
resilient than the West.

Moreover, the Eastern, or "Byzantine," Empire enjoyed important strategic advantages. The province of Asia Minor (Anatolia; the modern Turkey)
was its great reservoir of laborers, soldiers, and revenues. Protected from
Germanic incursions by the Black Sea and invulnerable Constantinople, Asia
Minor would remain for centuries the chief recruiting ground for the Byzantine
army and the most dependable source of imperial taxes. During the cataclys-
mic fifth century, while Germanic tribes were conquering the western provinces, Asia Minor was a bulwark of the Empire. Its tough, loyal troops provided the eastern emperors with an alternative to the dangerous policy of total
dependence on hired Germanic armies.

With the rich material and human resources of Asia Minor behind it,
the eastern capital at Constantinople held fast against the Germanic tide. Its
command of the commerce flowing between the Black Sea and the
Mediterranean made Constantinople the economic and political heart of the
Eastern Empire. So long as the great city remained secure behind its massive
landward and seaward walls, the Empire endured. Over the centuries,
Constantinople's walls repelled the attacks of Germanic and Asiatic tribes,

34

Persians and Muslims. One can well imagine why Germanic chieftains should have preferred the more vulnerable West.

The Eastern Empire had the further advantage, during the crucial fifth century, of being better governed than the Western Empire. A series of able rulers carefully husbanded their resources, fattened their treasury, and strengthened the fortifications of Constantinople while the Western Empire was collapsing. But the eastern emperors, skillful though many of them were, could have accomplished little had it not been for the superb strategic location of their capital and the enduring commercial and human resources of the lands they ruled.

Byzantine Government

The civilization of the Byzantine Empire was a synthesis of three elements: Roman government, Christian religion, and Greco-Oriental culture. From Rome the Eastern Empire drew its legal system, its bureaucracy, and its principles of administration. Indeed, Byzantine government was a direct offspring of the third- and fourth-century Roman political system. Byzantine autocracy had its roots in the glorification of late-Roman emperors such as Diocletian and Constantine; tight imperial control of the Byzantine Church harked back to the policies of Constantine and Theodosius I. The heavy taxation of late Roman times continued, and life in the Byzantine Empire remained burdensome and insecure.

The prevailing Byzantine mood, like the mood of the late Roman Empire, was one of defense and self-preservation. To the Byzantines, their state was the ark of civilization in an ocean of barbarism—the political embodiment of the Christian faith—and as such it had to be preserved at all costs. The appropriate virtues in such a state were entrenchment, not expansion; caution, not daring.

This defensive, conservative mood is evident in both the Byzantine bureaucracy and the Byzantine army. The bureaucracy, huge and precedent-bound, abhorred change and seldom took risks. Resisting the policies of Byzantium's more vigorous and imaginative emperors, it provided cohesion during the reigns of fools. The small, highly trained Byzantine army also clung to a policy of few risks. Its generals practiced their art with cunning and caution, well aware that the preservation of the Empire might depend on the survival of their armies.

Byzantine Christianity

The Byzantine emperors drew invaluable strength from the loyalty of their Christian subjects. Orthodox Christians within the Empire held their ruler to be more than a mere secular sovereign. He was God's vice-regent, and his was the decisive voice in all matters affecting Christian governance, practice, and doctrine. He was the protector of the Holy Church; his armies fought not merely for the Empire but for God; his warriors were not mere soldiers but crusaders. Christianity had become a potent stimulus to patriotism, and the Christian emperors of Byzantium enjoyed popular support to a degree unknown in the days of pagan Rome.

But the emperor's dominating position in Byzantine Christianity was a source of weakness as well. Religious controversy was now a matter of direct imperial concern, and heresy became a threat to the state. The fifth and sixth centuries were singularly rich in doctrinal disputes, and in the end these conflicts cost the Empire dearly. The most widespread heresy of the age was Monophysitism, a doctrine that arose in Egypt and spread into Syria and Palestine, creating a mood of hostility toward the orthodox emperors. The controversy between the orthodox and the Monophysites turned on the question of whether Christ's manhood and Godhood constituted two separate natures (as the orthodox said) or were fused together into one nature (Monophysitism). The Monophysite Christ possessed a single nature in which divinity tended to supersede humanity. Monophysitism has thus been seen as a return to the spiritualism of the ancient Near East, which tended to regard the physical world as evil or unimportant.

Monophysitism can also be viewed as a protest doctrine, upheld in districts that had been civilized long before the days of Roman rule by people whose commitment to Greco-Roman culture was tempered by their own, far older cultures. Even without Monophysitism, the inhabitants of Egypt and Syria might well have been expected to show separatist tendencies against embattled Byzantium. And Monophysitism, although far more than a mere excuse for rebellion, was nevertheless an appropriate vehicle for the antagonisms of Near Eastern peoples against a millennium of Greco-Roman domination.

The orthodox-Monophysite quarrel raged long and bitterly. The emperors, convinced that doctrinal unity was essential to the preservation of their state, followed first one policy, then another. Sometimes they persecuted the Monophysites, sometimes they favored them, and sometimes they worked out compromise doctrinal formulas that were intended to satisfy both sides but in fact satisfied neither. Whatever policy the emperors might follow, the controversy dragged on until the seventh century, when the disaffected Monophysite provinces were swallowed by the expanding Islamic world. Only then, at the Ecumenical Council of Constantinople in 680, did orthodoxy win its definitive victory within what remained of the Byzantine Empire.

Byzantine Culture

Roman government, Christian religion, Greco-Oriental culture—these were the three pillars of Byzantine civilization. And all three were shaped—and to a degree transformed—by the experience of the fourth-century Christian Empire. As a consequence of that experience, Byzantium inherited Roman government in its late, authoritarian form. Byzantine Christianity was a direct outgrowth of the Christianity of the later Roman Empire—its theology tightened and defined by the reaction to Arianism, its priestly hierarchy overshadowed by the power of the emperors. Just as Constantine had dominated the clergy at the Council of Nicaea in 325, so likewise did the Byzantine emperors, over the centuries, tend to dominate the patriarchs of Constantinople.

Byzantium's Greco-Oriental culture, too, was molded by the intellectual and cultural currents of the third, fourth, and fifth centuries. The Greek culture that Byzantium inherited was by no means the culture of classical Athens—with its superbly proportioned architecture, its advances into uncharted regions of speculative thought, and its controlled, tensely muscular sculpture. That tradition had undergone successive modifications in the ages that followed and, above all, during the third- and fourth-century Empire. The mood of otherworldliness that gradually permeated Roman culture resulted in a transformation of the classical spirit. There had always been a potent spiritual-mystical element in Greco-Roman culture, coexisting with the traditional classical concern with the earthly and concrete. Now the mystical element grew stronger. More and more of the better minds turned to theology, scriptural study, and the quest for individual salvation. Artists were less interested in portraying physical perfection than in portraying sanctity. The new Christian art depicted slender, heavily robed figures with solemn faces and deep eyes—windows into the soul. Techniques of perspective, which artists of the classical era had developed to a fine degree, mattered less to the artists of the new age (as they have mattered less to artists of our own century). Deemphasizing physical realism, the artists of the late Empire embellished their works with rich, glittering colors that conveyed a sense of heavenly radiance and religious solemnity.

Such was the artistic tradition Byzantium inherited. It conformed so perfectly to the Byzantine spirit that the artists of the Eastern Empire were able to produce enduring masterpieces without ever departing far from its basic aesthetic canons. Majestic churches rose in the Byzantine style—churches such

Mosaic of female martyrs; Sant' Apollinare Nuovo, Ravenna (sixth century).

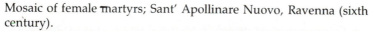

San Vitale, Ravenna (526-547): Interior.

as Sancta Sophia in Constantinople, San Vitale in Ravenna, and St. Mark's in Venice—whose interiors shone with glistening mosaics portraying saints and monarchs, Christ and the Virgin, on backgrounds of gold. Here was an art vastly different from that of Greek antiquity, with different techniques and different goals, yet as valid and as successful as the art of classical Athens.

In this new, transcendental environment, Greek culture was significantly altered, but Byzantine civilization remained Greek nonetheless. Greek was the language of most of its inhabitants, and despite their deep commitment to the Christian faith, they never forgot their ancient Greek heritage. Indeed, the transition from late Roman to Byzantine civilization is marked by an increasing dissociation from the Latin-Roman past. Greek became the language of the imperial court. The Byzantine Church, under the emperor and the patriarch of Constantinople, gave no allegiance and little thought to the Roman pope. Byzantine scholars ignored their Latin to the point where they could no more be expected to read a Latin literary text than could a modern professor of accounting or American history. But they continued through the centuries to scrutinize the literature and philosophy of the ancient Greeks.

THE BYZANTINE CENTURIES

The Age of Justinian

The first major creative surge of Byzantine civilization occurred during the reign of Justinian (527–565). In many respects Justinian stands as the last of the Roman emperors. He and his court still conversed in the Latin tongue. He was driven by the vision of reviving the old Roman Empire by reconquering its lost western provinces. And it was under his direction that the vast heritage of Roman law was assembled into a single, coherent body of jurisprudence. But Justinian was a Byzantine no less than a Roman—and he would surely have perceived no distinction between them. His reign witnessed a golden age of Byzantine art and the climax of imperial autocracy that typified Byzantine culture over the centuries that followed.

The achievements of Justinian's reign were products not only of his own determination and ambition but also of the wise and cautious rule of his predecessors, who endured the worst of the Germanic invasions, nurtured the financial resources of the Empire, and gradually accumulated a sizable surplus in the treasury. Justinian was also fortunate in that the Germanic kingdoms of the West, which he had determined to conquer, were losing much of their early vigor. Theodoric, king of the Ostrogoths, died in 526, a year before Justinian ascended the Byzantine throne, and the Vandal monarchy of North Africa was becoming increasingly disorganized and corrupt.

✳ Byzantine Chronology

330:	Constantine founds Constantinople
395:	Final division of Eastern and Western Empire
527–565:	Reign of Justinian
533–534:	Conquest of Vandal North Africa
535–555:	Gothic Wars; conquest of Italy
541–543:	Great plague
548:	Death of Empress Theodora
568:	Lombards invade Italy
610–641:	Reign of Heraclius; Islamic conquests of Syria, Palestine, and Egypt
680:	Ecumenical Council of Constantinople: orthodoxy triumphs over Monophysitism
690s:	Muslims conquer Byzantine North Africa
717–718:	Great Muslim siege of Constantinople
867–1056:	Macedonian dynasty: reconquest of Balkans; conversion of south Slavs
976–1025:	Reign of Basil the Bulgar-Slayer
c. 980–1015:	Reign of Prince Vladimir of Kiev, who converts to Byzantine Christianity
1071:	Seljuk Turks rout Byzantines at Manzikert; loss of Asia Minor
1453:	Fall of Constantinople to Ottoman Turks

San Vitale, Ravenna: Mosaic of Theodora and her Court.

Justinian was aided immeasurably by his wife and co-ruler, Empress Theodora, a woman no less ambitious than he and even more resolute. Formerly a public entertainer and courtesan, Theodora was gifted with extraordinary practical intelligence. Together, she and Justinian brought new energy and boldness to the old, conservative regime. The plans to rebuild Constantinople, reform Roman law, and reconquer the West are usually ascribed to Justinian himself, but since he consulted Theodora on all matters of policy, it is often impossible to distinguish her ideas from his. In any event, without Theodora's iron will, none of these policies could have been carried out. Early in the reign a great urban riot resulted in the burning of much of Constantinople. With the city in flames and rioters advancing on the imperial palace, Justinian was on the point of abandoning his imperial office and fleeing in panic when Theodora restored his courage. Refusing to depart, she announced that she intended to die an empress. As a result of her determination, the riots were quelled and the regime survived.

The audacious policies of Justinian and Theodora, though reasonably successful in their own time, left the empire exhausted and unstable. Justinian applied his considerable knowledge of theology to the tangled problem of reconciling the orthodox and the Monophysites (he himself was orthodox, whereas Theodora had Monophysite leanings), but his complex compromise satisfied neither group. After the riot and conflagration, he devoted immense

Sancta Sophia, Constantinople: full interior. The four disks were added many centuries later by the Muslims and carry messages from the Koran.

funds to the rebuilding of Constantinople on an unprecedented scale. The most notable product of his construction program was the church of Sancta Sophia—one of Byzantium's foremost works of art. Gold, silver, ivory, and dazzling mosaics adorned its interior, and a vast dome seemed almost to float on air above it. The total effect was such as to stun even Justinian: he is said to have exclaimed on its completion, "Glory to God who has judged me worthy of accomplishing such a work as this! O Solomon, I have outdone thee!"*

It was at Justinian's bidding that a talented group of lawyers set about to assemble the immense mass of legal precedents, juridical opinions, and imperial edicts that constituted the legacy of Roman law. These materials were arranged into a vast, systematic collection known in later centuries as the *Corpus Juris Civilis*—the "body of civil law." Justinian's *Corpus* not only became the keystone of future Byzantine jurisprudence but also served as the vehicle in which Roman law returned to Western Europe in the twelfth century to challenge the age-long domination of Germanic legal custom. The appearance of the *Corpus Juris Civilis* in the twelfth-century West was of incalculable importance to the development of sophisticated and rational legal systems in

*Unlike the temple of Solomon, Sancta Sophia still stands: see above.

the European states. Indeed, its effect is still very much apparent in the legal codes of modern nations. But the importance of the *Corpus Juris Civilis* extended even beyond this. Roman law had formerly contained strong elements of popular sovereignty, but in Justinian's hand it acquired some of the autocratic flavor of the Byzantine state. Thus, in the late-medieval and early-modern West it tended to support the rise of royal absolutism, acting as a counterpoise to the limited-monarchy notions of Germanic legal tradition. The monarchs of late-medieval and early-modern Europe found much to admire in Justinian's precept that the emperor's decree is law.

Historians are prone to criticize Justinian for lavishing the limited resources of his empire on the chimerical policy of reconquering the West. In one sense they are correct: the reconquest did drain the treasury and prostrate the Empire, and the victories of Justinian's western armies proved in time to be largely ephemeral. Yet Justinian, keenly sensitive to the Roman imperial tradition, could not rest until he had made one all-out attempt to recover the lost provinces and to reestablish imperial authority in the city of Rome. His armies, small but led by brilliant generals, conquered the strife-torn Vandal kingdom of North Africa with ease in 533–534 and succeeded in wresting a long strip of the Spanish Mediterranean coast from the Visigoths. For twenty years his troops struggled against the Ostrogoths in Italy, crushing them at length in 555 but only after enormous effort and expense. The campaigns in Italy, known as the "Gothic Wars," ravaged the Italian peninsula and left Rome itself in ruins. The Visigothic sack of 410 was a minor incident compared with the havoc wrought by Justinian's armies. (See map below.)

During the final years of his reign, Justinian ruled almost the entire Mediterranean coastline, but his vastly expanded empire was impoverished and

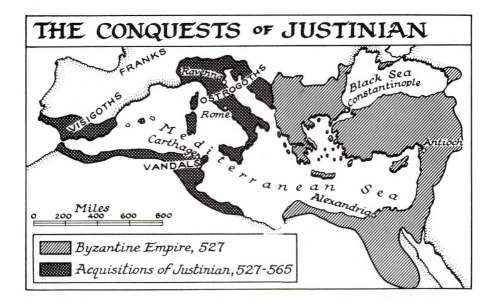

THE CONQUESTS OF JUSTINIAN

Byzantine Empire, 527
Acquisitions of Justinian, 527–565

San Vitale, Ravenna (526–547): Exterior.

bankrupt. Theodora died in 548, leaving Justinian demoralized and irresolute. Moreover, a devastating outbreak of plague swept across Byzantium and Western Europe in 541–543 and recurred sporadically over the next two centuries, taking a fearful toll of human lives and crippling the Byzantine economy. But even without the plague, Byzantium would have found it difficult to hold its newly conquered territories. With his military attention focused westward, Justinian was powerless to prevent a great flood of Slavic peoples and Bulgars from ravaging the Balkans. In 561, the Avars, warlike nomads from the Asian steppes, settled on the Danube shore and proceeded to subjugate the Slavs and Bulgars. Byzantium now found itself living in the shadow of a hostile Avar state, far more threatening than Vandal North Africa or Ostrogothic Italy.

Retrenchment and Revival

The Byzantine Empire aspired to be Roman yet was destined by its geographic setting to be Balkan and Near-Eastern. Justinian's western conquests were not enduring. In 568, three years after his death, a Germanic tribe known as the Lombards (Langobards or Long Beards) burst into Italy, further devastating that troubled land and carving out an extensive kingdom in northern Italy centering on the Po Valley. Byzantium retained much of southern Italy and clung to Ravenna and other cities along the Adriatic coast, but its hold on Italy was appreciably loosened. Shortly afterward, the Visigoths reconquered the Byzantine territories in southern Spain, and eventually, in the 690s, Byzantine North Africa—the former Vandal state—fell to the Muslims. In 751 the Lombards seized Ravenna, reducing still further the Byzantine presence in Italy.

Justinian's successors were forced to abandon his ambitious policies and face the hard necessities of survival, turning their backs on the West to face more immediate threats from hostile peoples to the north and east. The Persian Empire pressed dangerously against Byzantium's eastern frontier, and the Avars with their Bulgar and Slavic subjects won control of most of the Balkans.

The great crisis occurred during the reign of Emperor Heraclius (610–641), when Persian armies occupied Syria, Palestine, and Egypt, and when, in 626, Constantinople just barely withstood a furious combined siege of Persians and Avars. Heraclius crushed the Persian army at last in 628 and recovered the lands that had been lost to Persia. He succeeded also in reestablishing imperial suzerainty over the Balkans. But no sooner had the Persians been defeated than the Muslim armies exploded out of Arabia to wrest Syria, Palestine, and Egypt from the Empire and put Constantinople once again in grave danger. The Muslims besieged the city on several occasions, most determinedly in 717–718, at which time the dogged Byzantine defense may have prevented not only the Empire but much of eastern and central Europe from being absorbed into the Arab world. The Empire withstood the powerful northward thrust of Islam, retaining Constantinople, Asia Minor, and an unsteady overlordship in the Balkan peninsula, thereby preserving the division of medieval western Eurasia into the three great cultures of Byzantium, Islam, and Western Christendom. The Christian kingdoms of the West were able to develop behind the shield of Constantinople's walls.

The Macedonian Emperors and the Conversion of the Slavs

Byzantium had won the time necessary for the gradual conquest and conversion of southeastern Europe. In the course of the seventh century it had lost to Islam such great urban centers as Damascus, Alexandria, Antioch, and Carthage, with the result that the Empire became far smaller and poorer, yet more homogeneous, more unified in religion and culture, and more tightly centered on Constantinople, the one great city remaining.

After several generations of retrenchment, Byzantium began to expand once again under the dynasty of "Macedonian" emperors (867–1056). A rich literary and artistic revival was accompanied by a series of important territorial conquests, and by a surge in missionary activity that resulted in the conversion of countless Slavic peoples to Eastern Orthodox Christianity.

The Macedonians reconquered northern Syria for a time and pushed their frontiers in Asia Minor northeastward. But their most significant military accomplishment, in the long run, was the establishment of firm Byzantine rule over the Balkan Slavs and Bulgars. The most celebrated ruler of the dynasty, Basil II, "the Bulgar-Slayer" (976–1025), campaigned year after year in the Balkans, demolishing a Bulgarian army in 1014 and eventually crushing all resistance to Byzantine imperial authority.

In the meantime, beginning in the middle years of the ninth century, the process of Byzantine religious conversion and acculturation among the peoples of southeastern Europe began in earnest. Missionaries such as Saints Cyril and Methodius, "the Apostles to the Slavs," evangelized tirelessly among the south Slavs and Russians. In the later ninth century the first Slavonic alphabet was developed by Byzantine missionaries—reputedly by Cyril and Methodius themselves—for the purpose of creating a Slavic vernacular Bible and liturgy. Thus the Slavonic written language and the Slavonic Christian Church came into being side by side. Ultimately, the evangelism of the Macedonian age brought Russia and much of the Balkans into the Orthodox Church and into the sphere of Byzantine culture. The enduring effects of this process are exemplified by the Slavonic alphabet used to this day in portions of the Balkan peninsula and throughout the Soviet Union: it is known as the "Cyrillic alphabet," after St. Cyril.

The Conversion of Russia

The age of the Macedonian emperors was concurrent with the rise of Russia— far beyond the political boundaries of the Empire. Byzantium had always had economic and political interests on the northern shore of the Black Sea. In the ninth and tenth centuries, trade flourished between the Black Sea and the Baltic and linked the Byzantine Empire with the vigorous commerce of the Viking world. Numerous Byzantine coin hoards dating from this era have been unearthed in Scandinavia, and Norsemen were widely employed as Byzantine mercenaries. Swedish Vikings probed deep into Russia in the ninth century and established a dynasty in the Russian trading center of Novgorod, ruling over the native Slavic population and later intermarrying with it. In the tenth century a ruler of Novgorod captured the strategic Russian commercial town of Kiev, which became the nucleus of the first important Russian state.

The Macedonian emperors at Constantinople took pains to maintain warm diplomatic relations with Kievan Russia. Basil the Bulgar-Slayer received crucial military aid from Prince Vladimir of Kiev and promised in return to give his own sister to Vladimir in marriage. The result of this union was nothing less than the conversion of Kievan Russia. Vladimir, on marrying his Byzantine princess, agreed to adopt Christianity, and his people quickly followed him. Kiev never submitted politically to the Byzantine emperors, but its people became spiritual subjects of the Byzantine church.

In the course of the eleventh century, Kievan Russia disintegrated politically, and in the thirteenth century it was brought under the yoke of Mongol invaders, but its Christian-Byzantine culture survived these political disasters. In the sixteenth century, after the Byzantine Empire itself was demolished, the Christian princes of Moscow assumed the imperial title (Caesar—Czar). As Constantinople had been the "Second Rome," they intended Moscow to become the "Third Rome," and they asserted their dominion over both church and state much as their imperial "predecessors" at Constantinople had done.

Some scholars have even suggested that the present rulers of the Soviet Union, with their control of both the state and the Communist ideological apparatus, are perpetuating in secular form the Byzantine tradition of imperial control over church and state.

Military Disaster and Cultural Survival

The dynamism and grandeur of the Macedonian age came to an end in the eleventh century with the passing of the Macedonian dynasty (1056) and the westward migration of a powerful new Asian tribe, the Seljuk Turks, into the Middle East. Recently converted to Islam, the Seljuks had made a puppet of the Islamic caliph at Baghdad. In 1065 they wrested Armenia from the Byzantines, and when an imperial army attempted to drive them from Asia Minor, it was annihilated at the epochal Battle of Manzikert in 1071.

Manzikert is one of the great turning points in Byzantine history. Even though the Seljuk Turks did not adequately follow up their triumph, the disaster crippled the Empire by breaking the age-long Byzantine hold on Asia Minor. In the same fatal year of 1071, the Normans in southern Italy conquered the vital Byzantine Adriatic port of Bari, marking the virtual end of Byzantium's presence in the West. By now, Western Christendom was acquiring the wealth and power of a great civilization, and prostrate Byzantium was forced to beg aid from the papacy and the Franks. The century of Manzikert ended with the First Crusade and the fall of Jerusalem (1099), not to Byzantine warriors but to French crusaders. Byzantium tottered on until the mid-fifteenth century, but it was never again the same. Its years of expansion were over, and its energies were thenceforth consumed in its struggle against destruction.

Yet Byzantine culture survived the blow of Manzikert. Art and learning continued to flourish through Byzantium's final centuries. When at length Constantinople fell to the Ottoman Turks in 1453, Byzantium was in the midst of an impressive Classical-Humanist revival that had a significant impact on the Italian Renaissance.

To the end, Byzantium revered its Classical heritage. As a custodian of Greco-Roman culture, the Eastern Empire provided an invaluable service to the emerging civilization of Western Europe. Roman law and Greek philosophy and literature were studied in Constantinople at a time when they were all but unknown in the West. The influence of Byzantine art on medieval Western Christendom was, in the words of a modern historian, "far-flung and everywhere beneficial: and whatever else the West disliked and despised about the East, its mosaics and enamels, its textiles and ivories, its pearl and onyx, its painting and its gold work were eagerly coveted and jealously guarded in western treasuries."*

*Romily Jenkins, *Byzantium, The Imperial Centuries,* Vintage Books, New York, 1969, p. 385.

Yet Byzantium's government was never able to transcend the rigid autocracy of the late Roman Empire or the defensive mood that it implied. Byzantium's creative impulses, though impressive and sometimes awesome, were inhibited by its devotion to an ancient and holy tradition that could be altered only slowly and very cautiously, if at all. The task of Byzantine artists and scholars was not to innovate but to preserve. They would not have appreciated Pablo Picasso. Similarly the Byzantine Church dedicated itself to safeguarding a body of sacred truth already revealed and complete. Byzantine Christianity was more deeply mystical than Western Christianity, but less open to liturgical and doctrinal change, less interested in serving the outer world through schools, hospitals, and charities, less inclined to construct daring new theological systems on rational foundations.

Byzantium contributed much to Western Europe. It was a military bastion and a cultural treasure chest, and its maritime trade stimulated the economic awakening of western commercial centers such as Venice, Genoa, and Pisa. But it was on the Slavic peoples of Eastern Europe that Byzantine culture left its deepest imprint. There, Eastern Orthodox Christianity remains a powerful force to this day, and memories of Byzantium still linger. In the Soviet Union the Orthodox Church was long under siege, yet like Byzantium, it has displayed a remarkable capacity for survival. And any traveler who has had to cope with Soviet administrators, hotel managers, Intourist agents, shopkeepers, customs inspectors, or Aeroflot officials will be keenly aware that the Byzantine bureaucratic tradition lives on.

4

Early Western Christendom

CONTINUITY AND CHANGE

Western Europe: The Land and its People

Until recently, historians had visualized transalpine Western Europe in late Roman or early medieval times as a sparsely populated and largely untamed wilderness. This misconception turns up, among other places, in a widely used textbook on medieval history: "North of the Mediterranean Basin, Western Europe was lightly settled and little developed" in A.D. 500.* But the traditional "untamed wilderness" picture of post-Roman Europe—and pre-Roman Europe as well—has now been discarded. Archaeological investigations throughout much of Western Europe have demonstrated that human settlement was far more widespread—and more complex—than had previously been suspected. As the Romans expanded into the Balkans, Gaul, and Britain, they found populous and flourishing agricultural villages in large number. They encountered hillforts sheltering well-organized communities, farms tilled with large and highly effective plows, and networks of fields, stock corrals, and homesteads linked together by boundaries and trackways into what archaeologists describe as managed landscapes. The lands across the Alps through which Julius Caesar campaigned had undergone many millennia of economic and cultural development from the Stone Age to the Bronze Age (c. 3000 B.C.) and finally, after 100 B.C., the Iron Age. The half-millennium of Roman occupation witnessed the building of cities on the Greco-Roman model—Lyons, Cologne, Vienna, London, and many others.

   With this new knowledge, together with the benefit of hindsight (a form of cheating known as "history"), Europe's potential becomes obvious. Its weather is bracing but not intimidating—a happy compromise between the languid, narcotic mildness of southern California, and the torrid summers and arctic winters that can sometimes afflict mid-America. (A guidebook for British tourists visiting the United States warns them of the violent temperature ex-

*C. W. Hollister, *Medieval Europe: A Short History*, 5th ed., Random House, Inc. New York, 1982 p. 51.

tremes of the Middle West.) Northwestern Europe's dependable, year-round rainfall and the fertile soils of its numerous river valleys encourage agricultural productivity—so much so that a first-century Greek geographer could describe the region as "producing in perfection all the fruits of the earth necessary for life."

By the fifth century, Europe's climate was better still. Between roughly A.D. 400 and 1200 Europe was less rainy, and warmer by several degrees, than it had previously been or than it is now. The summer growing season was longer, and vineyards flourished some 300 miles further north than they do today. Marshes and bogs receded, and the North Atlantic welcomed seafarers with less ice and milder storms.

The Western European heartlands form a vast plain that fans out from the Pyrenees and the Alps northeastward across France and Germany and on through Eastern Europe to the Urals. In Roman and early medieval times, as in preceding millennia, this fan-shaped plain was the invasion route of countless tribes migrating westward out of Russia and beyond. Crossing the plain are several low, mineral-rich mountain ranges and a remarkable network of broad rivers fed by the year-round rains. Europe has been shaped and nourished by its rivers: they connect interior settlements with the sea and with each other, facilitating communication and commerce. Most of Europe's major cities were built on riverbanks—Paris, London, Milan, Cologne, and many others—so that even though they lay far from the sea, they could function as ports. A further stimulus to commerce is Europe's long, irregular coastline, with its huge bays and peninsulas, and accessible offshore islands such as Sicily, Sardinia, and the British Isles. Taken altogether, Europe's climate, rich soils, rivers, and coastline create an ideal environment for human habitation and commercial enterprise.

Before the Roman conquests and long thereafter, most of Western Europe north of the Alps was inhabited by Celts—and by still earlier settlers whom they had subdued. The Celts were a creative people, skilled at music and poetry, metalwork, and textile making. The Romans were amused at their barbaric custom of wearing pants instead of tunics ("breeches" is a Celtic word). Most Celts were farmers, living in villages surrounded by cultivated fields. Others engaged in commerce across vast reaches of western, central, and even eastern Europe. The Celts built fortified towns along their trade routes, some of which became important provincial cities in Roman times. But it would be misleading to describe their far-flung settlements as a "Celtic Empire" (as some careless scholars have done), for the Celts were split into hundreds of independent tribes that united only occasionally, briefly, and grudgingly into larger confederations. They fought hard against the Romans, but in the long run they could not match the military resources of a Mediterranean empire.

Under the Roman conquerors, Celtic agricultural villages continued to function much as before. In time, the majority of these communities were incorporated into the great estates of the provincial Roman aristocracy (itself part Celtic through intermarriage). The farmer-villagers became unfree peas-

Physical map of Europe.

ants and were forced to pay rents and dues to their lords. But they continued to inhabit their villages and till their fields; it was in their landlords' interest that they should do so.

The Germanic conquerors, as we have seen, took only portions of the old Roman estates (or of their tax revenues) while establishing new ones on much the same pattern. And in the meantime, important churchmen—bishops and abbots—were themselves acquiring extensive lands through the accumulation of pious gifts. But whether under new lords or old, lay or ecclesiastical, the villagers worked on.

Post-Roman Europe

In the aftermath of the Germanic invasions, Western Europe lost much of the administrative structure of the Roman Empire. But the Church preserved a great deal of the old classical legacy, and bishops exercised both spiritual and political authority across considerable areas. By A.D. 600 the municipal governments of antiquity had all but disappeared north of the Alps, and archaeological investigations have disclosed a process of urban economic collapse. But many of the towns endured as centers of ecclesiastical administration. They remained the sites of the bishops' cathedral churches and the headquarters of episcopal (bishops') government over surrounding districts.

Many towns became important pilgrimage centers, for the more important cathedral churches possessed relics—the bodies or clothing of departed saints—which were regarded as agents of spiritual power and physical healing. The cathedral at Tours, for example, possessed the body of the noted miracle-worker, St. Martin (bishop of Tours, 372–397), which was said to have healed many who touched his tomb. Holy men such as St. Martin were revered in their lifetimes as transmitters of divine power, wisdom, and love to the communities in which they lived, and their sacred bodies were thought to retain this function after death.

The urban bishoprics, with their relics and vast estates, played a major role in the economy of the Germanic successor states. So, too, did the large monasteries with their surrounding fields, and often with wonder-working relics of their own. Bishops and abbots were the social and economic equals of the lay aristocracy; together they formed the landholding elite of the post-Roman West. The great estates—whether lay, ecclesiastical, or royal—were tilled by slaves or by semiservile, rent-paying villagers in an economic environment that was becoming increasingly localized and self-contained. A small-scale luxury trade persisted, but the agrarian communities of the sixth and seventh centuries produced most of what they needed, and since lives were meager, needs were few.

There is reason to believe that some Western European farmlands were abandoned altogether and resettled only much later. Aerial photographs of the southern French countryside disclose fields of a typically medieval pattern—radiating outward from a central village. But often these radiating fields appear superimposed on earlier Roman patterns—square or rectangular fields, systematically laid out. Since no governmental authority of the early Middle Ages had either the power or the will to effect such a fundamental change in field patterns, one can only conclude that the Roman fields had reverted to wilderness, and generations thereafter had been resettled and reshaped. Aerial photographs do not permit precise dating, but the silent catastrophe they record may well have resulted from the violence and depopulation following Rome's collapse in the West, aggravated by a great plague cycle that commenced in the 540s.

Germanic invasions and Germanic settlements transformed the ethnic character of Western Europe. First in Gaul, then elsewhere, the Germanic settlers gradually fused with the indigenous population. In the process, free Germanic farmers often descended into the ranks of the semiservile Celtic villagers (or villains). At the aristocratic level, the pattern of life was influenced by the Germanic warrior ideology—the heroic virtues of the comitatus and its warlord—while the civility of Roman villa life diminished accordingly.

On the other hand, the ideas of the late Empire and Christianity gradually liberalized Germanic legal attitudes toward women, who rose steadily from their earlier status as perpetual minors. Widows could now be guardians of their children; daughters could inherit lands; husbands could no longer divorce their wives at will. The blending of Roman and Germanic landholders into a single class—combining elements from both cultures—gave rise to the aristocracy of medieval Europe.

Government and Intellectual Life

Except for Theodoric, the Germanic kings proved inept at carrying on the Roman administrative traditions they had inherited. They allowed the imperial tax system to break down and permitted the privilege of minting coins to fall into private hands. Lacking a firm conception of public authority, they tended to regard their kingdoms as private estates to be exploited or alienated according to their whims. By showering lands and political privileges on aristocrats and churchmen and treating what remained as personal property, they succeeded in combining the worst features of anarchy and tyranny.

During the late Roman Empire, Western Europe had been overtaxed and overgoverned; now it was radically undergoverned. The Germanic monarchs did little to enliven the economy or ameliorate the general impoverishment. The Church strove to fill the vacuum by dispensing charity and glamorizing the virtue of resignation, but it was ill-equipped to cope with the troubled countryside of the post-Roman West. Its organization was confined largely to the shrinking towns and walled monasteries. Only gradually were rural parishes organized to meet the needs of the peasantry. Not until after the eighth century did the country parish become a characteristic feature of the Western Church. In the meantime peasants were fortunate if they saw a priest once a year. The monarchy and the Church were better known among the peasantry as acquisitive landlords than as fountains of justice and divine grace.

The intellectual life of the West suffered accordingly. The culture of old Rome was decaying, and the new civilization of Western Europe had scarcely begun to develop. The leading scholars of the era were bishops, most of whom were from families of the old Roman aristocracy. One such bishop, Gregory of Tours (d. 594), remarked that "all but five of the bishops of the see of Tours were connected with my family." Gregory of Tours' *History of the Franks* is our best source for the reigns of Clovis and his successors. It is in some respects an impressive work of history, but it is written in ungrammatical Latin (for which he apologizes to his readers) and filled with the most improbable miracles. The world that Gregory portrays was dominated by savage cruelty and beclouded by fantasy. Both the story that he presents and the way in which he presents it attest to the decline of literary culture in sixth-century Gaul.

Pope Gregory the Great (d. 604), another bishop of aristocratic Roman background, was awarded a place alongside Ambrose, Jerome, and Augustine as one of the Doctors of the Latin Church. Pope Gregory's writings are marked by profound practical wisdom and psychological insight, but they do not approach the level of the fourth-century Doctors in philosophical depth and scholarly sophistication. Pope Gregory watered down Augustinian theology for the benefit of his own naive contemporaries. The lofty theological issues with which Augustine grappled are overshadowed in Gregory's thought by a concentration on such secondary matters as demons and relics.

Bishop Isidore of Seville (d. 636) was known as the foremost scholar of his generation. His most impressive work, the *Etymologies*, was intended to be an encyclopedia of all knowledge. It was a valuable work for its time and was studied for centuries thereafter. But its value was diminished by Isidore's lack of critical powers. He included every scrap of information that he could find, whether likely or unlikely, profound or superficial. In fairness to Isidore, it should be said that he was victimized by the credulity of the ancient writers on whom he depended and was left adrift by the weakness of the Latin scientific tradition. Nevertheless, as the greatest mind of his age he betrays a certain lack of sophistication. On the subject of monsters he writes as follows:

> The Cynocephali are so called because they have dogs' heads and their very barking betrays them as beasts rather than men. These are born in India. The Cyclopses, too, hail from India, and they are so named because they have a single eye in the midst of the forehead.... The Blemmyes, born in Libya, are believed to be headless trunks, having mouth and eyes in the breast; others are born without necks, with eyes in the shoulders.... They say the Panotii in Scythia have ears so huge that they cover the whole body with them.... The race of the Sciopodes is said to live in Ethiopia. They have one leg apiece, and are of a

marvelous swiftness, and...in summertime they lie on the ground on
their backs and are shaded by the greatness of their feet.

Finally, with a touch of skepticism, Isidore concludes:

Other fabulous monstrosities of the human race are said to exist, but
they do not; they are imaginary.

The Germanic Kingdoms

The century between A.D. 500 and 600 witnessed important changes in the
political superstructure of Western Christendom. In A.D. 500 Theodoric's
Ostrogothic regime dominated Italy, the Vandals ruled North Africa, the
Visigoths governed Spain, Clovis and his Franks were conquering Gaul, and
the Anglo-Saxons were expanding their settlements in Britain. A century later,
two of these states had been destroyed by Justinian's armies: North Africa
was now Byzantine rather than Vandal, and the Ostrogothic kingdom of Italy
had collapsed.

By 600 pagan Anglo-Saxon tribes had occupied much of Britain, dispossessing many of the indigenous Celtic inhabitants and driving others into the
western hills of Cornwall and Wales. Anglo-Saxon Britain was now a confused cluster of small, independent kingdoms in which the process of Christian
conversion was just beginning.

Gaul in 600 was thoroughly dominated by the Franks under the successors of Clovis, founder of the "Merovingian" dynasty.* The Merovingian kings
followed the practice of dividing the kingdom among the sons of a deceased
ruler. Often the sons would engage in civil war until, as it sometimes happened, one of them emerged as sole monarch of the Franks. At his death, the
kingdom would be divided among his own sons, and the bitter comedy would
be repeated. Merovingian government became less and less effective, and the
Frankish Church became increasingly disorganized.

The monarchy of Visigothic Spain, which shed its Arianism and embraced Catholicism in 589, managed in the 620s to reconquer its Mediterranean
shore from Byzantium (whose attention was focused on the Persians just then).
But the Visigothic kings allowed their power to slip little by little into the hands
of the landed aristocracy. As Gregory of Tours explained, the Visigoths "had
adopted the reprehensible habit of murdering on the spot any king who dis-
pleased them and replacing him with someone they preferred." The regime
was an easy prey for the conquering Muslims in the early 700s.

The century since Theodoric's reign had been a disastrous one for Italy.
The horrors of Justinian's Gothic wars were followed by the invasion of the
Lombards. By 600 the decimated peninsula was divided between the Byzantines in Ravenna and the south and the Lombards in the north. The papacy, under nominal Byzantine jurisdiction, dominated the lands around Rome
and sought to preserve its fragile independence by playing Lombard against

*Named after Clovis's half-mythical ancestor, Merovech.

EUROPE AROUND 600

Byzantine. At critical moments, however, it looked to the Byzantines as its defenders.

MONKS AND POPES

Such was the condition of Western Europe in 600—violent, politically unstable, culturally feeble. Yet this was the society out of which Western civilization was born, the formative epoch in which apparently minor trends would one day broaden into traditions that would govern the course of European history. Even in 600 some of these trends can be discerned. Although Classical culture was not flourishing, it was at least surviving. If Isidore of Seville was no Augustine, he was at least a deeply learned scholar. The Church, although tainted by the ignorance and corruption of its environment, still retained its capacity to inspire, enlighten, and civilize.

Far to the north, Ireland had been won for Christianity in the fifth century by St. Patrick and other missionaries; by 600 it had developed an astonishingly creative Celtic-Christian culture. Lacking the city-based substructure of episcopal organization on the Continent, Irish Christianity developed its own distinctive organizational structure based on great, autonomous monasteries rather than urban bishoprics. The Celtic Church did have bishops, but they did not rule dioceses; their functions were spiritual and sacramental only. They had no administrative power and usually lived in monasteries under the authority of an abbot.

Celtic monasticism became one of the great energizing forces of the age—in Ireland, in Scotland, on the Continent, and, eventually, among the English. Developing in relative isolation from the papacy, it originated a variety of customs and practices uniquely its own. During the sixth and seventh centuries, Irish monks excelled in the rigor of their scholarship, the depth of their sanctity, the austerity of their lives, and the scope of their missionary work. Irish monastic schools were perhaps the best in Western Europe at the time, and a rich Irish artistic tradition culminated in the illuminated manuscripts of the eighth century, which were the wonder of their age and still excite admiration in our own. Irish missionaries, striving to deepen and expand monastic life on the Continent, founded a number of important religious houses in the Frankish kingdom and as far afield as northern Italy, and Frankish aristocratic abbey founders often adapted Irish monastic customs, usually in modified form, for the governance of their own monastic communities.

Monasticism

Monasticism had a dynamic impact on the culture of the early Middle Ages. Monastic life is not peculiar to Christianity but is found in many religions—Buddhism and Judaism, to name two. The Essenes, for example, whose cult may have produced the famous Dead Sea scrolls, constituted a kind of Jewish monastic order. There have always been religious people who long to withdraw from the world and devote their lives to uninterrupted communion with God, and among late Roman and medieval Christians, this impulse was particularly strong. Monasticism came to be regarded as the most perfect form of the Christian life—the consummate embodiment of Christ's own words: "Anyone who has forsaken home, brothers, sisters, father, mother, wife, children, or lands for my name's sake will be repaid a hundred times over and inherit everlasting life" (Matthew, 19:29).

This impulse toward withdrawal and renunciation first affected Christianity in the third century when the Egyptian St. Anthony retired to the desert to live the ascetic life of a godly hermit. In time the fame of his sanctity spread, and a colony of ascetics gathered around him to draw inspiration from his holiness. Anthony thereupon organized a community of hermits who lived together but had no communication with one another—like apartment dwellers in an

American city. Similar hermit communities soon arose throughout Egypt and spread into other regions of the Empire. Hermit saints abounded in the fourth and fifth centuries. One of them, a Syrian holy man named Simeon Stylites, achieved the necessary isolation by living atop a sixty-foot pillar for thirty years, evoking widespread admiration and imitation.

In the meantime a more down-to-earth type of monasticism was developing. Beginning in early fourth-century Egypt and then expanding quickly throughout the Roman Empire, monastic communities of men or women, based on a cooperative rather than a hermit life, were attracting numerous dedicated Christians who found insufficient challenge in the increasingly complacent post-Constantinian Church. The holy individualism of the desert and pillar saints thus gave way to a more ordered monastic life.

St. Benedict and his Rule

St. Benedict of Nursia (*c.* 480–*c.* 550) contributed much to Western monasticism, tempering its flamboyant holiness with common sense and realistic principles of organization. Like other Christian leaders of his time, Benedict was a Roman of good family. Born in the province of Nursia, in the mountains of central Italy, he was sent to Rome for his education. But he fled the worldly city before completing his studies and took up the hermit life in a cave near the ruins of Nero's country palace. In time, word of his saintliness circulated and disciples gathered around him. As it turned out, Benedict was more than a simple ascetic; he was a man of keen psychological insight—a superb organizer who learned from the varied experiences of his youth how the monastic life might best be lived. His tremendously influential monastic rule discloses not only his personal genius but also a sense of order and discipline that was characteristically Roman.

Benedict founded a number of monasteries and attracted within them not only prospective saints but ordinary people as well—including the offspring of wealthy Roman families. At length he built his great monastery of Monte Cassino atop a mountain midway between Rome and Naples. His sister and disciple, St. Scholastica, established herself in a nearby hermitage and visited him once a year to talk of spiritual matters. Scholastica was to become the patron saint of all Benedictine nunneries, while Benedict's abbey at Monte Cassino remained for many centuries one of the chief centers of religious life in Western Europe.

Pope Gregory the Great described the Rule of St. Benedict as "conspicuous for its discretion." Modern scholars have discovered that it was derived from an earlier, anonymous monastic rule, but St. Benedict gave it a novel quality of humane practicality. It provided for a busy, closely regulated life, simple but not ruthlessly austere. Although designed for communities of men, it was readily adaptable to nunneries. Benedictine monks and nuns were decently clothed, adequately fed, and seldom left to their own devices. Theirs was a life dedicated to God and the attainment of personal sanctity through prayer and service, yet it was also a life that could be led by any serious Christian. It was rendered all the more attractive by the increasing brutality of the world outside.

The monastic day was filled with carefully regulated activities: communal prayer, devotional reading, and work—field work, household work, manuscript copying, according to need and ability. Benedictine communities included priests to conduct the Eucharist and other sacraments, but it was by no means necessary that all monks be inducted into the priesthood—and most were not. Monks and nuns alike were pledged to the fundamental obligations of poverty, chastity, and obedience. Benedictines must resist the three great worldly temptations of money, sex, and ambition by relinquishing all personal possessions, living a celibate life, and obeying the abbot or abbess. The heads of Benedictine houses were elected for life and were the unquestioned rulers of their abbeys. They were strictly responsible to God and were instructed to govern justly in accordance with the Rule. Benedict cautioned abbots not to "sadden" or "overdrive" their monks or give them cause for "just murmuring." Here especially is the quality of discretion to which Pope Gregory alludes and which was such a significant element in the Rule's success.

Contributions of the Benedictines

Within two or three centuries of Benedict's death, the Rule had spread throughout Western Christendom. The result was not a vast hierarchical monastic organization but rather a host of individual, autonomous monasteries sharing a single rule and way of life, yet administratively unrelated. Benedict had visualized his monasteries as spiritual sanctuaries into which pious Christians might withdraw from the world. But the chaotic and illiterate society of early Western Christendom, desperately in need of the discipline and learning of the Benedictines, could not permit them to abdicate from secular affairs.

In reality, therefore, the Benedictines had an enormous impact on the world they renounced. Their schools produced most of the small group of literate Europeans who kept the art of writing alive during the early Middle Ages. They served as a cultural bridge, transcribing and preserving the writings of Latin antiquity in a society that was overwhelmingly nonliterate. Scribal work could be demanding and exhausting, as we learn from occasional postscripts tacked onto the ends of medieval manuscripts: "The art of writing is difficult; it tires the eyes, breaks the back and cramps the arms and legs." "The end has come; give me a pot of wine." "Give the poor scribe a pretty girl" (presumably a passing erotic fantasy, not to be taken literally).

This preservation of a cultural lifeline to Classical-Christian antiquity was by no means the only contribution of the Benedictines to early Western Europe. They spearheaded the penetration of Christianity into the forests of Germany and later into Scandinavia, Poland, and Hungary. They served as scribes and advisers to princes and were drafted into high ecclesiastical offices. As recipients of gifts of land from pious donors over many generations, they held

and managed large estates, some of which were models of intelligent agricultural organization and technological innovation. For although the Benedictine was pledged to *personal* poverty, a Benedictine abbey might acquire
immense *corporate* wealth. With the coming of feudalism, Benedictine abbots
became great vassals responsible for political and legal administration and military recruitment over the large areas under their control. Above all, as islands of learning and security in an ocean of ignorance and political chaos,
the Benedictine monasteries were the spiritual and intellectual centers of the
developing Classical-Christian-Germanic synthesis that underlay European civilization. In short, Benedictine monasticism became the supreme civilizing influence in the early Christian West.

Pope Gregory the Great (590–604)

In its early years, however, the Benedictine movement was very nearly destroyed. A generation after Benedict's death, Monte Cassino was pillaged by
the Lombards (*c.* 577) and its monks were scattered. Some of them took refuge in Rome, where they came into contact with the pious, well-born monk
and future pope, Gregory the Great. Though not himself a Benedictine,
Gregory was deeply impressed by their accounts of Benedict's holiness and
his Rule. Gregory wrote a biography of the saint that achieved tremendous
popularity in the years that followed and drew widespread attention and support to Benedictine monasticism. Most of the biography deals with Benedict's
miracles, but Gregory also wrote admiringly of the Benedictine Rule. Some
scholarly specialists doubt that Gregory had actually seen the Rule, but I sus-
pect they are mistaken, for Gregory advised his readers that they could "find
all of Benedict's administrative acts in this *Book of the Rule*," and one can reasonably suppose that the honest and unassuming pope knew whereof he
spoke.

   We have already encountered Pope Gregory as a scholar—a popularizer
of Augustinian thought. His theology, although highly influential in subsequent centuries, failed to rise much above the intellectual level of his age. His
real genius lay in his keen understanding of human nature and his ability as
an administrator and organizer. His *Pastoral Care*, a treatise on the duties and
obligations of a bishop, is a masterpiece of practical wisdom and common
sense. It answered a great need of the times and became one of the most
widely read books in the Middle Ages.

   Gregory loved the monastic life and ascended the papal throne with genuine regret. On hearing of his election he went into hiding and had to be
dragged into the Roman basilica of St. Peter's to be consecrated. But once
resigned to his new responsibilities, Gregory bent every energy to the extension of papal authority. He believed fervently that the pope, as successor of
St. Peter, was the rightful ruler of the Church. He reorganized the financial
structure of the papal estates and used the increased revenues for charitable
works to ameliorate the wretched poverty of his age. His integrity, wisdom,

and administrative ability won him an almost regal position in Rome and central Italy, as Lombards and Byzantines struggled for control of the peninsula. The reform of the Frankish Church was beyond his immediate powers, but he set in motion a process that would one day bring both France and Germany into the papal fold when he dispatched a group of monks to convert the pagan Anglo-Saxons.

The Conversion of England

The mission to England was led by the monk St. Augustine (not to be confused with the great theologian of an earlier day, St. Augustine of Hippo). In 597, Augustine and his followers arrived in the English kingdom of Kent and began their momentous work. England was then divided into a number of independent Germanic kingdoms, of which Kent was momentarily the most powerful, and Augustine was assured a friendly reception by the fact that Queen Bertha, wife of King Ethelbert of Kent, was a Frankish Christian. With Bertha's support, the conversion proceeded swiftly, and on Whitsunday, 597, King Ethelbert and thousands of his subjects were baptized. The chief town of the realm, Canterbury ("Kent City"), became the headquarters of the new Church, and Augustine himself became Canterbury's first archbishop. Under his influence Ethelbert issued the first written laws in the Anglo-Saxon language.

During the decades that followed, the fortunes of English Christianity rose and fell with the varying fortunes of the Anglo-Saxon kingdoms. Kent declined after King Ethelbert's death, and by the mid-600s political power had shifted to the northernmost of the Anglo-Saxon states, Northumbria. This remote outpost became the scene of a deeply significant encounter between the two great creative forces of the age: Irish-Celtic Christianity moving southward from its monasteries in Scotland and Roman Christianity moving northward from Kent and influenced increasingly by the Benedictine Rule.

Although the two movements shared a common faith, they had different cultural backgrounds, different notions of monastic life and ecclesiastical organization, and different systems for calculating the date of Easter. The Roman Easter date won official recognition at a synod convened at the nunnery of Whitby in 664; there King Oswy of Northumbria decided in favor of Roman-Benedictine Christianity, and papal influence in England was assured. In 669, five years after the Synod of Whitby, the papacy sent the scholarly Theodore of Tarsus to assume the archbishopric of Canterbury and reorganize the English Church into a coherent system of bishops and dioceses. As a consequence of Northumbria's conversion and Archbishop Theodore's tireless efforts, England, only a century out of paganism, became Europe's most vigorous and creative Christian society.

But in England, as elsewhere, old pagan customs lingered on for centuries among the common people, blending into Christianity in interesting ways. Here, for example, are some of the charms that were performed in Anglo-Saxon England long after its conversion:

Against the Elfin Race: Make a salve [of various herbs including] wormwood, bishopswort, lupine, viper's bugloss, crow leek, garlic. Put the herbs into a vessel, place them under the altar, sing nine masses over them, then boil them in butter and sheep's grease...etc.

To drive away a dwarf: pound the dung of a white dog into dust, mix it with flour, and bake it into a cake; give it to the afflicted person to eat before the time of the dwarf's arrival.

If someone is demented, take the skin of a porpoise, make it into a whip, and flog him with it: he will soon be well. Amen.

The Northumbrian Renaissance

The Irish-Benedictine encounter in seventh-century Northumbria produced a notable cultural awakening known as the "Northumbrian Renaissance." The two traditions influenced and energized one another to such an extent that the evolving civilization of the Christian West reached a pinnacle in this remote land. Boldly executed illuminated manuscripts in a curvilinear style both Celtic and Germanic in inspiration, a new script, a vigorous vernacular epic poetry, an impressive architecture—all contributed to the luster of Northumbrian culture in the late 600s and early 700s. The Northumbrian Renaissance centered on the great monasteries founded by Irish and Benedictine missionaries at Lindisfarne, Wearmouth, Jarrow, and elsewhere. It was at the Benedictine abbey of Jarrow that the supreme scholar of the age, St. Bede the Venerable, spent his life.

Bede entered Jarrow as a child and remained there until his death in 735. The greatest of his many works, the *Ecclesiastical History of England*, displays a critical sense far superior to that of Bede's medieval predecessors and contemporaries. The *Ecclesiastical History*, our chief source for early English history, is the first major historical work to employ the modern chronological framework based on the Christian era (A.D.—Anno Domini—the year of the Lord). Bede's chronological scheme reflects his deep sense of historical unity and purpose: the transformation of the world—and particularly of England—through the spread of the Christian gospel and the monastic life. The *Ecclesiastical History* reflects a remarkable cultural breadth and a penetrating mind; it establishes Bede as the foremost Christian intellect since Augustine of Hippo. And the progress of the Classical-Germanic synthesis is made clear by the fact that Bede, unlike the major scholars of the 500s and 600s, was not a well-born Roman but a man of Germanic roots.

By Bede's death in 735, the Northumbrian kings had lost their political hegemony, and Northumbrian culture was beginning to fade. But the tradition of learning was carried from England back to the Continent during the eighth century by a group of Anglo-Saxon Benedictine missionaries. In the 740s the English monk St. Boniface reformed the Church of Francia, infusing it with Benedictine idealism, systematizing its organization, and binding it more closely to the papacy. Pope Gregory had now been in his grave

Illuminated page from the *Lindisfarne Gospels*
(*c.* A.D. 700), illustrating the curvilinear style characteristic of the Northumbrian Renaissance.

for 140 years, but his spirit was still at work. St. Boniface and other English
missionaries founded new Benedictine monasteries among the Germans east
of the Rhine and began the long, difficult task of Christianizing and civilizing
Germany, just as Augustine and his monks had once Christianized Kent. By
the later 700s the cultural center of Christendom had shifted southward again
from England to the rising empire of the Frankish leader, Charlemagne.* Significantly, the leading scholar in Charlemagne's kingdom was Alcuin, a
Benedictine monk from Northumbria, a student of one of Bede's own pupils.

The Church and Western Civilization

The West differed from the Byzantine East in innumerable ways, the most
obvious being its far lower level of civilization. But just as important is the
fact that the Western Church was able to develop more or less independently
of the state. Church and state often worked hand in hand in the Christian
West, but religion and secular politics were never merged to the degree that

*See pp. 84 ff.

they were in Constantinople and, indeed, in most ancient civilizations. Early Western Christendom was marked by a separation between cultural leadership, which was ecclesiastical and monastic, and political power, which was in the hands of the Germanic kings and Roman-Germanic aristocracies. This split contributed much to the fluidity and dynamism of Western culture. It produced a creative tension that tended toward change rather than crystallization. Like St. Augustine's two cities, the warrior culture of the Germanic states and the Classical-Christian culture of church and monastery remained always in the process of fusion, yet never completely fused. The interplay between these two worlds shaped the development of early medieval civilization.

5

The Explosion of Islam

BACKGROUND AND ORIGIN

Islam, Byzantium, and Western Christendom were the three major civilizations of medieval western Eurasia, and of the three, Western Christendom remained for many centuries the most primitive. It had much to learn from Islam and Byzantium, and its developing synthesis of Classical, Christian, and Germanic traditions was shaped in many ways by its two neighboring civilizations. The influence of these neighbors was impeded, however, by Europe's hostility toward the "infidel" Muslims and the "effete, treacherous" Byzantines. In the eighth and ninth centuries Western Europe's contacts with Islam were limited largely to the battlefield. Only after about A.D. 1000 did the West begin to draw on the rich legacy of Muslim thought and culture.

Islam today is a distinctive culture and a living religion extending across an immense stretch of South Asia, the Middle East, and North Africa—from the Philippines and Indonesia to Pakistan to the Arab world of southwest Asia and Mediterranean Africa. This vast Islamic belt was created by a militant, compelling religion that burst into the world in seventh-century Arabia and spread outward with remarkable speed. In the first hundred years of its existence, Islam shattered the Christian domination of the Mediterranean Basin, destroyed the Persian Empire, seized Byzantium's richest provinces, absorbed Spain, pressed into the heart of France, and expanded far into southern Asia.

Muhammad (c. 571–632)

For countless centuries prior to the time of the prophet Muhammad, nomadic tribes from the Arabian Peninsula (the modern Saudi Arabia) had repeatedly invaded the rich civilized districts of Palestine, Syria, and Mesopotamia to the north. Many Semitic invaders and empire builders of the ancient Near East had come originally from the Arabian Desert—the Amorites, the Chaldeans, the Canaanites, even the Hebrews. These peoples had quickly assimilated the ancient civilization of the Fertile Crescent and developed it in new, creative ways. But their kinfolk who stayed in Arabia remained primitive and disorganized.

In Muhammad's time most Arabians were still nomadic and polytheistic, but by then new civilizing influences were beginning to make themselves felt. A great caravan route running northward from southern Arabia served as an important link in a far-flung commercial network between the Far East and the Byzantine and Persian Empires. Along this route cities developed to serve the caravans, and with city life came a degree of civilization. Indeed, the greatest of these trading cities, Mecca, became a bustling commercial center that sent its own caravans northward and southward and grew wealthy from their profits. As the tribal life of Mecca and other caravan cities began to give way to commercial life, new foreign ideas challenged old ways and old viewpoints. It was in Mecca, around the year 571, that the prophet Muhammad was born.

At Muhammad's birth the Emperor Justinian had been dead for six years. Muhammad's contemporaries include such men as Pope Gregory the Great and Bishop Isidore of Seville. When the Benedictine mission from Rome landed in Kent in 597 to begin the conversion of England, Muhammad was in his twenties, as yet unknown outside his own immediate circle.

The future architect of one of the world's great religions was born of a lesser branch of Mecca's leading clan. With little formal education he became a caravan trader, and his travels brought him into contact with Judaism, Christianity, and Persian Zoroastrianism. A sensitive man with a powerful, winning personality, he underwent a mystical experience while in his late thirties and began to set forth his new faith by preaching and writing. He won little support in Mecca apart from his wife and relatives and a few converts from the underprivileged classes. The ruling merchants of Mecca were immune to the teaching of this "low-born upstart." They seem to have feared that his new religion would discredit the chief Meccan temple, the *Kaaba*, which housed a sacred meteoritic stone and was a profitable center of pilgrimages. Their belief that Muhammad's faith would ruin Mecca's pilgrim business was a staggering miscalculation, but their hostility to the new teaching forced Muhammad to flee Mecca in 622 and settle in the town of Medina, 280 miles northward on the caravan route.

The flight to Medina, known among the Muslims as the "Hegira," was a momentous turning point in the development of Islam and marks the beginning date of the Muslim calendar. Muhammad quickly won the inhabitants of Medina to his faith and became the city's political chief as well as its religious leader. Indeed, under Muhammad's direction religious and civil authority were fused; the sacred community was at once a state and a church. In this respect Muhammad's community at Medina foreshadowed the great Islamic state of later years.

The Medinans made war on Mecca, raiding its caravans and blockading its trade until, in 630, Mecca was incorporated into the sacred community. During the two remaining years of his life Muhammad, now an almost legendary figure in Arabia, received the voluntary submission of many tribes in the peninsula. By the time of his death in 632 he had united the Arabians as never before into a coherent political-religious group, well-organized, well-armed, and inspired by a powerful new monotheistic religion. The energies of these desert people were now channeled toward conquest.

The Islamic Religion

Faith was the cement with which Muhammad unified Arabia. The new faith was called *Islam*, the Arabic word for "surrender." Muhammad taught that his followers must surrender to the will of Allah, the single, almighty God of the universe. Muhammad did not regard himself as divine but rather as the last and greatest of a long line of prophets of whom he was the "seal." Among his predecessors were Moses, the Old Testament prophets, and Jesus.

Islam respected the Old and New Testaments and was relatively tolerant toward Jews and Christians—the "peoples of the book." But the Muslims had a book of their own, the *Koran*, which superseded its predecessors and was believed to contain the pure essence of divine revelation. The *Koran* is the comprehensive body of Muhammad's teachings, the bedrock of the Islamic faith: "All men and jinn in collaboration," so it was said, "could not produce its like." Muslims regard it as the word of Allah, *dictated* to Muhammad by the angel Gabriel from an original "uncreated" book in heaven. Accordingly, its divine inspiration and authority extend not only to its precepts but also to its every letter (of which there are 323,621), making any translation a species of heresy. Every good Muslim must read the *Koran* in Arabic, and as Islam spread, the Arabic language spread with it.

The *Koran* is perhaps the most widely read book ever written. More than a manual of worship, it was the text from which non-Arabian Muslims learned their Arabic. And since it was the supreme authority not only in religion but also in law, science, and the humanities, it became the standard text in Muslim schools for every imaginable subject. Muhammad's genius is vividly illustrated by his success in adapting a primitive language such as seventh-century Arabic to the sophisticated religious, legal, and ethical concepts that one encounters in his sacred book.

Muhammad offered his followers the assurance of eternal salvation if they led upright, sober lives and followed the precepts of Islam. Above all, they were bound to a simple confession of faith: "There is no god but Allah, and Muhammad is his prophet." Muslims were also obliged to engage in specified prayers and fasting, to journey as pilgrims to Mecca at least once in their lifetimes, and to work devoutly toward the welfare and expansion of the sacred community. Holy war was the supremely meritorious activity, for service to the faith was identical with service to the state. Public law in Islamic lands had a religious sanction, and the fusion of religion and politics, which Muhammad created at Medina, remained a fundamental characteristic of Islamic society. There was no Muslim priesthood, no Muslim "church" apart from the state: Muhammad's political successors, the caliphs, were defenders of the faith and guardians of the faithful. The tension between church and state that troubled and enlivened medieval Europe was thus unknown in the Muslim world.

THE ISLAMIC EMPIRE

The Early Conquests: 632–655

Immediately after Muhammad's death in 632, the explosive energy of the Arabs, harnessed at last by the teachings of the Prophet, broke upon the world. The spectacular conquests resulted in part from the youthful vigor of Islam, in part from the weakness and exhaustion of its enemies. The Persian and Byzantine Empires had just concluded a long, desperate conflict that left both powers spent and enfeebled. And the Monophysites of Syria and Egypt remained hostile to their orthodox Byzantine masters.

The Arabs entered these tired, embittered lands afire with religious zeal. They did not seek converts to their new faith—Islam was regarded in its early generations as a religion for the Arab community only—nor did they have any master plan of conquest. Most of the early campaigns began as plundering expeditions prompted by the wealth and luxuries of the civilized world, but with each victory the momentum grew. Striking into Syria, the Arabs annihilated a huge Byzantine army in 636, captured Damascus and Jerusalem, and by 640 had occupied the entire land, detaching it more or less permanently from Byzantine control. In 637 they inflicted an overwhelming defeat on the army of the Persian Empire and entered the Persian capital of Ctesiphon, gazing in bewilderment at the opulence and wealth of the great city. Within another decade they had subdued all Persia and reached the borders of India. In later years they penetrated deeply into the Indian subcontinent and laid the religious foundations of the modern Muslim states of Pakistan and Bangladesh.

Eventually, most Persians came to accept the new faith, abandoning Zoroaster for Muhammad and thus preparing themselves for the great role they would later play in Islamic politics and culture. Yet despite mass conversions to Islam during the 700s, the Persians retained important elements of their ancient culture. Their distinctiveness from the Arab world to the west and south is reflected even today in the hostility between Arab Iraq and Persian Iran.

Meanwhile, Muslims were pushing westward into Egypt. In the 640s, they captured Alexandria—the great metropolis that had for centuries been a center of Greek science and, later, Jewish and Christian theology. With Egypt and Syria in their hands, the Muslims took to the sea, challenging the long-established Byzantine domination of the eastern Mediterranean. They took the island of Cyprus, raided ancient Rhodes, and won a major victory over the Byzantine fleet.

Muslim Chronology

c. 571–632:	Muhammad
622:	The Hegira
632–655:	The first conquests: Syria, Persian Empire, Egypt
655–661:	Civil war: Umayyads versus Ali
661–750:	Umayyad Dynasty; new conquests: North Africa, Spain
717–718:	Arabs besiege Constantinople
732:	Arabs defeated at Tours
750–1258:	Abbasid dynasty at Baghdad
786–809:	Harun-al-Rashid; zenith of Abbasid power

The Civil War: 655–661

In 655 Islamic expansion ceased momentarily as the new empire became locked in a dynastic struggle. The succession to the caliphate was contested between the Umayyads, a leading family in the old Meccan commercial elite, and Ali, the son-in-law of Muhammad himself. Ali headed a faction that was to become exceedingly powerful in later centuries. His followers insisted that the caliph must be a direct descendant of the Prophet. As it happened, Muhammad had left no surviving sons and only one daughter, Fatima, who married the Prophet's cousin, Ali.

In 661 the Umayyad forces defeated Ali in battle and initiated an Umayyad dynasty of caliphs that moved the Islamic capital to Damascus in Syria and ruled there for nearly a century. But the legitimist faction that had once supported Ali persisted as a dedicated minority, throwing its support behind various descendants of Ali and Fatima. In time, the political movement evolved into a dissenting religious cult known as "Shi'ism," which held that the *true* caliphs—the descendants of Muhammad through Fatima and Ali—were sinless, infallible, and possessed of a body of secret knowledge not contained in the *Koran.* Shi'ism became an occult underground doctrine, which occasionally rose to the surface in the form of civil insurrection. In the tenth century the Shi'ists gained control of Egypt and established a "Fatimid" dynasty of caliphs in Cairo. Shi'ism inspired a band of Muslim desperadoes known as the "Assassins." In various forms, the Shi'ist movement survives to this day. It is, for example, the doctrine of the majority of Muslims in Iran.

The Umayyad Dynasty: 661–750

The intermission in the Muslim expansion ended with the Umayyad victory over Ali in 661. And even though the Islamic capital was now Damascus rather than Medina, the old Arabian aristocracy remained in firm control. Constantinople was now the chief military goal, but the great city repulsed a series of powerful Muslim attacks between 670 and 680. The Byzantine defense was aided by a secret weapon known as "Greek fire"—a liquid containing quicklime that ignited on contact with water and could only be extinguished by

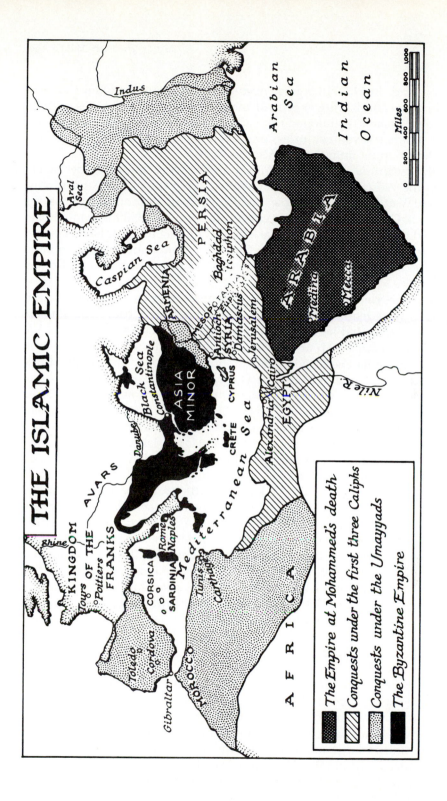

THE ISLAMIC EMPIRE

Indus

Aral Sea

Caspian Sea

Arabian Sea

Indian Ocean

PERSIA

ARMENIA

Baghdad
Ctesiphon
MESOPOTAMIA
Antioch
SYRIA
Damascus
Jerusalem

ARABIA

Medina

Mecca

Miles
0 200 400 600 800 1,000

Black Sea

Danube

Constantinople

ASIA MINOR

CYPRUS

CRETE

Mediterranean Sea

Alexandria
Cairo
EGYPT

Nile

AVARS

Rhine

KINGDOM OF THE FRANKS

Poitiers
Tours

Rome
Naples

CORSICA
SARDINIA

Tunis
Carthage

MOROCCO

Gibraltar

Toledo
Cordova

AFRICA

The Empire at Mohammed's death
Conquests under the first three Caliphs
Conquests under the Umayyads
The Byzantine Empire

vinegar or sand. In 717–718 a great Arab fleet and army assaulted Constantinople in vain, and having expended their energies and resources without success, the Muslims abandoned their effort to take the city. Byzantium survived for another seven centuries, effectively barring Muslim inroads into southeastern Europe until the late Middle Ages.

In the meantime, however, Muslim armies were enjoying spectacular success in the West. From Egypt they moved along the North African coast into the old Vandal kingdom, now ruled by distant Byzantium. In 698 the Muslims took Carthage. In 711 they crossed the Straits of Gibraltar into Spain and crushed the Visigothic kingdom at a blow, bringing the Spanish Christians under their dominion and driving the Christian princes into mountain hideaways in the Pyrenees, where central control had been weak even in Roman times. Next the Muslims moved into southern Gaul and threatened the kingdom of the Merovingian Franks. In 732, a century after the Prophet's death, the Muslims were halted at last on a battlefield between Tours and Poitiers by a Christian army led by the Frankish warrior Charles Martel.

The Muslim army at Tours was small and makeshift in comparison with the great force that had besieged Constantinople in 717–718. But together these two battles brought an end to the era of major Islamic encroachments upon the territories of the two Christian civilizations. The remainder of the Middle Ages witnessed a continuance of Christian-Islamic warfare and some territorial change—most of Spain, for example, had reverted to Christian control by the middle of the thirteenth century. But by and large, Islam, Byzantium, and Western Christendom had achieved equilibrium by the mid-700s and remained in balance for centuries to come.

Throughout the rest of the Middle Ages, the three civilizations tended to expand not at one another's expense but away from each other—Byzantium into the Balkans and Russia, Islam into South Asia, Western Christendom into Germany, Scandinavia, Hungary, and Poland. The Crusades were, ultimately, only a minor exception to this generalization; the Christian reconquest of Spain and the victory of the Seljuk Turks over the Byzantines in Asia Minor were much more important exceptions. But it was not until the fourteenth century, when the Islamic Ottoman Turks swept into the Balkans, that the balance of the three powers was upset altogether.

The Golden Age of the Abbasids

In 750, eighteen years after the battle of Tours, the Umayyads were overthrown. Their successors, the Abbasids (750–1258), were Arabians—as caliphs had always been. But the Abbasids, unlike their Ummayad predecessors, encouraged the political participation of the highly civilized conquered peoples, now converting in large numbers to Islam. It was above all the Islamized Persian aristocracy whom the Abbasids favored, and shortly after the victory of the new dynasty, the Islamic capital was moved from Damascus to Baghdad on the Tigris River in present-day Iraq, in the western part of the old Persian

Empire. This move marked an eastward shift in Islam's political interests, which relieved some of the pressure against Constantinople and the West. In 751 the Muslims won a major victory over a Chinese army at the battle of Talas in Central Asia, and in later years Islam expanded deep inside India and onward to the great offshore islands of Indonesia.

The rise of the Abbasids marks the end of the Arabian aristocracy's monopoly on political power. The new government at Baghdad was run by a medley of races and peoples, and individuals of humble origin could rise high in the service of the caliph. As one disgruntled aristocrat observed, "Sons of concubines have become too numerous among us; O God, lead me to a land where I shall see no bastards."

Baghdad, under the early Abbasid caliphs, became one of the world's great cities. It was the center of a vast commercial network spreading across the Islamic world and far beyond. Silks, spices, and fragrant woods flowed into its wharves from India, China, and Indonesia; furs, honey, and slaves were imported from Scandinavia; and gold, slaves, and ivory from tropical Africa. Baghdad was the hub of a far-flung banking system with branches in other cities across the Islamic world. A check could be drawn in Baghdad and cashed in Morocco, 4000 miles to the west. The Abbasid imperial palace, occupying fully a third of the city, contained innumerable apartments and public rooms, quarters for eunuchs, harems, and government officials, and a remarkable reception room known as the "hall of the tree," which contained an artificial tree of gold and silver on whose branches mechanical birds chirped and sang. (The Byzantine imperial throne room in Constantinople boasted a similar contrivance.)

The culture of Baghdad reached its height under the Abbasid caliph, Harun-al-Rashid (786–809), whose opulence and power became legendary. Harun was accustomed to receiving tribute from the Byzantine Empire itself. When on one occasion the tribute was discontinued, he sent the following peremptory note to the Emperor Nicephorus at Constantinople:

I*n the name of God, the merciful, the compassionate.*
From Harun, the commander of the faithful,
  to Nicephorus, the dog of a Roman.
Verily I have read thy letter, O son of an infidel mother.
  As for the answer, it shall be for thine eye to see,
  not for thine ear to hear. Salaam.

The letter was followed by a successful military campaign that forced the unlucky Byzantines to resume their tribute.

The era of Harun-al-Rashid was notable too for its vigorous intellectual life. Islamic scholars studied and synthesized the learned traditions of Greece, Rome, Persia, and India. In Baghdad, Harun's son and successor founded the House of Wisdom—a great intellectual institute that was at once a library, a university, and a translation center. Here and elsewhere Islamic scholars pushed their learning far beyond the point it had reached under the Umayyads. Drawing from various older traditions, Islamic culture had come of age with remarkable speed. At a time when Charlemagne was struggling to civilize his rustic, illiterate Franks, Harun reigned over glittering Baghdad.

The Abbasid government drew heavily from the administrative techniques of Byzantium and, especially, Persia. A sophisticated, complex bureaucracy ran the affairs of state from the capital at Baghdad and kept in touch with the provinces through a multitude of tax-gatherers, judges, couriers, and spies. Although no more sensitive to social justice than other governments of its day, the Abbasid regime did increase the amount of land under cultivation by draining swamps and undertaking extensive irrigation works. The status of peasants and unskilled laborers was kept low by the competition of multitudes of slaves, many of them from sub-Saharan Africa.

The teachings of the *Koran* had tended to raise the status of Arab women above the level of pre-Islamic Arabia, with its male-dominated tribal culture and its unrestrained polygamy (Muhammad limited his male followers to four wives only). But the Abbasid era witnessed the spread of severely antifeminist customs, partly Persian in inspiration: the seclusion of women in private quarters such as harems, the hiding of women's faces and bodies behind veils and draperies. For all the brilliance of Abbasid civilization, women were distinctly better off in the monogamous environments of Byzantium and Western Christendom.

The elite culture of the Islamic empire had little effect on the impoverished masses, women and men alike. Apart from their fervent Islamic faith, they retained much the same primitive way of life that they had known for the previous two thousand years.

The Decline of Abbasid Power

The Abbasids were unable to maintain their power throughout the vast reaches of the Islamic empire. Communications were limited by the speed of sailing vessels and camels, and governors of remote provinces required sufficient independence and military strength to defend themselves from infidel attacks. Such local independence and power could easily ripen into full autonomy. The Abbasid revolution of 750 was followed by a long process of political disintegration as one province after another broke free of the control of the caliphs at Baghdad. Even in the palmy days of Harun-al-Rashid, the extreme western provinces—Spain, Morocco, and Tunisia—were ruled by independent local dynasties. Spain, indeed, had never passed under Abbasid control but remained under the domination of Umayyad rulers. And by the later ninth century the trend toward disintegration was gaining momentum as Egypt, Syria, and eastern Persia (Iran) broke free.

By then the Abbasid caliphs were slowly losing their grip on their own government in Baghdad. Ambitious army commanders gradually usurped power, establishing control over the tax machinery and the other organs of government. In the later tenth and eleventh centuries the Fatimid caliphate

of Cairo rose to great power, extending its authority to Syria and briefly occupying Baghdad itself. Since about the mid-tenth century, the Abbasid caliphs of Baghdad had been controlled by members of a local Persian aristocratic dynasty who took the title of "sultan" and ruled what was left of the
Abbasid state. A century later, in 1055, the chief of the Seljuk Turks conquered
Baghdad, assumed the title of "Grand Sultan," and then turned his forces
against Byzantium with the devastating effects already mentioned. Seljuk
power declined in the twelfth century, to be followed by a period of further
Islamic political disintegration concurrent with the Crusades. By the later
twelfth century Islam recovered itself in Syria and Egypt, and in the course of
the thirteenth century the crusaders were driven out. In that same century
the emasculated Abbasid caliphate was destroyed. The Mongols took Baghdad
in 1258, massacred its inhabitants (allegedly 800,000 people), and brought to
an end the dynasty and the office that had ruled Baghdad, in fact or in name,
for five centuries.

Economic and Religious Change

The political troubles that the Abbasids endured from about 950 to 1258 were
accompanied by a serious economic decline. Trade dried up, money became
scarce, and Islamic rulers, whether in Baghdad, Cairo, or Damascus, were
forced to reward their political underlings with land or revenue rights rather
than wages. Thus, imperialism gave way to localism, and wealth tended increasingly to be identified with land rather than with commerce.

     The general unrest of the period encouraged waves of popular protest,
both socioeconomic and religious. A quasi-heretical, mystical movement
known as "Sufism" became immensely popular throughout the Islamic world.
For centuries the Sufi movement, although never tightly coordinated, had provided the chief impetus to missionary work among the infidel. These Sufi mystics, often illiterate, always fervent, had achieved the conversion of millions
of people in Africa, India, Indonesia, Central Asia, and China. And it was
they, rather than the orthodox religious scholars and lawyers, who could bring
hope to the Muslim masses in times of trouble. Drawing from the Neoplatonic
notion that reality rests in God alone, the Sufis sought mystical union with
the divine and stressed God's love over the orthodox emphasis on God's authority. The orthodox Islamic scholars contended vigorously against this mystical trend, but by the tenth century Sufism was the most powerful religious
force among the people of Islam. It affects Islamic personal devotion to this
day.

Islamic Culture: Conversion and Diffusion

Throughout the epoch of political disintegration, the Muslim world remained
united by a common culture and a common faith. It continued to struggle
vigorously with Byzantium for control of the Mediterranean and managed, at

various times between the ninth and eleventh centuries, to occupy the key islands of Crete, Sicily, Sardinia, and Corsica. As early as the reign of Harun-al-Rashid, most of the inhabitants of Syria, Egypt, and North Africa had converted to Islam, even though these lands had once supported well-organized Christian churches. The Muslims did not ordinarily persecute the Christians; they merely taxed them. And the prolonged tax burden was probably a more effective instrument of conversion than ruthless persecution would have been.

The intellectual awakening of Harun-al-Rashid's day continued unabated for another four centuries. The untutored Arab from the desert became the cultural heir of Greece, Rome, Persia, and India, and within less than two centuries of the Prophet's death, Islamic culture had reached the level of a mature, sophisticated civilization. Its mercurial rise was a consequence of the Arabs' success in absorbing the great civilized traditions of their conquered peoples and employing these traditions in a cultural synthesis both new and unique. Islam borrowed, but never without digesting. What it drew from other civilizations it transmuted and made its own.

The political disintegration of the ninth and tenth centuries was accompanied by a diffusion of cultural activity throughout the Muslim world. During the tenth century, for example, Cordova, the capital of Umayyad Spain, acquired prodigious wealth and became the center of a brilliant cultural flowering. With a population of half a million or more, Cordova was another Baghdad. No other city in Western Europe could remotely approach it in population, wealth, or municipal organization. It was the wonder of the age—with its mansions, mosques, aqueducts, and baths, its bustling markets and shops, its efficient police force and sanitation service, its street lights, and its splendid, sprawling palace, flashing with brightly colored tiles and surrounded by minarets and sparkling fountains.

All across the Islamic world, from Cordova to Baghdad and far to the east, Muslim scholars and artists were developing the legacies of past civilizations. Architects were molding Greco-Roman forms into a graceful and distinctive new style. Philosophers were studying and elaborating the writings of Plato and Aristotle, despite the hostility of orthodox Islamic theologians. Physicians were expanding the ancient medical doctrines of Galen and his Greek predecessors, describing new symptoms, and identifying new curative drugs. Astronomers and astrologers were tightening the geocentric system of Ptolemy, preparing accurate tables of planetary motions, and giving the stars Arabic names that are used to this day—names such as Altair, Deneb, Aldebaran, and (regrettably) Zubenelgenubi. The renowned astronomer-poet of eleventh-century Persia, Omar Khayyam, devised a calendar of singular accuracy. Muslim mathematicians borrowed creatively from both Greece and India. From the Greeks they learned geometry and trigonometry. And from the Hindus they developed algebra (Arabic: *al Jabr*) and appropriated the so-called Arabic numerals—the set of nine number symbols plus the zero—which were ultimately passed on to the West to revolutionize European mathematics.

Interior of the mosque at Cordova (tenth century).

Islamic literature excelled in works of both poetry and prose. Muslim poets endeavored to perfect individual verses rather than to create long, coherent poems. The quatrains of Omar Khayyam's *Rubaiyat* seem to have been arranged in alphabetical order rather than conforming to any overall plan. The chapters of the *Koran* itself, which had been left unorganized by Muhammad, were assembled shortly after his death in order of decreasing length, with no attempt at structural unity. The enduring value of these works lies in the power and beauty of their individual chapters and verses.

The Arab conquests during the century after Muhammad changed the historical course of North Africa and Southwest Asia decisively and permanently. In the end, the term "Arab" applied to every Muslim from Morocco to Iraq, regardless of ethnic background. Within its all-encompassing religious and linguistic framework, Arab culture provided a new stimulus and a new orientation to the long-civilized peoples of former empires. With its manifold ingredients, the rich Islamic heritage would one day provide nourishment to the thought of the twelfth- and thirteenth-century West. Later, in 1453, Islamic armies would bring Byzantium to an end and make Constantinople a Muslim city. Later still, in the sixteenth and seventeenth centuries, their armies would be at the gates of Vienna. Only in the nineteenth century did Islam become clearly subordinate to the West militarily and politically. And today there are clear signs that this subordination has ceased.

6

Carolingian Europe

THE CULTURAL, ECONOMIC, AND POLITICAL BACKGROUND

In the course of the eighth century, Western Christendom began to emerge as a coherent civilization. It did so under the Carolingian Empire—a vast constellation of territories welded together by the Frankish king Charlemagne and his talented predecessors. Here for the first time the various cultural ingredients—Classical, Christian, and Germanic—that went into the making of European civilization achieved a degree of synthesis. Charlemagne was a Germanic king who surrounded himself with Germanic warrior-aristocrats. But he also consorted with well-educated churchmen, trained in Classical scholarship, and took very seriously his role as protector and sustainer of the Western Church. Although his empire was fundamentally Germanic, its intellectual life, limited though it was, drew heavily from the Classical-Christian tradition. The fusion of these ingredients was evident in the life of the Carolingian court, in the rising vigor of the Carolingian Church, and in the person of Charlemagne himself.

Charlemagne's Francia stood in sharp contrast to contemporary Byzantium and the Abbasid Empire of Islam. Baghdad and Constantinople were the centers of opulent, mercantile civilizations. Charlemagne's Franks were half-civilized rustics. But it was beginning to dawn on a few of his subjects that they were a people apart, *Europeans,* agents of a new, distinctive civilization rooted in Athens and Jerusalem, Germany and Rome, and bound together—much as the Byzantines and Muslims were—by a common faith, a common scholarly language, and a common heritage.

The new Europe was spiritually and intellectually enlivened by the wide-ranging Benedictines, who disseminated a cultural tradition based on the Bible, the writings of the Latin Doctors and their contemporaries, and the surviving masterpieces of Latin literature. This evolving culture was bound together politically by a new dynasty of Frankish monarchs, the Carolingians.*

Carolingian Europe differed profoundly from the Western Roman Empire of old. It was a land without large cities, thoroughly agrarian in its economic organization, with its culture centered on the monastery, the cathedral, and the traveling royal court instead of the urban marketplace. And although Charlemagne extended his authority into Italy, the center of his activities and interests remained northern Francia. In a word, the new Europe no longer faced the Mediterranean; its axis had shifted northward.

Agricultural Technology

The relative brightness of the age of Charlemagne was the product of creative processes that had been at work during the preceding centuries. Benedictine evangelism and Northumbrian culture contributed much to the Carolingian revival. So, too, did the gradual development of agrarian technology that increased the productivity of north European farmlands.

By the opening of the eighth century, heavy compound plows had long been in widespread use throughout northern Europe, in contrast to the light scratch plow of the ancient Mediterranean world. The heavy plows—with wheels, colters, plowshares, and moldboards—cut deeply into the soil, pulverized it, and turned it aside, thus creating a drainage system of ridges and furrows. Well suited to the thick lowland soils and rainy climate of northern Europe, the heavy plow, drawn by teams of oxen, made it possible to cultivate vast, fertile areas in which the scratch plow was ineffective. Peasants pooled their oxen, fields, and labor in order to exploit the heavy plow, and in so doing they laid the foundation for the agricultural communities of medieval Europe with strong village councils to apportion labor and resources.

Newly opened farmlands were often fertile enough to permit more frequent crop rotation than had previously been feasible. By the Carolingian age, parts of northern Europe were just beginning to adopt a three-field system of cultivation in place of the two-field system typical of Roman times. Formerly, a typical farm had been divided into two fields, one of which was planted each year and allowed to lie fallow the second year to recover its fertility. But the rich northern soils, tilled by the heavy plow, did not require a full year's rest between crops. Instead, they were sometimes divided into three fields, each of which underwent a three-year cycle of autumn planting, spring planting, and fallow. Three-field agriculture developed slowly and irregularly. In time, however, it had an important impact on the European economy, for it increased food production, made possible a more varied and nutritious diet, and enabled plow teams to be used with greater effectiveness by spreading their work more evenly over the year.

*They were so named by later historians after their most illustrious representative, Charles the Great, or Charlemagne (Latin: *Carolus Magnus*).

The early Middle Ages also profited from a trend toward mechanization. The water mill, which was used occasionally in antiquity for grinding grain, had now come into more widespread use and was often to be seen on Carolingian farms. During the centuries following Charlemagne's death, the water mill was put to new uses—to power the rising textile industry of the eleventh century and to drive triphammers in forges. Thus, the technological progress of Merovingian and Carolingian times continued into the centuries that followed. By 1000 the development of metal shoes for horses and oxen greatly increased their work-lives, while the use of a more efficient horse collar increased the horse's effectiveness as a cart animal and prompted some cultivators in especially fertile areas to substitute horses for oxen in their plow teams (the horse was more expensive to feed but drew the plow more swiftly). And in the twelfth century the windmill made its debut in the European countryside. These new devices, some of them borrowed from peoples to the east, resulted in the increased productivity that underlay the prosperous civilization of the High Middle Ages (c. 1050–1300). Slowly the custom of human slavery declined as human power gave way more and more to the power of animals and machines. The decline of slavery has also been attributed to the impossibility of maintaining an oppressed and hostile work force on the land without the enforcement machinery of an effective state.

Carolingian Europe profited from the earlier phase of this drawn-out revolution in agrarian technology, but its major impact was yet to come. In Carolingian times, as before, agrarian villages, fields, and farmsteads continued to be challenged by widespread wilderness areas of forests, swamps, and trackless wastelands. A few Carolingian peasants worked on their own isolated farms; others inhabited free villages; most continued to live as semiservile villagers on the estates of lay and ecclesiastical lords. And all remained near the subsistence level, in part because since about 700 the population had been rising to match its increased productivity. During a great famine in 791, for example, peasants were driven to cannibalism and were even reported to have eaten members of their own families. Conditions may have been improving, but only very gradually, and a single bad year could be disastrous.

The Rise of the Carolingians

The Merovingian dynasty, founded by Clovis, had weakened over the centuries. A fundamental problem that the Merovingians shared with other early-medieval monarchs was the necessity of giving away portions of their crown lands, generation after generation, in order to attract loyal followers. By the later 600s, the Merovingians were impoverished, and power had passed to the landed aristocracy. Meanwhile, as a consequence of the Merovingian policy of dividing royal authority and crown lands among the sons of a deceased king, Francia had split into several distinct districts, the most important of which were Neustria (Paris and northwestern France), Austrasia (the heavily

Germanized northeast including the Rhinelands), and Burgundy in the southeast (see map, p. 88).

During the seventh century there emerged from the landholding aristocracy of Austrasia the family known to historians as the "Carolingians." Supported by a handful of allied and related families, the Carolingians managed to eliminate or assimilate rival families until they had achieved supremacy in Austrasia. Their family charisma was enhanced by the fact that they could claim a saint in their ancestry (Gertrude of Nivelles) and another "possible" saint (Arnulf, bishop of Metz). The Carolingians became "mayors" of the Austrasian royal household—that is, they held the chief administrative office in the itinerant court of Austrasia and made the post hereditary. As the Merovingians became increasingly land-poor and powerless, the Carolingians became the real masters of Austrasia. Carolingian mayors built up their power by gathering around them considerable numbers of trained warriors, in the tradition of the old Germanic comitatus. These men became "vassals" of the Carolingians, placing themselves under the mayor's protection, accepting his food, shelter, and support, and pledging him their loyalty. Other aristocrats also had private armies of vassals, but the Carolingians, with far the greatest number of followers, dominated the scene.

In 687 a Carolingian mayor named Pepin of Heristal led his Austrasian army to a decisive victory over the Neustrians at the battle of Tertry, and the Carolingians thenceforth controlled both districts. With Neustria in their grip they were able to dominate Burgundy, and when the Muslims moved into Gaul in the early 730s, the Franks stood united against them under the vigorous Carolingian mayor Charles Martel—Pepin of Heristal's bastard son.

Charles Martel (714–741)

Charles Martel ("The Hammer") was a skillful, ruthless military chieftain. Not only did he turn back the Muslims at the battle of Tours (732), he also won

Carolingian Chronology

687:	Pepin of Heristal, Carolingian mayor of Austrasia, defeats Neustria; Carolingian hegemony established
714–741:	Rule of Charles Martel
732:	Arabs defeated at Tours
741–768:	Rule of Pepin the Short
751:	Pepin crowned king of the Franks; Merovingian dynasty ends
754:	Death of St. Boniface
768–814:	Reign of Charlemagne
772–804:	Charlemagne's Saxon wars
800:	Charlemagne crowned Roman Emperor
814–840:	Reign of Louis the Pious
842:	Oaths of Strasbourg
843:	Treaty of Verdun

victory after victory over Muslims and Christians alike, consolidating his power over the Franks and extending the boundaries of the Frankish state. Charles Martel rewarded his military followers with estates in the conquered lands, and with further estates that he confiscated from the Frankish church. Although churchmen complained loudly, there was little they could do to oppose the hero of Tours and master of the Franks.

The Carolingians followed the same policy of divided succession among male heirs that had so weakened the Merovingians. But, as it happened, the Carolingian rulers over several generations had only one long-surviving heir. Frankish unity was maintained not by policy but by luck. When Charles Martel died in 741, his lands and authority were divided between his two sons, Carloman and Pepin the Short. But Carloman ruled only six years, retiring to a Benedictine monastery in 747 (voluntarily)—leaving the field to his brother Pepin. Carloman represented a new kind of Germanic ruler, deeply affected by the spiritual currents of his age, whose piety foreshadowed that of numerous saint-kings of later centuries. Christian culture and Germanic political leadership were beginning to merge.

Missions from England

At the time of Charles Martel's death in 741, English Benedictine monks had long been engaged in evangelical work among the Germanic peoples east of the Rhine. The earliest of these missions were directed at the Frisians, a maritime people who were settled along the coast of the Netherlands. The first of the Benedictine evangelists were monks from Northumbria. They brought to the Continent not only the organizational discipline and devotion to the papacy that had been characteristic of the Northumbrian Benedictines but also the venturesome missionary fervor the Celtic monks had contributed to the Northumbrian revival. So it was that Benedictine monks such as Wilfrid of Ripon and Willibrord left their Northumbrian homeland during the later 600s to evangelize the Frisians. The course of Western civilization was deeply affected by the transfer to Francia and Germany of the vibrant culture and Roman-Benedictine discipline of Northumbrian Christianity. Wilfrid of Ripon, Willibrord, and their devoted followers represent the first wave of a movement that was ultimately to infuse the Frankish empire of Charlemagne with the spiritual life that had developed in Anglo-Saxon England during the century following St. Augustine's mission to Kent.

The key figure in this cultural movement was the English Benedictine, St. Boniface. Reared in monasteries of southern England, Boniface left his native Wessex in 716 to do missionary work among the Frisians. From then until his death in 754 he devoted himself above all other tasks to Christianizing the Germanic peoples. Boniface was a man of energy, learning, and wisdom. A great number of his letters survive, many of which request support from his compatriots in Wessex and advice from Rome. On three occasions he visited the papal court, and from the beginning his work among the Germans was performed under papal commission. In 732 the papacy appointed him archbishop in Germany, and some years later he was given the episcopal see at Mainz as his headquarters. Throughout his career he was a devoted representative of the Anglo-Saxon church, the Benedictine Rule, and the papacy. As he put it, he strove "to hold fast the Catholic faith and unity, and to yield submission to the Church of Rome as long as life shall last for us."

Boniface also worked with the backing of the Carolingian mayors—Charles Martel and his sons, Carloman and Pepin the Short. Armed with the Christian faith and the Benedictine Rule, and supported by England, Francia, and Rome, Boniface labored among the Germanic tribes in Frisia, Thuringia, Hesse, and Bavaria. There he won converts, founded new Benedictine monasteries in the German wilderness, and erected the organizational framework of a disciplined German church. He suffered moments of discouragement, as when he wrote to an English abbot, "Have pity upon an old man tried and tossed on all sides by the waves of a German sea." Yet Boniface accomplished much, and the monasteries which he established—particularly the great house of Fulda in Hesse—were to become centers of learning and evangelism that played a great role in converting and civilizing the peoples of Germany.

During the decade following Charles Martel's death in 741, Boniface devoted much of his energy to Francia, where the church stood in desperate need of reform. Many areas had no priests at all; numerous peasants were scarcely removed from paganism; and priests themselves are reported to have hedged their bets by sacrificing animals to Germanic gods. Charles Martel, although willing enough to support Boniface's missionary endeavors among the Germanic pagans, did not want reformers interfering with his own Frankish church and perhaps raising awkward questions about his policy toward church lands. Carloman and Pepin, however, encouraged Boniface to reform the Frankish church, and beginning in 742 he held a series of synods for that purpose. Working closely with the papacy, he remodeled the Frankish ecclesiastical organization on the disciplined pattern of England and papal Rome. He reformed Frankish monasteries along the lines of the Benedictine Rule, saw to the establishment of monastic schools, encouraged the appointment of dedicated bishops and abbots, and worked toward the development of an adequate parish system to bring the Gospel to the countryside. Thus Boniface laid the groundwork for both the new church in Germany and the reformed church in Francia. In doing so, he served as one of the chief architects of the Carolingian cultural revival. And the bishops and abbots of his reformed Frankish church became valuable supporters and servants of the Carolingian regime.

The Franco-Papal Alliance

Boniface's introduction of Roman discipline and organization into the Frankish church was followed almost immediately by the consummation of a political alliance between Rome and Francia. It may well have been at Boniface's prompting that the Carolingian mayor, Pepin the Short (741–768), sought papal support for his seizure of the Frankish crown. Although the Merovingian monarchs had become impoverished puppet-kings, they retained the enormous prestige always enjoyed by a Germanic royal dynasty. If the Carolingians hoped to replace the Merovingians on the Frankish throne, they would have to call on the most potent spiritual sanction available to their age: papal consecration. In supporting Boniface and his fellow Benedictines, the Carolingian mayors had fostered papal influence in the Frankish church. Now, seeking papal support for a dynastic revolution, Pepin the Short could reasonably expect a favorable response from Rome.

For their part, the popes were seeking a strong, loyal ally against the Byzantines and Lombards who had long been contending for political supremacy in Italy. The Carolingians, with their policy of aid to the Benedictine missionaries and their support of Boniface's reforms, must have seemed strong candidates for the role of papal champion. And by the mid-eighth century a champion was badly needed. For many years the papacy had been trying to establish its own autonomous state in central Italy, the "Republic of St. Peter." In pursuing this goal, the popes had often turned to Byzantium for protection against the Lombards, who, although Christian, remained an ominous threat to papal independence. By 750 the popes could no longer depend on Byzantine protection for two reasons: (1) the Byzantine emperors had recently embraced a doctrine known as "iconoclasm," which the papacy regarded as heretical, and (2) Lombard aggression was rapidly becoming so effective that the Byzantine army could no longer be counted on to defend the papacy.

The iconoclastic controversy was the chief religious dispute of the Christian world in the eighth century. It was a conflict over the use of statues and pictures of Christ and the saints. These icons had gradually come to assume an important role in Christian worship. Strictly speaking, Christians might venerate them as symbols of the holy persons whom they represented, but in fact there was a tendency among the uneducated to worship the objects themselves. A line of reform emperors in Constantinople, beginning with Leo the Isaurian (717–741), sought to end the practice of worshiping images—vigorously fostered by the numerous monks of the Eastern Empire—by banning icons altogether. This new policy, known as "iconoclasm," served the interests of the Byzantine emperors by weakening the power of the eastern monasteries, which controlled far more land than the emperors would have wished. But the iconoclastic decrees offended a great many Byzantines, image worshipers and intelligent traditionalists alike. In the West little support was to be found for the policy of banning images. The papacy in particular opposed iconoclasm as heretical and contrary to the Christian tradition. Although it ultimately failed in the Byzantine Church, iconoclasm in the 750s was a center of controversy that aroused intense enmity between Rome and Constantinople. The papacy was deeply apprehensive of depending on the troops of a heretical emperor for its defense.

Even without the iconoclastic controversy it was becoming increasingly doubtful that the papacy could count on the military power of Byzantium in Italy. By 750 the Lombards were on the march once again, threatening not only Byzantine holdings but also the territories of the pope himself. In 751 the Lombards captured Ravenna, which had long served as the Byzantines' Italian capital, and the papal position in Italy became more precarious than ever.

Accordingly, the alliance was struck. Pepin sent messengers to Rome with the far from theoretical query, "Is it right that a powerless ruler should continue to bear the title of king?" The pope answered that by the authority of the Apostle Peter, Pepin was henceforth to be king of the Franks, and ordered that he should be anointed into his royal office by a papal representative. The anointing ceremony was duly performed at Soissons in 751. It had the purpose of buttressing the new Carolingian dynasty with the strongest of spiritual sanctions. Not by force alone, but by the supernatural potency of the royal anointing was the new dynasty established on the Frankish throne. Appropriately, this ceremony—the symbolic junction of the power of Rome and Francia—was performed by the aged Boniface.

With Pepin's anointment, the last of the Merovingians were shorn of their long hair (a symbol of their royalty) and packed off to a monastery. Three years thereafter Boniface, now nearing eighty, returned to his missionary work in Frisia and met a martyr's death. In the same year, 754, the pope himself traveled northward to Francia where he personally anointed and crowned Pepin at the royal monastery of St. Denis, thereby conferring every spiritual sanction at his disposal on the upstart Carolingian monarchy. At the same time he sought Pepin's military support against the Lombards.

Pepin obliged, leading his armies into Italy, defeating the Lombards, and granting a large portion of central Italy to the papacy. This "Donation of Pepin" was of lasting historical significance. It had the immediate effect of relieving the popes of the ominous Lombard pressure. In the long run, it became the nucleus of the Papal States, the "Patrimony of St. Peter," which would remain a characteristic feature of Italian politics until the later nineteenth century. For the moment, the papacy had been rescued from its peril. It remained to be seen whether the popes could prevent their new champion from becoming their master.

Pepin the Short, like all successful monarchs of the early Middle Ages, was an able war leader. As the first Carolingian king, he followed in the warlike tradition of his father. Besides defeating the Lombards in Italy, he drove the Muslims from Aquitaine and maintained domestic peace. He died in 768, leaving Francia larger, more powerful, and better organized than he had found it.

Charlemagne (768–814)

Pepin was a remarkably successful monarch, but he was overshadowed by his even more successful son. Charlemagne was a talented military com-

Ninth-century golden reliquary in the shape of
Charlemagne's head.

mander, a statesman of rare ability, a friend of learning. And he exhibited a
strong sense of responsibility for the welfare of the society over which he ruled.
In this last respect he advanced well beyond his Merovingian predecessors in
developing a conception of Christian kingship.

Charlemagne towered over his contemporaries both figuratively and literally. He was 6'3½" tall, thick-necked, and pot-bellied, yet imposing in appearance for all that. Thanks to his able biographer, Einhard, whose *Life of
Charlemagne* was written a few years after the emperor's death, Charlemagne
has come down to posterity as a three-dimensional figure. Einhard, who was
dwarfish in stature, wrote enthusiastically of his oversized hero. The Roman
historian Suetonius was Einhard's model, and he lifted whole passages from
Suetonius's *Lives of the Twelve Caesars,* adapting many other phrases from the
work to his own purposes. Yet there is much in Einhard's *Life* that represents
his own appraisal of Charlemagne's deeds and character. Reared at the mon-

astery of Fulda, Einhard served for many years in Charlemagne's court and so gained an intimate knowledge of the emperor. Einhard's warm admiration for Charlemagne emerges clearly from the biography, yet the author was able to see Charlemagne's faults as well as his virtues:

> Temperate in both eating and drinking, he hated drunkenness in anybody, particularly in himself and those of his household. But he found it difficult to abstain from food and often complained that fasts injured his health. . . . His meals usually consisted of four courses, not counting the roast, which his huntsmen used to bring in on the spit. He was fonder of this than of any other dish. While at the table he listened to reading or music. The readings were stories and deeds of olden times; he was also fond of St. Augustine's books, especially of the one entitled *The City of God*. So moderate was he in the use of wine and all sorts of drink that he rarely allowed himself more than three cups in the course of a meal.*

Einhard comments at length on Charlemagne's military and political career, but the most fascinating passages in the biography deal with the emperor's way of life and personal idiosyncrasies that disclose him as a human being rather than as a shadowy hero of legend:

> While he was dressing and putting on his shoes, he not only gave audience to his friends, but if the Count of the Household told him of any lawsuit in which his judgment was necessary, he had the parties brought before him forthwith, considered the case, and gave his decision, just as if he were sitting on the judgment seat.

Einhard also was at pains to show Charlemagne's thirst for learning. He portrays the emperor as a fluent master of Latin, a student of Greek, a speaker of such skill that he might have passed for a teacher of rhetoric, a devotee of the liberal arts, and in particular a student of astronomy who learned to calculate the motions of the heavenly bodies. Einhard concludes this impressive discussion of Charlemagne's scholarship with a final tribute that unwittingly discloses the emperor's severe limitations:

> He also tried to write, and used to keep tablets and blank pages in bed under his pillow so that in his leisure hours he might accustom his hand to form the letters; but as he did not begin his efforts at an early age but late in life, they met with poor success.

Charlemagne could be warm and talkative, but he could also be hard, cruel, and violent, and his subjects came to regard him with both admiration and fear. He was possessed of a strong, if superficial, piety that prompted him to build churches, collect relics, and struggle for a Christian cultural revival in Francia. But it did not prevent him from filling his court with concubines and other disreputable characters. In short, Charlemagne, despite his

---

*The size of the cup is not provided.

military and political genius, was a man of his age, in tune with its most progressive forces yet by no means removed from its past.

The Expansion of the Empire

Above all else Charlemagne was a warrior-king. He led his armies on yearly campaigns as a matter of course. When his magnates and their retainers assembled around him annually on the May Field, the question was not whether to go to war but whom to fight. It was only gradually, however, that Charlemagne developed a coherent scheme of conquest built on a notion of Christian mission and addressed to the goal of unifying and systematically expanding the Christian West. At the behest of the papacy, he followed his father's footsteps into Italy. There he conquered the Lombards completely in 774, incorporated them into his growing state, and assumed for himself the Lombard crown. Thenceforth he employed the title "King of the Franks and the Lombards."

In 778 Charlemagne launched a campaign against the Spanish Muslims that met with little success. He did manage subsequently to establish a border district on the Spanish side of the Pyrenees Mountains known as the "Spanish March" (march = frontier). In later generations the southern portion of Charlemagne's Spanish March evolved into the county of Barcelona, which remained more receptive to the influence of French institutions and customs than any other district in Spain. A relatively minor military episode in Charlemagne's Spanish campaign of 778—an attack by a band of Christian Basques against the rearguard of Charlemagne's army as it was withdrawing across the Pyrenees into Francia—became the inspiration for one of the great epic poems of the eleventh and twelfth centuries: the *Song of Roland.* The unknown author or authors of the poem transformed the Basques into Muslims and made the battle a heroic struggle between the rival faiths. Charlemagne was portrayed as a godlike conqueror, phenomenally aged, and Roland, the warden of the Breton March and commander of the rearguard, acquired a fame in literature far out of proportion to his actual historical importance.

Charlemagne devoted much of his strength to the expansion of his eastern frontier. In 787 he conquered and absorbed Bavaria, organizing its easternmost district into a forward defensive barrier against the Slavs. The East March, or *Ostmark,* became the nucleus of a new state later to be called Austria. In the 790s Charlemagne pushed still farther to the southeast, destroying the rich and predatory Avar state, which had long tormented eastern Europe. For many generations the Avars had been enriching themselves on the plunder of their victims and on heavy tribute payments from Byzantium and elsewhere. Charlemagne had the good fortune to seize a substantial portion of the Avar treasure; it is reported that fifteen four-ox wagons were required to transport the hoard of gold, silver, and precious garments back to Francia. The loot of the Avars contributed significantly to the resources of Charle-

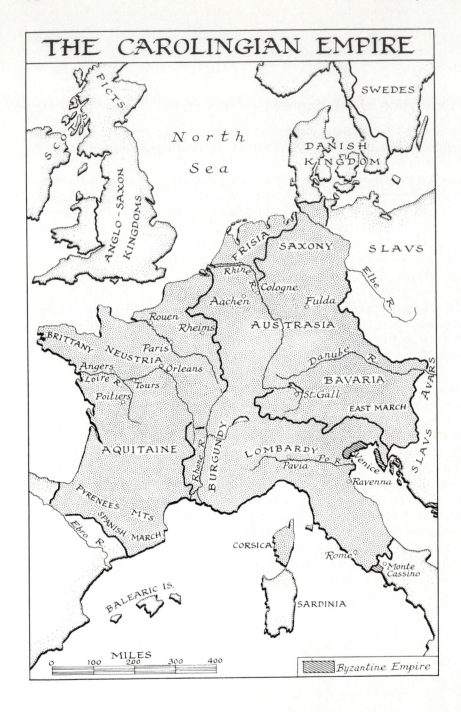

THE CAROLINGIAN EMPIRE

PICTS

SWEDES

SCOTS

North

Sea

DANISH KINGDOM

ANGLO-SAXON KINGDOMS

FRISIA

SAXONY

SLAVS

Rhine R.

Cologne

Elbe R.

Aachen

Fulda

Rouen

Rheims

AUSTRASIA

BRITTANY

NEUSTRIA

Paris

Danube R.

Angers

Orleans

BAVARIA

Loire R.

Tours

AVARS

Poitiers

St.Gall

EAST MARCH

AQUITAINE

Rhone R.

BURGUNDY

LOMBARDY

Po R.

Venice

SLAVS

Pavia

Ravenna

PYRENEES MTS

SPANISH MARCH

Ebro R.

CORSICA

Rome

Monte Cassino

BALEARIC IS.

SARDINIA

MILES

0   100   200   300   400

Byzantine Empire

magne's treasury and broadened the scope of his subsequent building program and patronage to scholars and churches.

Charlemagne's most prolonged military effort was directed against the pagan Saxons of northern Germany. With the twin goals of protecting the Frankish Rhinelands and bringing new souls into the Church, he campaigned for some thirty-two years, conquering the Saxons repeatedly and baptizing them by force, only to have them rebel when his armies withdrew. In a fit of savage exasperation he ordered the execution of 4500 unfaithful Saxons in a single day in 782. At length Saxony submitted to the remorseless pressure of Charlemagne's soldiers and the monks who followed in their wake. By 804 Frankish control of Saxony was well established, and in subsequent decades Christianity seeped gradually into the Saxon soul. A century and a half later, Christian Saxons were governing the most powerful state in Europe and were fostering a significant artistic and intellectual revival that was to enrich the culture of tenth-century Christendom.

The Imperial Coronation of A.D. 800

Charlemagne's armies, by incorporating central Germany into the new civilization, had succeeded where the legions of ancient Rome had failed. No longer a mere Frankish king, Charlemagne, by 800, was the master of the West. A few small Christian states remained outside his jurisdiction—the principalities of southern Italy, the kingdoms of Anglo-Saxon England. But with a handful of exceptions such as these, Charlemagne's political sway extended throughout Western Christendom. On Christmas Day 800, his immense accomplishment was given formal recognition when Pope Leo III placed the imperial crown on his head and acclaimed him "Emperor of the Romans." From the standpoint of legal theory, this dramatic act reconstituted the Roman Empire in the West after a 324-year intermission. In another sense it was the ultimate consummation of the Franco-papal alliance of 751.

Charlemagne's imperial coronation has evoked heated controversy among historians. According to Einhard, Pope Leo III took Charlemagne by surprise and bestowed on him an unwanted dignity. Charlemagne had such an aversion to the title of Emperor, so Einhard reports, "that he declared he would not have set foot in the church the day that it was conferred, although it was a great feast day, if he could have foreseen the pope's design."

Many modern historians have tended to be skeptical, arguing that Charlemagne was too powerful—too firmly in control of events—to permit a coronation that he did not wish. It has been pointed out that scholars in Charlemagne's court, beguiled by the dream of empire, may well have urged him on. Some historians have stressed the fact that Byzantium lacked an emperor in 800 and that Charlemagne disclosed his interest in the Roman imperial crown by engaging unsuccessfully in marriage negotiations with the Byzantine empress Irene. Conversely, it has been suggested that the coronation was largely a product of internal Roman politics during the years 799–

800. In any event, the acclamation that Charlemagne received from the people of Rome immediately after his coronation had obviously been well rehearsed, and it is hard to believe that Charlemagne did not know what was afoot.

Most likely Charlemagne's imperial coronation of 800, like the royal coronation of Pepin the Short in 751, represents a blend of papal and Carolingian interests. For some years Charlemagne had been attempting to attain a status comparable to that of the Byzantine emperors. To take one example, he modified the practice, traditional among Germanic kings and aristocrats, of traveling constantly with his court, consuming the surplus food of one estate and moving on to the next. In 794 he established a permanent capital at Aachen in Austrasia, where he sought, though vainly, to create a Constantinople of his own. Aachen was called "New Rome," and an impressive palace-church was built in the Byzantine style—almost literally a poor man's Sancta Sophia. Even though Charlemagne's "Mary Church" at Aachen was a far cry from Justinian's masterpiece, it was a marvel for its time and place and made a deep impression on contemporaries. Einhard describes it as a beautiful basilica adorned with gold and silver lamps, with rails and doors of solid brass, and with columns and marbles from Rome and Ravenna. It was the product of a major effort on Charlemagne's part—an effort not only to create a beautiful church but also to ape the Byzantines. The coronation of 800 may well have been an expression of this same imitative policy.

The papacy, on the other hand, may well have regarded the coronation as an opportunity to regain some of the initiative it had lost to the all-powerful Charlemagne. To be sure, the Carolingians had been promoted from kings to emperors, but their empire thenceforth bore the stamp "Made in Rome." In later years the popes would insist that what they gave they could also take away. If the papacy could make emperors, it also could depose them. Indeed, it was only shortly before that the papal chancery had produced a famous forged document called the "Donation of Constantine"* in which the first Christian emperor allegedly gave to the pope the imperial diadem and governance over Rome, Italy, and all the West. The pope is alleged to have returned the diadem but kept the power of governance. Later popes, drawing on the "Donation of Constantine," regarded Charlemagne's imperial successors as stewards exercising political authority by delegation from the papacy, wielding their power in the interests of the Roman Church.

So convincing was this theory of papal supremacy in the eyes of the popes that it justified the use of a forgery to support the case. The "Donation of Constantine" was not an effort to rewrite history but an attempt to buttress the papal position by manufacturing evidence for an event that had actually occurred, so the papacy supposed, but for which the documentation had unfortunately perished.

*Probably sometime in the 740s.

Interior of the "Mary Church" in Aachen
(796–804). The Byzantine arches and the basic
structure are similar to those of San Vitale in
Ravenna (see p. 38).

But although Charlemagne respected the papacy, he was unwilling to
cast himself in the subordinate role papal theory demanded of him. He was
careful to retain the title "King of the Franks and the Lombards" alongside
his new imperial title. When the time came to crown his son emperor, Charlemagne excluded the pope from the ceremony and did the honors himself. In
these maneuvers we are witnessing the prologue to a long, bitter struggle
over the correct relationship between empire and papacy—a struggle that
reached its crescendo in the eleventh, twelfth, and thirteenth centuries. For
the present, however, Charlemagne's power was unrivaled and the popes
were much too weak to resist him. The warm Carolingian-papal relations of

Pepin's day continued, and the papacy was nearly smothered in Charlemagne's affectionate embrace.

Carolingian Theocracy

At no time since has Europe been so nearly united as under Charlemagne. And never again would Western Christendom flirt so seriously with theocracy. The papal anointing of Pepin and Charlemagne gave the Carolingian monarchy a sacred, almost priestly quality. Charlemagne used his immense authority to govern not only the body politic but the imperial Church as well. The laws and regulations of his reign, known as "capitularies," dealt with both ecclesiastical and secular matters. At his Synod of Frankfurt in 796, he issued legislation on Christian doctrine. Driven by a sense of responsibility for systematizing church discipline, and by the need to incorporate dependable educated churchmen into the structure of Carolingian government, he was a far greater force in the Carolingian Church than was the pope. Indeed, the significant intellectual revival known as the "Carolingian Renaissance" grew out of Charlemagne's concern for the welfare of the Church and the perpetuation of ecclesiastical culture as essential buttresses of the Carolingian state.

CAROLINGIAN CIVILIZATION

The Carolingian Renaissance

The term "Carolingian Renaissance" can be misleading. Charlemagne's age produced no serious abstract thought and little original philosophical or theological work. It produced no Thomas Aquinas or Leonardo da Vinci. If we look for a "renaissance" in the ordinary sense of the word, we are bound to be disappointed. The intellectual task of the Carolingian age was less exalted: to rescue Continental culture from the pit of ignorance into which it was sinking. Nevertheless, it would be pointless to abandon the tradition of calling the Carolingian revival a "renaissance." As one perceptive historian wrote, "'Renaissance' is no more misleading than any other word. It achieves indeed the sort of sublime meaninglessness which is required in words of high but uncertain import."

As with so many other aspects of the era, the Carolingian Renaissance bears the stamp of Charlemagne's will and initiative. It was he who saw the desperate need for schools in his kingdom and sought to provide them. There could be no question of establishing institutions of higher learning. None existed north of the Alps, and none would emerge until the High Middle Ages. All that the Carolingians could do was to promote primary and secondary education, and this itself was an immensely difficult task. Francia had no professional class of teachers either lay or clerical. The only hope for educational reform lay with the Church, which had an almost complete monopoly on literacy. So Charlemagne tried to force the cathedrals and monasteries of his realm to operate schools that would preserve and disseminate the rudiments of Classical-Christian culture. A capitulary of 789 commands that "In every episcopal see and in every monastery, instruction shall be given in the psalms, musical notation, chant, the computation of years and seasons, and grammar, and all books used shall be carefully corrected."

A curriculum of the sort proposed in this capitulary can hardly be described as sophisticated or demanding, yet many Carolingian monasteries and cathedrals fell considerably short of the modest standards that it sought to establish. Still, Charlemagne succeeded in improving vastly the quantity and quality of schooling in his empire. There was even an attempt to make village priests provide free instruction in reading and writing. Only a minute fraction of Charlemagne's subjects acquired literacy. But those few provided an all-important learned nucleus that kept knowledge alive and transmitted it to future generations. It was above all in the monastic schools that learning flourished—in houses such as Fulda, Tours, and Reichenau. During the turbulent generations following Charlemagne's death many of these monastic schools survived to become seedbeds of the far greater intellectual awakening of the eleventh and twelfth centuries.

As an integral part of his effort to raise the intellectual standards of his realm and sustain Christian culture, Charlemagne assembled scholars at his court from all over Europe. One such scholar was the emperor's biographer, Einhard, from eastern Francia. Another was the poet-historian Paul the Deacon, of the great Italian Benedictine house of Monte Cassino. Paul the Deacon's *History of the Lombards* provides an invaluable account of that Germanic tribe and its settlement in Italy. From Spain came Theodulf, later bishop of Orléans and abbot of Fleury, a tireless supporter of Charlemagne's educational reforms and a poet of considerable talent. The most important of these Carolingian scholars was Alcuin of York, the last significant mind to be produced by the Northumbrian Renaissance. Alcuin, along with his countrymen of an earlier generation—Wilfrid of Ripon, Willibrord, and Boniface—represents the vital connecting link between the Christian cultural life of seventh- and eighth-century England and the intellectual upsurge of Carolingian Francia.

Alcuin performed the essential task of preparing an accurate new edition of the Bible, purged of the scribal errors that had crept into it over the centuries, thereby saving Christian culture from the confusion arising from the corruption of its most fundamental text. For many years the chief scholar in Charlemagne's court school, Alcuin spent his final years as abbot of the wealthy and venerable monastery of St. Martin of Tours. He was extraordinarily well educated for his period, and his approach to learning typified the whole philosophy of the Carolingian Renaissance: to produce accurate copies of important traditional texts, to encourage the establishment of schools, and in every way possible to cherish and transmit the Classical-Christian cultural tradition, without, however, adding to it in any significant way. "There is nothing better for us," Alcuin wrote, "than to follow the teachings of the Apostles and the Gospels. We must follow these precepts instead of inventing new ones or propounding new doctrine or vainly seeking to increase our own fame by the discovery of new fangled ideas."

Alcuin and his fellow scholars were neither intellectual innovators nor men of conspicuous holiness. Drawn by Charlemagne's wealth and power and enriched by his patronage, they struggled to improve the scholarly level of the Carolingian Church, but they showed little concern for deepening its devotional life or exploring uncharted regions of speculative thought. They had the talents and inclinations—and the limitations—of a school teacher. At best they were scholars and humanists; in no sense could they be described as philosophers or mystics.

Accordingly, Alcuin, Theodulf, Einhard, Paul the Deacon, and others like them regularized the liturgy of the Church and encouraged the preaching of sermons. Carrying forward some of the monastic reforms begun by Boniface, they persuaded Charlemagne to command that all monasteries establish schools and follow the Benedictine Rule (an accurate and official copy of which was obtained at Monte Cassino). Although these commands were not everywhere obeyed, they did contribute to the standardization of monastic life and the preservation of literacy. A new official script was developed—the Carolingian minuscule—that derived in part from the Irish and Northumbrian scripts of the previous century. Thenceforth the Carolingian minuscule superseded the often illegible scripts earlier employed on the Continent. Its letters were clearly and separately formed (rather like modern printing which derives from it), and individual words were separated by spaces, unlike the practice that was common among earlier scribes of runningtheirwordstogether. As a result, reading became much easier than before and gradually more widespread. Throughout the realm monks set about copying manuscripts on an unprecedented scale. If Classical-Christian culture was advanced very little by these activities, it was at least preserved. Above all, its base was broadened. In the task they set themselves, the Carolingian scholars were eminently successful.

The Renaissance after Charlemagne

It was characteristic of the powerful theocratic tendencies of the age that this educational achievement was accomplished through royal rather than papal initiative. Germanic monarchy and Classical-Christian culture had joined hands at last. With the breakdown of European unity after Charlemagne's death, the momentary fusion of political and cultural energies dissolved, yet the intellectual revival continued. A deeply spiritual movement of monastic reform and moral regeneration began in Aquitaine under the leadership of the ardent and saintly Benedict of Aniane. Soon the influence of this movement took hold at the court of Charlemagne's son and successor, Louis the Pious. Louis gave St. Benedict of Aniane the privilege of visiting any monastery in the empire and tightening its discipline in whatever way he chose, to the chagrin of numerous abbots and monks. And in 817 a significantly expanded version of the Benedictine Rule, based on the strict monastic regulations of Benedict of Aniane, was promulgated for all the monasteries of the Empire and given the weight of imperial law. Benedict of Aniane's reform represents a marked shift from the spiritually superficial monastic regulations of Charlemagne's day to a deep concern for the Christ-centered life. The elaborated Benedictine Rule of 817 lost its status as imperial law in 840, with the death of Louis the Pious, but it remained an inspiration to subsequent monastic reform movements in the centuries that followed.

While Carolingian spiritual life was deepening in the years after Charlemagne's death, Carolingian scholarship continued to flourish in the cathedral and monastic schools. In keeping with the Carolingian intellectual program of preserving the Classical-Christian tradition, learned churchmen of the Carolingian Renaissance's "second generation" devoted themselves to preparing encyclopedic accounts of existing knowledge. Although unoriginal, these works contributed significantly to the process of cultural transmission. For example, Raban Maur (d. 856), abbot of Fulda, produced a learned collection of all information available to him on all subjects that occurred to him—on the pattern of Isidore of Seville's *Etymologies*. Raban Maur also carried forward the Carolingian educational tradition by writing a handbook on the instruction of the clergy that had a great impact on the operation of monastic schools.

The one original scholar in this second generation was the Irishman John Scotus Erigena, or John the Scot (the "Scots" in his day were inhabitants of Ireland rather than Scotland). He served for years in the court of Charlemagne's grandson, King Charles the Bald, himself a man of some learning. John the Scot was not only a philosopher but a wit as well, at least if we can believe the legend of a dinner table conversation between John and King Charles. The king, intending to needle his court scholar, asked him whether there was anything separating a Scot from a sot. "Only the dinner table," was John's reply.

John Scotus was a student of Neoplatonism and the only Western European scholar of his age to master the Greek tongue. He translated into Latin an important Greek philosophical treatise, *On the Celestial Hierarchy*, written by an anonymous late-fifth-century Christian Neoplatonist known as the Pseudo-Dionysius. This author was incorrectly identified in the Middle Ages as Dionysius the Areopagite, a first-century Athenian philosopher who is described in the *Acts of the Apostles* as being converted to Christianity by St. Paul. He was further misidentified as St. Denis, evangelist of the Gauls and first bishop of Paris, who was beheaded by pagans in the third century and in whose honor the great royal monastery of St. Denis was built. Accordingly, the writings of the Pseudo-Dionysius passed into the Middle Ages with the commanding credentials of an early Christian author, a Pauline convert, and a martyred missionary who brought Christianity to Gaul. In reality, the importance of the Pseudo-Dionysius lay in his providing a Christian dimension to the philosophical scheme of Plotinus and other pagan Neoplatonists. The unknowable and indescribable Neoplatonic god—the center and source of the concentric circles of reality—was identified as the God of the Christians. Such a god could not be approached intellectually but only by means of a mystical experience; hence the Pseudo-Dionysius became an important source of inspiration to later Christian mystics.

Stimulated by the work of the Pseudo-Dionysius, which he translated from Greek into Latin, John Scotus went on to write a highly original Neoplatonic treatise of his own, *On the Divisions of Nature.* In its blurred distinction between God and the created world, the treatise reflected the Neoplatonic tendency toward pantheism. It was controversial in its own time and even more so in later centuries.

The intellectual revival instigated by Charlemagne echoed through subsequent generations. In the monasteries and cathedrals of the ninth and tenth centuries, particularly in the German districts of Charlemagne's old empire, documents continued to be copied, schools continued to operate, and commentaries and summaries of ancient texts continued to appear. By the eleventh century, Europe was ready to build on its sturdy Carolingian foundations.

The Dynamics of Carolingian Expansion and Decline

The Carolingian Empire was ephemeral. Rising out of a chaotic past, it disintegrated in the turbulent era that followed. The Carolingians had achieved their early successes, under Pepin of Heristal and Charles Martel, not only because of strong leadership but also because of the sizable landed resources that the family came to control and the loyal, well-armed vassals and aristocratic supporters whom these resources could attract. Carolingian armies were better organized and better disciplined than those of most neighboring powers. No rival principality made such effective use of armored horsemen as did the Carolingians. And once Carolingian expansion was underway, it fed on its own momentum. Conquests brought plunder and new lands with which the Carolingians could enrich themselves and reward their supporters. Indeed, it became Carolingian policy to install loyal Franks, mostly Austrasians, as counts and dukes of the conquered provinces. Accordingly, the interests of the Frankish landholding aristocracy became ever more closely tied to the political and military fortunes of the Carolingian family. As long as the Carolingians could bring in profits from military campaigns, they commanded the enthusiastic obedience of disciplined followers. A Frank would gladly obey Charlemagne if it meant a cut of the Avar treasure or a lordship in Italy or Saxony. In short, Carolingian expansion was like a snowball, growing as it rolled, rolling as it grew.

Yet even at its height, Charlemagne's empire remained economically primitive and undergoverned. Towns were small and scattered, and the roads that linked settled areas were miserably poor. There was some trade, most of it dependent on the river network: Carolingian villages often had to obtain their iron, salt, and wine from outside sources, and the great lay and ecclesiastical landholders imported luxury goods such as jewelry and precious fabrics. Charlemagne did what he could to encourage such trade: he established a silver coinage of good quality (though most ordinary transactions continued to be based on barter or food rents); he concluded a reciprocal agreement with an English king guaranteeing the safety of merchants; he encouraged the construction of roads, bridges, and lighthouses; and he even contemplated building a canal to link the Rhine and Danube Rivers. But by Byzantine or Islamic standards, Carolingian commerce trickled rather than gushed.

Despite the plunder of conquests, Charlemagne had nowhere near the funds sufficient to support a salaried bureaucracy. Like his predecessors, he had to depend on the competence and loyalty of landholding regional officials: dukes, lords of the marches (margraves), and, most commonly, counts of the nearly 300 counties of the Empire. These men were royal officials, pledged to obey the king-emperor. But pledges are frail threads, and the Carolingian counts were in a position to act independently when loyalty no longer suited their interests. Many were drawn, of necessity, from aristocratic Frankish families with landed power bases of their own. Moreover, in place of salaries the counts were granted the use of extensive royal lands from which they could not easily be dislodged. And because of the vast distances and poor communications, they had to be entrusted with broad powers over the royal tribunals, taxation systems, and military recruiting arrangements in their counties. Charlemagne kept track of his regional administrators by sending out pairs of inspectors known as *missi dominici* (envoys of the lord) to make certain that his orders were being obeyed and his revenues were not being pocketed. The *missi dominici*, consisting usually of one churchman and one layman, typified the theocratic trend of Charlemagne's reign. They were moderately effective, but only because they represented a monarch who had the power to punish and reward. A count who owed his office to Charlemagne and whose authority over potentially troublesome provincials depended on Charlemagne's continued backing would receive the *missi dominici* with respect. Provincial officials obeyed royal commands and capitularies not out of patriotic allegiance to the Carolingian state but because of their devotion to Charlemagne's person—a devotion based on the bonds of common interest that linked the conquering monarch and his highly favored aristocracy.

These bonds had always been fragile, and when the Carolingian Empire ceased expanding, as it did after the final submission of Saxony in 804, they began to loosen. As the flow of lands and plunder dried up, aristocratic loyalty diminished, and the Empire started disintegrating. Disaffection and rebellion clouded the final decade of Charlemagne's life and brought political chaos to the reign of his son and heir, Louis the Pious. Once the snowball stopped rolling, it began to melt.

Carolingian Europe: An Overview

The Carolingian Empire, impressive though it was, lacked a vigorous commercial life and other necessary ingredients of a flourishing civilization. Its revenues were small and its administrative institutions grossly inadequate to the needs of a great state. Beneath the military and cultural veneer, Carolingian Europe was still only half-civilized.

But even though Charlemagne's "Roman Empire" was merely a shadow of its ancient namesake, one cannot help respecting its founder for doing so much with so little, for making such an effort to transcend his own primitive past. The historian Karl Werner caught the spirit of Charlemagne's policy when he described it as a "grand design"—not simply a royal-aristocratic partnership in pursuit of conquest and loot, but a new conception of the ruler and the state. Werner is well aware of the Carolingians' brutality and the flimsiness of their administration, but that is by no means the whole story:

> Their willingness to use all the help available—for example, the
> Anglo-Saxon missionaries and the papacy; their eagerness to discover
> and take over whatever they believed to be good, reliable and
> authentic, and to spread it; these Carolingian qualities, which reached
> their peak under Charlemagne, were not only an achievement that will
> always be remarkable; they helped refashion the high nobility and
> exercised an immeasurable influence on the future development of
> Europe, long after their dynasty had vanished.

7

The New Invasions

THE LATER CAROLINGIANS

Tentative though it was, the Carolingian revival might conceivably have evolved much further had it not been for a series of new invasions. During the ninth and tenth centuries Western Christendom was hammered by the attacks of three separate peoples: the semi-nomadic Hungarians (Magyars) from the east, the Saracens (Muslims) from the south, and the seafaring Vikings from the north. Europe emerged from its ordeal with a political organization radically different from that of the Carolingian Empire.

Louis the Pious (814–840)

One cannot ascribe the political fragmentation of Carolingian Europe entirely to these outside forces. Charlemagne himself, in keeping with Frankish tradition, planned to divide his state among his several sons. As it happened, however, Charlemagne outlived all but one of them. The luck of the Carolingians was still running, and when the great conqueror died in 814, his realm passed intact to his remaining heir, Louis the Pious.

Although Louis was by no means incompetent, his military and political talents were less impressive than those of his father Charlemagne, his grandfather Pepin the Short, and his great-grandfather Charles Martel. And with the cessation of Carolingian expansion a few years prior to his accession, Louis could not reward his aristocratic followers on the scale to which they had long been accustomed. During the generations of Carolingian expansion, the Frankish aristocracy had become far richer than before and far more powerful. Now, with the flow of lands and booty cut off, many great landholders deserted the monarchy and looked to their own interests.

Louis the Pious was well named. He ran Charlemagne's minstrels and concubines out of the imperial court. He gave his wholehearted support to the monastic reforms of Benedict of Aniane. And far more than his hardheaded father, Louis committed himself to the dream of a unified Christian Empire—

a City of God brought down to earth. But empires cannot be sustained on dreams alone, and Louis lacked the resources necessary to maintain cohesion throughout the wide dominions that the Carolingians had won. He was the first of his line to conceive the notion of bequeathing supreme political authority to his eldest son, thereby making the unity of the kingdom a matter of policy rather than luck. But ironically, he turned out to be the last Carolingian to rule an undivided Frankish realm. His bold plan for a single succession was foiled by the ambitions of his younger sons, who rebelled openly against him, vied with him for aristocratic support, and plunged the Empire into civil war.

The Oaths of Strasbourg and the Treaty of Verdun

When Louis the Pious' troubled reign ended in 840, his three surviving sons struggled for the spoils. The eldest, Lothar, claimed the indivisible imperial title and supreme power over the entire realm. The other two sons, Louis the German and Charles the Bald, fought to win independent royal authority in East and West Francia, respectively.

The battle among the brothers symbolized a fundamental tension within the Empire between imperial unity and regionalism. The principle of unity, represented by Lothar, was more an abstraction than a reality, for even at its height the Carolingian Empire had been a loosely joined cluster of separate principalities, differing in language, culture, and administrative traditions. The Empire's linguistic diversity was made vividly clear when Charles the Bald and Louis the German met at Strasbourg in 842 to seal their alliance against Lothar. Charles took his oath of allegiance in the German vernacular so that Louis' East Frankish army could understand him, whereas Louis for the same reason swore his loyalty in the Romance language of Charles' West Franks— the ancestor of modern French. The Oaths of Strasbourg disclose that the kingdoms claimed by Charles and Louis were not artificial creations but were rooted in separate cultural and linguistic traditions.

The controversy was resolved by the Treaty of Verdun in 843. Lothar was forced to submit to the combined might of his younger brothers, and the Empire was divided permanently. The Treaty of Verdun, along with subsequent settlements, marked the disintegration of the Carolingian Empire into its component parts, which themselves dimly foreshadowed the political structure of modern Europe. Lothar was permitted to keep the imperial title but was denied any superior jurisdiction over the realms of Louis the German and Charles the Bald. Louis ruled East Francia, which became the nucleus of modern Germany. Charles the Bald became king of West Francia, which evolved into modern France. Lothar retained a long, narrow strip of territory that stretched for some thousand miles northward from Italy through Burgundy, Alsace, Lorraine, and the Netherlands, embracing considerable portions of western Germany and eastern France. This Middle Kingdom included the two "imperial capitals"—Rome and Aachen—but its frontiers were diffi-

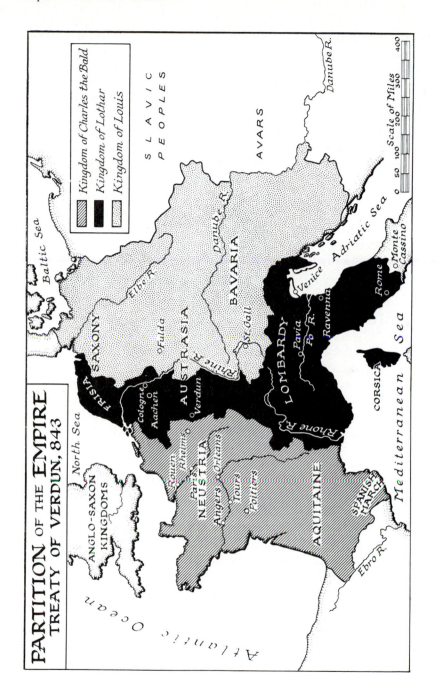

PARTITION OF THE EMPIRE
TREATY OF VERDUN, 843

Kingdom of Charles the Bald
Kingdom of Lothar
Kingdom of Louis

Scale of Miles
0 50 100 200 300 400

SLAVIC PEOPLES

AVARS

Baltic Sea

North Sea

Atlantic Ocean

ANGLO-SAXON KINGDOMS

FRISIA

SAXONY

AUSTRASIA

Elbe R.

Danube R.

Danube R.

BAVARIA

St. Gall

Rhine R.

Fulda

Cologne
Aachen
Verdun

Rouen
Rheims
Paris
NEUSTRIA
Orléans
Angers
Tours
Poitiers

AQUITAINE

SPANISH MARCH

Ebro R.

Rhone R.

LOMBARDY

Pavia
Po R.
Ravenna

Venice

Rome

Monte
Cassino

CORSICA

Adriatic Sea

Mediterranean Sea

cult to defend, and it lacked cohesion. At Lothar's death in 855 it was sub-divided among his three sons, one of whom inherited Carolingian Italy along with the old Lombard crown and the increasingly insignificant imperial title. From the ninth century to the twentieth, fragments of Lothar's Middle King-dom have been the source of endless bitter territorial disputes between Germany and France.

The struggles among Charlemagne's grandsons occurred against a back-ground of Viking, Hungarian, and Saracen invasions, which accelerated the tendency toward political fragmentation brought about by internal weak-nesses. As it turned out, even the more modest political units arising from the Treaty of Verdun were too large—too far removed from the desperate re-alities of the countryside—to cope successfully with the incessant raids of Viking shipmen or Hungarian horsemen. During the ninth and tenth centu-ries Carolingian leadership was visibly failing. The ineffectiveness of the later Carolingians is graphically illustrated in their names: Charles the Fat, Charles the Simple, Louis the Child, Louis the Blind, Louis the Stammerer.

THE INVASIONS

The Saracens, Hungarians, and Vikings who plundered the declining Carolingian state were in part drawn by its growing political instability and in part impelled by forces operating in their own homelands. Europe suffered much from their marauding, yet it was strong enough in the end to survive and absorb the invaders. And these invasions were the last that Western Christendom was destined to endure. From about A.D. 1000 to the present, the West has had the unique opportunity of developing on its own, sheltered from alien attacks that have so disrupted other civilizations over the past thou-sand years. As the historian Marc Bloch said, "It is surely not unreasonable to think that this extraordinary immunity, of which we have shared the priv-ilege with scarcely any people but the Japanese, was one of the fundamental factors of European civilization."

Yet in the ninth and tenth centuries Europe's hard-pressed peoples had no way of knowing that the invasions would one day end. A Frankish writer of the mid-ninth century described the Viking attacks in these chilling words:

> The number of ships grows larger and larger; the great host of
> Northmen continually increases; on every hand Christians are the
> victims of massacres, looting, and arson—clear proof of which will
> remain as long as the world itself endures. The Northmen capture every
> city they pass through, and none can withstand them.

In southern Gaul people prayed for divine protection against the Saracens: "Eternal Trinity, deliver thy Christian people from the oppression of the pagans." To the north thy prayed, "From the savage nation of the Northmen, which lays waste our realms, deliver us, O God." And in northern Italy: "Against the arrows of the Hungarians be thou our protector."

Saracens and Hungarians

The Saracens of the ninth and tenth centuries, unlike their Muslim predecessors in the seventh and early eighth centuries, came as brigands rather than conquerors and settlers. From their pirate nests in Africa, Spain, and the Mediterranean islands they preyed on shipping, plundered coastal cities, and sailed up rivers to carry their devastation far inland. Saracen bandit lairs were established on the southern coast of France (today's "French Riviera"), from which the marauders conducted raids far and wide through the countryside and kidnapped pilgrims crossing the Alpine passes. Charlemagne had never possessed much of a navy, and his successors found themselves helpless to defend their coasts. In 846 Saracen brigands raided Rome itself, profaning its churches and stealing its treasures. As late as 982 a German king was severely defeated by Saracens in southern Italy, but by then the raids were tapering off. Southern Europe, now bristling with fortifications, had learned to defend itself and was even beginning to challenge Saracen domination of the western Mediterranean.

The Hungarians or Magyars—fierce nomadic horsemen from the Asiatic steppes—settled in the land now known as Hungary. From the late 800s to 955 they terrorized Germany, northern Italy, and eastern and central France. Hungarian raiding parties ranged across the land, seeking defenseless settlements to plunder, avoiding fortified towns, outriding and outmaneuvering the armies sent against them. In time, however, they became more sedentary, gave more attention to their farms, and lost much of their nomadic mobility. In 955 King Otto the Great of Germany crushed a large Hungarian army at the battle of the Lechfeld and brought the raids to an end at last. Within another half-century, the Hungarians had adopted Christianity and were becoming integrated into the community of Christian Europe.

Vikings

The Vikings, or Norsemen, from Scandinavia were the most fearsome invaders of all. Then, as now, the Scandinavians were divided roughly into three groups: Danes, Swedes, and Norwegians. Only gradually did these groups jell into unified kingdoms; in the early years of Viking expansion Scandinavia was a patchwork of petty states. The population consisted of landowning aristocrats, free farmers, and slaves. As elsewhere, women were subordinated to men, and there were instances of Viking lords having several wives. But, for the most part, Viking women enjoyed a somewhat greater freedom of action than their counterparts in Western Christendom: they could own and grant property, marry whomever they chose, and govern the affairs of their family if their husbands were absent or dead. The Viking economy was based on grain growing and the raising of cattle and sheep, but good lands for farming and pasturing were limited largely to Denmark and southern Sweden. The land shortage and accompanying property disputes resulted in incessant private warfare. Only a few small towns developed, as commercial centers for goods imported from the distant and far-flung lands where Viking seafarers traded and plundered.

During the great age of Viking expansion in the ninth and tenth centuries the Danes, who were brought cheek to jowl with the Carolingian Empire by Charlemagne's conquest of Saxony, focused their attention on France and England. The Norwegians raided and settled in Scotland, Ireland, and the North Atlantic. The Swedes concentrated on the East—the Baltic shores, Russia, and the Byzantine Empire. Yet the three Norse peoples had much in common, and the distinctions among them were by no means sharp. It is therefore proper to regard their raids, their astonishing explorations, and their far-flung commercial enterprises as a single great international movement.

Though the breakdown of Carolingian unity doubtless acted as a magnet to Viking marauders, their raids on the West began as early as Charlemagne's later years. The basic causes for their outward thrust must be sought in Scandinavia, where the population had apparently increased by the later 700s to a level that the primitive Norse agriculture was unable to support. The pressure of overpopulation was probably aggravated by the growth of centralized royal power, which cramped the more restless spirits and drove them to seek adventures and opportunities abroad. A third factor was the development of improved Viking ships, eminently seaworthy, propelled by both sail and oars, and capable of carrying crews of forty to a hundred warriors at speeds up to ten knots. In these longships Viking warriors struck the ports of northern Europe. They sailed up rivers far into the interior, plundering towns and monasteries and taking great numbers of captives, whom they sold as slaves in the markets of Spain and the Mediterranean. Sometimes they would steal horses and ride across the countryside to spread their devastation still further.

Europeans were accustomed enough to war, yet they regarded the Viking raids as something new and terrifying. Carolingian armies were unaccustomed to naval warfare, whereas the Vikings were marvelously skilled at building and navigating ships. Coming from a land of mountainous coasts and deep fjords, they had long used ships for traveling, fishing, fighting, and even entombment. Moreover, Christian warriors, fearful for their souls, tended to respect the sanctity of monasteries, which to the pagan Vikings were ideal targets—at once wealthy and defenseless. The monastic chroniclers of the time, accustomed to peace within their walls, may have exaggerated the violence of the Viking age and the ferocity of Viking armies. Yet the Viking impact on northern France, England, and Russia was real, and it was lasting.

Attacks against England and the Continent

England was the first to suffer from Viking attacks. In 793 Norse brigands annihilated the Northumbrian monastery of Lindisfarne. In 794 they plundered Jarrow, where Bede had lived and died. And other major abbeys of

THE VIKING, HUNGARIAN AND MUSLIM INVASIONS

Atlantic Ocean

ICELAND

VIKINGS

NORWAY

SWEDEN

SCOT-LAND

IRELAND

DENMARK

ENGLAND

Rhine R.

Aachen

Rouen

Paris

Seine R.

Loire R.

Tours

Dnieper R.

Kiev

Danube R.

HUNGARIANS

Danube R.

Black Sea

LOMBARDY

PROVENCE

Marseilles

CORSICA

Rome

Monte Cassino

Naples

Constantinople

SARDINIA

BALEARIC IS.

SICILY

MUSLIMS

Mediterranean Sea

Vikings

Muslims

Hungarians

MILES

0   200   400   600   800

Northumbria suffered a similar devastation. Thenceforth the Anglo-Saxon kingdoms were tormented by incessant Viking raids.

In 842 the Danes plundered London. A few years thereafter they began to establish permanent winter bases in England, which freed them from the necessity of returning to Scandinavia after the raiding season. By the later 800s they had turned from piracy to large-scale occupation and permanent settlement. One after another the Anglo-Saxon kingdoms were overrun until at length, in the 870s, only the southern kingdom of Wessex remained free of Danish control. And even Wessex came within a hair's breadth of falling to the Danes.

To mariners such as the Vikings, the English Channel was a boulevard instead of a barrier, and their raiding parties attacked the English and French shores indiscriminately. They established permanent bases at the mouths of large rivers and sailed up them to plunder monasteries and sack towns. Antwerp was ravaged in 837, Rouen in 841, Hamburg and Paris in 845, Charlemagne's old capital at Aachen in 881.

But many European princes fought doggedly to protect their lands. King Alfred the Great of Wessex saved his kingdom from Danish conquest in the late 870s and began the task of rolling back the Danish armies in England. King Arnulf of East Francia won a decisive victory over the Norsemen in 891 at the battle of the Dyle and thereby decreased the Viking pressure on Germany—although it was at this very time that the Hungarian raids were beginning. West Francia continued to suffer for a time, but in about 911 King Charles the Simple created a friendly Viking buffer state in northern France by concluding a treaty with a Norse chieftain named Rolf. The Vikings in Rolf's band had been conducting raids from their settlement at the mouth of the River Seine. Charles, less simple than his name would imply, reasoned that if he could make Rolf his ally, the Seine settlement might prove an effective barrier against further raids. Rolf became a Christian, married Charles the Simple's daughter, and recognized at least in some sense the lordship of the French monarchy. Thus his state acquired a degree of legitimacy in the eyes of Western Christendom. Expanding gradually under Rolf and his successors, it became known as the land of the Northmen, or "Normandy." Over the next century and a half the Normans became, as one historian put it, "more French than the French." They adopted French culture and the French language, built castles and founded monasteries, yet they retained much of their former adventurousness and wanderlust. In the eleventh century Normandy was producing some of Europe's best warriors, crusaders, administrators, and monks.

The North Atlantic and Russia

France, England, and Germany formed only a part of the vast Viking world of the ninth and tenth centuries. By the mid-800s Norwegians and Danes had conquered the greater part of Ireland, and between 875 and 930 they settled remote and desolate Iceland. There a distinctive Norse culture arose which for several centuries remained only slightly affected by the main currents of Western civilization. In Iceland the magnificent oral tradition of the Norse saga flourished and was eventually committed to writing, to provide epic entertainment during long, dark Icelandic winters. The Norsemen of Iceland were perhaps the greatest sailors of all. They settled on the coast of Greenland in the late 900s, and in the eleventh century they established temporary settlements on the northern coast of North America itself (Newfoundland), anticipating Columbus by half a millennium. Indeed, the Greenland settlement survived until about the time of Columbus's voyage, succumbing only then to gradually falling temperatures and to the seal-hunting Eskimos moving southward with the advancing ice.

To the east, Swedish Vikings overran Finland and penetrated far southward along the rivers of European Russia to trade with Constantinople and Baghdad. The Swedes attacked Constantinople in 860, 907, and 941, and their efforts won them valuable trading privileges from the Byzantine emperors. Some Swedish Vikings took service in the Byzantine imperial guard.

In Russia, a Swedish dynasty established itself at Novgorod in the later ninth century, ruling over the indigenous Slavic population. In the tenth century a Norse prince of Novgorod captured the south-Russian city of Kiev, which became the capital of the powerful, well-organized state of Kievan Russia. Deeply influenced by the culture of its subjects, the dynasty at Kiev became more Slavic than Scandinavian. Around the turn of the millennium, as we have seen, Prince Vladimir of Kiev adopted Byzantine Christianity. Submitting himself and his subjects to the spiritual authority of the patriarch of Constantinople, Vladimir opened Russia to the influence of Byzantine culture (see p. 42).

Twilight of the Viking Age

The development of centralized monarchies in Denmark, Norway, and Sweden, which may well have been a factor in driving enterprising Norse seafarers to seek their fortunes elsewhere, ultimately resulted in taming the Viking spirit. As Scandinavia became increasingly civilized its kings discouraged the activities of roaming warrior bands, and its social environment gave rise to a more humdrum life. Far into the eleventh century, England continued to face the attacks of Norsemen, but these invaders were no longer pirate bands; instead, they were royal armies led by Scandinavian kings. The nature of the Scandinavian threat had changed, and by the late eleventh century the threat had ceased altogether. Around the year 1000 Christianity was winning converts all across the Scandinavian world. In Iceland, in Russia—even in the kingdoms of Scandinavia itself—the Norsemen were adopting the religion of the monks whom they had formerly terrorized. Scandinavia was becoming a part of Western European culture.

Even at the height of the invasions, the Norsemen excelled at commerce as well as piracy. They were the greatest seafarers of the age. They introduced Europe to the art of ocean navigation and enlarged the commercial horizons of Western Christendom. The scope of the Scandinavian trade network is suggested by the saga story of a tenth-century merchant from Russia selling an Irish princess to an Icelandic farmer in a Norwegian town. Whether true or not, and disregarding the affront to Irish royalty, the tale reflects the cosmopolitanism and enterprise that Viking voyagers injected into the conservative, landbound culture of Carolingian Europe.

8

Europe Survives the Siege

The invasions of the ninth and tenth centuries wrought significant changes in the political and social organization of Western Europe. In France political authority tended to crumble into local units as unwieldy royal armies failed to cope with the Viking raids. But elsewhere the invasions had the effect of augmenting royal power. The German monarchy, after a period of relative weakness, underwent a spectacular recovery in the tenth century, while in England the hammerblows of the Danes had the ultimate result of unifying the several Anglo-Saxon states into a single kingdom. In general, Europeans rallied behind whatever leadership could provide an effective defense— whether kings, magnates, or, as in northern Italy, urban bishops.

THE ENGLISH RESPONSE

In the later eighth century, on the eve of the Viking invasions, England was politically fragmented, as it had been ever since the Anglo-Saxon conquests. But over the centuries the several smaller kingdoms had gradually passed under the control of four larger ones: Northumbria in the north, Mercia in the Midlands, East Anglia in the southeast, and Wessex in the south. The Danish attacks of the ninth century, by destroying the power of Wessex's rivals, cleared the field for the Wessex monarchy and thereby hastened the trend toward consolidation that was already underway. But if the Danes were doing the Wessex monarchy a favor, neither side was aware of it during the troubled years of the later ninth century. For a time it appeared that the Danes might conquer Wessex itself.

King Alfred (871–899)

At the moment of crisis a remarkable leader, Alfred the Great, rose to the throne of Wessex. Alfred did everything in his power to save his kingdom from the Vikings. He fought ferocious battles against them. He even resorted to bribing them. In the winter of 877–878 the Danes, in a surprise attack, in-

Chronology of the Age of Siege and Its Aftermath

England	France	Germany
793: First Danish raid	814–840: Louis the Pious	814–840: Louis the Pious
871–899: Reign of Alfred	840–877: Charles the Bald	840–876: Louis the German
878: Battle of Edington	843: Treaty of Verdun	843: Treaty of Verdun
c.954: Reconquest	c.911: Normandy	891: Vikings defeated
of Danelaw	recognized	by Arnulf
completed		936–973: Reign of Otto
		the Great
		955: Otto defeats
		Hungarians at
		the Lechfeld
978–1016: Reign of Ethelred	987: Capetians replace	962: Otto crowned
1017–1035: Reign of Canute	Carolingians	Roman Emperor
1042–1066: Reign of Edward		973–983: Reign of Otto II
the Confessor		983–1002: Reign of Otto III
1066: Norman		1003: Gerbert of
Conquest of		Aurillac dies
England		1039–1056: Reign of Henry III

vaded Wessex and forced Alfred to take refuge, with a handful of companions, on the Isle of Athelney in a remote swamp. Athelney was England's Valley Forge. In the following spring Alfred rallied his forces and smashed a Danish army at the battle of Edington. This victory turned the tide of the war; the Danish leader agreed to take up Christianity, to withdraw from the land, and to accept a "permanent" peace.

But other Danes under other leaders refused to honor the peace, and Alfred in his later campaigns extended his authority to the north and east. In 886 he captured London—even then England's chief city—and shortly thereafter a new peace treaty gave Alfred most of southern and southwestern England. The rest of England—the "Danelaw"—remained independent of the Wessex monarchy, but virtually all of non-Danish England was now united under a single king.

Like all successful leaders of the age, Alfred was an able warrior. But more than that, he was an imaginative organizer who systematized military recruitment and built a navy, seeing clearly that Christian Europe could not hope to drive back the Vikings without challenging them on the seas. He lavished his resources on a crash program of fortifying and garrisoning towns, which thereafter served both as defensive strongholds and as places of sanctuary for the agrarian population in time of war. They served as commercial centers as well and provided a significant stimulus to English commerce long thereafter. And gradually, as the Danish tide was rolled back, fortified centers were built to secure the territories newly reconquered. Alfred clarified and rationalized the laws of his people, enforced them strictly, and ruled with an authority such as no Anglo-Saxon king had exercised before his time.

ENGLAND
ABOUT 885

Scale of Miles
0   20   40   60   80 100

Scots

Picts

Tay

Firth of Forth

North

ENGLISH

NORTHUMBRIA

• LINDISFARNE

Sea

Picts

Tees

Whitby

York

IRELAND

Irish Sea

DANELAW

WALES

ENGLISH MERCIA

Trent R.

Ouse

EAST
ANGLIA

Severn R.

Thames R.   London

SURREY

KENT   Canterbury

WESSEX   SUSSEX

DEVON

English Channel

CORNWALL

Alfred was also a scholar and patron of learning. His intellectual environment was even less promising than Charlemagne's. The great days of Bede, Boniface, and Alcuin were far in the past, and by Alfred's time, Latin—the key to Classical-Christian culture—was almost unknown in England. Like Charlemagne, Alfred gathered scholars from far and wide—England, Wales, the Continent—and set them to work teaching Latin and preparing Anglo-Saxon translations of classical Latin works, to be available at the royal court and at episcopal centers throughout his kingdom. Alfred himself participated in the work of translation, helping to render such books as Boethius' *Consolation of Philosophy*, Pope Gregory's *Pastoral Care*, and Bede's *Ecclesiastical History* into the native tongue. In his translation of Boethius, Alfred added a regretful comment of his own: "In those days one never heard of ships armed for war." And in his preface to the *Pastoral Care* he alluded with nostalgia to the days "before everything was ravaged and burned, when England's churches overflowed with treasures and books." Alfred's intellectual revival, even more than Charlemagne's, was a salvage operation rather than an outburst of originality. The Viking pillaging of English monasteries and bishoprics had threatened the survival of literacy and, indeed, of Christianity itself; it was this desperate situation that Alfred's educational program sought to correct. He was both modest and accurate when he described himself as one who wandered through a great forest collecting timber with which others could build.

Alfred's task of reconquest was carried on by his able successors in the first half of the tenth century. By the mid-900s all England was in their hands, and the kings of Wessex had become the kings of England. Great numbers of Danish settlers still remained in northern and eastern England—the amalgamation of Danish and English customs required many generations. But the creative response of the Wessex kings to the Danish threat had brought political unity to the Anglo-Saxon world. Out of the agony of the invasions the English monarchy was born.

The Renewal of the Danish Attacks: Ethelred and Canute

For a generation after the Anglo-Saxon conquest of the Danelaw, from about 955 to 980, England enjoyed relative peace and prosperity. English fleets patrolled the shores, fortresses began to evolve into commercial centers, and churchmen, working closely with the monarchy, addressed themselves to the task of monastic reform. But the Danish inhabitants of northern and eastern England remained only half committed to the new English monarchy, and with the accession of a child-king, Ethelred "the Unready" (978–1016), the Danish invasions resumed.*

---

*"Unready" is the traditional but incorrect translation of Ethelred's nickname. "Ethelred the Unred" is closer to the original but has the disadvantage of making absolutely no sense to those unacquainted with the Anglo-Saxon tongue. It was a kind of joke: the name "Ethelred" meant "noble counsel"; "Ethelred the Unred" meant "Noble counsel the Uncounseled" or something of the sort and was perhaps more amusing in the tenth century than it is today.

The new invasions evolved into a campaign of conquest directed by the Danish monarchy. The English defense was plagued by incompetence, treason, and panic. In 991 Ethelred began paying a tribute to the Danes, known thereafter as *danegeld*. In later years the danegeld evolved into a land tax that was exceedingly profitable to the English monarchy, but at the time it was a sign of desperation and resulted in a massive outflow of English wealth. In 1016 Ethelred died, and in the following year King Canute of Denmark became the ruler of the English.

King Canute (1017–1035) was known to later generations as "Canute the Great," and appropriately so. He conquered Norway as well as England, and joining these two lands to his kingdom of Denmark, he became the master of a huge empire centering on the North Sea, held together by the wealth of England. A product of the new civilizing forces at work in eleventh-century Scandinavia, Canute was no footloose Viking. He issued law codes, practiced Christianity, and kept the peace. Devoting much of his time to England, he cast himself as an Anglo-Saxon king in the old Wessex tradition. After an initial bloody purge of potential troublemakers, he respected and upheld the ancient customs of the land and gave generously to monasteries: "Merry sang the monks of Ely," we are told, "as Canute the king rowed by."

But Canute's Danish-Norwegian-English empire was hopelessly disunited and failed to survive his death in 1035. When the last of his sons died in 1042, the English realm fell peacefully to Edward the Confessor, a member of the old Wessex dynasty who had grown up in exile in Normandy.

The Aftermath

King Edward the Confessor ruled England in relative peace. But his childless marriage ensured a disputed succession on his death in 1066 and set the stage for the Norman Conquest. When William the Conqueror, duke of Normandy, invaded England and won its crown in 1066, he inherited a prosperous kingdom with well-established political and legal traditions—a kingdom still divided by differences in custom but with a deep-seated respect for royal authority. With the timber that Alfred collected, his successors built an ample and sturdy edifice.

THE FRENCH RESPONSE

In England the invasions resulted in royal unification; in France they encouraged a breakdown of political authority into regional and local units. This difference can be explained in part by the fact that France, unlike England, was too large for the Vikings to hope to conquer. Although many of them settled in Normandy, the chief Norse threat to France came in the form of plundering expeditions rather than conquering armies. Distances were too great, communications too primitive, the aristocracy too firmly entrenched, and the kingdom-wide army too unwieldy for the monarchy to assume strong leadership in defending the realm. Military responsibility descended more and more to dukes, counts, and local nobles, who were better able to protect their regions from sudden Viking assaults.

As the monarchy waned, the dukes and counts evolved from Carolingian royal officials into territorial princes only loosely tied to the king. Their former custody of royal lands, tribunals, tax revenues, and military conscription ripened into hereditary authority. Lands and powers that they had once administered for the king they now administered for themselves, transforming France into a mosaic of largely independent duchies and counties.

The Carolingian kings of France became increasingly powerless until at length, in 987, the crown passed permanently from the Carolingian dynasty to the Capetian dynasty. Much later on, during the twelfth and thirteenth centuries, the Capetian family would produce some of France's most celebrated kings, but for the time being the new dynasty was nearly as feeble as its predecessor. The Capetian power base was the region around Paris and Orléans in north-central France—an area known as the "Ile de France," which was no greater in size and wealth than any of a number of French principalities of the period. In theory the Capetian monarch was king of the French, but on the basis of his limited jurisdiction and revenues, he was merely one prince among many.

Nobles, Knights, and Castles

The process of disintegration did not stop at the duchy-county level. Within these principalities, and often between them, lay clusters of estates ruled by important lords who lacked the ducal or comital title but nevertheless exercised considerable authority and commanded large resources. These lords might or might not support their regional princes, depending on the lord's interests and the prince's strength. Contemporary observers tended to regard the great landholders, whether dukes, counts, or untitled lords, as constituting a single class known as "nobles." Descended for the most part from powerful families of the Carolingian era and before, the nobles had the responsibility for maintaining peace and public order—and the capacity to wage war against Viking invaders and against each other.

Within each noble household was a group of military retainers—vassals—who by the late tenth century had come to be known as "knights." Midway in status between the great noble families and the peasantry, the knights constituted the lower level of a two-tiered warrior aristocracy. Both nobles and knights were trained in the techniques of mounted combat. They shared a common military vocation, were similarly equipped with arms, armor, and warhorses, and of course were exempt from agricultural labor. Indeed, great aristocrats came increasingly to describe themselves as "knight-nobles," higher in status than common knights, yet knights nonetheless. But whereas nobles possessed large estates, ordinary knights held few if any lands, and whereas nobles led armies into battle, knights followed and obeyed. Only later did it become common for knights to hold land and to marry into noble families.

The trend toward regional defense against invaders gave rise, during the tenth century, to a military innovation of surpassing importance: the castle. The earliest castles bore little resemblance to the great turreted fortresses of the later Middle Ages; many were nothing more than small, square towers, usually of wood, planted on hilltops or artificial mounds and encircled by wooden stockades. But when effectively garrisoned, they could be powerful instruments not only of defense but of territorial control as well. Many castles were built by nobles. Others were built (or seized) by ambitious men of less exalted status known as "castellans," who assembled knightly retinues of their own, subjected surrounding territories to their control, and ascended in time into the old nobility.

The coming of castles changed the character of the aristocracy by giving great families a specifically located center of power. Soon they began identifying themselves by the name of their chief castle, their "family seat." Nobles previously known simply by their first names—Amaury, Geoffrey, Roger—became Amaury de Montfort, Geoffrey de Mandeville, Roger de Beaumont, hereditary lords of the castles of Montfort, Mandeville, and Beaumont. Castles thus provided the nobility with a new sense of family identity. And as the castle and lordship passed over generations from father to eldest son, the family tended increasingly to regard itself not simply as a group of relatives but as members of an hereditary line of descent. The result was a much clearer idea of family ancestry and (as one historian has expressed it) "a strengthening of family solidarity within the framework of lineage." When in time members of the knightly class began settling on estates, they too took the name of their estate as their family name and, like the nobility, evolved into a class of hereditary landholders.

Feudalism

During the era of invasions and unrest, many knights and nobles of northern France came to hold estates conditionally, in return for military and other service to a greater lord. An estate held on these terms was called a "fief" (rhyming with beef), and the relationship of landholding to service is known as "feudalism" (after *feudum*, the Latin word for fief). The holder of a fief became the vassal of his lord, swearing him lifelong loyalty in a solemn oath of homage. The granting of estates in exchange for loyalty and service was a convenient way for a lord to support a retinue of mounted warriors in an age in which money was scarce and land abundant.

Often such feudal arrangements would extend down through several levels of lordship. In theory at least, the great territorial princes held their duchies and counties as fiefs of the king of France (though they did not always bother to swear him homage, and they were as apt to fight against him as for him). Lesser nobles, in turn, might hold estates as vassals of counts or dukes, while granting smaller fiefs to vassals of their own. A single person might thus be both the vassal of a greater lord and the lord of lesser vassals.

Bridgenorth Castle, England. Built by the rebellious
earl of Shropshire, *c.* 1101, this dramatic stronghold, situated at the summit of the hilltop town of
Bridgenorth overlooking the River Severn, is now
surrounded by a public park. It was successfully
besieged by the king of England in 1102, was used
as a headquarters by sheriffs of Shropshire long
thereafter, and was blown up in 1646 during the
English Civil War.

The feudal concepts of vassalage and conditional land tenure were deeply
rooted in the European past. One such root was the oath of fidelity and service
that bound a warrior to his lord in Carolingian and Merovingian times. Another root was the late-Roman and early-medieval concept of granting an estate—a *benefice*—in return for certain services. Charlemagne, as we have seen,
permitted his counts and dukes the use of royal estates in return for their
military and administrative service to his regime, and the entire Carolingian
political structure had been bound together by oaths of personal loyalty—rendered to the king by his great magnates and to the magnates by their own
followers.

Only in the tenth and eleventh centuries, and only in portions of France, did these elements coalesce into the pattern of fiefs, lords, and vassals known as "feudalism." The term "feudal system," so widely used by historians, conveys a misleading impression of order and universality. In reality feudal relationships coexisted with entirely different arrangements—lands held unconditionally, landless knights supported in noble households, political power based on public sovereign authority rather than on personal lordship over vassals, and loyalties based on kinship or wages rather than on homage. Even when relationships were feudal, they were not necessarily systematic. A single vassal, for example, might acquire several estates by swearing homage to several lords. The resulting confusion of loyalties is suggested in this twelfth-century document:

> I, John of Toul, affirm that I am the vassal of the Lady Beatrice,
> countess of Troyes, and of her son Theobald, count of Champagne,
> against every creature living or dead, excepting my allegiance to Lord
> Enjourand of Coucy, Lord John of Arcis, and the count of Grandpré. If
> it should happen that the count of Grandpré should be at war with the
> countess and count of Champagne in his own quarrel, I will aid the
> count of Grandpré in my own person, and will aid the count and
> countess of Champagne by sending them the knights whose services I
> owe them from the fief which I hold of them.

Like much historical evidence, this document can be interpreted in more than one way. It suggests that feudal arrangements could be confused and complex, but it also represents an effort to bring order out of the chaos of multiple allegiances. In this last respect it typifies the tendency, beginning in the eleventh century and growing in the twelfth, to systematize feudal practices that had originally sprouted like dandelions in an ill-kept lawn.

Under the influence of strong territorial princes, feudal rights and obligations came to be defined with increasing precision (though the definitions varied from region to region). Typically, the vassal owed service in his lord's army—his own personal service and, often, that of additional knights from his household or estates. The vassal might also be obliged to join his lord's retinue on tours of the countryside (large retinues were status symbols), to serve in his lord's court of justice, to feed and house the lord and his retinue on their visits, to help raise a ransom should the lord be captured in battle, and to give the lord money on specified occasions—for example, the knighting of the lord's eldest son, the marriage of his eldest daughter, and the succession of a son to his father's fief. Early in its history the fief became hereditary, but the lord retained the right to confiscate it should his vassal die without heirs, to enjoy its revenues during a minority (while rearing and training the minor heir), and to exercise the power of veto over the marriage of an heiress. Often, indeed, the lord chose the heiress' husband for her, sometimes charging him a stiff price for her hand and inheritance.

In return for these rights, the lord was duty-bound to protect his vassals, to deal with them justly, and to defend their fiefs against enemy attacks.

In short, the lord-vassal relationship involved obligations in both directions. The essence of feudalism was the notion of reciprocal rights and duties. The relationship of a prince to his greater subjects resembled that of a lord to his vassals, and medieval aristocracies never permitted their rulers to forget that bad lordship justified the repudiation of homage.

Because of its diversity, feudalism is heartbreakingly difficult to define. Some scholars would abolish the word altogether; others would prefer the term "feudalisms" to "feudalism." I continue to find feudalism a useful word if employed with caution—no more misleading than humanism, democracy, communism, capitalism, classicism, or renaissance (which some scholars would also like to abolish). If feudalism cannot be precisely defined, it can at least be described. The great French historian Marc Bloch described it well:

> A subject peasantry; widespread use of the service tenement (that is, the fief) instead of a salary, which was out of the question; the supremacy of a class of specialized warriors; ties of obedience and protection which bind man to man and, within the warrior class, assume the distinctive form called vassalage; fragmentation of author-ity—leading inevitably to disorder; and in the midst of all this, the survival of other forms of association, family and state...such then seem to be the fundamental features of European feudalism.

The French Principalities

We have seen how Carolingian royal authority disintegrated into regional prin-cipalities and often into still smaller units. As one historian expressed it, "Dirty, bloodstained, and exhausted lords surrounded by brutal warriors, making their way from primitive wooden castles to austere monastic refuges, must have been common sights on the West Frankish roads."* But as the invasions di-minished, the process of disintegration was gradually reversed. New princi-palities emerged as ambitious noble families succeeded in combining groups of counties, through marriages and conquests, into large territorial blocs. By the early twelfth century the French principalities, old and new, were grow-ing steadily in wealth and power. The dukes of Aquitaine and Normandy and the counts of Flanders, Anjou, Blois, Champagne, and Burgundy were in most practical respects the equals of the king of France.

These great princes continued to base their power on the control of lands, tribunals, and public taxes and services that had formerly pertained to the Carolingian monarchy. The Carolingian system of government was not de-molished but merely fragmented. Indeed, in some important respects it was improved. A number of territorial princes adopted the novel and sensible prac-tice of administering their dominions not through powerful regional landhold-ers but through salaried officials who could be transferred or removed at will. The princes ruled not only as lords of fief-holding vassals but also through

*Jean Dunbabin, *France in the Making, 843–1180,* Oxford University Press, Oxford, 1985, p. 241.

the exercise of public authority and the control of increasingly efficient and flexible administrations. In time their governance became more intensive and effective than that of the old Carolingian Empire. They had the advantage of ruling compact territorial units and the further advantage of controlling a growing number of castles (increasingly built of stone), which served as military and political power centers throughout their principalities. And as the eleventh century progressed, they benefited from an accelerating commercial revival.

The princes themselves contributed to this revival in a variety of ways. They established new agricultural settlements on depopulated lands. They supported monastic reform (which usually brought marked improvement to the management of monastic estates) and encouraged the construction of water mills. They founded hundreds of new abbeys and smaller priories as centers of princely influence and agrarian development. And they opened up new lands for cultivation by clearing forests and draining bogs. The counts of Flanders organized and encouraged an elaborate program of dike building to reclaim land from the sea and convert it to sheep farming. The counts of Champagne sponsored a series of annual fairs for long-distance merchants and— for a price—guaranteed them safe passage through the county.

The growth of agricultural productivity and vitalization of commerce increased the revenues of the princes. With their new wealth they enlarged their administrations, armies, and networks of castles to the point where they could overawe their vassals and bring relative peace to their principalities. In late-eleventh-century Normandy and Flanders, no magnate could build a castle without ducal or comital permission, and the dukes of Normandy claimed the right to occupy a vassal's stronghold on demand.

The rise of strong principalities by no means put an end to military violence. Warfare was almost incessant—between rival princes and between lesser magnates within principalities or in the turbulent regions between them. The territorial princes of southern France proved much less successful than those elsewhere in bringing order to their lands. But in central and northern France, for the first time since Roman antiquity, princely regimes were acquiring the administrative, military, and financial resources necessary for effective governance. As such, they mark a vital stage in the development of political cohesion from the loosely governed Carolingian Empire to the beginnings of the modern European state.

THE GERMAN RESPONSE

The invasions gave birth to unified monarchy in England while undermining it in France. Germany's response was different still: first the emergence of powerful, semi-independent duchies; then a resurgence of royal power.

Although East Francia (Germany) was subject to Viking attacks, the greater threat came from Hungarian horsemen to the east. When the late-

Carolingian kings of Germany proved unable to cope with the Hungarian raids, authority descended, as in France, to the great regional officials of the realm—the dukes, who had formerly administered their duchies as agents of the monarchy.

Following their accustomed policy, the Carolingians had patterned their German duchies on earlier tribal divisions. During the turbulent years of the ninth century, these "tribal duchies" became virtually autonomous. Their dukes took direct control of royal lands and powers and dominated the churches within their districts. The process should be now be all too familiar.

In the early tenth century Germany was dominated by five duchies: Saxony, Swabia, Bavaria, Franconia, and Lorraine. The first three had been incorporated only quite recently into the Carolingian state, whereas the western duchies of Franconia and Lorraine were much more strongly Frankish in outlook and organization. The five "tribal" dukes might well have become the masters of Germany. Their ambitions were frustrated by two related factors: (1) their failure to curb the Hungarians, and (2) the reinvigoration of the German monarchy under an able, new dynasty. The Carolingian line came to an end in Germany in 911 with the death of King Louis the Child. He was succeeded first by the duke of Franconia and then, in 919, by the duke of Saxony—the first of an illustrious line of kings whose power was based on their domination of the powerful Saxon duchy.

Otto I

The Saxon monarchy struggled vigorously to assert its authority over the tribal duchies. With the duchy of Saxony under their power, the Saxon kings quickly won direct control over Franconia and Lorraine as well, and a protectorate over the kingdom of Burgundy. But the semi-independent dukes of the two southern duchies, Swabia and Bavaria, presented greater problems. The real victory of the monarchy occurred in the reign of the second and ablest of the Saxon kings, Otto I (936–973).

Otto I, or "Otto the Great," directed his considerable talents toward three goals and achieved them all: (1) the defense of Germany against the Hungarian invasions, (2) the recovery of royal lands and powers within the remaining tribal duchies, and (3) the extension of German royal control to the crumbling, unstable Middle Kingdom that the Treaty of Verdun had assigned to Emperor Lothar back in 843. We have already seen how this Middle Kingdom began to fall to pieces after Lothar's death. By the mid-tenth century it had become a political shambles. Parts of it had been taken over by Germany and France, but its southern districts—Burgundy and Italy—retained a chaotic independence. The dukes of Swabia and Bavaria both had notions of seizing these territories. Otto the Great, in order to forestall the development of an unmanageable rival power to his south, led his armies into Italy in 951 and assumed the title "King of Italy."

From 951 onwards events developed rapidly. Otto the Great had to leave Italy in haste to put down a major uprising in Germany. His triumph over the rebels enabled him to establish his power there more strongly than ever. In 955 he won the crucial victory of his age when he crushed a large Hungarian army at the battle of the Lechfeld, bringing the Hungarian raids to an end at last. Otto's triumph at the Lechfeld served as a vivid demonstration of royal power—a vindication of the monarch's claim that he, not the dukes, was the true defender of Germany. With the Hungarians defeated, Germany's eastern frontier now lay open to the gradual penetration of German-Christian culture. The tribal duchies were overshadowed; the monarchy was supreme. Otto the Great now towered over his contemporaries as the greatest monarch since Charlemagne.

Not long after his victory over the Hungarians, Otto turned his attention to still another crisis. Since his departure from Italy, a Lombard magnate had seized the Italian throne and was harassing the pope. In response to a papal appeal—which dovetailed with his own interests—Otto returned to Italy in force and recovered the Italian throne. In 962 the pope hailed Otto as "Roman Emperor" and placed the imperial crown on his head. It is this event, rather than the coronation of Charlemagne in 800, that marks the true genesis of the medieval Holy Roman Empire.

Although the events of 962 are reminiscent of 800, Otto's empire was vastly different from Charlemagne's. Above all, Otto and his imperial successors exercised no jurisdiction over France or the remainder of Western Christendom. The medieval Holy Roman Empire had its roots deep in the soil of Germany, and most of the emperors subordinated imperial interests to those of the German monarchy. From its advent in 962 to its long-delayed demise in the early nineteenth century, the Holy Roman Empire remained fundamentally a German phenomenon.*

The German orientation of Otto's empire is illustrated by the fact that neither he nor the majority of his successors over the next two centuries made any real effort to establish tight control in Italy. Only when they marched south of the Alps could they count on the obedience of the Italians; when they returned to Germany, they left behind them no real administrative structure but depended almost solely on the fickle allegiance of certain Italian magnates and bishops. The German emperors were never successful in straddling the Alps.

In Germany conditions were quite different. There the coming of feudalism was delayed for more than a century after Otto's imperial coronation. The great magnates became vassals of the king but normally had no vassals of their own. The chief tool that Otto and his successors used in governing their state was the Church. Otto extended his authority over the churches of the various tribal duchies, making the great bishops and abbots of Germany

---

*The term "Holy Roman Empire" was not actually employed until the twelfth century. It is used here for convenience and with apologies to the purist. A later cynic observed that the Holy Roman Empire was neither holy nor Roman nor an empire. In a recent exam, a student gave this oft-quoted statement a surprising twist: the Holy Roman Empire "was neither holy, Roman, nor empirical in nature."

THE HOLY ROMAN EMPIRE IN 962

The Holy Roman Emperor with orb and scepter: manuscript illumination from the Gospel Book of Otto III. A.D. 1000.

the king's men. They were ideal royal officials, for they could not pass on their estates to heirs, and when a bishop or abbot died, his successor was handpicked by the king. Thus the loyalty and political capacity of the king's administrator-churchmen were assured. After 962, the German monarchy was sometimes successful even in appointing popes. There would come a time when churchmen would rebel at such treatment, but in Otto's reign the time was still far off.

Otto's claims to proprietorship of the imperial Church were supported by both tradition and theory. Otto was regarded as more than a mere secular monarch. He was *rex et sacerdos*, king and priest, sanctified by the holy anointing ceremony that accompanied his coronation. He was the vicar of God— the living symbol of Christ the King—the "natural" leader of the Church in his empire. And he led it firmly and aggressively, reorganizing bishoprics, establishing new ones across the northern and eastern reaches of his empire, and defending them with his armies against hostile Danes and Slavs. Otto's religious foundations drew German churchmen and settlers far eastward into the lands of the Slavs, extending the German frontier to the boundaries of Poland. The combined expansion of church and empire into pagan lands brings to mind Charlemagne's campaigns, generations earlier, against Otto's native Saxony.

The Ottonian Renaissance

Otto's reign provided the impulse for an impressive intellectual revival that reached its culmination under his two successors, Otto II (973–983) and Otto III (983–1002). This "Ottonian Renaissance" produced a series of able administrators and scholars, the greatest of whom was the churchman Gerbert of Aurillac—later Pope Sylvester II (d. 1003). Gerbert visited Spain and returned with a comprehensive knowledge of Islamic science. With this event the infiltration of Arab thought into Western Christendom began.

Gerbert had an encyclopedic though unoriginal mind. A master of classical literature, logic, mathematics, and science, he advocated the Greco-Arab doctrine that the earth was spherical. It was rumored that he was a wizard in league with the Devil—but these rumors were dampened by his elevation to the papacy. Gerbert was no wizard but an advance agent of the intellectual awakening that Europe was about to undergo.

In 1024 the Saxon dynasty died out and was replaced by a Franconian line known as the "Salian dynasty" (1024–1125). Working hand in glove with the German church, the Salians improved and expanded the royal administration and ultimately came to exercise even greater authority than Otto I. In the mid-eleventh century the strongest of the Salian emperors, Henry III (1039–1056), ruled unrivaled over Germany and appointed popes as freely as he selected his own bishops. In 1050, at a time when the French monarchy still dozed, Emperor Henry III dominated central Europe and held the papacy in his palm.

THE ITALIAN RESPONSE

When Charlemagne conquered Lombard Italy in 774, he was faced with the problem of reorganizing a kingdom much different from his own. For one thing, urban life had retained far more vitality in Italy than elsewhere in Western Christendom. For another, the Lombard royal administration that Charlemagne inherited differed sharply from the administration of Carolingian Francia. The Lombard kings had managed to exercise strong authority only in a region of northern Italy that came to be known as the Lombard Plain, or simply Lombardy. They ruled only loosely over the Lombard dukes of Friuli to the northeast (near Venice) and Spoleto to the south. Still further south, below Rome, Lombard royal authority was nonexistent. Here a congregation

of small powers waged incessant war with one another: independent duchies, coastal towns (Amalfi, Naples, Salerno), Saracen bandits' nests, and
Byzantine enclaves left from Justinian's conquests.

Kings, Dukes, and Counts

Characteristically, Charlemagne installed Frankish counts on the Lombard
Plain in the places of Lombard royal officials, and in Friuli and Spoleto
Lombard dukes gave way to new dukes drawn from Carolingian officialdom.
Charlemagne never established his authority south of Rome, and even in
Lombardy the new Carolingian order did not have time to jell. Within a generation or two, Carolingian royal authority was faltering. And by the late 800s
the north Italian crown had become the object of a brutal and confused power
struggle involving the dukes of Spoleto and Friuli and other ambitious
families.

    None of these contending dynasties could hope to hold the crown for
long without establishing control over the Lombard Plain. Consequently, as
one family after another seized the throne, it would place its own supporters
in the controlling positions as counts in Lombardy. As a result of these policies, the old Carolingian aristocracy was replaced throughout the Lombard
Plain by a new aristocracy dependent on one or another of the short-lived
royal dynasties. Thus Lombardy, unlike France, experienced a nearly complete break with the Carolingian past. Whereas most of the principalities of
France were ruled by descendants of Carolingian counts and dukes, the counties of Lombardy were not. And whereas the power of the French principalities was growing, that of the Lombard counties was diminishing for want of
dynastic continuity.

The Rise of the Cities

As the position of the Lombard counts weakened, the cities that they governed grew more and more independent. With the coming of the Hungarian
and Saracen invasions, it was the Italian cities, under the leadership of their
bishops, that became the chief centers of resistance. The contending Italian
kings depended increasingly on their cities to repel the invaders and had no
choice but to grant the urban bishops extensive powers and privileges—the
right to build walls and fortified towers and the right to collect tolls and public revenues with which the defensive works might be financed. By the early
900s the cities had won full exemption from the counts' jurisdiction. The bishops acquired control not only of the cities' defenses but of their revenues and
courts of justice as well.

    Generations thereafter, Lombard townspeople would seize these privi-
leges from their bishops and would subject the surrounding countryside to
the authority of their cities. These processes occurred only with the economic
revival of the eleventh century and amidst the concurrent struggle between

Italy, *c.* 1000.

pope and emperor. But even in the early tenth century, forces were at work
that would one day transform northern Italy into a land of self-governing city-
states.

Throughout the 900s, however, the bishops remained firmly in power.
Ruling and defending their cities, they became the decisive force in northern
Italian politics. The royal dynasties required their support, and more than once
the opposition of bishops cost a monarch his crown. Indeed, it was at the
urging of a group of important Lombard bishops that Otto the Great intervened in the mid-900s, bringing an end to the royal dynastic squabbles by
incorporating northern Italy into his empire.

Otto the Great and his imperial successors ruled northern Italy from a
distance. Except on the rare occasions when they led their armies southward
across the Alps, they based their authority on the support of the urban bishops, whose powers endured and grew under German rule. In this respect,
Otto's conquest changed nothing, but it did furnish Italy the vitally impor-

tant benefits of relative peace and stability after a century of anarchy. The emperors helped relieve Italy of the Muslim menace, both by leading armies against Muslim enclaves and by providing a settled environment that encouraged urban growth and commercial revival. By the late 900s, the north Italian ports of Genoa and Pisa were developing a vigorous and widespread Mediterranean trade and a growing merchant class. In the course of the next century, Genoa and Pisa seized the offensive from the Muslims, expelling them from the important Mediterranean islands of Sardinia and Corsica and launching raids against Muslim ports in Spain and North Africa. Other Italian coastal cities, beyond the lands ruled by the German emperor, were taking to the sea as well: Amalfi, Salerno, and Naples in southern Italy and, above all, the republic of Venice on the northern shore of the Adriatic Sea.

Long a Byzantine dependency, Venice had achieved virtual independence by the ninth century and yet continued to send fleets to assist Byzantium in its wars. By carefully cultivating its relations with both Constantinople and Islamic North Africa, Venice developed a flourishing triangular trade. And during the 900s Venice evolved into the foremost commercial center in Western Christendom. In a Europe that was overwhelmingly agrarian, the Venetians developed the first state to live by trade alone. Enriched by the exporting of salt from their lagoons and glass from their furnaces, and by the profits of commerce, they produced little food but purchased it instead in the markets of other north Italian towns. A Lombard writer remarked with astonishment that "These people neither plow nor sow nor gather grapes," but "buy grain and wine in every market place."

In this respect Venice was unique, but other Italian ports—Genoa, Pisa, Amalfi—were following her into the lucrative Mediterranean trade. And their burgeoning commercial life stimulated the growth of inland cities such as Milan, Bologna, and Florence. Milan's population in A.D. 1000, although probably no more than about 20,000, made it the largest city in Lombardy and one of the most populous in Western Christendom. With the closing of the age of invasions, Italy had thus achieved the reversal of two age-long historical trends: its cities were growing once more, and its well-armed fleets were at last challenging the Byzantine and Muslim domination of Mediterranean commerce.

THE ORGANIZATION OF AGRICULTURE

During the tenth and eleventh centuries the commercial city remained a rarity in Western Christendom. Almost everywhere wealth and power were associated with the holding of land. And beneath the social layer of nobles and knights, the great majority of Europeans labored on the soil.

To discuss the typical medieval farm is as difficult as to discuss the typical American business, for medieval agriculture exhibited countless variations. Nevertheless some features of agrarian life recur throughout the more fertile and heavily populated portions of northwestern Europe. Certain generalizations can be made about medieval agrarian institutions, if we bear in mind that numerous exceptions to any of them can be found.

Any discussion of medieval husbandry must begin by distinguishing between two fundamental institutions: the village and the manor. The village, the basic unit of the agrarian economy, consisted of a population nucleus ranging from about a dozen to several hundred peasant families living in a cluster, encircled by their fields. In regions where the soil was poor, peasant families might live in separate farms or hamlets, but across the fertile lowlands of northern France, England, and Germany, village life was the norm.

The manor, on the other hand, was an artificial unit—a unit of jurisdiction and economic exploitation controlled by a single lord. The lord might be a king or a great nobleman or churchman with numerous manors under his control. Or he might be a simple knight with only one or two manors at his disposal. The manor—the unit of jurisdiction—was often geographically identical with the village, but some manors embraced two or more villages, and an occasional large village might be divided into two or more manors. In any case, the agrarian routine of plowing, planting, and harvesting was based on the village organization, whereas the peasants' dues, obligations, and legal and political subordination were based on the manor.

The Village

The peasants of the early Middle Ages, like the Romans and Celts before them, tended to live in agrarian settlements consisting of scattered individual farms or small clusters of them. The agricultural community which had been an important element in the European landscape since prehistoric times, underwent fundamental changes between approximately the ninth and twelfth centuries, the chronology of this change varying from region to region. Before it occurred, rural communities were rootless, flimsy, and impermanent, consisting of ramshackle cottages that lasted no more than a lifetime (at most) and were easily abandoned if the villagers chose to relocate their village (as they often did). Around the turn of the millennium, these scattered, ephemeral settlements began to merge into villages of the later medieval and modern type, with their houses set close together, often centered on a village green, or a well or pond, and surrounded by great fields. Agrarian communities of this sort are known as "nucleated villages"—i.e., a nucleus of houses encircled by fields. The causes of this process of village formation are not entirely clear. Perhaps a particularly large cluster of farms began to attract the inhabitants of the neighboring district through the power or initiative of a central lordship or through community consensus.

Village formation was stimulated by the emergence of castles or stone manor houses, which served as "anchors" to the agrarian community. Another stimulus was the development of "parishes"—small ecclesiastical districts centering on a local church, which tended increasingly to be built of stone, thereby becoming a second anchor. The social and religious life of villagers typically centered on their parish churches, which provided the village community a sense of permanence.

At about this same period it became common for the village population to include a substantial group of artisans—wheelwrights, blacksmiths, carpenters, coopers, and joiners. With the help of these craftsmen, peasant families began building larger and better-constructed cottages. In short, as has recently been argued,* the European village of high- and late-medieval and early modern times—with its church, its castle or manor house, its nucleus of sturdily built cottages surrounded by fields, and its organized community of artisans—was by *c.* 1000 or 1050 a recent creation.

The lands surrounding these villages would normally be divided into either two or three large fields. Two had been the traditional number and remained so throughout southern Europe. But the agrarian economy had been shifting in some districts of northern Europe from a two-field to a three-field system of rotation. The peasants of a three-field village would plant one field in the spring for fall harvesting, plant the second field in the fall for early summer harvesting, and let the third field lie fallow throughout the year. The next year the fields would be rotated and the process repeated. Although three-field agriculture was becoming common in northern Europe, it was necessarily limited to areas where soil fertility was sufficient to sustain more intensive cultivation. Many villages continued to function with only two fields, while others might have four, five, or even more, all subject to complex rotation arrangements.

The arable lands surrounding the village were known as "open fields" and were normally divided into unfenced strips, each about 220 yards long. Typically, a single peasant family possessed several strips, scattered throughout the fields, from which it produced its own food for consumption, sale, or the rendering of manorial dues. But the village community pooled its plows, draught animals, and toil. Collective farming was necessary because plows were expensive and had to be shared, and because no one peasant owned sufficient oxen to make up the team of several beasts (often four) necessary to draw the heavy plow. The details of this collective process were usually worked out in the village council and were guided by custom.

The necessity of cooperation in farming their open fields forced European villagers to learn how to regulate the inevitable disputes that would arise over field boundaries and plowing rights. A stimulating book has stressed the importance of community relationships in medieval society, as opposed to the traditional emphasis on hierarchical relationships.† Villagers were under strong practical pressure to develop skill at manipulating and resolving their conflicts, and they acquired the ability to carry on their agrarian routine without the constant intervention of manorial lords or their bailiffs and without de-

---

*Jean Chapelot and Robert Fossier, *The Village and House in the Middle Ages*, University of California Press, Berkeley, 1985.
†Susan Reynolds, *Kingdoms and Communities in Western Europe, 900–1300*, Clarendon Press, Oxford, 1984.

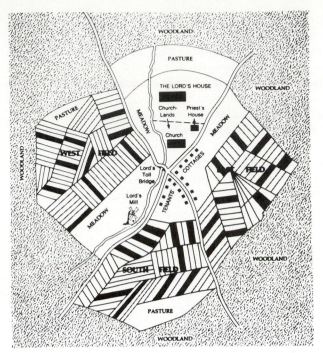

Diagram of a typical manor.

structive community violence. It has been suggested (though not all would agree) that these skills contributed to the later emergence of cooperative commercial enterprises and effective local government in the principalities of medieval Western Europe.

The shape, contour, and method of cultivation of the open fields varied from place to place, depending as they did on the topography of the region and the fertility of the soil. The strips themselves were often determined by the heavy plow and the necessity of reversing the ox team as seldom as possible (though there are instances of strip fields cultivated by light plows). The length of the strips frequently depended on the distance a team could draw the plow without rest. A group of four strips, which constituted the normal day's work of a plow team, became the basis of our modern acre.

The open fields were fundamental to the village economy and, indeed, to the entire agrarian system of northern Europe. But there was more to the village community than the cluster of peasants' huts and the encircling fields. Besides their scattered strips in the fields, peasants ordinarily had small gardens adjacent to their huts where vegetables and fruits could be raised and fowl kept to provide variety to their diet. The village also included a pasture where the plow animals might graze, and a meadow from which hay was cut to sustain the precious beasts over the winter. Some village communities kept sheep on their pasture as a source of cheese, milk, and wool. Certain districts, particularly in Flanders and northern England, took up sheep raising on a scale so large as almost to exclude the growing of grains.

Attached to most village communities was a wooded area from which fuel and building materials could be gathered. It also served as a forage for pigs, which provided most of the meat in the peasants' diet. There was commonly a stream or pond nearby that supplied the community with fish, a water mill for grinding grain, and a large oven that the community used for baking bread. By the eleventh century, as we have seen, some village communities were organized as parishes, with village churches and parish priests who were allotted lands of their own in the open fields. A single priest might frequently acquire the revenues of several village churches, living in style and delegating his priestly responsibilities to a local vicar—often of peasant birth.

The village community was economically self-sufficient only to a degree. There was always a certain amount of regional trade, and crucial items such as salt and metals often had to be imported from fairly distant sources. Thus, villagers had some incentive to produce food surpluses for trade. This incentive was intensified when the commercial revival of the eleventh and twelfth centuries vastly increased the market for grain.

The commercial revival was itself supported by the increased agricultural productivity brought about by early-medieval innovations in agrarian organization and technology. Commercial expansion thus depended on food surpluses (as we have seen in the case of Venice) while at the same time encouraging further surpluses. As towns and commerce grew, the village economy was integrated more and more into region-wide trade networks, and enterprising peasants were provided a means of acquiring considerable wealth in exchange for surplus grain. The expanding grain market in turn encouraged the creation of new fields from forests and marshes. By the mid-eleventh century the limited horizons of the early-medieval village were visibly widening.

The Manor

Superimposed on the economic structure of the village was the jurisdictional structure of the manor. In the eleventh century the manorial regime was only incompletely established in England and was scarcely evident at all in Scandinavia, Italy, and parts of northern Germany and southern France. But throughout much of northern France and, later, southern England and elsewhere, most peasant villagers were bound to manorial lords.

Some agrarian laborers were outright slaves, but slavery was declining during the early Middle Ages and had become uncommon by the end of the eleventh century. Some peasants were of free status, owing rents to their lord but little or nothing more. A few were landless laborers working for a wage. But the great middle stratum of the peasantry consisted of serfs—people of unfree status, bound to their lords and usually bound also to their land, like the peasantry of late-Roman times. In return for their strips in the open fields, serfs owed various dues to their manorial lords, chiefly in kind, and were normally expected to labor for a certain number of days each week—often three—on the lord's fields. The insecure conditions of the invasion era prompted many free peasants to relinquish their freedom in exchange for the protection of nearby lords, often bishops or abbots who could offer both military aid and the supernatural support of a local saint whose venerated relics they possessed. A monastic land survey of around A.D. 900 records "fourteen freemen who have handed over their property to the [abbey's] manor, the condition being that each shall do one day's work a week."

The lord drew his sustenance from the dues of his peasants and from the produce of his own fields. The lord's fields were strips scattered among the strips of the peasants and were known collectively as his *demesne*. Theoretically, the fields of the manor were divided into two categories: the lord's demesne (perhaps one-fourth to one-third of the total area) and the peasants' holdings. But in actuality the demesne strips were intermixed with the peasants' strips. The lord's demesne might be cultivated by slaves or hired hands. But in the eleventh century much of the demesne labor was performed by landed serfs who also paid their lord a percentage of the produce of their own fields and rendered him fees for the use of the pasture, the woods, and the lord's mill and oven. These at least were some of the more common peasant obligations.

The lord also enjoyed significant jurisdictional authority over his peasants. The administrative center of the manor was the manorial court, usually held in the lord's castle or manor house. Here a rough, custom-based justice was meted out, disputes settled, misdeeds punished, and obligations enforced. Since most lords possessed more than one manor, authority over individual manors was commonly exercised by an agent known as a "bailiff" or "steward" who supervised the manorial court, oversaw the farming of the demesne, and collected the peasants' dues. In addition to the peasants' demesne labor, the lord was entitled to certain payments deriving from his political and personal authority over his tenants. He might levy a *tallage*—a manorial tax that was theoretically unlimited in frequency and amount but was usually circumscribed by custom. He was normally entitled to payments when a peasant's son inherited the holdings of his father and when a peasant's daughter married outside the manor.

In theory, serfs had no standing before the law. But most lords were restrained from exploiting them arbitrarily by the force of custom. Some lords ignored this restraint and abused their serfs pitilessly. But custom was strong in the Middle Ages and could protect serfs in many ways. They were by no means chattel slaves: they could not normally be sold away from their lands or families, and after paying their manorial dues, they were entitled to the remaining produce of their fields. The serf's condition was hardly enviable, but it was better than the slavery of ancient times.

THE POST-CAROLINGIAN CHURCH

The existence of parish churches in eleventh-century villages illustrates the deeply significant fact that the long process of Christianizing Europe was by now well advanced. Whatever the intellectual and moral shortcomings of the village priests or vicars may have been, they were at least representatives of the international Church operating at the most immediate local levels throughout the European countryside.

At a rather more elevated level, Benedictine monasticism remained a potent force in European society. The Benedictines offered a continuous round of prayers, copied manuscripts, supplied knights from their estates to secular armies, and served as counselors to princes. Perhaps even more than in Carolingian times, they played a major role in political life. This close association with secular politics sometimes resulted in abuses and corruption. Abbeys often found themselves under the direct "protection" of lay lords, who might pack monasteries or nunneries with their unmarriageable kinfolk, appoint cronies or younger siblings as abbots or abbesses, or even assume the abbatial function themselves. Aristocratic intervention in monastic affairs is understandable in view of the great wealth of the abbeys and the fact that many were founded by nobles as "family houses." But the results of such intervention on the Benedictine spiritual life were, at best, mixed.

Bishops and archbishops, too, were commonly appointed and controlled by lay lords. It was not unusual for a noble family to reserve a local bishopric, generation after generation, for its own junior members. Some bishops, on the other hand, wielded independent power over large districts, and there were times when bishops waged war against lay nobles. More often, however, bishops and nobles worked together in relative harmony, springing as they did from the same aristocratic milieu and sometimes the same family. All too frequently the interests and policies of such bishops were more worldly than spiritual and were directed more toward the advancement of their families than toward the welfare of the Christian community. These problems affected the mid-eleventh-century episcopacy from bottom to top, extending even to the papacy—which itself had become the grand prize of contending noble families in the city of Rome.

Abuses of these sorts gave rise throughout Western Europe to powerful countermovements of church reform, typical of which was the reform movement centered on the Burgundian abbey of Cluny. Founded in 909 by the duke of Aquitaine, Cluny was free of local aristocratic and episcopal control and subject only to the pope, whose authority was feeble and remote, and it was blessed with a series of able and long-lived abbots. Cluny followed Benedict of Aniane's modifications of the original Benedictine Rule. Its monks devoted themselves to an elaborate sequence of daily prayers and liturgical services and a strict, godly life. Richly endowed, holy, and seemingly incorruptible, Cluny was widely admired. Gradually it began to acquire daughter houses until, in time, it became the nucleus of a great congregation of reform

A seventeenth-century engraving of the abbey of Cluny, which was largely
demolished a century later during the French Revolution.

monasteries extending across Europe—each of them headed by a prior who
was subject to the abbot of Cluny. In the mid-eleventh century the congregation of Cluny was both powerful and wealthy, and its new abbey church,
completed in the early twelfth century, was the most splendid building of its
time in all Western Europe.

As the lay world became more and more exposed to Christianity, as kings
such as Edward the Confessor in England and Henry III in Germany demonstrated their concern for the welfare of their churches, the Church itself
tended increasingly to come to terms with lay society. Through the ceremony
of anointing, kings became virtual priest-kings. Indeed, contemporary political theory taught that the Church and the world were one—a single, God-
oriented organism in which churchmen and lay lords each had appropriate
roles to play.

EUROPE ON THE EVE OF THE HIGH MIDDLE AGES

During the centuries between the fall of the Roman Empire in the West and
the great economic and cultural revival of the later eleventh century, the foundations were built on which Western civilization rose. Kingdoms emerged that
would play dominant roles in the history of the modern world—England,
Germany, France—and distinctive customs and institutions were developing
that would define and vitalize Europe across the next millennium. A Classical-

Christian cultural tradition was becoming absorbed, adapted, and fused with the customs of the Germanic peoples.

By the mid-eleventh century Europe's commerce was reviving, and the population was growing again. Indeed, the troubled era following the breakdown of Charlemagne's empire had a much livelier commerce than was once believed. Trade continued and even intensified during the post-Carolingian years along Europe's great river valleys—the Rhine, Seine, Po, Loire, Danube, Thames, and others. It was the growing wealth of the river valleys that had attracted Viking, Hungarian, and Saracen raiders, and as the invasions diminished, Europe's commerce surged. French princes, English kings, and German emperors alike encouraged markets and fairs and sought to control and systematize the minting of silver coins. The commerce of the Italian towns flourished under the Ottos and their successors, and when Otto the Great opened a rich silver mine in Rammelsberg in the 970s, a new wave of money flowed out across northern Europe.

By 1050 both England and Germany were comparatively stable, well-organized kingdoms. The Church was poised for a great movement of reform and centralization. The French monarchy was still weak, but by the end of the following century it would be on its way toward dominating France. Meanwhile, French principalities such as Champagne, Flanders, Normandy, and Anjou were well along the road to political coherence. Warfare was still commonplace, but it was beginning to lessen as Europe moved toward political stability. Above all, the invasions were over—the siege had ended. Hungary and the Scandinavian world were being absorbed into Western Christendom, and Islam was by now on the defensive. The return of prosperity, the increase in food production, the rise in population, the quickening of commerce, the intensification of intellectual activity—all betokened the coming of a new age. Western civilization was on the verge of a creative explosion.

SUGGESTED READINGS

GENERAL WORKS

Bernard Hamilton, *Religion in the Medieval West* (1986). A brief, skillful introductory account.

David Herlihy, *Medieval Households* (1985). An absorbing, provocative study of the transformation of households and family units between late Antiquity and the Renaissance.

George Holmes, ed., *The Oxford Illustrated History of Medieval Europe* (1988). An authoritative, beautifully illustrated work of scholarly collaboration aimed at the general reader.

Robert Latouche, *The Birth of Western Economy* (1966). A stimulating account of early medieval economic trends, emphasizing the importance of the small farm.

C. H. Lawrence, *Medieval Monasticism: Forms of Religious Life in Western Europe in the Middle Ages* 2d ed., (1989). This erudite, gracefully written account is the best short work on Western monasticism.

Jeffrey B. Russell, *A History of Medieval Christianity* (1968). A short, clearly written work that interprets Church history across the Middle Ages in terms of the opposing forces of prophecy and order.

EARLY CHRISTIANITY

Peter Brown, *Augustine of Hippo: A Biography* (1969). An extraordinarily sensitive study of Augustine's life and times.

Henry Chadwick, *Augustine* (1986). A brief, lucid introduction to Augustine's thought.

Jean Daniélou and Henri Marrou, *The Christian Centuries*, vol. 1: *The First Six Hundred Years* (1964). Comprehensive and clearly written.

Judith Herrin, *The Formation of Christendom* (1987). A learned, meticulous, and constantly thought-provoking study of the evolution of Christian Europe, East and West, from late Antiquity into the Carolingian era.

James J. O'Donnell, *Cassiodorus* (1979). A skillful biography of a well-born Christian administrator-scholar whose ninety-year life of service to the monarchy and Church in Italy spanned the entire, eventful sixth century.

136

Ramsay MacMullen, *Christianizing the Roman Empire*, A.D. *100–400* (1984). An excellent, brief, up-to-date survey written in a lively style.

R. A. Marcus, *Christianity in the Roman World* (1974). A clear, brief, learned overview of Christianity from its origins to the end of the Western Empire.

Joann McNamara, *A New Song: Celibate Women in the First Three Christian Centuries* (1983). A perceptive study that argues persuasively that the development of communal life for celibate Christian women constituted a dramatically new opportunity for women to adopt a lifestyle previously unavailable to them.

Michael Walsh, *The Triumph of the Meek: Why Early Christianity Succeeded* (1986). A highly readable, up-to-date, beautifully illustrated book for the nonspecialist reader.

THE LATER EMPIRE AND THE GERMANIC INVASIONS

Peter Brown, *The World of Late Antiquity:* A.D. *150–750* (1971). A sympathetic study of social and cultural change in Eastern and Western Europe and the Middle East.

Walter Goffart, *Barbarians and Romans,* A.D. *418–584: The Techniques of Accommodation* (1980). A challenging, highly original work that argues strongly against the idea of Western Europe sinking under a barbarian deluge and stresses the separateness of individual Germanic groups.

Richard Krautheimer, *Three Christian Capitals: Topography and Politics* (1983). A penetrating and highly original study of architecture, society, and culture in late-antique Rome, Constantinople, and Milan.

Lucien Musset, *The Germanic Invasions: The Making of Europe,* A.D. *400–600* (1975). Discusses the state of scholarly investigations and controversies; not for beginners.

Clare Stancliffe, *St. Martin and His Hagiographer: History and Miracle in Sulpicius Severus* (1983). A sensitive, persuasive study of St. Martin of Tours, the growth of his cult, the genre of early medieval saints' lives, and the mentality and world view of late Antiquity.

Raymond Van Dam, *Leadership and Community in Late-Antique Gaul* (1985). An original and persuasive reinterpretation of the receding imperial administration, the regional and local aristocracy, the evolution of Christian communities and heresies, and the growing social importance of the cult of saints and relics—St. Martin of Tours in particular—in late-Roman and early-medieval Gaul.

Stephen Williams, *Diocletian and the Roman Recovery* (1985). An up-to-date, engagingly written account that portrays Diocletian as a masterful ruler who reconstituted a faltering empire.

BYZANTIUM

Robert Browning, *The Byzantine Empire* (1980). A sympathetic chronological treatment of Byzantine politics, culture, literature, philosophy, and art.

Deno J. Geanakoplos, *Interaction of the "Sibling" Byzantine and Western Cultures in the Middle Ages and Italian Renaissance* (1976). A learned discussion of Byzantine-Western interactions across thirteen centuries.

Romilly Jenkins, *Byzantium: The Imperial Centuries* (1969). A fine account of the period from Heraclius to the battle of Manzikert, particularly valuable on the age of the Macedonian emperors.

George Ostrogorsky, *History of the Byzantine State* (rev. ed., 1969). The most comprehensive single-volume account of Byzantine political history.

Steven Runciman, *The Byzantine Theocracy* (1977). A brief survey of relations between the Byzantine Church and Empire stressing the emperor's role as God's viceroy.

Speros Vryonis, *Byzantium and Europe* (1969). A short, well-illustrated interpretive survey picturing Byzantium as "a society and culture midway between those of Islam and the Latin west."

THE WEST BEFORE THE CAROLINGIANS

James Campbell, ed., *The Anglo-Saxons* (1982). An aptly illustrated survey of Anglo-Saxon history and archaeology.

Roger Collins, *Early Medieval Spain: Unity in diversity (400–1000)* (1983). An outstanding, highly original account stressing regional diversity and rehabilitating, to a degree, the Visigothic monarchy.

Patrick Geary, *Before France and Germany* (1987). A brief survey, incorporating the most recent historical interpretations and archaeological findings, which emphasizes the vitality and significance of the Merovingian era in Frankish history.

Richard Hodges and David Whitehouse, *Mohammed, Charlemagne, and the Origins of Europe: Archeology and the Pirenne Thesis* (1983). A contribution, making much use of archaeological evidence, to the ongoing debate over Henri Pirenne's challenge to the traditional view of the fall of the Roman Empire (see Pirenne, below).

Edward James, *The Franks* (1988). Readable and original, this work employs historical and archaeological evidence to cast new light on the Franks from later Roman to Carolingian times.

Peter Lasko, *The Kingdom of the Franks* (1971). A splendidly illustrated account of the Merovingian Franks, emphasizing Frankish art.

Bryce Lyon, *The Origins of the Middle Ages: Pirenne's Challenge to Gibbon* (1972). A brief, illuminating study of conflicting historical interpretations of the early medieval West.

Henri Pirenne, *Mohammed and Charlemagne* (1955 reprint). The firmest statement by the great Belgian scholar of his thesis that Roman civilization endured in the West until the eighth century. This book should be read in connection with Hodges and Whitehouse and with Bryce Lyon (above).

Jeffrey Richards, *The Popes and the Papacy in the Early Middle Ages, 476–752* (1979). A welcome effort to view the early-medieval papacy without the distorting lens of later papal ideologies.

J. M. Wallace-Hadrill, *Early Germanic Kingship in England and on the Continent* (1971). Authoritative studies of kingship from the early Germanic peoples through Charlemagne and Alfred.

———, *The Frankish Church* (1983). An erudite, witty, and original study of the Church in both Merovingian and Carolingian Francia.

Suzanne Fonay Wemple, *Women in Frankish Society: Marriage and the Cloister, 500 to 900* (1981). A meticulously documented analysis of Frankish women in both the Church and the family, arguing changes in status between Merovingian and Carolingian times.

ISLAM

G. E. Von Grunebaum, *Medieval Islam* (2nd ed., 1961). A learned and original work, the best on the subject.

P. K. Hitti, *History of the Arabs* (10th ed., 1970). Broad, yet full; a monumental work. For a brief survey by the same author, with a particularly beguiling subtitle, see *The Arabs: A Short History* (1956).

Archibald Lewis, *The Islamic World and the West: A.D. 622–1492* (1970). A thoughtfully selected collection of essays by modern historians and original sources in English translation.

W. M. Watt and Pierre Cachia, *A History of Islamic Spain* (1967). A good, short survey from the fall of the Visigothic kingdom to the fall of Granada in 1492, particularly full on the tenth-century golden age of Cordova.

CAROLINGIAN AND POST-CAROLINGIAN EUROPE

Bernard S. Bachrach, *Early Medieval Jewish Policy in Western Europe* (1977). Argues that anti-Semitic policy among early-medieval Christian princes was only sporadic and was often politically motivated.

Geoffrey Barraclough, *The Crucible of Europe* (1976). A clearly written political analysis of Western Europe c. 800–1050.

March Bloch, *Feudal Society* (2 vols., 1961; originally published in 1940). A masterpiece, challengingly written and boldly original for its time. Bloch treats feudalism in a broad sociological sense.

Ute-Renate Blumenthal, ed., *Carolingian Essays* (1983). Well-selected discussions and reinterpretations of the Carolingian era.

Jacques Boussard, *The Civilization of Charlemagne* (1968). This important work, which was immediately translated from the French, remains the best single book in English on the age of Charlemagne.

Jean Chapelot and Robert Fossier, *The Village and House in the Middle Ages* (1985). A pioneering reinterpretation based on a synthesis of history and archaeology.

Georges Duby, *The Early Growth of the European Economy: Warriors and Peasants from the Seventh to the Twelfth Century* (1974). A path-breaking work of synthesis by the most innovative and influential living historian of the medieval French economy and society.

F. L. Ganshof, *Feudalism* (2nd ed., 1961). A short, somewhat technical survey of medieval feudal institutions by a great Belgian scholar.

———, *Frankish Institutions under Charlemagne* (1968). A masterful work of institutional history.

Gwyn Jones, *A History of the Vikings* (rev. ed., 1984). An impressive work of scholarly synthesis, stylishly written.

K. J. Leyser, *Rule and Conflict in an Early Medieval Society: Ottonian Saxony* (1979). A work of impressive erudition that casts new light on Otto I, Saxon aristocratic women, and contemporary ideas of sacral kingship.

Donald F. Logan, *The Vikings in History* (1983). A lively survey stressing the Vikings' positive contributions to European history.

H. R. Loyn, *The Governance of Anglo-Saxon England* (1984). Brief, clear, and authoritative.

——, *The Vikings in Britain* (1977). A brief synthesis that treats a variety of evidence sensitively, expertly, and clearly.

Rosamund McKitterick, *The Frankish Kingdoms under the Carolingians, 751–987* (1983). Written in a dense style, this is nevertheless the best book on the subject. Good luck with it!

Thomas F. X. Noble, *The Republic of St. Peter: The Birth of the Papal States, 680–825* (1984). This admirable book makes the important point that the popes were not merely bystanders in the policies of the Byzantines, Lombards, and Franks but had firm political ambitions of their own.

Barbara Rosenwein, *Rhinoceros Bound: Cluny in the Tenth Century* (1982). This methodologically innovative study demonstrates how the abbey of Cluny contributed to the needs of its surrounding society for security and order.

Paul Sachs, *Icelandic Sagas* (1984). A skillful introductory account.

Peter Sawyer, *Kings and Vikings* (1982). A succinct survey and reinterpretation of the Viking age.

SOURCES

Alfred the Great, ed. Simon Keynes and Michael Lapidge (1983). Newly translated excerpts from original sources.

Bede, *The Age of Bede,* ed. J. F. Webb and D. H. Farmer (rev. ed., 1983). Translated writings of Bede and his contemporaries.

——, *A History of the English Church and People,* trans. Leo Shirley Price.

Einhard, *Life of Charlemagne,* trans. S. E. Turner.

Eusebius, *The History of the Church,* trans. G. A. Williamson.

Gregory of Tours, *History of the Franks,* trans. Ernest Brehaut.

Gregory the Great, *Dialogues, Book II: St. Benedict,* trans. Myra L. Uhlfelder. Pope Gregory I's biography of St. Benedict of Nursia.

For a collection of translated medieval sources that follows the organization of this present volume, see *Medieval Europe: A Short Sourcebook,* ed. C. Warren Hollister, Joe W. Leedom, Marc A. Meyer, and David S. Spear (1982).

PART TWO

The High Middle Ages
The Flowering of Medieval Culture

THE HIGH MIDDLE AGES (c. 1050–1300): AN OVERVIEW

Part One of this book was organized more or less chronologically—except for our breathless sprints through Byzantium and Islam. Part Two shifts to a topical organization. We will explore the 250 years conventionally labeled the "High Middle Ages" from a variety of historical perspectives: economic and social change, territorial expansion, the deepening and broadening of religious life, the struggle between papacy and empire, the evolution of England and France into coherent states, and concurrent developments in literature, art, and thought.

High-medieval civilization rested on the material foundation of a somewhat earlier medieval commercial revival. Indeed, some historians would prefer to begin the High Middle Ages some years earlier than 1050—perhaps in 1000 or 950. The process was gradual, commencing in the tenth century, gathering momentum in the eleventh, achieving full speed in the twelfth. Across these years devices such as the tandem harness and redesigned horse collar resulted not only in substituting animal for human labor but also in increasing the energy available for cultivation. The heavy plow, drawn by a team of oxen, was the machine most crucial to high-medieval agriculture, but horses were important as well. They were of enormously greater significance in the High Middle Ages than in Roman times because the new horse collar allowed them to pull loads with their shoulders instead of their necks. Additional energy was supplied by tens of thousands of water mills and, later, by windmills. Advances in agriculture produced food in greater abundance and greater variety than before: protein-rich peas and beans became for the first time an important element in the European diet, and there was greater consumption of cheese and eggs, fish and meat.

Consequently, Europe's population was not only much larger in 1300 than in 1050 but probably healthier, too, and more energetic. The best scholarly guesses put the population of Western Christendom at about thirty-five or forty million in the eleventh century and at twice that by 1300. To feed the millions of new mouths, the process of land clearing accelerated.

With the rise in population and food production came a decisive shift toward urbanization. Although society remained primarily agricultural throughout the Middle Ages and long thereafter, by 1300 cities had become a crucial factor in the European economy, culture, and social structure. Milan rose in population from about 20,000 to something like 100,000, and Venice, Florence, and Genoa reached comparable size. Urban populations north of the Alps tended to be lower, but by 1300 cities of 25,000 or 50,000 were not uncommon, and Paris was approaching 100,000.

Although small by present standards, the high-medieval cities transformed Europe for all time to come. They were themselves the products of a tremendous intensification of commerce, which the economic historian Robert S. Lopez described as a commercial revolution. "For the first time in history," he wrote, "an underdeveloped society succeeded in developing itself, mostly by its own efforts." The awesome cathedrals of Europe's high-medieval cities have long been viewed as symbols of an "Age of Faith," but they could only have risen in a period that was also an age of commerce.

The economic transformation of the High Middle Ages was accompanied by far-reaching changes in political and social organization, as well as in mental attitudes. Europe evolved during these generations from a preliterate to a literate society. While it is true that most Europeans of 1300 could not read (or at least not very well), they had nevertheless come to depend on written records—deeds, letters, government surveys—to define their rights, property, and status. Whereas much had previously been left to memory and oral tradition, by 1300 English freeholders and even some serfs were having their property transactions recorded in writing. The production and preservation of government documents increased spectacularly: surviving papal letters number about 35 per year around 1100 but rise to 3600 per year by the early fourteenth century, and the same thousand-fold explosion of paperwork occurred at royal courts.

Financial records, too, were becoming more and more widespread and systematic. Annual written accounts of royal revenues commenced in England around 1110, in France around 1190. Taken altogether, these new records bear witness to increasingly effective and complex royal administrative systems which by 1300 were evolving into modern states. All across Europe, skills such as reading, writing, and mathematical calculation were becoming vital to the functioning of secular and ecclesiastical governments, urban businesses, and even agricultural enterprises. Possessors of these skills, the reasoners and reckoners, sifted into positions of control throughout society, changing its attitudes and its character. Schools sprang up everywhere, and the age of the university dawned.

The growing complexity of high-medieval society opened much greater possibilities than before for social mobility. Clever social nobodies could rise to power in royal and ecclesiastical administrations. Committed Christians could now choose from a rapidly increasing number of new monastic orders. And to restless serfs and poor freeholders, the city beckoned. Most sons and daughters continued to follow in their parents' footsteps, but the more daring and ambitious found opportunities to break from the family pattern. The result was greater social vitality and, for many, increased anxiety. One's career choice was no longer as predetermined as before, and it could be a traumatic experience to move from a small community of 100 or 200 familiar faces into a city of 10,000 or 20,000 strangers. Some historians have seen as a consequence of this fluidity an increased awareness of self and a growth of introspection. More people were collecting and preserving their personal letters; autobiographies began to appear for the first time since St. Augustine wrote his *Confessions*.

One of the twelfth-century's best known autobiographers, Peter Abelard, also pioneered the development of a new, rational attitude toward the universe. The seeds of such an attitude had existed in the Judeo-Christian doctrine that the world was created by God yet separate from God. Nevertheless, early-medieval people viewed the world as a theater of miracles: a storm or fire was a divine punishment for sin; a military victory was a mark of God's approval. But in the view of Abelard, and of many who followed him, God's creation was a natural order that could function by its own rules, without constant divine tinkering. Miracles were possible, of course, but they were rare. The spread of this idea encouraged a growing skepticism toward the judicial ordeal—the appeal to God for a "miracle on demand" to determine guilt or innocence.* The ordeal came under attack in the twelfth century, and a papal council of 1215 prohibited priests from participating in it, thereby dooming the procedure to gradual extinction. The judgment of God gave way to the testimony of witnesses and the deliberations of juries.

These deeply significant shifts in attitude toward self and toward the world, and the vast economic and social changes that accompanied them, have been described as Europe's coming of age. Such biological metaphors are obviously inadequate; historians might argue endlessly (if they chose to) over the date of Europe's puberty or adulthood. But whether the High Middle Ages are seen as childhood's end, or the opening phase of Europe's "modernization," or the time of economic "take off" (or, for that matter, the climax of the Age of Faith), the changes described in these pages were essential preconditions for modern European civilization. Behind the seventeenth-century scientific revolution lay the high-medieval idea of a universe functioning by natural rules and open to rational inspection. Behind the fifteenth-century invention of printing lay the high-medieval shift from a preliterate to a literate society. Behind the nineteenth-century industrial revolution lay the commercial revolution of the twelfth and thirteenth. Our word "civilization" is derived from the Latin *civitas*—"city." In this strict sense, Europe became civilized in the High Middle Ages.

*See pp. 27–28.

9

Town, Countryside, and Economic Take-off

THE COMMERCIAL REVOLUTION

Towns and Commerce

There had been towns in Western Europe ever since antiquity. The administrative-military towns of the Roman Empire evolved into the cathedral towns of the early Middle Ages, with their episcopal courts and churches and the sacred legends and relics of their saints. As commerce revived in the tenth and eleventh centuries, old towns were invigorated and new ones emerged as centers of trade and production. The high-medieval city remained faithful to its saints and religious establishments, while at the same time expanding its commercial districts and developing its political and legal institutions. Church, commerce, and urban government coexisted in a balanced relationship within the city's walls, but where trade was lively merchants spilled outside the walls into new suburbs. It was commerce that transformed Europe's cities into economic centers that, for the first time, earned their own way from the activities of their traders and artisans.

The commerce of early post-Carolingian Europe owed much to the activities of Jewish merchants, who linked Western Christendom with the wealthier civilizations of Islam and Byzantium. Commercial activity intensified between the ninth century and the eleventh as Jewish merchants in European towns conducted a regional and international trade in such commodities as cloth, grain, salt, slaves, and wine. They enjoyed the great advantage of commercial contacts with Jewish communities in Islamic and Byzantine cities, and shared with these communities a familiarity with accounting techniques, commercial contracts, and other business methods otherwise unknown in the West. During the eleventh and twelfth centuries Christians moved increasingly into commercial life, first in Italy, then to the north. By then the commercial revolution was well underway.

As it gathered momentum, commercial settlements began springing up all across Western Europe—sometimes as suburbs of older cathedral towns, sometimes outside the walls of monasteries, and often around one or another of the many fortresses that had risen in post-Carolingian Europe. These strongholds were generally known by some form of the Germanic word *burgh,* and in time the term came to apply to the town itself rather than the fortress that spawned it. By the twelfth century a burgh, or *borough,* was an urban commercial center, inhabited by *burghers* or *burgesses,* who constituted a new class known later as the *bourgeoisie.*

The earliest and largest commercial towns were those of northern Italy, where the immense opportunities of international commerce were first exploited. As we have seen, Venetian merchants had long been trading with Constantinople and Islam, while other Italian ports—Genoa, Pisa, and Amalfi—soon followed Venice into the profitable markets of the eastern Mediterranean. We have seen, too, how the ramifications of their far-flung trade brought vigorous new life to towns of interior Italy such as Milan and Florence. During the High Middle Ages the Muslims were virtually driven from the seas; Italian merchants dominated the Mediterranean, bringing Eastern goods to the markets of Italy, and carrying them overland across the Alps into Germany and France.

Meanwhile the towns of Flanders were growing wealthy from the commerce of the north—from trade with northern France and the British Isles, the Rhineland and the shores of the Baltic Sea. Flanders itself was a great sheep-raising district, and its towns became centers of woolen textile production. In time, the towns were processing more wool than Flemish sheep could supply, so that from the twelfth century onward Flemish merchants began to import wool on a large scale from England. By then Flanders was the industrial center of northern Europe, and its textile industry the supreme manufacturing enterprise of the age. It was the exporting of textiles more than anything else that reversed Europe's age-long trade deficit.

As isolated settlements became linked into a single network of commerce, agricultural specialization increased significantly. Money and merchants made it possible for local areas to concentrate on whatever goods they could produce most efficiently, using their profits to import other necessities. Thus, the Paris basin exported grain, Scandinavia exported timber, Germany exported salt and fish, England exported wool and beer, Flanders exported cloth, and Burgundy exported wine. A thirteenth-century visitor to a Burgundian religious house reported that the surrounding lands were devoted exclusively to vineyards: "they send their wine to Paris, because they have a river at hand that flows there, and they sell it for a good price from which they buy all their food and all their clothes."

Throughout Western Christendom commerce was lubricating the economy with an ever-increasing flow of money, causing Marbod of Rennes, writing around A.D. 1100, to burst into poetry: "Money! He's the whole world's Master. His the voice that makes men run: Speak! Be quiet! Slower! Faster! Money orders—and it's done."

With the increasing abundance of money, princes could now collect their taxes in silver coins rather than in goods and could govern through salaried officials and wage war with hired troops. Enterprising peasants could accumulate liquid wealth. Aristocrats could pamper themselves with imported luxury goods. And burghers, the chief beneficiaries of the new economy, could honor their civic saints (and express their civic pride) by building vast, richly decorated churches. Often, too, they honored themselves by building elaborate town halls.

Urban Liberties

The new urban class emerged from a society that had heretofore been almost exclusively agrarian. The town dwellers were drawn primarily from the wealthier peasantry but also included vagabonds, runaway serfs, ambitious younger offspring of the lesser nobility, and, in general, the surplus of a mushrooming population. At an early date traders began to form themselves into merchant guilds to protect themselves against exorbitant tolls and other exactions levied by the landed aristocracy. A town was almost always situated on the territories of some lord—baron, bishop, count, duke, or king. And the merchants found that only by collective action could they win the privileges essential to their calling: freedom from servile dues, freedom of movement, freedom from inordinate tolls at every bridge or castle, and the rights to own town property, to be judged by the town court rather than the lord's court, to execute commercial contracts, and to buy and sell freely.

By the twelfth century, lords were issuing charters to their towns that guaranteed many or all of these privileges. Some lords were forced to do so in response to urban riots and revolts; others did so voluntarily, recognizing the economic advantages of having flourishing commercial centers in their territories. Indeed, some farsighted lords began founding and chartering new towns on their own initiative, laying out streets on a gridiron plan within the new walls, and attracting commercial settlers by offering generous privileges.

The first urban charters varied greatly from one another, but in time it became common to pattern them after certain well-known models. The privileges enjoyed by the burghers of Newcastle-on-Tyne under King Henry I of England, and the charter granted by the French king Louis VI to the community of Lorris, were copied repeatedly throughout England and France. In effect, such privileges recognized towns as semiautonomous political and legal entities, each with its own local government, its own court, its own tax-collecting agencies, and its own customs. These urban communes paid well for their charters and continued to render regular taxes to their lord. But—and this is all-important—they did so as political units. Individual merchants were freed from the harassments of their lords' agents. Townspeople enforced their own law in their own courts, collected their own taxes, and paid their dues to their lord in a lump sum. In short, they had won the invaluable privilege of handling their own affairs.

One should not conclude, however, that the medieval towns were even remotely democratic. It was the prosperous merchants and master craftsmen who profited chiefly from the charters, and it was they who came to control the town governments, ruling over the towns' less exalted inhabitants. Some towns witnessed the beginnings of a significant split between large-scale producers and wage-earning workers. Indeed, the medieval town was the birthplace of European capitalism. For as time progressed towns tended to become centers of industry as well as commerce. Manufacturing followed in the footsteps of trade. And although most industrial production took place in small shops rather than large factories, some enterprising manufacturers employed considerable numbers of workers to produce goods, usually textiles, on a large scale. Normally, these workers did not labor in a factory but instead worked in their own shops or homes. Since the entrepreneur sent raw materials out to the workers, rather than bringing the workers to the materials, this mode of production has been called the "putting-out system." As a direct antecedent of the factory system, it was a crucial phase in the early history of capitalism.

Craft Guilds and Artisans

The more typical medieval manufacturers worked for themselves in their own shops, producing their own goods and selling them directly to the public. As early as the eleventh century, these artisans were organizing themselves into craft guilds, distinct from merchant guilds. In order to limit competition and ensure the quality of their goods, the craft guilds established strict admission requirements and stringent rules on prices, wages, standards of quality, and operating procedures. Young artisans would learn their trade as apprentices in the shops of master craftsmen. After a specified period, sometimes as long as seven years, the apprenticeship ended. With good luck and rich parents, the apprentice might then become a master. But young artisans normally had to work for some years beyond their apprenticeships as day laborers—"journeymen"—improving their skills and saving their money until they could establish their own shop and become guild members. Toward the end of the High Middle Ages, as prosperity waned and urban society crystallized, it became increasingly common for artisans to spend their whole lives as wage earners, never becoming masters.

Throughout the High Middle Ages and beyond, women took an active part in town life. Since the master craftsman's shop was also his home, the modern distinction between home and workplace, between public and private spheres of activity, did not exist (nor did it in aristocrats' castles or peasants' huts). This blurring of domestic and business life worked to women's advantage: a master's wife and daughters could learn his skills just as his apprentices could—by observing and practicing. Indeed, master craftsmen and their wives normally shared authority over apprentices, on the assumption that the wife was well acquainted with her husband's craft. Widows commonly carried on the businesses of their deceased husbands—and the tendency for urban women in their teens to marry established businessmen in their late 20s or early 30s resulted in an abundance of lively, prosperous widows. Even while still married, women sometimes owned and operated their own businesses, distinct from their husbands. And women dominated such economic activities as the spinning of silk, the manufacture of female headgear and purses, and, in Paris, the managing of hotels and taverns. Women could also be members of some guilds, though by no means all. And town records show women collecting taxes, lending and exchanging money, illuminating and copying books, working as druggists and barbers, and engaging on their own in a wide variety of craft and merchant enterprises.

Economic and Cultural Vitalization

There were many who made their fortunes in commerce and manufacturing. Europe was astir with new life, and for one who was clever and enterprising, the possibilities were vast. In the twelfth and thirteenth centuries, merchants were moving continuously along the roads and rivers of Europe. A series of annual fairs on the overland trade routes provided them with excellent opportunities to sell their goods. As commerce grew, credit and banking grew with it, and by the thirteenth century several Italian banking families had amassed huge fortunes.

Money and religious piety blended in the new towns to vitalize the Christian culture of the High Middle Ages. It was money that built the cathedrals, supported the Crusades, financed the charities of Christian princes, and gave life and substance to the magnificent religious culture of the thirteenth century—money and of course an ardent faith. For townspeople, by and large, exhibited a piety that was more vibrant and intense than that of the peasantry and aristocracy. The surge of urban piety became a crucial factor in the development of high-medieval Christianity—spawning cathedrals and hospitals, universities and colleges, saints and heretics. The most famous saint of the era, Francis of Assisi, and the best known heretic, Peter Waldo, were both townsmen. In the electric atmosphere of the new cities, Christianity acquired an emotional content unknown to the villages and manor houses.

At some point in the course of the medieval commercial revolution, perhaps toward the end of the twelfth century, commerce outdistanced agriculture to become the dominating force in the European economy that it has remained ever since. What occurred was more than a great boom: it was a permanent change, and of such historic magnitude that several scholars have described it as Europe's economic "take-off." In centuries thereafter, Europe would endure depressions, plagues, and devastating wars, but it would never revert to the primarily agrarian economy of the early Middle Ages.

Twelfth-Century London

We can gain some impression of life in a medieval city by looking at London as it existed toward the end of the twelfth century. With a population of about

30,000, London was by far the largest city of its time in the British Isles and one of the leading commercial centers of northwestern Europe. Many of England's bishops, abbots, and barons maintained townhouses there, and the king himself conducted much of his business at a palace (which stands to this day) in London's western suburb of Westminster. The Londoners were served by 139 churches, whose bells pealed across the city and its suburbs to mark the hours of the day.

London's narrow streets were lined with houses and shops, most of them built of wood. Fire was an ever-present danger. The streets were mostly unpaved and during the day were crowded with people, dogs, horses, and pigs. (Half a century earlier a crown prince of France was killed when his horse tripped over a pig in the streets of Paris.) But from the perspective of the twelfth century, London was a great, progressive metropolis. The old wooden bridge across the River Thames was being replaced by a new London Bridge made entirely of stone. Sanitation workers were employed by the city to clear the streets of garbage. There was a sewer system—the only one in England—consisting of open drains down the centers of streets. There was even a public lavatory.

By today's standards, the city was a small, filthy, odoriferous firetrap. But twelfth-century Londoners were proud of it. One of them, William fitz Stephen, writing around 1175, describes it in these glowing words:

> Among the noble and celebrated cities of the world, London, the capital
> of the kingdom of the English, extends its glory farther than all others
> and sends its wealth and merchandise more widely into far distant
> lands. It holds its head higher than all the rest. It is fortunate in the
> healthiness of its air, in its observance of Christian practice, in the
> strength of its fortifications, in its natural setting, in the honor of its
> citizens, and in the modest behavior of its wives. It is cheerful in its
> sports and the fruitful mother of noble men....*

All medieval cities were fortified, and London more strongly than most:

> It has on the east the Tower of London, very great and strong.... On
> the west there are two powerful castles, and from there runs a high and
> massive wall with seven double gates and with towers along the north
> at regular intervals....

Within these walls, London was a hive of commercial activity:

> Those engaged in businesses of various kinds—sellers of merchandise,
> hirers of labor—go off every morning into their various districts
> according to their trade. Besides, there is a public cook shop in London,
> located on the riverbank in the district where wines are offered for sale
> in ships and in the cellars of the wine merchants. Each day, at this cook
> shop, you will find food according to the season—dishes of meat,
> roasted, fried, and boiled; large and small fish; coarser meats for the

*Among the noble "men" born in twelfth-century London, William fitz Stephen proudly includes the Empress Matilda.

poor and more delicate for the rich, such as venison and large and
small birds....

The delicacies offered by this medieval Colonel Sanders could be enjoyed
not only by Londoners but also by visitors from afar:

> To this city merchants delight to bring their trade by sea from every
> nation under heaven. The Arabian sends gold; the Sabaean spice and
> incense. The Scythian brings arms, and from the rich, fat lands of
> Babylon comes palm oil. The Nile sends precious stones; the
> Norwegians and Russians send furs and sables; nor is China absent
> with her purple silk. The French come with their wines.

William fitz Stephen goes on and on. He describes London's entertainments and sports: the miracle plays, the annual Carnival Day with its rooster
fights and athletic contests, when ball teams from various London guilds and
schools competed in the fields outside the city's walls. "On feast days throughout the summer, the young men engage in the sports of archery, running,
jumping, wrestling, slinging stones, hurling javelins beyond a certain mark,
and fighting with sword and buckler." And in winter,

> Swarms of young men come out to play games on the ice. Some,
> gaining speed in their run, slide sideways over a vast expanse of ice,
> their feet set well apart. Others make seats out of a large lump of ice,
> and while one person sits on it, the others, with linked hands, run in
> front and drag him along behind them. So swift is their sliding motion
> that sometimes their feet slip, and they all fall on their faces. Others,
> more skilled at winter sports, put on their feet the shin bones of
> animals, binding them firmly around their ankles, and then, gripping
> iron-shod poles, which they strike from time to time against the ice,
> they are propelled as swiftly as a bird in flight.

William fitz Stephen is prone to exaggeration. He speaks of the health-
iness of London's air, and yet we know that London had a smog problem
even in the twelfth century. The author's chamber-of-commerce viewpoint
contrasts sharply with the testimony of a twelfth-century Jewish merchant
from France, who gives this warning to a friend about to leave for England:

> If you go to London pass through it quickly.... Every evil or malicious
> thing that can be found anywhere on earth you will find in that one city.
> Steer clear of the crowds of pimps; don't mingle with the throngs in eating
> houses; avoid dice and gambling, the theater and the tavern. You will
> meet with more braggarts there than in all of France. The number of
> parasites is infinite. Actors, jesters, smooth-skinned lads, Moors, flatterers,
> pretty boys, effeminates, degenerates, singing girls and dancing girls,
> quacks, belly dancers, sorceresses, extortioners, night wanderers,
> magicians, mimes, beggars, buffoons: all this tribe fill all the houses. So if
> you don't want to deal with evildoers, don't go to London.

The same Jewish merchant gives equally bad news about other English
towns. In Exeter both men and beasts are provided the same food. Bath, ly-

ing amidst "exceedingly heavy air and sulphurous fumes, is at the gates of hell." At Bristol, "there is nobody who is not or has not been a soap maker." Ely stinks perpetually from the surrounding marshes. And York is "full of Scotsmen—filthy and treacherous creatures, scarcely men."*

The warnings of the French merchant are reinforced by a recent calculation of the murder rate in thirteenth-century London: 12 homicides per 100,000 people, thirty times the per-capita murder rate of modern Britain (though only half the rate of Los Angeles or New York in the 1980s). The violence of medieval London may be attributable in part to the existence (in 1309) of 354 taverns and more than 1300 ale shops—a fact that provides added meaning to the term "High Middle Ages." Ale consumption seems to have been still more heroic in the medieval English countryside, where the murder rate was even higher than in the towns.

The Jews of Medieval Europe

Well might a twelfth-century Jewish merchant be unenthusiastic about urban life in England—or, for that matter, throughout much of Western Christendom. For in a civilization that was almost unanimously Christian, members of a minority faith were apt to suffer. In most regions of Christian Europe, Jews had long been subjected to legal disabilities and popular bias. And their condition worsened in the High Middle Ages with the growth of Christian self-awareness, militancy, and popular devotion to the suffering Christ. Good Christian theology insists that Christ died for the sins of all humanity, but popular sentiment often held that he was murdered by the Jews. And there were those who arrived at the grotesque conclusion that the "murder" should be avenged. The persecution of Jews—and of other dissenting groups such as heretics and magicians—represents the wormy underside of high-medieval Christian piety.

Jews had played a vital part in the earlier phases of medieval urban growth, as we have seen. They were active in the commercial life of Italian cities throughout the early Middle Ages, and in 875 King Charles the Bald brought a community of Jews home with him from a visit to Italy and settled them in his kingdom. Soon they spread into numerous cities of France and Germany and finally into England in the wake of the Norman Conquest of 1066. Wherever they settled, they stimulated commerce through their mercantile expertise.

Ever since the Christian conversion of the Roman Empire, however, Jews had been at best second-class citizens. A Church council of 451 had prohibited Christians from marrying Jews, having dinner with them, or even going to Jewish physicians. Jews were not to hold Christian slaves, to take Christian

*These views are ascribed to the merchant by the English chronicler Richard of Devizes, who may himself have invented the whole business.

oaths of fealty, or to be lords over Christians. Such rules were not strictly enforced in the early Middle Ages, but by the later twelfth century, Jews were required to wear special badges or hats so that Christians might be warned to keep their appropriate social distance.* The papacy was never a great friend of Jews, but it did endeavor to protect them from the violence of popular prejudice, and Jewish intellectuals responded by supporting the growth of papal authority. An eleventh-century pope wrote to the bishops of Spain,

> We are pleased with the account we have recently heard concerning the way you have protected the Jews who live among you from destruction by those who are setting out to fight the Saracens. For these warriors, moved by stupidity or perhaps blinded by avarice, wished to behave like savages, destroying those whom divine, fatherly love may well have intended for salvation.... Indeed, the cases of the Jews and Saracens are altogether distinct: warfare is rightful against the Saracens, who persecute Christians and drive them from their own towns and lands; but the Jews are everywhere ready to do service.

As this passage suggests, crusades against Islam could escalate Christian anti-Semitism to the point of bloodthirsty violence. Such was the effect of the First Crusade to the Holy Land in 1096. It dawned on some crusaders that their mission to extend Christian power over infidels abroad might be prefaced by slaughtering the "infidel" minority in Christendom itself. The Jews of France and England survived the crusading fervor largely unscathed, but those of Central Europe did not. According to one Christian writer, the crusaders

> should have traveled their road for Christ, recalling the divine commands and holding to the discipline of the Gospel, while instead they turned to madness and shamefully, wantonly, cruelly cut down the Jewish people in the cities and towns through which they passed.

Massacres of Jews did not begin with the Crusades, but they became more frequent thereafter. Most were products of prejudice among common Christian town dwellers, whipped to a frenzy by popular rumors that Jews desecrated the transfigured bread of the Holy Eucharist, or that they murdered Christian infants (as they had allegedly murdered Christ). A pope decreed in 1272 "that Jews arrested on such an absurd pretext be freed from captivity."

Here again the papacy was assuming responsibility for protecting Jews from mindless grassroots savagery, and the responsibility was shared by kings and emperors. But these enthroned guardians demanded much of the Jews in return for protection. They borrowed heavily from Jewish burghers, milked them through arbitrary taxes, seized the property and loan accounts of Jews who had died without heirs, and charged enormous sums for the rights to

---

*Similar stigmas were imposed on the Coptic Christians of medieval and early-modern Egypt by their Muslim rulers.

travel freely, enjoy a fair trial, and pass their property on to their heirs. As the High Middle Ages closed, Jews were subjected to ever more intense persecution. Whereas the Fathers of the early Church had advocated the toleration of Jews as witnesses to the faith of the Old Testament, many churchmen and theologians had become convinced by the mid-thirteenth century that the Judaism of their own times, with its emphasis on the Talmud, constituted an heretical lapse from the original, Mosaic Faith. Jews should therefore be punished for blasphemy if they refused to convert to Christianity.

In the years around 1300, Jews were being expelled *en masse* from one kingdom after another by monarchs who coveted their wealth. By then their services as moneylenders were no longer essential; Italian bankers were providing an alternative source of credit. Many Jews subsequently filtered back or were invited to return when royal policy shifted. But by the time of the fifteenth-century Renaissance they were being segregated into ghettos. And persecution continued unabated throughout most of Europe for centuries thereafter.

The Jews of the High Middle Ages have usually been associated almost exclusively with such activities as moneylending and commerce. But while it is true that Jews were excluded from Christian guilds and forbidden to be lords of Christian peasants, recent scholarship suggests that many Jews, particularly in southern Europe, blended almost invisibly into the general urban society. Their activities were less strictly limited in the south than in the north, and it is certain that, throughout Christendom, moneylending and commerce occupied only a small, highly visible minority of medieval Jews. Still, they differed from Christians in ways other than faith alone: they achieved a much higher literacy rate than their Christian contemporaries (every substantial Jewish community had its own school), and their contribution to medieval medicine, Biblical scholarship, and philosophy was all out of proportion to their numbers. The Spanish Jew Moses Maimonides (1135–1204), in his highly creative use of Aristotle, did much to shape Christian philosophy in the thirteenth century. In the areas of medicine and commerce, too, the contacts of European Jews with their Jewish counterparts in Islam and Byzantium contributed much to the ending of Europe's isolation.

THE LANDHOLDING ARISTOCRACY

The commercial revival had a substantial impact on medieval aristocratic life in the north-European countryside. For one thing, the much-increased circulation of money gradually eroded the tenure-service relationship of early-medieval feudalism. Rulers came to depend less on the military and administrative services that vassals performed in return for their fiefs and resorted increasingly to the use of mercenary troops and paid officials—first in England and later on the Continent. Beginning in the twelfth century, English fiefholders were often asked to pay a tax called *scutage* ("shield money") in lieu of personal service in a royal campaign, and in time this practice spread to France and elsewhere.

Moreover, money and commerce made new luxuries available to the landed aristocracy: pepper, ginger, and cinnamon for baronial kitchens; finer and more colorful clothing, jewelry, fur coats for the cold winters (and to impress the less fortunate); and—for the castle—carpets, wall hangings, and more elaborate furniture. These amenities, in turn, drove many nobles deeply into debt, thus increasing the business (and unpopularity) of Jewish lenders. Many aristocrats, women and men alike, regarded overspending as a virtue—the mark of a generous spirit. A monk gives us this disapproving picture of the late-eleventh-century magnate, Hugh, earl of Chester, whose life-style was grander than most, yet not atypical:

> He was a great lover of the world and its pomp, which he regarded as
> the greatest blessing of the human lot. He was always in the vanguard
> in battle, lavish to the point of prodigality, a lover of games and
> luxuries, entertainers, horses, dogs, and similar vanities. He was always
> surrounded by a huge following, noisy with swarms of boys both
> low-born and high-born. Many honorable men, clerics and knights,
> were also in his entourage, and he cheerfully shared his wealth and
> labors with them.... He kept no check on what he gave or received. His
> hunting was a daily devastation of his lands, for he thought more
> highly of hawkers and hunters than of peasants or monks. A slave to
> gluttony, he staggered under a mountain of fat, scarcely able to move.
> He was given over to carnal lusts and sired a multitude of bastards by
> his concubines.

Along with their improvidence, many aristocrats displayed an almost childlike absence of emotional control. They were (to lapse into modern psychological jargon) in touch with their feelings. Always ready to take offense, a baron could be carried away by a fit of rage. An act of savage violence—a murderous assault or a pillaging campaign—might be followed by remorse so overwhelming that the baron would lavish wealth on the Church or embark on a distant pilgrimage or crusade. Similarly, contemporary records disclose instances of aristocratic women doing away with their own or their family's enemies through poison. But the significant role of women as benefactors of religious houses and hospitals owed less to guilt than to religious sensibilities. Benefactors far outnumbered poisoners, and the two groups seldom overlapped.

The medieval aristocracy was, above all, a military class, trained from early youth in the practice of mounted combat. As we saw in the last chapter, the aristocracy was two-tiered, divided between nobles (the great landholders) and knights (their followers). With the passing of generations, however, the social boundary between nobles and knights grew indistinct. The term "knight" gradually acquired high prestige: the Church emphasized more and more the idea of Christian knighthood, the crusading movement glamorized the "knights of Christ," and fictional knights such as Roland, Tristan, Lancelot,

and Galahad became heroes of high-medieval literature. The dubbing ceremony was shared by nobles and knights alike, and under the influence of the
Church it became a kind of "sacrament of knighthood." In the end even the
grandest nobles were proud to be called "knights" and to share with less
wealthy warriors a common code of knightly behavior known as "chivalry"
(from *cheval*, the French word for "horse"). Common knights, in the meantime, were acquiring more extensive lands, along with privileges and jurisdictional rights formerly limited to the old nobility. They were building fortified dwellings on their estates and marrying into old noble families. By the
thirteenth century, knights and nobles had blended into a single aristocratic
order.

For all the romantic images surrounding the medieval conception of the
knight, he was, essentially, a warrior. Mounted on a charger and clad in helmet and chain mail, he was a kind of military "machine"—the medieval equivalent of the modern tank. The analogy becomes still closer when, in the fourteenth century, chain mail gave way to plate mail in response to the coming
of the longbow.

Warfare was all too common in the High Middle Ages, not only among
kings and great princes, but also between neighboring barons. In time the
growing authority of monarchs and princes curtailed private wars, particularly in England. But it was a slow process and did not seriously affect the
French countryside until well into the thirteenth century. Fighting was what
aristocrats has been trained for; it was the chief justification for their existence. They were viewed (ideally) as the protectors of Church and society, but
most of them were interested primarily in defending and extending their own
estates. And to some, nothing was more fulfilling than to do battle with the
enemy—any enemy. As a twelfth-century French writer puts it,

> I tell you that I never eat or sleep or drink so well as when I hear the
> cry, "Up and at 'em!" from both sides, and when I hear the neighing of
> riderless horses in the brush and hear shouts of "Help! Help!" and see
> men fall...and the dead pierced in the side by gaily-pennoned spears.

War could ravage the land, destroying farms and churches, but it was less
dangerous to the aristocracy than might be imagined. Great battles were rare,
and even when they occurred, the knight was well protected by his armor. Most
medieval warfare consisted of castle sieges and the harrying of an enemy's possessions (including his peasants). The great risk was to be taken captive in battle, which obliged the victim to raise a large ransom in return for his release. On
the other hand, a skillful and lucky knight might take many captives in the course
of his campaigning and enrich himself from their ransoms.

In peacetime, tournaments took the place of battles. The Church legis-
lated against tournaments, fruitlessly but with good reason. For they often
involved day-long mock battles among groups of as many as a hundred
knights, in the course of which a participant might be killed, maimed, or taken

for ransom. The aristocracy relished these melees as opportunities to train for war or to collect ransoms—or simply for the fun of fighting.

Magnates had more sober tasks to perform as well: presiding at the castle court, giving counsel to their lords, and managing their revenues and estates—a responsibility that they took more and more seriously as the commercial revolution increased the circulation of money and encouraged a profit mentality. For recreation, aristocrats went hunting or hawking in their private forests. Besides the sheer enjoyment of it, hunting rid the forests of dangerous beasts—wolves and wild boars—and provided tasty venison for the baronial table. Lords and ladies alike engaged in falconry, a sport which consisted of releasing a trained falcon to soar upward, kill a wild bird in flight, and return it to earth uneaten. Both hunting and falconry were refined during the High Middle Ages into complex arts.

Indeed, the process of gradual refinement characterized high-medieval aristocratic life as a whole, and it was much needed. Most baronial castles of the eleventh and early twelfth centuries were nothing more than square wooden towers of two or three stories. They were usually set atop hills or artificial mounds and surrounded by barracks, storehouses, stables, workshops, kitchen gardens, manure heaps, and perhaps a chapel—all enclosed, along with assorted livestock, within a large stockade. The tower (or "keep") was apt to be stuffy, leaky, gloomy, and badly heated. Since it was built for defense not comfort, its windows were narrow slits for outgoing arrows, and its few rooms had to accommodate not only the lord and lady and their family but servants, retainers, and guests as well. It was a world of enforced togetherness in which only the wealthiest of aristocratic couples could enjoy the luxury of a private bedchamber.

By the late thirteenth century, however, rich aristocrats were living in much more commodious dwellings, usually built of stone and mortar. The advent of chimneys in the twelfth century, replacing the central fire, made it possible to heat individual rooms and thus contributed to the spread of the modern notion of privacy—private bedrooms and separate servants' quarters. Privacy remained relatively rare, for great lords now commanded larger retinues than before. But the sweaty, swashbuckling life of the eleventh-century baron had evolved by 1300 into a new, courtly life-style of good manners, troubadour songs, and gentlemanly and ladylike behavior. In much of Christendom war had become less incessant, and the barracks atmosphere was softening. The old military elite was becoming a "high society," increasingly conscious of itself as a separate class. Distinguished from lesser folk by its good breeding and good taste, the aristocracy became more exclusive and rigidly defined than in its earlier, less stylish days.

Aristocratic Women

It stands to reason that a society of landholding warriors would relegate women to supporting roles. Women were indeed subordinated to men in

Fourteenth-century minnesingers and coat of arms.
Minnesingers were a class of 12th-to-14th century
German poets and musicians whose major themes
were romance and courtly love.

many respects, but not in all. Shortly after the Norman Conquest of England
in 1066, so we are told by a contemporary monk,

> certain Norman women, consumed by raging lust, sent message after
> message to their husbands urging them to return at once, and adding
> that, unless they did so with all possible speed they would find other
> husbands for themselves.... Many men left England heavy-hearted and
> reluctant, because they were abandoning their king while he struggled
> in a foreign land. They returned to Normandy to oblige their wanton
> wives.

The monk who relates this story objects to the women's initiative, but their
all-conquering husbands rushed home nonetheless.
Women were subordinated to men in virtually all premodern societies—
less so in Western Christendom than, for example, in Islamic civilization, where

the veil and harem flourished. We have traced in earlier chapters the gradual improvement of women's status in the later Roman Empire and the ways in which late-Roman and Christian influences softened the antifeminine attitudes embodied in early-Germanic law codes. According to an early Anglo-Saxon law, "If a free man lies with another free man's wife, he shall pay the husband [a sum of money] and shall buy the husband another wife." By the tenth century, however, Anglo-Saxon women were holding property on a sizable scale and were willing it to their sons and daughters, sometimes in equal portions.

Christianity itself could be highly inconsistent in its attitude toward women. St. Paul—at once a Christian evangelist and a Roman citizen—injected a typically Roman antifeminine bias into the Christian mainstream. He conceded that in God's eyes there was no distinction between men and women or between slave and nonslave: "All are one in Christ." But this heavenly equality did not, in St. Paul's opinion, extend to earthly affairs: "Let your women keep silent in churches," he wrote, "for it is not permitted to them to speak.... And if they want to learn anything, let them ask their husbands at home."

Medieval Christianity echoed some of St. Paul's antifeminism. Women could not be priests; they could hold no church office except as an abbess or lesser official in a nunnery (though "double monasteries" admitting both men and women were occasionally presided over by abbesses). Holy men were apt to regard women as threats to male purity, and thus as objects. The canons of a thirteenth-century priory expelled the nuns from their community on these grounds:

> Recognizing that the wickedness of women is greater than all the other wickedness in the world, and that there is no anger like that of a woman, and that the poison of snakes and dragons is easier to cure and less dangerous to men than associating with women, we and our whole community have unanimously decreed—for the preservation of our souls no less than of our bodies and property—that we will on no account receive any more nuns, to the increase of our damnation, but will avoid them as we would avoid poisonous beasts.

Many churchmen would have taken strong exception to this tirade. Meister Eckhart, writing in the fourteenth century, observed that God had made woman "from man's side, so that she should be equal with man—neither below nor above." And a thirteenth-century Dominican argued that God had favored women over men from the beginning:

> For God made man from the vile earth, but he made woman in Paradise. Man he formed of slime, but woman of man's rib. She wasn't formed of a lower limb of man—for example, of his foot—lest man should regard her as his servant, but of his midmost part, so that he should regard her as his fellow....

Geoffrey Chaucer, writing in the fourteenth century, tells the story of an oft-married Wife of Bath whose fifth husband persisted in reading aloud to her from a "book of wicked wives," which recounted the evil deeds of innumerable wives from Biblical, Classical, and later times. As the Wife of Bath explained it,

When I saw that he would never stop
Reading this cursed book, all night no doubt,
I suddenly grabbed and tore three pages out
Where he was reading, at the very place,
And fisted such a buffet in his face
That backwards down into our fire he fell.

Alongside notions of wanton women and wicked wives, high-medieval Christianity developed a concept of idealized womanhood from its emphasis on Mary, the virgin mother of Jesus. As the great symbol of maternal compassion, Mary became the subject of countless miracle stories. Sinners who trembled at the prospect of God's judgment would turn their prayers to Mary, confident that she could persuade Christ to forgive them—for what son could refuse his mother? Many of Europe's greatest cathedrals were dedicated to Mary under the name of "Notre Dame"—our Lady.

The high-medieval troubadour songs and the rise of stylized courtesy in noble households resulted in still another kind of idealization. As romanticized ladies-fair, women were placed on pedestals, from which they are only now descending. This idealization of women was itself a kind of dehumanizing process; for high atop their pedestals, women remained objects still. But the pedestals tended to raise women from their former inferior status as threats to male purity, or objects of casual knightly seduction and rape, or victims of boorish, wife-beating husbands. The courtly lady remained an object, but a more revered and idealized object than before.

Such at least was the condition of noblewomen in much of the courtly literature. But one must always recall the gulf that separated social and literary convention from real life. Medieval lords and ladies did not ordinarily behave like characters in some courtly romance. Wife-beating persisted, and, on a lesser scale, husband-beating as well (recall the Wife of Bath). Wives of all classes were immobilized for long periods by the bearing and nursing of numerous offspring, necessary for the preservation of family lines in an era of high infant mortality. Eleanor of Aquitaine, one of the great women of twelfth-century Europe and a patroness of troubadours, had no less than eleven children but was survived by only two. She was imprisoned by her husband, King Henry II of England, for urging their sons to rebel, and spent many years in confinement. Only at her husband's death was she released to live out her final years as a valued adviser to her royal sons and as a wealthy and independent *grande dame* of the realm.

Other medieval queens and noblewomen often served as regents, ruling the dominions in their husbands' absences. In the thirteenth century Blanche of Castile, mother of King Louis IX (St. Louis), ruled France for eight years in her son's name until he came of age and again when he was off crusading. A person of uncommon intelligence and resolution, Blanche of Castile put down a major baronial rebellion at the beginning of St. Louis' reign through an adroit blend of warfare and diplomacy. "To all intents and purposes," writes a modern French historian, "she may be counted among the kings of France."

Blanche and Eleanor were probably exceptional. In general, medieval society was a warrior's world, and women were not expected to fight in battle. Still, the convention could occasionally be defied: Isabel of Conches, the wife of a Norman baron of about the year 1100, was described by a contemporary writer as generous, daring, and high-spirited: "In war she rode among the knights, dressed as a knight herself."

Isabel was a newsworthy exception to the male domination in warfare, but women could be influential in other ways as well. For if the aristocracy was a warrior class, it was also a class of hereditary landholders, and women could play a key role in the inheritance of land. In the absence of sons, a daughter might become a wealthy and coveted heiress; even if she had brothers, a well-born daughter might bring a large estate to her husband as a dowry and retain some control over it. Women, whether married or single, could sometimes hold and grant fiefs. They could own goods, make contracts and wills, and, under certain conditions, engage in litigation. A widow normally received a third of her husband's lands (their eldest son received the rest), and since aristocratic wives, like urban wives, were usually much younger than their husbands, landholding widows were commonplace.

A strong king might compel a wealthy maiden or widow to marry some royal favorite. Indeed, the granting of an heiress in marriage to a loyal courtier was an important element in royal patronage—and a source of royal revenue as well. In the financial accounts of King Henry I of England (1100–1135) one finds such items as these: "Robert de Venuiz renders account to the king for sixteen shillings eightpence for the daughter of Herbert the Chamberlain with her dowry"; "The sheriff of Hampshire renders account to the king for a thousand silver marks for the office, lands, and daughter of the late Robert Mauduit." And one great English heiress, the thrice-widowed Lucy, countess of Chester, was charged a handsome sum for the privilege of not having to marry again for five years.

Favorable marriages could bring wealth and greatness to a family. Many a family fortune was built on strategic marriages of heirs to heiresses. In a landed society such as medieval Europe's, marriages were crucial to a family's well-being, and marriages for love alone were luxuries that no noble family could afford. Medieval church law insisted that both partners must consent to their marriage. But family interests usually superseded the wishes of the bride and groom. Marriages based on family interests sometimes did, in time, become loving relationships, but they also encouraged the emphasis on extramarital romance in courtly literature—and sometimes in the real world as well. We have already encountered the numerous bastards of Earl Hugh. Eleanor of Aquitaine was suspected of an extramarital affair with her uncle. The Church condemned adultery as a mortal sin, but aristocratic society looked tolerantly on the escapades of well-born husbands. Their wives, however, were judged by a double standard that demanded wifely fidelity to ensure the legitimacy of family lines. Earl Hugh could sire bastards across the Cheshire countryside but expected his wife's children to be his own. This juxtaposition of male "wild-oat sowing" and female virtue has persisted into the present century.

Notwithstanding their dowry rights, wives were very much under their husbands' control according to feudal law. But in the actual day-to-day functioning of aristocratic life, the wife might exercise a great deal of power. In the castle, as in the urban shop-dwelling, home and workplace were one. The wife usually governed the castle and barony when her husband was absent (as husbands often were—on wars or Crusades). If the castle was attacked while the lord was away, his wife frequently commanded its defense.

Even when the lord was home, the wife might enjoy considerable authority. In medieval marriages as in modern ones, husband and wife might relate in a wide variety of ways. Some husbands were cruel and domineering. Others were ineffectual or senile, in which case—despite social and legal conventions—the wife ruled the castle. One such person was Avicia, countess of Évreux:

> The count of Évreux's intellect was by nature somewhat feeble as well as being blunted with age. And putting perhaps undue trust in his wife's ability, he left the government of his country entirely in her hands. The countess was distinguished for her wit and beauty. She was one of the tallest women in all Évreux and of very high birth.... Disregarding the counsels of her husband's barons, she chose instead to follow her own opinion and ambition. Often inspiring bold measures in political affairs, she readily engaged in rash enterprises.

The Norman monk who wrote these words clearly disapproved, but his description of the Countess Avicia shows us an aspect of aristocratic womanhood absent from the arid accounts of legal custom and the romances of the troubadours.

Medieval Children

Until recently, historians of the new and expanding field of childhood have viewed the Middle Ages as pitch dark. Medieval people, they argued, had no conception of childhood as a distinct phase of human life, but regarded children simply as unformed "little adults." Childhood thus had to be "invented" at some point in modern history (it was never clear exactly when). This is nonsense.

Even in the early Middle Ages, Gregory of Tours had written of a plague that was particularly fatal to young children: "And so we lost our little ones, who were so dear to us and sweet, whom we had cherished in our bosoms and dandled in our arms, whom we had fed and nurtured with such loving care. As I write I wipe away my tears."

With the advent of the High Middle Ages, children were cherished even more. The revolutionary high-medieval changes in commerce and social organization required increasing numbers of well-trained specialists in a wide variety of vocations—trading, manufacturing, estate management, ecclesiastical and secular governance—and, hence, much greater emphasis than before on the rearing and training of children. Schools sprang up on all sides; to the old monastic schools were now added an abundance of urban schools and village schools. It has been estimated that about half the boys and girls of early-fourteenth-century Florence were receiving at least a grammar school education. Other medieval cities probably did not do so well (we lack the figures), and widespread illiteracy continued in the countryside until fairly recent times. But there can be no question that high-medieval society invested heavily in the education of its children.

Aristocratic and urban children, particularly boys, were usually sent away from home at an early age for training in another noble household or urban business. Nevertheless, there is unmistakable evidence that many medieval parents were devoted to their children, whether at home or away. Despite the vexations of large families, and the danger of lavishing affection on a child who might not survive infancy, parents could love their children dearly and care for them tenderly. Voices began to be raised against the age-long custom of child-beating: the thirteenth-century writer, Vincent of Beauvais, cautioned that "children's minds break down under excessive severity of correction: they despair, they worry, and finally they hate. And this is most injurious, for where everything is feared, nothing is attempted."

Beginning in the twelfth century, books on the rearing and training of lay children began appearing in considerable number. One of the most popular of them, by the Spanish writer Raymond Lull, included sections on breast feeding, weaning, early education, and the care and nourishment of children. "Every person," Raymond Lull observed, "must hold his child dear."

Even the traditional Christian doctrine that baptism was necessary for salvation was modified in the twelfth century with respect to unbaptised babies. Previously they had been condemned to hell; now they were assigned to "limbo," where they could exist for eternity in innocent happiness even though denied the direct presence of God. There also emerged in high-medieval piety a special devotion to the Child Jesus, whose beauty and innocence were reflected, to a lesser degree, in all children. "O sweet and sacred childhood," wrote a Cistercian monk, "which brought back mankind's true innocence."

Actual child-rearing practices varied widely from family to family and class to class, and as in most ages they usually fell short of the social ideal. Warnings against excessive child-beating show not only that it was frowned on but that it continued. And infanticide, though severely forbidden, was never eliminated. Nevertheless, whether judging by the proliferation of schools, the popularity of books on child rearing, or the sympathetic literary portrayals of childhood, the people of the High Middle Ages placed a large emotional and material investment in their children. They were by no means blind to the existence of childhood; instead, they idealized it.

THE EVOLUTION OF AGRARIAN LIFE

The new social and economic conditions of the late eleventh and twelfth centuries gave rise to an expansion of arable land that transformed the north-European countryside. Swamps and marshes were drained, and in the Low Countries dikes were built to reclaim land from the sea. These clearing and draining operations were stimulated by the growing population and the rising money economy. Agricultural surpluses could now be sold to townspeople and thereby converted into cash. Consequently, peasants were motivated to produce as far in excess of the consumption level as they possibly could.

The initial result was to increase peasants' incomes and elevate their legal status. Slavery, common in Carolingian times, was diminishing by the eleventh century and virtually disappeared in the course of the twelfth. The tillers of the land were now chiefly freemen and serfs. Often the freeman owned his own small farm, but the serf was generally to be found on a manor. Normally, it will be remembered, the manor included the peasants' fields intermixed with the lord's fields (demesne), the produce of which went directly to the lord. Among the obligations that the serf usually owed his lord was labor service for a stipulated number of days per week on the lord's demesne. In Carolingian times, manorial lords had augmented the part-time serf labor by using slaves. But in the twelfth century, with slavery dying out, the lord was faced with a labor shortage on his demesne.

As a result of this problem, and in keeping with the trend toward transforming service obligations into money payments, some lords abandoned demesne farming altogether. They leased out their demesne fields to peasants and, in return for a fixed-money payment, released their serfs from the traditional obligation to work part-time on the demesne. At about the same time, many lords were translating the serf's rent-in-kind from his own fields into a money rent. By freeing the serf of his labor obligation, they transformed him, in effect, into a tenant farmer, thereby improving his legal status. The obligations of the peasant, like those of the feudal vassal, were gradually being placed on a cash basis.

Throughout much of the eleventh and twelfth centuries, lords were under pressure to improve the condition of their peasants in order to keep them from migrating to the towns or to newly cleared lands. Peasants were in demand, and enterprising land developers who were turning woods and marshes into fields competed for their services. As a consequence, the twelfth century witnessed the elevation of innumerable peasants from servile status to freedom. One of the clearest expressions of this trend was the emergence of rural communes—communities of peasants whose lord had granted a charter freeing them from servile obligations and permitting them to pay their dues collectively, on the pattern of the chartered town.

But even in the booming twelfth century, the reduction of demesne farming and the freeing of serfs occurred slowly and unevenly. And by the thirteenth, these trends were beginning to reverse. For population growth was gradually outstripping the increase in arable lands, creating a rise in land values and a surplus of peasant labor. As land became more valuable than laborers, lords throughout much of northern Europe began farming their demesnes more intensively than before, often employing landless peasants at low wages or strictly enforcing the labor services of their remaining serfs.

Moreover, the thirteenth century witnessed a growth of legal consciousness and a hardening of custom that gave rise to stricter class divisions and made it much more difficult for serfs to gain their freedom. On the other hand, a freeman might easily sink back into serfdom. It was the custom of some districts, for example, that a free peasant forfeited his freedom by marrying a servile woman, and a free woman suffered the same descent if she married a serf. In thirteenth-century England there are instances of landless free peasants submitting to serfdom in return for a plot of land. And quite apart from the matter of legal status, peasants of the thirteenth century, lacking the leverage they had enjoyed in the earlier generations of land clearance and labor shortage, were subjected to heavy economic exploitation by their lords. They were burdened with higher rents and taxes, higher fines at the lord's court, higher charges for the use of his mill, winepress, and ovens. And a peasant who refused to pay could be replaced by someone else from among the growing body of landless laborers that the high-medieval population explosion produced.

Again, these processes varied a great deal from place to place and from region to region. But generally speaking, the combined effects of population growth and land clearance profited lords and peasants alike throughout the later eleventh century and much of the twelfth, but worked to the peasants' disadvantage during the thirteenth, when land clearance and advances in farming techniques failed to keep pace with a continually rising population. Western Europe remained prosperous throughout most of the thirteenth century, but the easy years of limitless land were passing, and there was trouble ahead.

Life in a North-European Peasant Village

The life of a high-medieval peasant is almost beyond our imagining. Village life was tied to the cycle of the seasons and vulnerable to the whims of nature—drought, flooding, epidemics among humans and animals, crop diseases, the summer's heat and the winter's chill. Today we are insulated from nature by a screen of modern technological wonders: central heating, air conditioning, a secure food supply, plumbing, deodorants, modern medicine, and much more. We enjoy the protection of police and fire departments; we defy distance and terrain with our freeways and jets. All these things and others we take for granted, but they are all products of the recent past. They were un-dreamed of in the Middle Ages and remained unknown for many centuries thereafter.

From the viewpoint of modern middle-class America, the medieval peas-ant lived in unspeakable filth and poverty. A typical peasant's house con-sisted of a thatched roof resting on a timber framework, with the spaces be-tween the framing filled with webbed branches covered with mud and straw. The houses of wealthier peasants sometimes had two rooms, furnished with benches, a table, and perhaps a chest. But poorer peasants often lived in one-room cottages virtually bare of furniture.

The straw on which the family slept was apt to be crawling with ver-min. The smells of sweat and manure were always present, and therefore largely unnoticed. Flies buzzed everywhere. The cottage might shelter not only a large family but its domestic livestock as well: chickens, dogs, geese, occasionally even cattle. In winter animals provided added heat, and for the same reason, all family members usually slept in the same bed. Windows, if any, were small and few (and of course had no glass). The floor was usually of earth; it froze in the wintertime and turned damp and oozy with the com-ing of a thaw. Arthritis and rheumatism were common, along with countless other diseases whose cure lay far in the future. A simple fire served for cook-ing and heating, but in the absence of chimneys the smoke filled the room before escaping through holes or cracks in the ceiling. Candles were luxury items, and peasants had to make do with smoky, evil-smelling torches made of rushes soaked in fat. And there was always the danger that a stray spark might set the thatched roof afire.

The daily routine of a family of village-dwelling serfs might run more or less as follows: there would be a predawn breakfast—perhaps of coarse black bread (don't try it!) and diluted ale—after which the husband, wife, and post-toddling offspring would work from daybreak to nightfall. Peasants' work in-volved a close partnership between husband and wife; indeed, young peasant men were expected to marry before inheriting land, because women and chil-dren played essential roles in the peasant work force. The father and his sons did most of the heavy plowing. The wife and daughters took primary respon-sibility for the "inside" work—not only doing such domestic chores as cooking and cleaning, but also manufacturing the family's food and clothing: making cheese and butter, spinning and weaving cloth. They milked the cows, fed the livestock, tended the vegetable garden outside the cottage, and joined with the men in such activities as haymaking, thatching, shearing the sheep, sowing and reaping the grain, weeding the open fields, and sometimes even plowing. Or in the winter, when the fields were often frozen, the whole family might stay in-doors constructing or repairing their tools. The evening meal might consist of a pot of vegetable broth, more coarse black bread, more ale, and possibly an egg. Then it was early to bed, to rest for the toils of the following day.

Even this somber picture is a bit idealized. Often one or more members of the peasant family would be immobilized by illness (for which there were no available doctors and no effective medicines) or tormented by injuries, wounds, aches, and pains (no aspirin, just ale). Wives had to endure one pregnancy after another; childbirth was a mortal danger to mother and baby alike, and infant mortality was very high. (In medieval and early-modern Europe, approximately two-thirds of all children died before the age of ten, and well over one-third died during their first year.)

Occasionally famine would strike a large region, as in 1125 when a great August flood inundated numerous villages of eastern England: "Many people drowned and bridges collapsed and grain and meadows were utterly ruined, and famine and disease afflicted people and cattle." Worse still, the frequency of warfare meant that a peasant village might be pillaged or burned by its lord's enemy or might even become a battleground. From a twelfth-century French poem comes this chilling tale:

> They start to march. The scouts and the incendiaries lead. After them come the foragers who are to gather the spoils and load them into the great baggage train. The tumult begins. The peasants, having just come out to the fields, turn back uttering loud cries. The shepherds gather their flocks and drive them toward the neighboring woods in the hope of saving them. The incendiaries set the villages afire and foragers visit and plunder them. The distracted inhabitants are burned to death or led away with tied hands to be held for ransom. Everywhere alarm bells ring. Fear spreads from one side to another and becomes general. Everywhere one sees helmets shining, pennons floating, and horsemen covering the plain. Here money is seized; there cattle, donkeys, and flocks are taken. The smoke spreads; the flames rise; the terrified peasants and shepherds flee in all directions.

Such disasters were rare in the life of a single village, but when they occurred, the helpless inhabitants had no choice but to rebuild, replant, and pray for survival through a cold, hungry winter.

In a typical peasant village the most substantial buildings, as we have seen, were the lord's or bailiff's residence and the parish church. The lord's residence, the headquarters of the manor, was commonly surrounded by a walled enclosure that also contained a bakehouse, kitchen, barns, and other structures. To the manor house the peasants would bring portions of their crops, which they owed as customary dues. Here, too, they would bring their disputes to be settled in their lord's court. The parish church often stood at the center of the village. Its priest was seldom well-educated, though he might have learned the rudiments of reading and writing. He played a central role in the villagers' lives—baptizing infants, presiding at marriages and burials, and regularly celebrating the Mass. The church was likely to be painted inside with scenes from the Bible or the life of the local patron saint; such paintings provided an elementary form of religious instruction to an illiterate congregation.

The church usually doubled as a village meeting hall, and on festival days it might be used for dancing, drinking, and revelry. The feast days of the Christian calendar—Christmas, Easter, and many lesser holy days (holidays)—provided joyous relief from an otherwise grinding routine. In some districts the feast of Candlemas (February 2) was celebrated by a candlelight procession followed by a pancake dinner. On the eve of May Day the young men of some villages would cut branches in the forest and lay them at the doors of houses inhabited by young unmarried women. St. John's Day (midsummer) brought bonfires and dancing. And throughout the year, time could be found for informal sports—wrestling, archery, rooster fights, drinking contests, and a rough, primitive form of soccer.

But for most of their days the medieval peasants labored to raise the food on which their families and communities depended for survival. An English writer of the late tenth century attributes these words to an imaginary serf of his times:

> I work hard. I go out at daybreak, driving the oxen to the field, and then I yoke them to the plow. Be the winter ever so stark, I dare not linger at home for awe of my lord; but having yoked my oxen, and fastened plowshare and coulter, every day I must plow a full acre or more....I have a boy, driving the oxen with an iron goad, who is hoarse with cold and shouting. Mighty hard work it is, for I am not free.

Dietary Changes and Female Mortality

The last several paragraphs should banish any illusions about the happy medieval farmer (close to nature, living in rhythm with the seasons, free of urban anxieties, etc., etc.). But they must not blind us to the fact that conditions were improving. The spread of iron or iron-tipped tools, better plows, better systems of crop rotation, water mills, and windmills—all these contributed to the increase in food production and to gradual but significant improvements in the peasants' diet. The High Middle Ages saw a marked increase in the consumption of protein-rich and iron-rich foods—peas and beans (products of the new three-field rotation), cheese and eggs, fish and meat. Pork was beginning to appear more often on peasant tables, and the rabbit, introduced from Spain, had reached France by late-Carolingian times and England by the twelfth century. By the late Middle Ages, Europe had become, in the words of one historian, "the most meat-eating culture in the world."

These dietary improvements appear to have produced a shift of the most fundamental importance in the relative life expectancies of women and men. There is scattered but fairly consistent evidence that throughout Classical Antiquity and the early Middle Ages men outnumbered and outlived women. Back in the fourth century B.C., Aristotle had explained that men live longer than women because the male is a "warmer creature than the female," and while other classical writers differed on the explanation, they were agreed on the fact. Early-medieval estate surveys likewise disclose a preponderance of males to females, particularly in the older age groups. By the thirteenth and fourteenth centuries, however, writers are alluding to a surplus of women over men. The thirteenth-century scholar Albertus Magnus attributed women's greater longevity to the cleansing effect of menstruation and the fact that sexual intercourse drains the female less than the male. Whatever the merits of these hypotheses, they fail to explain the basic shift: more males than females until the High Middle Ages; more females than males from then until now.

The explanation may well be found in the increased consumption of iron-rich foods such as meat, beans, and other green vegetables. As a series of TV commercials has correctly pointed out, women require iron in much greater quantities than men. Menstruation, pregnancy, and breast-feeding drain iron from the body to such a degree that a woman of menstrual age requires twice as much iron as a man, and a pregnant woman requires three times as much. The scarcity of iron in the diet of common people of ancient and early-medieval times probably resulted in most women becoming severely anemic by their early twenties, and therefore highly vulnerable to death from a variety of diseases. The improved diet of the High Middle Ages would have seriously reduced the high rate of female mortality resulting from iron-deficiency anemia. The whole population would live longer and more energetic lives than ever before, but the effect of the new foods on women would be particularly striking—altering the sex ratio in women's favor throughout European society for all time to come.

Conclusion

This chapter has attempted to catch the flavor of life among the townspeople, aristocrats, and peasant villagers of the High Middle Ages. For all these groups I have tried to show not only what their lives were like but also how their lives were changing. Across the generations between about 1050 and 1300, the changes were most evident among the townspeople and aristocrats: the former were participants in a commercial and urban revolution of decisive significance to European history; the latter experienced a drastic transformation in taste and style as they moved from grim, square towers into elaborate, well-furnished castles echoing with the songs of troubadours.

Changes in the life of the peasant village were no less important. Villagers, too, were drawn increasingly into the web of a burgeoning money economy that provided markets and profits for surplus food. With the vast increase of cultivated fields, the European landscape was permanently transformed. And the gradual improvement of the peasant diet, too gradual to have been perceived at the time, may well have contributed a great deal to the vitality and longevity of Western man—and, more particularly, Western woman.

10

Conquests and Crusades

THE NEW FRONTIERS

Europe's frontiers were open and expanding in the High Middle Ages. The clearing of forests and the draining of swamps represent the conquest of a great internal frontier. It is paralleled by external expansion all along the periphery of Western Christendom that brought areas of the Arab, Byzantine, and Slavic worlds within the ballooning boundaries of European civilization and added wealth to the flourishing economy.

Western Europe had been expanding ever since Charles Martel repelled the Arabs in 732. Charlemagne had introduced Frankish government and Christianity into much of Germany and had established a Spanish bridgehead around Barcelona. The stabilization and conversion of Hungary, Scandinavia, Bohemia, and Poland around the turn of the millennium pushed the limits of Western civilization far northward and eastward from the original Carolingian core. Now, in the eleventh, twelfth, and thirteenth centuries, the population boom produced multitudes of landless aristocratic younger sons who sought land and military glory on Christendom's frontiers. And the ever-proliferating European peasantry provided a potential labor force for the newly conquered lands. While the warrior of the frontier was carving out new estates for himself, he was also storing up treasures in heaven by pushing Western Christianity into Muslim Spain, Sicily, Syria, and great tracts of Slavic Eastern Europe. Land, gold, and eternal salvation—these were the alluring rewards of the medieval frontier.

SPAIN

So it was that knightly adventurers from all over Christendom—and particularly from France—flocked southwestward into Spain during the eleventh century to aid in the reconquest of the Iberian Peninsula from Islam. The

CHRONOLOGY OF THE EUROPEAN FRONTIER MOVEMENT

Spain	Sicily	Holy Land
1002: Breakup of Caliphate of Cordova	c.1016: Norman infiltration begins	
1085: Capture of Toledo	1060—91: Sicily conquered	
1140: Aragon unites with Catalonia	1085: Death of Robert Guiscard	1095: Calling of First Crusade
	1130: Coronation of Roger the Great	1099: Crusaders take Jerusalem
1212: Christian Victory at Las Navas de Tolosa	1154: Death of Roger the Great	
1236: Castile takes Cordova		1187: Crusaders take Constantinople
		1291: Crusaders driven from Holy Land

Moorish Caliphate of Cordova had broken up after 1002 into warring frag-ments, providing the Christians a superb opportunity. The Christians, how-ever, were themselves divided into several kingdoms and seldom capable of united action. Taking the lead in the reconquest, the Christian kingdom of Castile captured the great Muslim city of Toledo in 1085. In later years Toledo became a crucial contact point between Islamic and Christian culture. Here Arab scientific and philosophical works were translated into Latin and then disseminated throughout Europe to challenge and invigorate western thought.

Early in the twelfth century the Spanish Christian kingdom of Aragon contested the supremacy of Castile and undertook an offensive of its own against the Moors. In 1140 Aragon was strengthened by its unification with the county of Barcelona—the Spanish March of Charlemagne's time. And meanwhile still another Christian state, Portugal, was establishing itself as an independent kingdom in the far west, facing the Atlantic. Yet more than a century following Toledo's fall in 1085, the reconquest made little progress. Muslim resistance stiffened, while the Christian kingdoms exhausted themselves fighting one another, or intervening in the affairs of southern France. It was not uncommon for a Christian prince to ally with Muslims against another Christian prince.

Finally, in 1212, Pope Innocent III proclaimed a cusade against the Spanish Muslims. The king of Castile advanced from Toledo with a pan-Iberian army and won a decisive victory over the Moors at the battle of Las Navas de Tolosa. Thereafter, Moorish power was permanently crippled. Cordova itself fell to Castile in 1236, and by the later thirteenth century the Moors were confined to the small southern kingdom of Granada where they remained in power until 1492. Castile now dominated central Spain, and the work of re-Christianization proceeded rapidly as Christian peasants were im-ported *en masse* into the newly conquered lands. Aragon, in the meantime,

THE RECONQUEST OF SPAIN

was overrunning the Muslim islands of the western Mediterranean and establishing a maritime empire.

The High Middle Ages thus witnessed the reconquest and Christianization of nearly all the Iberian Peninsula and its organization into three major Christian kingdoms: Castile, Aragon, and Portugal. Generations thereafter, Castile and Aragon would unite into the kingdom of Spain. And Spain, along with Portugal, would one day lead Europe's expansion into America, Africa, and the Far East. The high-medieval reconquest was an essential precondition for these Atlantic ventures.

SOUTHERN ITALY AND SICILY

Perhaps the most militant force in Europe's eleventh-century awakening was the warrior-aristocracy of Normandy. Largely Viking in ancestry, the Normans were by now thoroughly adapted to French culture. French in tongue, Christian in faith, feudal in social organization, they plied their arms across the length and breadth of Europe: in the reconquest of Spain, on the Crusades to the Holy Land, on the battlefields of England and France, and in southern Italy and Sicily.

Normandy itself was growing in prosperity and political centralization, and the pressure of an ever-increasing population drove greedy and adventurous Norman warriors far and wide on distant enterprises. The impression that they made on contemporaries is suggested by a passage from an Italian chronicler:

> The Normans are a cunning and revengeful people; eloquence and
> deceit seem to be their hereditary qualities. They can stoop to flatter,
> but unless curbed by the restraint of law they indulge in the licentious-
> ness of nature and passion and, in their eager search for wealth and
> power, despise whatever they possess and seek whatever they desire.
> They delight in arms and horses, the luxury of dress, and the exercise
> of hawking and hunting, but on pressing occasions they can endure
> with incredible patience the inclemency of every climate and the toil
> and privation of a military life.

The key figures in the Norman conquest of southern Italy were sons of a minor baron of northwest Normandy named Tancred de Hauteville. Tancred had twelve sons, and eight of them headed off to Italy in the 1030s and 1040s, poor in goods but rich in ambition. Even before the first of them arrived, other Norman adventurers had already been drifting south to serve as hired soldiers for the Byzantine coastal cities, Lombard principalities, and seaport republics that were struggling for power in the military-political snake pit of eleventh-century southern Italy. In the words of a contemporary observer, these Norman newcomers moved about the south Italian countryside "hoping to find someone willing to employ them; for they were sturdy men and well-built, and also most skilled in the use of arms." They made their presence felt, and before long were building principalities of their own.

In 1047 there arrived the most formidable of Tancred de Hauteville's sons, Robert Guiscard ("the cunning"). A contemporary Byzantine princess, Anna Comnena, describes him as a man

> of tyrannical temper, cunning in mind, brave in action, tall and
> well-proportioned. His complexion was ruddy, his hair blond, his
> shoulders broad, and his eyes all but emitted sparks of fire. His shout
> was loud enough to terrify armies...and he was ready to submit to
> nobody in all the world.

Robert Guiscard's wife, the Lombard princess Sichelgaita, was equally formidable. Tall and powerfully built, she participated fully in the wars and politics of her era. Princess Anna Comnena was awed and terrified by Sichelgaita's military prowess: "When dressed in full armor, the woman was a fearsome sight."

Robert Guiscard began his Italian career as a bandit leader. Swooping down from his hideaway in the barren mountains of southern Italy, he plundered villagers and travelers and terrorized the countryside. Successful at this,

he expanded his activities to conquest. And demonstrating his warlike prowess with victories over his neighbors, he gradually rose to become the leader
of the south-Italian Normans. In 1059 his authority over southern Italy was
recognized formally by the pope himself in the Treaty of Melfi: Guiscard agreed
to become a papal vassal and received in return the title of duke.

From the Treaty of Melfi onward, the conquests of the southern Normans
were "holy wars," and the papacy—which was becoming increasingly hostile
toward the Holy Roman Empire to its north—came more and more to depend
on the military support of Duke Robert Guiscard. In 1060, with papal blessings
Guiscard invaded the populous Muslim island of Sicily—driven less by Christian
zeal than by Norman greed. The island was prosperous and well-defended, and
its conquest consumed over thirty years. Once the invasion was well underway,
Guiscard turned the campaign over to a younger brother named Roger and
launched an attack against the Byzantine holdings in southern Italy. In 1071 he
captured Bari, Byzantium's chief Italian seaport. Then, returning to Sicily, he combined forces with his brother Roger to seize the great Muslim metropolis of
Palermo in 1072. Palermo had been one of the leading urban centers of the Islamic
world. It was larger and richer than any other city in Western Christendom, and
its bustling harbor was the key to the central Mediterranean. With Palermo, Bari,
and all of southern Italy under his control, Guiscard was now in a position to
dominate Mediterranean commerce.

His ambitions were limitless. In 1080, again with papal backing, he
launched a "crusade" against the Byzantine Empire, hungering for Constantinople itself. At the crucial battle of Durazzo, Guiscard's Normans were put
to flight by the Byzantines. But his wife Sichelgaita charged majestically after
them, her long hair streaming out beneath her helmet, shouting in a deafen-
ing voice, "How far will you flee? Stand and acquit yourselves like men!"
Seeing her approach at full gallop, spear upraised, the Normans ceased their
flight, returned to battle, and won the victory.

In 1084, in the midst of his Byzantine campaign, Robert Guiscard was
summoned back to Italy by Pope Gregory VII, whose conflicts with the Holy
Roman Empire had brought the emperor and his army to Rome. With Pope
Gregory besieged in a fortress within his own city, Robert Guiscard and
Sichelgaita returned to rescue him, and the news of their coming was enough
to send the emperor fleeing northward.

After a short siege, the Normans entered the ill-defended city in triumph,
rescued Pope Gregory, and restored him to power. Shortly afterwards, however, simmering hostility between Guiscard's army and the Roman townspeople exploded into violence. The Normans proceeded to plunder and burn
the city of Rome, causing greater devastation than the fifth-century Visigoths
and Vandals. Afterwards Guiscard's followers sold a number of Rome's leading citizens into Muslim slavery.

In 1085 Robert Guiscard died, with Sichelgaita at his side, in the midst
of still another campaign against Byzantium. His rags-to-riches career displays
in full measure the limitless opportunities and ruthlessness of his age. His

savage rescue of Pope Gregory VII was celebrated in the epitaph on his tomb in southern Italy:

> Here lies Guiscard, the terror of the world,
> Who out of Rome the Roman Emperor hurled. . . .

THE NORMAN KINGDOM OF SICILY

In the generations following Robert Guiscard's death, his Italian-Sicilian dominions became one of the wealthiest and best-governed states in medieval Europe. The lord-vassal structure of Norman feudalism was blended with the sophisticated administrative techniques of the Italian Byzantines and Sicilian Muslims. The mixing of cultures is vividly apparent in the Capella Palatina ("Palace Chapel": see p. 176), built by Norman rulers of the twelfth century in their palace at Palermo. The structural design of high nave and lower side aisles probably derives from other churches of Western Christendom; the interior glitters with mosaics in the Byzantine style; and the decor of the vaulted ceiling suggests a Muslim paradise, inhabited by djinns instead of Christian angels. The overall effect of the church, despite its diverse cultural ingredients, is one of unity—echoing the achievement of the southern Norman state in unifying peoples of many tongues and many pasts into a single, cohesive realm.

This achievement was given formal recognition in 1130 when a pope sanctioned the coronation of Guiscard's nephew, Roger the Great (d. 1154), as king of Sicily and southern Italy. The new Norman state came to be known officially as the "kingdom of Sicily," and its capital was the Sicilian metropolis of Palermo. But the kingdom, despite its name, included southern Italy as well. Roger the Great ruled strongly but tolerantly over the assorted peoples of his realm—Normans, Byzantines, Muslims, Jews, Italians, and Lombards—with their variety of faiths, customs, and languages. Palermo, with its superb harbor and magnificent palace, its impressive public buildings and luxurious villas, was at once a great commercial center and a crucial point of cultural exchange. Known as the city of the threefold tongue, Palermo drew its administrators and scholars from the Latin, Byzantine, and Arabic traditions.

The legal structure of the kingdom included elements from Justinian's *Corpus Juris* and subsequent Byzantine law, from Lombard law, and from Norman feudal custom. The royal court was the hub of an efficient, centralized bureaucracy with special departments of justice and finance. The administration profited from the inclusion of an important nonnoble professional class, devoted to the king and to the efficient execution of its duties. Drawing on the long experience of Byzantium and Islam, Roger's government was far in advance of most other states in Latin Christendom.

Under Roger and his successors the kingdom enjoyed a vital and diverse intellectual life. Its history was well chronicled by talented historians; the Muslim scholar Idrisi, the greatest geographer of his age, contributed a comprehensive geographical work that drew from Classical and Islamic

The Capella Palatina in Palermo (1132–1140).

sources. Idrisi dedicated his masterpiece to Roger the Great, and the treatise has been known ever since as "The Book of Roger." Sicily, like Spain, became a significant source of translations from Arabic and Greek into Latin. The Sicilian translators provided Western European scholars with a steady stream of texts drawn from both Classical-Greek and Islamic sources, and these texts, together with others passing into Europe from Spain, served as the essential foundations for the intellectual achievements of thirteenth-century Christendom.

In many ways Norman Sicily was Western Europe's most interesting and fruitful frontier state. Having been carved out partially at Byzantine and

Mosaic of Christ from the Cathedral in Monreale, Sicily: twelfth century.

Muslim expense, it was representative of twelfth-century Europe's advancing territorial frontier, and, as a vibrant center of cultural interplay, it demonstrated that the frontier was not only advancing but also open. Europe besieged had given way to a new, expanding Europe, exposed to the invigorating influences of surrounding civilizations. And nowhere was this cultural contact more intense than in Norman Sicily. East and West met in Roger the Great's glittering, sun-drenched realm, and worked creatively side by side to make his kingdom the most sophisticated European state of its day.

THE CRUSADES

The crusading movement, which proved so costly to Europe's Jews, was prompted by a major political crisis in the Near East. During the eleventh century a new warlike tribe from Central Asia, the Seljuk Turks, had swept into Persia, taken up the Islamic faith, and turned the Abbasid caliphs of Baghdad into their pawns. In 1071 the Seljuk Turks inflicted a nearly fatal wound on the Byzantine Empire by smashing a Byzantine army at the battle of Manzikert, and occupying Asia Minor.* Stories began filtering into the West of Turkish atrocities against Christian pilgrims to Jerusalem, and when the desperate Byzantine emperor, Alexius Comnenus, swallowed his pride and ap-

---

*For a discussion of the Seljuk Turks and the battle of Manzikert, see p. 46. The fall of Bari to Robert Guiscard in the same year was an added blow to Byzantium, though a less crippling one.

pealed to the West for help, Europe, under the leadership of a reinvigorated papacy, was ready to respond.

The Crusades represented a fusion of three characteristic medieval impulses: piety, pugnacity, and greed. All three were essential. Without Christian idealism, the Crusades would be inconceivable, yet the dream of liberating Jerusalem and the Holy Land from the infidel and reopening them to Christian pilgrims was reinforced mightily by the lure of new lands and vast wealth. The Crusaders were provided a superb opportunity to employ their knightly skills in God's service—and to make their fortunes in the bargain.

It was to Pope Urban II that Emperor Alexius Comnenus sent his envoys asking for military aid against the Turks, and Urban II, a masterful reform pope, was quick to grasp the opportunity. The Crusade presented many advantages to the Church. It enabled the papacy to put itself at the forefront of an immense popular movement and grasp the moral leadership of Europe. Moreover, the pope saw in the Crusade a partial solution to the problem of private warfare. For more than a century churchmen had been attempting to pacify Europe through a movement known as the "Peace of God," which prohibited military operations on noncombatants and their property. The partial success of this effort inspired a similar movement called the "Truce of God," which sought to outlaw warfare on holy days and during holy seasons (including Fridays through Sundays every week). The Crusade, strangely enough, was the climax of these earlier peace movements. For when Urban II proclaimed the Crusade, he also proclaimed a peace throughout the Latin West, forbidding all warfare between Christian and Christian. Although Urban's peace was not everywhere honored, it did have the effect of protecting the lordships of Crusaders against the designs of their stay-at-home enemies.

The Crusade also contributed to peace within Christendom by drawing off warlike members of the aristocracy and directing their ferocity outward toward the Muslims. Knights who had previously been condemned by the Church for violating the peace of Christendom were now lauded as soldiers of Christ fighting against the heathen. Thus Christian knighthood became a holy vocation; instead of begging the Church's forgiveness and doing acts of penance for their military violence, knights were invited to achieve salvation *through* the exercise of their warlike prowess. Indeed, the Church pictured crusading as an act of Christian love—toward persecuted fellow Christians in the East, and toward Christ himself, whose rightful lordship over the Holy Land had been usurped and polluted by nonbelievers. Just as a good vassal must help his lord recover a stolen lordship, so also must the Christian knight endeavor to restore Jerusalem to the Lord Christ.

The First Crusade

Accordingly, in 1095 Pope Urban II summoned Christian warriors to take up the cross and reconquer the Holy Land. He delivered a spellbinding address to the Frankish aristocracy at Clermont-Ferrand in central France, calling on them to emulate the brave deeds of their ancestors, to avenge the Turkish atrocities (which he described in bloodcurdling detail), to win the Biblical "land of milk and honey" for Christendom and drive the infidel from Jerusalem. Finally, he promised those who undertook the enterprise the highest of spiritual rewards: "Undertake this journey for the remission of your sins, with the assurance of the imperishable glory of the kingdom of Heaven."

The response was overwhelming. With shouts of "God wills it!" French warriors poured into the crusading army. By 1096 the First Crusade was underway. An international military force—with a large nucleus of knights from central and southern France, Normandy, and Norman Sicily—made its way across the Balkans and assembled at Constantinople. Altogether the warriors of the First Crusade numbered around twenty-five or thirty thousand, a relatively modest figure by modern standards but immense in the eyes of contemporaries. Emperor Alexius was gravely disturbed by the magnitude of the western European response. Having asked for military support, he had, as he put it, a new barbarian invasion on his hands. Cautious and apprehensive, he demanded and obtained from the Crusaders a promise of homage for all the lands they might conquer.

From the beginning there was friction between the Crusaders and the Byzantines, for they differed both in temperament and in aim. The Byzantines wished only to recapture the lost provinces of Asia Minor, whereas the Crusaders were determined on nothing less than the conquest of the Holy Land. Alexius promised military aid, but it was never forthcoming, and not long after the Crusaders left Constantinople, they broke with the Byzantines altogether. Hurling themselves southeastward across Asia Minor into Syria, they encountered and defeated Muslim forces, captured ancient Antioch after a long and complex siege, and in the summer of 1099 took Jerusalem itself.

The Crusaders celebrated their capture of Jerusalem by plundering the city and pitilessly slaughtering its Muslim inhabitants (as they had slaughtered Jews on their journey eastward). A Christian eyewitness describes the sack of Jerusalem in these words:

> If you had been there you would have seen our feet colored to our
> ankles with the blood of the slain. But what more shall I relate? None of
> them were left alive; neither women nor children were
> spared. . . . Afterward, all, clergy and laymen, went to the Sepulcher of
> the Lord and his glorious temple, singing the ninth chant. With fitting
> humility they repeated prayers and made their offering at the holy
> places that they had long desired to visit.

With the capture of Jerusalem after only three years of vigorous campaigning, the goal of the First Crusade had been achieved. No future crusade was to enjoy such success as the first, and during the two centuries that followed, the original conquests were gradually lost. For the moment, however, Europe rejoiced at the triumph of its Crusaders. Most of them returned to their homes and received heroes' welcomes. Others remained in Latin Syria to enjoy the fruits of their conquests. A long strip of territory along the eastern Mediterranean shore had been wrested from Islam and was now divided,

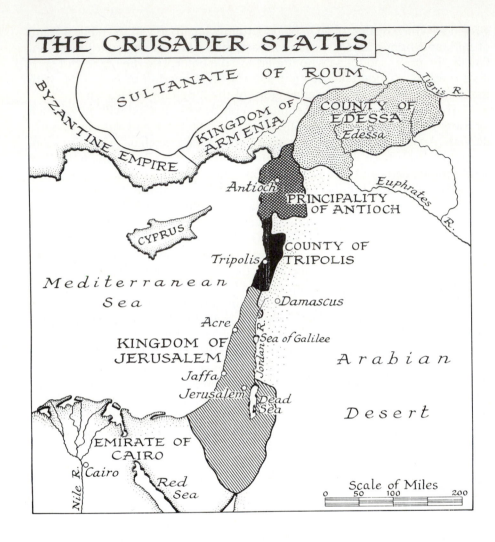

THE CRUSADER STATES

according to feudal principles, among the Crusader knights. These warriors consolidated their conquests by erecting elaborate castles, whose ruins survive to this day as tourist attractions and guerrilla hideouts.

The conquered lands were organized into four Crusader States: the county of Edessa, the principality of Antioch (ruled by a son of Robert Guiscard), the county of Tripolis, and the kingdom of Jerusalem. This last was the most important of the four states, and the king of Jerusalem was theoretically the overlord of all the crusader territories. In fact, however, he had difficulty enforcing his authority outside his own kingdom, and sometimes even within it. Indeed, the knights who settled in the Holy Land were far too proud and warlike for their own good, and the Crusader States were tormented from the beginning by rivalries and dissensions.

The Second and Third Crusades

Gradually over the years, the Muslims began to recover their lands. One churchman attributed the Crusaders' reverses to their wickedness: "They devoted themselves to all kinds of debauchery and allowed their womenfolk to spend whole nights at wild parties; they mixed with trashy people and drank the most delicious wines." Another cleric offered this explanation: "It is no wonder that the Christians suffer losses from Saracens, rats, and locusts, when they neglect to pay their church dues properly." Whatever the reasons, the crusader county of Edessa fell before Islamic pressure in 1144, and the disaster gave rise to a renewal of crusading fervor in Europe.

A Second Crusade (1147–1148) was inspired by the preaching of the renowned abbot, St. Bernard of Clairvaux (see pp. 193–194), who used his powerful influence to protect Jews from the violence they had suffered during the First Crusade. Led by the kings of France and Germany, the Second Crusade began with high hopes but ended in defeat. The Crusaders returned home shamefaced and emptyhanded, prompting St. Bernard to describe the campaign as "an abyss so deep that I must call him blessed who is not scandalized thereby."

The 1170s and 1180s witnessed the rise of a new, unified Islamic state centered in Egypt and galvanized by the skilled leadership of a warrior-prince named Saladin. Chivalrous as well as able, Saladin negotiated a truce with the Crusader States, but the rise of his new principality was nevertheless an ominous threat to Latin Syria. The truce was broken by a Christian robber baron, a characteristic product of grassroots feudal enterprise, who persisted in attacking Muslim caravans. Saladin responded by moving against Jerusalem, and in 1187 he captured it. Jerusalem was not to be retaken by a Christian army for the remainder of the Middle Ages.

This new catastrophe resulted in still another major crusading effort. The Third Crusade (1189–1193) was led by three of medieval Europe's most illustrious monarchs: Emperor Frederick Barbarossa of Germany, King Philip Augustus of France, and King Richard the Lion-Hearted of England.* But Frederick Barbarossa drowned on the way, and most of his army trudged back to Germany; Philip Augustus quarreled with King Richard and went home; and Richard failed to take Jerusalem. Worse yet, Richard fell into hostile hands on his return journey and became the prisoner of Frederick Barbarossa's son, Emperor Henry VI, who released his royal captive only after England had paid the staggering sum of 100,000 pounds—quite literally a king's ransom.

The Fourth Crusade

Within a decade Europe was ready for still another attempt on Jerusalem. Although lacking the distinguished royal leaders of the previous campaign, the Fourth Crusade (1201–1204) had as its instigator the most powerful of the medieval popes, Innocent III. Like the First Crusade, it was led not by kings but by great territorial princes such as Baldwin IX, count of Flanders. It was,

*All three will be encountered in subsequent chapters.

withal, the oddest of the Crusades. It never reached the Holy Land at all, yet in its own way it was spectacularly successful.

The Crusaders resolved to avoid the perils of overland travel by crossing to the Holy Land in Venetian ships. Unfortunately, the Crusade leaders enormously overestimated the number of their followers and, as a result, contracted with the Venetians for many more ships than were necessary, and at a far greater cost than the Crusaders could afford. The doge of Venice nevertheless agreed to take what money the Crusaders had and to transport them to the Holy Land if in return they would do him an errand on the way. They were to recapture for Venice the port of Zara, which had recently come into the hands of the king of Hungary. Pope Innocent III was infuriated by this bargain that diverted the crusading army against a king who was not only a Catholic Christian but a papal vassal as well. The Crusaders were excommunicated when they attacked Zara, and Innocent washed his hands of the whole enterprise.

Nevertheless, the warriors went doggedly on. Capturing Zara in 1202, they were then diverted still again, this time by a political dispute in Constantinople involving the succession to the Byzantine throne. One of the two claimants, having recently fled to the West, contacted the Crusaders and begged their support, promising them immense wealth, aid against the Muslims, and reunion of the Eastern and Western Churches under Rome. Rising to the challenge, the crusading army moved on Constantinople. The emperor-in-residence panicked and fled the city, and a delegation of citizens, realizing that further resistance was useless, opened Constantinople's gates to the Crusaders. Their imperial claimant was installed in power but was murdered shortly afterwards by one of his anti-Latin countrymen. Meanwhile, the Crusaders had withdrawn from the city as a result of growing hostility and violence between Greeks and Latins. But now, having expended considerable effort in what was apparently a fruitless cause, they resolved to take the city for themselves. Their plan was to elect a new Byzantine emperor from their own ranks and to divide the Eastern Empire among them.

Accordingly, in 1204 the Crusaders besieged Constantinople, took it by storm, and subjected it to three long-remembered days of pillage and massacre. The impregnable Byzantine capital had fallen at last to enemy conquerors; the Crusaders had succeeded where hordes of Muslims, Persians, Bulgars, Avars, and Germanic tribesmen had failed. Count Baldwin IX of Flanders became emperor, and he and his successors ruled in Constantinople for over half a century. A nucleus of the old Byzantine state held out in Asia Minor, nursing its grievances and gathering its strength, until in 1261 the Latin Empire was overthrown and Greek emperors reigned once again in Constantinople. But the Fourth Crusade had delivered a blow from which Byzantium never entirely recovered.

The wealth of Constantinople permanently diverted the warriors of the Fourth Crusade from the Holy Land. The Eastern and Western Churches were temporarily reunited: a Latin patriarch now sat in Constantinople, and a Latin hierarchy presided over a captive Greek Church. Innocent III, who had absolved the Crusaders from excommunication after the fall of Zara and had excommunicated them anew for attacking Constantinople, readmitted them once again to communion when he realized the "great blessings" that had befallen Christendom by the capture of the schismatic city.

The Crusaders, for their part, returned to Europe with immense booty from the Byzantine metropolis: precious gems, money, and gold. The greatest prize of all was the immense store of relics that the Westerners liberated from the Byzantine capital and brought home. Bones, heads, and arms of saints, Jesus' crown of thorns, St. Thomas the Apostle's doubting finger, and many similar treasures passed into Western Europe at this time. Perhaps more important, the West was given direct access to the intellectual legacy of Greek and Byzantine civilization. But the old hostility between Greeks and Latins was aggravated by the events of the Fourth Crusade into a virtually insurmountable wall of hatred. On a recent visit to Istanbul (the former Constantinople), I found my local guide still muttering about those accursed Crusaders.

Later Crusades

During the thirteenth century, the papacy called for Crusades not only against Muslims in the Holy Land and Spain but also against Albigensian heretics in southern France and even the Holy Roman Emperor. In 1212 a visionary, ill-organized enterprise known as the "Children's Crusade" ended in tragedy. Thousands of boys and girls flocked into the ports of southern Europe, gripped by religious fervor and convinced that the Mediterranean would dry up before them to provide them a miraculous pathway into the Holy Land. Many of them returned home sadder but wiser, and the rest were sold into Muslim slavery.

The next major crusading effort, the Fifth Crusade (1217–1221), was directed not at the Holy Land but at Egypt—the real center of Muslim power in the Near East. The Crusaders captured the key Egyptian port of Damietta in 1219 and refused a Muslim offer to trade Jerusalem for it. But dissension tore the Crusader ranks, and when they moved against Cairo they were caught between a Muslim army and the flooding Nile. The results were military disaster, the abandonment of Damietta, and another joyless homecoming.

Three additional Crusades of importance were undertaken in the thirteenth century, and together they mark a highly significant shift from papal to royal initiative. The first, led by the brilliant emperor, Frederick II, was at once the most fruitful and least violent of the three. Frederick negotiated with the sultan of Egypt rather than fighting him and in 1229 obtained possession of Jerusalem by treaty. The triumph was ephemeral, however, for Jerusalem returned to Muslim hands in 1244. And because of the absence of bloodshed, Frederick II's Crusade was never dignified by being given a number.

The Sixth and Seventh Crusades were led by the saint-king of France, Louis IX. One was undertaken against Egypt in 1248, the other against Tunisia in 1270. Both failed, and the second cost St. Louis his life. Crusades continued to be organized and mounted in subsequent generations, but in 1291 the fall of Acre—the last Christian bridgehead on the Syrian coast—brought an end to the Crusader States in the Holy Land. The reigning pope described this catastrophe as "a doleful cup of bitterness."

One scholar has called the Crusades "medieval Europe's Lost Weekend." But they were more than simply a romantic and bloody fiasco. During the greater part of the High Middle Ages, Christian lords ruled portions of the Holy Land. Their activities caught the imagination of Europe and held it for two centuries, uniting Western Christendom in a single vast effort. At the same time European merchants established permanent bases in Syria and enormously enlarged their role in international commerce. When the Crusaders departed, the merchants remained, continuing their commercial domination of the eastern Mediterranean and, after the capture of Constantinople, the Black Sea as well.

The Crusades gave rise to several religious orders of Christian warriors, bound by monastic rules and dedicated to fighting the Muslims and advancing the crusading cause in every possible way. One such order was the Knights Hospitalers, which drew chiefly on the French for its membership. Another was the Knights Templars, an international brotherhood that acquired great wealth through pious gifts and intelligent estate management and gradually became involved in far-flung banking activities. A third order, the Teutonic Knights, was composed chiefly of Germans. In the thirteenth century the Teutonic Knights transferred their activities from the Holy Land to northern Germany, where they devoted themselves to the eastward thrust of German-Christian civilization against the Slavs. Orders of a similar sort arose on other frontiers of Western Christendom. The Knights of Santiago de Compostela, for example, were dedicated to fighting the Muslims in Spain and furthering the Christian reconquest of the Iberian peninsula. These crusading orders, bridging as they did the two great medieval institutions of monasticism and knighthood, represent the ultimate synthesis of the military and the Christian life. They were widely admired in their time for "going in war to fight, and returning in peace to rest and pray, so that they behave like knights in battle and like monks in convent."

THE GERMAN EASTWARD EXPANSION

Eastern Germany was still another of medieval Europe's expanding frontiers. The German eastward drive was not a product of active royal or papal policy but rather a movement led by local aristocrats, in particular the dukes of Saxony. It was a gradual advance with a great deal of momentum behind it. Over a drawn-out period between about 1125 and 1350, it succeeded in pushing the eastern boundary of German settlement far to the north and east at Slavic expense (see the map on p.185). German military gains were consolidated by the building of innumerable agrarian villages and by a massive eastward migration of German peasants. Consequently, the new areas were not only conquered, they were in large part Christianized and permanently Germanized.

THE GERMAN EASTWARD PENETRATION

■	German before 800
▨	800 – 1400
░	Large minorities 1400
▧	Small minorities 1400

FINNS

SWEDES

DANES

ESTONIANS

LETTS

Baltic Sea

Dvina R.

RUSSIANS

Königsberg

Niemen R.

Lübeck

Elbe R.

Berlin

Magdeburg

Weser R.

Leipzig

Oder R.

POLES

Vistula R.

Breslau

Cracow

Dniester

Dresden

Rhine R.

Prague

BOHEMIANS

MORAVIANS

G E R M A N S

Danube R.

Vienna

Buda

Theiss R.

HUNGARIANS

ITALIANS

Drave R.

Venice

Po R.

CROATS

Danube R.

Adriatic Sea

Scale of Miles

0   100   200   300   400

The later phases of the German push were spearheaded by the Teutonic Knights who penetrated temporarily far northward into Lithuania, Latvia, and Estonia, and even made an unsuccessful bid to conquer Russia. During the fourteenth and fifteenth centuries the Teutonic Knights lost some of their conquests, but much of the German expansion proved to be permanent. The epoch between 1125 and 1350 witnessed the conquest and Germanization of large portions of modern East Germany and western Poland.

THE CLOSING OF THE HIGH-MEDIEVAL FRONTIERS

In the later thirteenth and early fourteenth centuries European expansion was coming to an end. The internal frontiers of forest and swamp had by then been won. The best farmlands had been reclaimed. And Europe's external frontiers were everywhere hardening, sometimes even receding as in the Holy Land. But by then the high-medieval territorial expansion had made its essential contribution to Europe's economic future. The expansion was at once a product of commercial growth and a powerful stimulus to further growth. At a time when European cities were still relatively small, Christian knights won for the Latin West such wealthy metropolises as Palermo, Toledo, Antioch, Cordova, and Constantinople. As a result of their capture, and of the extension of Christian maritime dominion into the eastern Mediterranean and the Black and Baltic Seas, money and precious goods flooded back into the towns and river valleys of the European heartland. The transformation that they wrought would never be undone.

11

New Paths to God: Monks, Friars, and Religious Rebels

THE CHURCH IN THE HIGH MIDDLE AGES

During the High Middle Ages, frontiers of all sorts were being explored and extended. Scholars were pioneering in new intellectual frontiers; artists and writers were adding ever-new dimensions to Western culture. Administrators were pushing forward the art of government. And underlying all these changes—which will be explored in the next chapters—was a deepening of the religious impulse that expressed itself in many different ways: in the rise of a vigorous papacy dedicated to reform and the creation of a Christian world order,* in the development of new forms of monasticism, in the rapid expansion of ecclesiastical administration and Church activities, in the intensification of lay piety, and in the growth of heresy.

Medieval religion followed many different paths. It could be devoutly orthodox, it could be anticlerical, and it could be openly heretical. Yet its basic institutional expression was the Catholic Church, and the most obvious characteristic that the vast majority of Western Christians had in common was their Catholicism. Nationalism was just then emerging, and the perspectives and allegiances of most Europeans tended to be at once local and international. In the twelfth and thirteenth centuries the majority of people were still parochial in their outlook, only vaguely aware of what was going on beyond their immediate surroundings. But alongside their localism was an element of cosmopolitanism—a consciousness of belonging to the international commonwealth of Western Christendom, fragmented politically, but united by a common faith, by the growing power of the papacy, and by a shared enthusiasm toward the Crusades.

*See Chapter 12.

187

The Church in the High Middle Ages was a powerful unifying influence. It had made notable progress since the half-heathen pre-Carolingian era. A flourishing parish system was by now spreading across the European countryside to bring the sacraments and a modicum of Christian instruction to the peasantry. New bishoprics and archbishoprics were formed, and old ones were becoming steadily more active. The papacy never completely succeeded in breaking the control of kings and secular lords over their local bishops, but by the twelfth century it was coming to exercise a very real authority over European bishops. And the growing efficiency of the papal bureaucracy evoked the envy and imitation of the rising royal governments.

The Sacraments

The buoyancy of high-medieval Europe is nowhere more evident than in the accelerating impact of Christian piety on European society. The sacraments of the Church introduced a significant religious dimension into the life of ordinary Europeans: their births were sanctified by the sacrament of *baptism*, in which they were cleansed of the taint of original sin and initiated into the Christian fellowship. At puberty they received the sacrament of *confirmation*, which reaffirmed their membership in the Church and gave them the additional grace to cope with the problems of adulthood. Christian couples were united in the sacrament of *matrimony*. And if a man chose the calling of the Christian ministry, he was spiritually transformed into a priest and "married" to the Church by the sacrament of *holy orders*. As death approached, the sacrament of *extreme unction* prepared the soul for its journey into the next world. And throughout their lives, Christians could receive forgiveness from the damning consequences of mortal sin by repenting their past transgressions and receiving the comforting sacrament of *penance*. Finally they might partake regularly of the central sacrament of the Church—the *Eucharist*—receiving the body of Christ into their own bodies by consuming the Eucharistic bread. Thus, the Church through its seven sacraments brought God's grace to all its members, great and humble, at every critical juncture of their lives. The sacramental system, which only assumed final form in the High Middle Ages, was a source of comfort and reassurance: it made communion with God not merely the elusive goal of a few mystics but the periodic experience of all believers. And, of course, it established the Church as the essential intermediary between God and humanity.

The Evolution of Piety

The ever-increasing scope of the Church, together with the rising self-awareness of the new age, resulted in a deepening of popular piety throughout Western Europe. The High Middle Ages witnessed a shift in religious attitude from the awe and mystery characteristic of earlier Christianity to a new emotionalism and dynamism. This shift is evident in ecclesiastical architec-

ture, as the earthbound Romanesque style gave way during the twelfth century to the tense, upward-reaching Gothic.* A parallel change is evident in
devotional practice, as the divine Christ sitting in judgment gave way to the
tragic figure of the human Christ suffering on the cross for the sins of humanity. And it was in the High Middle Ages that the Virgin Mary came into
her own as the compassionate intercessor for hopelessly lost souls. A legend
of the age told of the devil complaining to God that the tender-hearted Queen
of Heaven was cheating hell of its most promising candidates. Christianity
became, as never before, a doctrine of love, hope, and compassion. The God
of Justice became the merciful, suffering God of Love.

Like most human institutions, the medieval Church fell short of its ideals.
Despite its theoretically centralized command structure (popes to archbishops to bishops to priests), lines of communication had a way of getting
clogged. Ecclesiastical courts were deluged with jurisdictional disputes in
which abbots sought exemption from the control of bishops, and bishops from
archbishops. A bishop who ignored or deliberately "misunderstood" papal
commands was difficult to dislodge. And communications could be terribly
slow. It might take half a year for an archbishop of Canterbury to journey to
Rome, consult with the pope, and return to England.

Furthermore, an immense gulf separated the religious beliefs of popes
and theologians from those of common townspeople and peasants. The supernatural ideas of ordinary people in any society, including our own, will
include a variety of odd notions (a relative of mine transcribes messages from
the dead; a "nonfiction" bestseller insists that the pyramids were built by space-
men). It should come as no surprise that popular attitudes in prescientific societies tend to be at least as implausible. The God of the high-medieval theologians was a God of love and reason. But in the popular mind he became a
kind of divine magician who could shield his favorites from the hunger, pain,
disease, and sudden death that afflicted all humanity until quite recent times
and afflicts much of humanity still.

To such people, religion offered three desperately needed things: the
hope of eternal salvation from a harsh, threatening world; an explanation for
human suffering (as a spiritual discipline necessary for paradise); and the promise of a better life here and now. Of course religion continues to offer these
things, but in the Middle Ages, when human need was more intense and
more immediate, the popular practice of the Christian religion was quite unlike what it is today. There was a far greater emphasis on acquiring divine
favor through mechanical means such as charms, pilgrimages, holy images,
and the relics of saints.

The most cherished relics of all were those associated with Christ and
the Virgin Mary. Since both were believed to have ascended bodily into
heaven, relics of the usual sort were ruled out, but there remained pieces of

*See pp. 271 ff.

their clothing, fragments of the True Cross, vials of Christ's blood and the Virgin's milk, Christ's baby teeth, his umbilical cord, and the foreskin removed at his circumcision. Reading Abbey, founded in southern England in the 1120s, had acquired hundreds of relics by the end of the twelfth century, including twenty-nine relics of Christ, six of the Virgin Mary, nineteen of the Old Testament patriarchs and prophets, and fourteen of the apostles. As a result of its avid collecting, Reading became a prosperous pilgrimage center—yet it was merely one of many. Chartres had the Virgin Mary's tunic; Canterbury had the body of St. Thomas Becket; Santiago de Compostela had the bones of St. James the Apostle (except for his arm, which was at Reading); Paris acquired Christ's crown of thorns after it had been taken from Constantinople following the Fourth Crusade. Indeed, there was scarcely a town or rural district in all Christendom that did not possess some relic or protective image.

Each medieval trade honored its own particular saint. Potters offered special devotions to St. Gore, painters to St. Luke, horse doctors to St. Loy, dentists to St. Apolline. And there was an appropriate saint for almost every known disease. Plague sufferers prayed to St. Roch; St. Romane specialized in mental illnesses, St. Clare in afflictions of the eye, St. Agatha in sore breasts. In southern France a cult developed around a watchdog who was said to have been mistakenly killed by his master while defending his master's infant child; peasants began bringing their sick and deformed children to the grave of the sainted dog in expectation of miraculous healing. The healing powers associated with saints, human or not, satisfied a widespread longing for supernatural protection against dangers and afflictions that seemed beyond human comprehension. The doubts of the theologians were drowned out by the clamor of popular demand.

Such attitudes received innocent encouragement from ill-educated parish priests and from bishops and abbots anxious to attract floods of pilgrims to their churches. The relic cult could be justified up to a point by the Catholic doctrine of the Communion of Saints—the caring fellowship of all Christians, whether in this world or the next. But in its obsession with the supernatural powers of material objects, popular belief carried a residue from long-ago days of pagan magic.

The high-medieval Church suffered not only from popular credulity but from corruption as well. Corrupt churchmen were in evidence throughout the era—a result of the unfortunate necessity of staffing the Church with human beings. Some historians have delighted in cataloging instances of larcenous bishops, gluttonous priests, and licentious nuns. But cases such as these were clearly exceptional. The great shortcoming of the high-medieval Church was not gross corruption but rather a creeping complacency that resulted sometimes in a shallow, mechanical attitude toward the Christian religious life and an obsession with ecclesiastical property. The medieval Church had more than its share of saints, but among much of the clergy the profundity of the Faith was often lost in the day-to-day affairs of the pastoral office, the management of large estates, disputes over land and privileges, and ecclesiastical status seeking. Anyone familiar with modern politicians and academic administrators will appreciate the problem.

Changes in Monastic Life

The drift toward complacency has been a recurring trend in Christian monasticism. Again and again, the idealism of a monastic reform movement has been eroded and transformed by time and success until, at length, new reform movements arise in protest against the growing worldliness of old ones. This cycle has been repeated countless times. Indeed, the sixth-century Benedictine movement was itself a protest against the excesses and inadequacies of earlier monasticism. St. Benedict had regarded his new order as a means of withdrawing from the world and devoting full time to communion with God. But despite Benedict's ideal, the order became involved in teaching, evangelism, and ecclesiastical reform, and by the tenth and eleventh centuries the whole Benedictine movement had become immersed in worldly affairs. Benedictine monasteries controlled extensive lands, operated Europe's best schools, supplied contingents of knights to feudal armies, and worked closely with secular princes in affairs of state.

Early in the tenth century the Cluniac movement, which was itself Benedictine in spirit and rule, arose in protest against the worldliness and complacency of contemporary Benedictine monasticism.* For more than two centuries thereafter, the congregation of Cluny was a powerful force for Christian reform and social peace, though the monastic devotional life remained uppermost in the minds of Cluniac monks. During the twelfth century, however, Cluniac houses were showing traces of the very complacency against which they had originally rebelled. Prosperous, respected, and secure, Cluny was too content with its majestic abbeys and priories, its elaborate liturgical program, and its bounteous fields to give its wholehearted support to the radical transformation of society for which many Christian reformers were now struggling.

Chronology of High Medieval Monasticism and Heterodoxy

909:	Founding of Cluny
1084:	Establishment of Carthusian Order
1098:	Establishment of Cîteaux
1112–1153:	Career of St. Bernard of Clairvaux as a Cistercian
1128:	Original rule of the Knights Templars
c.1173:	Beginning of the Waldensian movement
1208:	Innocent III calls the Albigensian Crusade
1210:	Innocent III authorizes the Franciscan order
1216:	Dominican Rule sanctioned by the papacy
1226:	Death of St. Francis

*See pp. 133–134.

As the twelfth century progressed, the Benedictines saw their educational monopoly gradually broken by the rising schools and universities of the new towns. These urban schools produced increasing numbers of well-trained scholars who in time overshadowed the Benedictines as scribes and advisers to princes. With the steady advance of urbanization, the traditional Benedictine contributions to society diminished.

Still, the Benedictines retained their great landed wealth. The Benedictine monastery was scarcely the sanctuary from worldly concerns that St. Benedict had planned. The larger Benedictine monasteries and nunneries accepted novices only from the aristocracy and required in return a substantial entrance gift from the novice's family—usually a landed estate. Aristocratic parents designated younger offspring for monastic careers at the time of their birth and sent them off to monasteries or nunneries well before adolescence for education and training in the religious life. In short, future monks and nuns, like future brides and grooms, found their lives shaped by parental decisions based on family strategy. They themselves had little choice in the matter. Some developed into devoted servants of God; others simply went through the motions.

Carthusians and Cistercians

A great many new religious orders emerged during the High Middle Ages. They were founded by ardent reformers and peopled by men and women who had chosen their religious vocations for themselves, as adults. The increasing possibility of career choices resulted, among many, in a heightened sense of self-awareness. It was not so much a rise of individualism (in the modern, rather lonely sense) as a new freedom to choose between a number of different kinds of communal life—a discovery of self through community. This opportunity for self-conscious choice was provided by the growing numbers of towns, guilds, newly founded peasant communes, and, above all, new monastic orders. And the fact that their members had joined out of free choice, and after serious self-examination, gave the new orders a spiritual intensity absent from traditional Benedictine monasticism.

Perhaps the most demanding of the new orders, the Carthusians, emerged in eastern France in the late eleventh century and spread across Christendom in the twelfth. Isolated from the outside world, the Carthusians lived in small groups, worshiping together in communal chapels, but otherwise living as hermits in individual cells. This austere order has survived to the present day and, unlike most monastic movements, its discipline has seldom waned. Yet even in the spiritually charged atmosphere of the twelfth century it was a small movement, offering a way of life for only an heroically holy minority. Too ascetic for the average Christian, the Carthusian order was much admired but seldom joined.

The greatest monastic force of the twelfth century, the Cistercian order, managed for a time to be both austere and popular. The mother house of the order, Cîteaux, was established by a little group of Benedictine dissenters in 1098 on a wild, remote site in eastern France. The Cistercian order grew slowly at first, then gradually acquired momentum. In 1115 Cîteaux had four daughter houses; by the end of the century it had five hundred.

Like Cîteaux, many of its houses were deliberately built in remote wilderness areas. The abbeys themselves were stark and undecorated in contrast to the elaborate Cluniac architecture of the time. Cistercian life was stark as well—less severe than that of the Carthusians but far more so than that of the Cluniacs. The Cistercian order admitted no children but only adults certain of their religious vocation. They also admitted peasant lay brothers, known as *conversi*, who worked the Cistercian fields and were bound by vows of chastity and obedience but were permitted to follow a less demanding form of the Cistercian life than the monks. The admission of *conversi* into the order represents a compassionate outreach to the illiterate peasantry and, at the same time, a solution to the labor shortage on Cistercian lands.

The Cistercian monks and nuns sought to revive the simple, austere life of the early Benedictines. Their houses were unheated, even in the chill north-European winters; their diet was limited to black bread, water, and a few stewed vegetables; they were forbidden to speak except when it was absolutely essential. The numerous Cistercian houses were bound together not by the authority of a central abbot, as at Cluny, but by an annual council of all Cistercian abbots meeting at Cîteaux. Without such centralized control it is unlikely that the individual houses could have clung for long to the strict ascetic ideals on which the order was founded.

The key figure in twelfth-century Cistercianism was St. Bernard, whom we have already encountered preaching the Second Crusade. Bernard joined the community of Cîteaux in 1112 as a young man; three years later he became the founder and abbot of Clairvaux, one of Cîteaux's earliest daughter houses. St. Bernard of Clairvaux was the foremost Christian of his age—a mystic, an eloquent religious orator, an exceptionally gifted writer, and a crucial figure in the meteoric rise of the Cistercian order. His moral influence was so immense that he became Europe's leading arbiter of political and ecclesiastical disputes. Besides inducing the king of France and the Holy Roman emperor to participate in the Second Crusade, he persuaded Christendom to accept his candidate in the years following a hotly disputed papal election in 1130. On one occasion he even succeeded in reconciling the two great warring families of Germany, the Welfs and Hohenstaufens. He rebuked the pope himself: "Remember, first of all, that the Holy Roman Church, over which you hold sway, is the mother of churches, not their sovereign mistress—that you yourself are not the lord of bishops, but one among them." And he took an uncompromising stand against one of the rising movements of his day: the attempt to reconcile the Catholic faith with human reason, led by the brilliant philosopher Peter Abelard. In the long run Bernard failed to halt the growth of Christian rationalism, but he succeeded in making life miserable for Abelard and in securing the official condemnation of certain of Abelard's teachings.*

*See pp. 287–288.

Above and beyond his obvious talents for diplomacy and persuasion, St. Bernard won the devotion of twelfth-century Europe through his reputation for sanctity. He was widely regarded as a saint in his own lifetime, and stories of his miracles circulated far and wide. Pilgrims flocked to Clairvaux to be healed by his touch. This aspect of Bernard's reputation made his skillful preaching and diplomacy even more effective than it would otherwise have been. For here was a holy man, a miracle worker, who engaged in severe fasts, overworked himself to an extraordinary degree, wore coarse clothing, and devoted himself singlemindedly to the service of God.

On one occasion St. Bernard commanded Duke William of Aquitaine to reinstate certain bishops whom the duke had driven from their sees. When, after much persuasion, the duke remained obstinate, St. Bernard celebrated a High Mass for him. Holding the consecrated host in his hands, Bernard advanced from the altar toward the duke and said,

> We have besought you, and you have spurned us. The united
> multitude of the servants of God, meeting you elsewhere, have
> entreated you, and you have scorned them. Behold! Here comes to you
> the Virgin's Son, the Head and Lord of the Church which you
> persecute! Your Judge is here, at whose name every knee shall
> bow.... Your Judge is here, into whose hands your soul is to pass! Will
> you spurn him also? Will you scorn him as you have scorned his
> servants?

The duke threw himself on the ground and submitted to Bernard's demands.

Bernard's career demonstrates the essential paradox of Cistercianism. For although the Cistercians strove to dissociate themselves from the world, Bernard was drawn into the vortex of secular affairs. Indeed, as the twelfth century progressed, the entire Cistercian movement became increasingly involved in the world outside. And like the later Puritans and Quakers, the Cistercians discovered that their twin virtues of austere living and hard work resulted in an accumulation of wealth and, eventually, a corrosion of their spiritual simplicity. Their efforts to clear fields around their remote abbeys contributed to the advance of Europe's internal frontiers. They consolidated and managed their lands with considerable skill and introduced improvements in the breeding of horses, cattle, and sheep. The English Cistercians became the great wool producers of the realm. Altogether the Cistercians exerted a progressive influence on European husbandry and came to play a prominent role in the agrarian economy. Economic success brought ever-increasing wealth to the order. Cistercian abbey churches became more elaborate, and the austerity of Cistercian life was progressively relaxed. In later years there emerged new offshoots, such as the Trappists, which returned to the strict observance of the early Cistercians.

Monasticism in the World

The Cistercians had endeavored to withdraw from the world yet became a powerful force in twelfth-century Europe. At roughly the same time, other orders were being established with the deliberate aim of participating actively in society and working toward its regeneration. The Augustinian Canons, for example, submitted to the rigor of a rule, yet carried on normal ecclesiastical duties in the world, serving in parish churches and cathedrals. The fusion of monastic discipline and worldly activity culminated in the twelfth-century crusading orders—the Knights Templars, Knights Hospitalers, Teutonic Knights, and similar groups—whose ideal was a synthesis of the monastic and the military life for the purpose of expanding the political frontiers of Western Christendom. These and other efforts to direct the spiritual vigor of monastic life toward the regeneration of Christian society typify the visions and hopes of the new, emotionally charged piety of twelfth-century Europe.

Heresies and the Inquisition

The surge of popular piety also resulted in a flood of criticism against the Church itself. It was not that churchmen had grown worse, but rather that the laity had begun to judge them by more rigorous standards. Popular dissatisfaction toward the workaday Church spurred the rush toward the austere twelfth-century monastic orders. Yet the majority of Christians could not become monks, and, for them, certain new heretical doctrines began to exert a powerful appeal.

The heresies of the High Middle Ages flourished particularly in the rising towns of southern Europe. The eleventh-century urban revolution had caught the Church unprepared. The new towns were becoming centers of a burgeoning lay piety, yet the Church, with its roots in the older agrarian order, seemed unable to minister effectively to the vigorous and widely literate new burgher class. Too often the urban bishops appeared as political oppressors and enemies of burghal independence rather than spiritual directors. Too often the Church failed to understand the town dwellers' problems and aspirations or to anticipate their growing suspicion of ecclesiastical wealth and power. Although most townspeople remained loyal to the Church, a minority, particularly in the south, turned to new, anticlerical sects. In their denunciation of ecclesiastical wealth, these sects were doing nothing more than St. Bernard and the Cistercians had done. But many of the anticlerical sects crossed the narrow line between orthodox reformism and heresy by preaching without episcopal or papal approval. Far more important, they denied the exclusive right of the priesthood to perform sacraments.

One such sect, the Waldensians, was founded by a merchant of Lyons named Valdez, later known as Peter Waldo. Around 1173, he gave all his possessions to the poor and took up a life of apostolic poverty. He and his followers sought the Church's permission to preach in the towns. The Church refused, after some confusion and delay, because of its uneasiness about the preaching of untrained lay people who, among the Waldensians, included women as well as men. The Church preferred to leave religious instruction in the hands of ordained males. But Peter Waldo and his followers continued their preaching. This act of defiance, along with their growing doubts about the special spiritual status of the priesthood, earned them the condemnation of the Church.

Similar groups, some orthodox, some heretical, arose in the communes of Lombardy and were known as the *Humiliati*. These groups proved troublesome to the local ecclesiastical hierarchies, but generally they escaped downright condemnation, unless they themselves took the step of denying the authority of the Church. Many of them did take that step, however, and by the opening of the thirteenth century, heretical, anticlerical sects were spreading across northern Italy and southern France, and even into Spain and Germany.

The most popular heresy in southern France was associated with a group known as the *Cathari* (the pure) or the Albigensians—after the town of Albi where they were particularly strong. The Albigensians represented a fusion of two traditions: (1) the anticlerical protest against ecclesiastical wealth and power, and (2) an exotic theology derived originally from Persia. The Albigensians recognized two gods: the god of good who reigned over the universe of the spirit, and the god of evil who ruled the world of matter. The Old Testament God, creator of the material universe, was their god of evil; Christ, whom they regarded as a purely spiritual being with a phantom body, was the god of good. The Albigensians believed in reincarnation, and their goal was to break free of the cycle of physical rebirth. Their morality stressed a rigorous rejection of all material things—of physical appetites, wealth, worldly vanities, and sexual intercourse—in the hope of one day escaping from the prison of the body and ascending to the realm of pure spirit. In reality this severe ethic was practiced only by a small elite of spiritual men and women known as *perfecti* ("perfect ones"); the rank and file normally ate well, made love, and participated only vicariously in the rejection of the material world—by criticizing the affluence of the Church. Indeed, their opponents accused them of gross licentiousness. And although such accusations were grotesquely exaggerated, it does seem likely that some Provençal nobles were attracted to the new teaching by the opportunity of appropriating Church lands in good conscience.

As the thirteenth century dawned, the Albigensian heresy was spreading so swiftly that it posed a dangerous threat to the unity of Christendom and the authority of the Church. Pope Innocent III, recognizing the gravity of the situation, tried with every means in his power to eradicate the heresy. He pressed for the reform of the southern French clergy by the removal of incompetent and corrupt clerics; he urged the nobility to help suppress the Albigensians (whom he regarded as traitors against God); and he encouraged the revitalization of the faith through orthodox preaching. When none of these measures succeeded, he responded to the murder of a papal legate in southern France in 1208 by summoning a crusade against the Albigensians.

The Albigensian Crusade was a savage affair that succeeded only after two decades of bloodshed. The French monarchy intervened in its final stages and brought it to a successful conclusion at last in 1229. Southern France recovered quickly from the ravages of the Crusade, with some help from the kings of France who now extended their authority to the Mediterranean. The power of the Albigensians was crushed, and there remained only the task of mopping up some hard-core survivors and ensuring that the region would thereafter remain staunchly orthodox.

To serve these ends an institution emerged that will always stand as a grim symbol of the medieval Church at its worst: the Inquisition. Christian persecution of heretics dates from the fourth century, but it was not until the High Middle Ages that heterodox views presented a serious problem to European society. Traditionally, the task of converting or punishing heretics was handled at the local level, but in the early 1230s the papacy established a central tribunal for the purpose of standardizing procedures and increasing efficiency. The procedures of the Inquisition included torture, secret testimony, conviction on the testimony of only two witnesses, the denial of legal council to the accused, and other practices offensive to the Anglo-American legal tradition but not especially remarkable by the standards of the times. Many of these methods, including torture, were drawn from the customs of Roman law.

The Inquisition aroused strong regional opposition, but less on humanitarian grounds than on the grounds that papal officials were usurping the traditional rights of bishops and lay lords. Most inquisitors endeavored to act fairly, and the great majority of persons whom they convicted of heresy were given prison sentences or lesser penances (such as wearing crosses over their clothing) instead of being condemned to death. The Inquisition was the first Western European institution to employ imprisonment on a large scale. And inquisitors often felt frustrated by the difficulty of their task. An inquisitor of the 1230s complained,

> Serious problems beset the investigator from every side. On the one hand, his conscience torments him if an individual be punished who has neither confessed nor been proven guilty. On the other, it causes even more anguish to the mind of the inquisitor, familiar through much experience with the falsity, cunning, and malice of such persons, if by their wily astuteness they escape punishment to the detriment of the faith, since they are thereby strengthened, multiplied, and rendered more crafty.

The Inquisition cannot be justified, but, like all historical episodes, it can be explained. To the medieval Catholic, heresy was a hateful thing, a betrayal of Christ and a source of infection to others. Human beings have often found it difficult to respond calmly to attacks on their most deeply cherished beliefs, and if we regard the Inquisition simply as an act of senseless cruelty perpetrated long ago by people very different from ourselves, then we will have learned nothing from it.

MENDICANTISM

The thirteenth-century Church found another answer to the heretical drift that was far more compassionate and effective than the Inquisition. In the opening decades of the century two new religious orders emerged—the Dominican and Franciscan—which were devoted to a life of poverty, preaching, and charitable deeds. Rejecting the life of the cloister, they dedicated themselves to religious work in the world—particularly in the towns. Benedictines had traditionally taken vows of personal poverty, but their monasteries could and did acquire great corporate wealth. The Dominicans and Franciscans, on the contrary, were pledged to both personal and corporate poverty. They would accept no lands, whether developed or undeveloped, and they drew their earliest members not from the aristocracy but from lower levels of society. Appropriately, they were known as "mendicants"—"beggars." Through their preaching and works of charity, they drained urban heresy of much of its former support by demonstrating to townspeople that Christian orthodoxy could be both relevant and compelling.

The Dominicans

St. Dominic (1170–1221), a well-educated Spaniard, spent his early manhood in Castile serving as an Augustinian Canon. In his mid-thirties he traveled to Rome, met Pope Innocent III, and followed the pope's bidding to preach in southern France against the Albigensians. For the next decade, between 1205 and 1215, he worked among the heretics, leading an austere, humble life. His eloquence and simplicity won him considerable renown, but few converts.

The Dominican order evolved out of a small group of volunteers who joined Dominic in his work among the Albigensians. Gradually Dominic came to see the possibility of a far larger mission: to preach and win converts to the faith throughout the world. In 1215 Dominic's friend, the bishop of Toulouse, gave the group a church and a house in the city, and shortly thereafter the papacy recognized the Dominicans as a separate religious order and approved the Dominican rule.

The congregation founded by Dominic was to be known as the Order of Friars Preachers. It assumed its permanent shape during the years between its formal establishment in 1216 and Dominic's death in 1221, by which time it had grown to include some five hundred friars and sixty priories organized into eight provinces embracing the whole of Western Europe. The Dominicans stood in the vanguard of thirteenth-century piety. Their order attracted people of imagination and unusual religious dedication who could not be satisfied with the enclosed, tradition-bound life of earlier monasticism but were challenged by the austerity of the Dominican rule, the disciplined vitality of the order, and the goal of working toward the moral regeneration of society.

The Dominican rule drew freely from the earlier rule of the Augustinian Canons that Dominic had known in his youth, but added new elements and provided a novel direction for the religious life. The order was to be headed by a minister-general, elected for life, and a legislative body that met annually. It was to include communities of women as well as of men. The friars themselves belonged not to a particular house, but to the order at large. Their place of residence and sphere of activity were determined by the minister-general. Their life included such rigors as midnight services, total abstinence from meat, frequent fasts, and prolonged periods of mandatory silence. And the entire order was strictly bound by the rule of poverty Dominic had learned from his contemporary, St. Francis. Not only should poverty be the condition of individual Dominicans as it was of individual Benedictines, it was to be the condition of the order itself. The Dominican order was to have no possessions except churches and priories. It was to have no fixed incomes and no manors but was to subsist through charitable gifts.

The order expanded at a phenomenal rate during the course of the thirteenth century. Dominican friars carried their evangelical activities across Europe and beyond, into the Holy Land, Central Asia, Tartary, Tibet, and China. Joining the faculties of the rising universities, they became the leading proponents of Aristotelian philosophy and included in their numbers such notable scholars as Albertus Magnus and Thomas Aquinas. Dominic himself had insisted that his followers acquire broad educations before undertaking their mission of preaching and that each Dominican priory maintain a school of theology. Within a few decades after his death his order included some of the foremost intellects of the age.

The Dominicans were, above all, preachers, and their particular mission was to preach among heretics and non-Christians. Their contact with heretics brought them into close involvement with the Inquisition, and they themselves became the leading inquisitors. They took pride in their nickname *Domini canes*—"hounds of God"—which suggested their role as watchdogs of the Catholic Faith. To religious rebels, the nickname bore an ominous connotation.

The Dominican order still flourishes. The rule of corporate poverty was softened increasingly; finally, in the fifteenth century, it was dropped altogether in deference to the great truth that scholar-teachers cannot be expected to beg or do odd jobs. But long after their original mendicant ideals were modified, the Dominicans remained committed to their central mission of championing Catholic orthodoxy.

Saint Francis

Dominic's contemporary, St. Francis (c 1182–1226), is perhaps the most widely admired figure of the Middle Ages. A product of the medieval urban revolution, he was the son of a wealthy cloth merchant of Assisi in central Italy. As a youth he was generous, high-spirited, and popular, and in time he became the leader of a boisterous teenage gang. As one writer aptly expressed it, he "seems altogether to have been rather a festive figure."

In his early twenties St. Francis underwent a profound religious conversion that occurred in several steps. It began on the occasion of a banquet that he was giving for some of his friends. After the banquet Francis and his companions went into the town with torches, singing in the streets. Francis was crowned with garlands as king of the revelers, but after a time he disappeared and was found in a religious trance. Thereafter, he devoted himself to solitude, prayer, and service to the poor. He went as a pilgrim to Rome, where he is reported to have exchanged clothes with a beggar and spent the day begging with other beggars. Returning to Assisi, he encountered an impoverished leper, and notwithstanding his fear of leprosy, he gave the poor man all the money he was carrying and kissed his hand. Thenceforth he devoted himself to the service of lepers and hospitals.

To the consternation of his bourgeois father, Francis now went about Assisi dressed in rags, giving to the poor. His former companions pelted him with mud, and his father, fearing that Francis's almsgiving would consume the family fortune, disinherited him. Francis left home singing a French song and spent the next three years of his life in the environs of Assisi, living in abject poverty. He ministered to lepers and social outcasts and continued to embarrass his family by his unconventional behavior. It was at this time that he began to frequent a crumbling little chapel known as the Portiuncula. One day in the year 1209, while attending Mass there, he was struck by the words of the Gospel that the priest was reading:

> Everywhere on your road preach and say, "The Kingdom of God is at
> hand." Cure the sick, raise the dead, cleanse the lepers, drive out
> devils. Freely have you received; freely give. Carry neither gold nor
> silver nor money in your belts, nor bag, nor two coats, nor sandals, nor
> staff, for the workman is worthy of his hire.*

Francis at once accepted this injunction and immediately thereafter—even though a layman—began to preach to the poor.

Disciples now joined him, and when he had about a dozen followers he is said to have remarked, "Let us go to our Mother, the Holy Roman Church, and tell the pope what the Lord has begun to do through us and carry it out with papal approval." This may seem a naive approach to the masterful, aristocratic Pope Innocent III, yet when Francis came to Rome in 1210, Innocent sanctioned his work. Doubtless the pope saw in the Franciscan mission a potential orthodox counterpoise to the Waldensians, Albigensians, and other heretical groups who had been winning masses of converts from the Church by the example of their poverty and simplicity. For here was a man whose loyalty to Catholicism was beyond question and whose own artless simplicity might bring erring souls back into the Church. Already Innocent III had given his blessing to movements similar to that of Francis. An orthodox group of *Humiliati* had received his sanction in 1201, and in 1208 he permitted a converted Waldensian to found an order known as the "Poor Catholics," which was dedicated to lay preaching. In Francis's movement the pope must have seen still another opportunity to encourage a much-needed wave of reform within the orthodox framework. And it may well be that Francis's glowing spirituality appealed to the sanctity of Innocent himself, for the pope, even though a great man of affairs, was genuinely pious. However this may be,

*Matthew, 10:7–10.

This much restored frescoe in the Lower Church of St. Francis of
Assisi is the earliest known depiction of St. Francis. It is ascribed to
the thirteenth-century Italian painter Cimabue (*c.* 1240–1302).

thirteenth-century Europe deserves some credit for embracing a movement
that in many other ages would have been persecuted or ridiculed. Rome crucified Christ, whereas the medieval West took Francis to its heart and made
him a saint. But the hard edges of Franciscan religious austerity were blunted
in the process.

Immediately after the papal interview Francis and his followers returned to the neighborhood of Assisi. They were given the Portiuncula as their own chapel, and over the years it continued to serve as the headquarters of the Franciscan movement. Around it the friars built huts of branches and twigs. The Portiuncula was a headquarters but not a home, for the friars were always on the move, wandering in pairs over the country, dressed in peasants' clothing, preaching, serving, and living in conscious imitation of Christ.

During the next decade the order expanded at a spectacular rate. Franciscans were soon to be found throughout northern Italy; by Francis's death in 1226, Franciscan missions were active in France, Germany, England, Hungary, Spain, Morocco, Turkey, and the Holy Land, and the friars numbered in the thousands. The captivating personality of Francis himself was doubtless a crucial factor in his order's popularity, but it also owed much to the fact that its ideals harmonized with the highest religious aspirations of the age. Urban heresy lost some of its allure as the cheerful, devoted Franciscans began to pour into Europe's cities, preaching in the crowded streets and setting a living example of Christian sanctity.

The Franciscan ideal was based above all on the imitation of Christ. Fundamental to this ideal was the notion of poverty, both individual and corporate. The Franciscans subsisted by working and serving in return for their food and other necessities. Humility also was a part of the idea; Francis named his followers the "Friars Minor" (little brothers). Preaching was an important part of their mission, and it answered an urgent need in the cities where the Church had hitherto responded inadequately to the growing religious hunger of the townspeople. Perhaps most attractive of all was the quality of joyousness, akin to the joyousness that Francis had shown prior to his conversion, but directed now toward spiritual ends. Contemporaries referred to Francis affectionately as "God's own troubadour."

Pious people of other times have fled the world; the Albigensians renounced it as the epitome of evil. But Francis embraced it joyfully as the handiwork of God. In his "Song of Brother Sun" he expressed poetically his holy commitment to the physical universe:

Praise be to you, my Lord, for all your creatures,
Above all Brother Sun
Who brings us the day, and lends us his light;
Beautiful is he, radiant with great splendor,
And speaks to us of you, O most high.
Praise to you, my Lord, for Sister Moon and for the stars;
In heaven you have set them, clear and precious and fair.
Praise to you, my Lord, for Brother Wind,
For air and clouds, for calm and all weather
By which you support life in all your creatures.
Praise to you, my Lord, for Sister Water
Which is so helpful and humble, precious and pure.
Praise to you, my Lord, for Brother Fire,
By whom you light up the night;

And fair is he, and joyous, and mighty, and strong.
Praise to you, my Lord, for our sister, Mother Earth,
Who sustains and directs us,
And brings forth varied fruits, and plants,
and flowers bright.
Praise and bless my Lord, and give him thanks,
And serve him with great humility.

Early Franciscanism was too good to last. The order was becoming too large to retain its original disorganized simplicity. Francis was no administrator, and well before his death the movement was passing beyond his control. In 1219–1220 he traveled to Egypt in an effort to convert its Muslim inhabitants—a hopeless task, but Francis was never dismayed by the impossible—and while he was away it became apparent that his order required a more coherent organization than he had seen fit to provide it. Many perplexing questions now arose: With thousands of friars invading the begging market, what would become of the common tramp? Would Europe's generosity be overstrained? Above all, how could these crowds of friars be expected to cleave to the ideal without an explicit rule and without Francis's personal presence to inspire and guide them? In short, could the Franciscan ideal be practical on a large scale? For the movement was proliferating at a remarkable rate. Besides the Friars Minor themselves, a Second Order was established— a female order directed by Francis's friend, St. Clare—known as the "Poor Clares." And a third group, consisting of part-time Franciscans known as "Tertiaries," dedicated themselves to the Franciscan way while continuing their former careers in the world. The little band of Franciscan brothers had evolved into a multitude.

On his return from the Near East, Francis prevailed on a powerful friend, Cardinal Hugolino—later Pope Gregory IX—to become the order's protector. On Hugolino's initiative, a formal rule was drawn up in 1220 that provided a certain degree of administrative structure to the order. A probationary period was established for initiates, who, after completing it, were required to take lifetime vows. And the rule of absolute poverty was softened. In 1223 a shorter, somewhat laxer rule was instituted, and over the years and decades that followed, the movement continued to evolve from the ideal to the practical.

St. Francis himself withdrew more and more from involvement in the order's administration. At the meeting of the general chapter in 1220, he resigned his formal leadership of the movement with the words, "Lord, I give you back this family that you entrusted to me. You know, most sweet Jesus, that I no longer have the power and qualities to continue to take care of it." In 1224, St. Francis underwent a mystical experience atop Mt. Alverno in the Apennines, and legend has it that he received the *stigmata** on that occasion. It is not entirely clear how St. Francis reacted to the evolution of his order,

*The stigmata, which have been attributed to several saints, consist of wounds or scars, supposedly of supernatural origin, that correspond to those sustained by Christ in his crucifixion.

but in his closing years his mysticism deepened, his health declined, and he kept much to himself. At his death in 1226 he was universally mourned, and the order that he had founded remained the most powerful and attractive religious movement of its age.

As Franciscanism became increasingly modified by the demands of practicality, it also became increasingly rent with dissension. Some friars, wishing to draw on Francis's prestige without being burdened with his spiritual dedication, advocated an exceedingly lax interpretation of the Franciscan way. Others insisted on the strict imitation of Francis's life and struggled against its modification. These last, known in later years as "Spiritual Franciscans," sought to preserve the apostolic poverty and artless idealism of Francis himself. By the fourteenth century they had become vigorously antipapal and anticlerical.

The majority of Franciscans, however, were willing to meet reality halfway. Although the order neither acquired nor sought the immense landed wealth of the Benedictines or Cistercians, it soon possessed sufficient means to sustain its members. And although Francis had disparaged formal learning as irrelevant to salvation, Franciscan friars began devoting themselves to scholarship and took their places alongside the Dominicans in the thirteenth and fourteenth century universities. Franciscan scholars such as Roger Bacon played a vital role in the revival of scientific investigation, and the minister-general of the Franciscan order in the later thirteenth century, St. Bonaventure, was one of the most illustrious theologians of the age.

Necessary though they were, these compromises diminished the radical idealism that Francis had instilled in his order. In the progress from huts of twigs to halls of ivy, something precious was left behind. The Franciscans continued to serve society, but by the end of the thirteenth century they had ceased to inspire it.

THE PASSING OF THE HIGH MIDDLE AGES

The pattern of religious reform in the High Middle Ages is one of ebb and flow. A reform movement is launched with high enthusiasm and lofty purpose; it galvanizes society for a time and then succumbs gradually to complacency and gives way to a new and different wave of reform. But with the passing of the High Middle Ages, one can detect a gradual waning of spiritual vigor in orthodox Catholicism. The frontiers were closing as the fourteenth century dawned. Western political power was at an end in Constantinople and the Holy Land, and the Spanish reconquest had ceased. The economic boom was giving way to an epoch of depression, declining population, peasants' rebellions, and debilitating wars. And until the time of the Protestant Reformation, no new religious order was to attain the immense social impact of the thirteenth-century Franciscans and Dominicans. Popular piety remained strong, particularly in northern Europe where succeeding cen-

turies witnessed a surge of mysticism. But in the south a more secular attitude was beginning to emerge. Young men and women no longer flocked
into monastic orders; soldiers no longer rushed to crusades; papal excommunications no longer wrought their former terror. The electrifying appeal of a
St. Bernard, a St. Dominic, and a St. Francis was a phenomenon peculiar to
their age. By the fourteenth century their age was passing.

12

Worlds in Collision:
Papacy and Empire

THE FIRST PHASE: GREGORIAN REFORM

Papacy and Church in the Mid-Eleventh Century

The role of the popes in the changing religious patterns of the High Middle Ages was scarcely touched on in the previous chapter. For although the papacy contributed much to the spiritual development of the period, it was also closely associated with the politics of empire and kingdom, which is the central topic of this chapter. So we must return now to the mid-eleventh century, the age when Cluny still stood in the vanguard of European monasticism, when Cîteaux was yet an untouched wilderness, and the mendicant movement lay in the distant future.

With the dawning of the High Middle Ages there emerged a newly invigorated papacy, dedicated to ecclesiastical reform and the spiritual regeneration of Christian society. Almost at once the reform papacy became involved in a struggle with the Holy Roman Empire—a tragic conflict that dominated European politics for more than two centuries. On the eve of the conflict, Germany was the mightiest monarchy in Western Christendom, and the German king, or "Roman Emperor," dominated the papacy. By 1300 Germany was fragmented, and the papacy, after 250 years of political prominence, was on the brink of a long downward slide.

Prior to the beginnings of papal reform in the mid-eleventh century, a chasm had existed between the papal theory of Christian society and the realities of the contemporary Church. The papal theory, with a venerable tradition running back to late Roman times, envisaged a sanctified Christian commonwealth in which lords and kings accepted the spiritual direction of priests and bishops who, in turn, recognized the leadership of the papacy. The popes claimed to be the successors and representatives of St. Peter, who was thought to have been the first bishop of Rome—the first pope. Just as St. Peter was the chief of Christ's apostles, they argued, the pope was the monarch of the apostolic Church. And as eternal salvation was more important than earthly prosperity—as the soul was more important than the body—so the priestly power overshadowed the power of secular lords, kings, and emperors. The properly ordered society, the truly Christian society, was one dominated by the Church, which, in turn, was dominated by the pope. In the intellectual climate of the High Middle Ages this view caught the imagination of many thoughtful people. It provided a persuasive justification for the idea of papal monarchy.

The reality of mid-eleventh-century society was far different. Almost everywhere the Church was under the control of aristocratic lay proprietors. Manorial lords appointed their priests; dukes and kings selected their bishops and abbots. As we have seen, the Holy Roman emperors used churchmen extensively in the administration of Germany. In France, the Church provided warriors from its estates for feudal armies, advisers for kings and princes, and clerks for their administrations. The Church played a vital role in the operation of tenth- and early-eleventh-century society, but it was usually subordinate to the lay ruling class. From the lay standpoint it was an effective administrative tool, but from the spiritual standpoint it was sometimes inadequate and even corrupt. Monasteries all too frequently ignored the strict Benedictine Rule. Some priests had concubines, and many had wives, despite the canonical requirement of priestly celibacy. Lay lords often sold important ecclesiastical offices to unworthy self-seekers who then recouped the purchase price by exploiting their tenants and subordinates. This commerce in ecclesiastical appointments was known as *simony*—after Simon the Magician, a New Testament character who tried to purchase the Holy Spirit. Reformers regarded simony as shamefully corrupt. Traditionalists, however, defended it as an ecclesiastical version of a feudal inheritance tax. And to many bishops it was simply a shrewd investment. Archbishop Manasses of Reims, who had paid handsomely for his office and then enriched himself from it, is supposed to have said, "The archbishopric of Reims would be a good thing if only one didn't have to sing Mass because of it."

Ecclesiastical corruption was nowhere more evident than in Rome itself. The papacy of the earlier eleventh century had fallen into the soiled hands of the Roman nobility and had become a prize disputed among the several leading aristocratic families of the city. In 1032 the prize fell to a young aristocratic libertine who took the name of Benedict IX. His pontificate was scandalous even by contemporary Roman standards. Benedict sold the papacy, then changed his mind and reclaimed it. By 1046 his right to the papal throne was challenged by two other claimants; the papacy had fallen into a three-way schism.

Ecclesiastical Reform

Such were the conditions of the European Church as the mid-eleventh century approached. A Church dominated by lay proprietors had long existed in Europe and had long been accepted. But with the surge of lay piety that accompanied the opening of the High Middle Ages, the comfortable church-state relationship of the previous epoch seemed monstrously wrong to some sensitive reformers. This was the epoch in which Christians were beginning to join hermit groups such as the Carthusians; they would soon be flocking into the austere Cistercian order. Such people as these were responding to the spiritual awakening of their age by following the path of withdrawal from worldly society. Others chose the novel and adventurous approach of reforming the Church and the world. The dream of sanctifying society rather than withdrawing from it was shared by many Christians of the High Middle Ages. During the second half of the eleventh century it manifested itself in a powerful movement of ecclesiastical reform that was beginning to make itself felt across Western Christendom. At the heart of this movement was the reform papacy.

In general, the reformers fell into two groups. One consisted of moderates who sought to eliminate simony, enforce clerical celibacy, and improve the moral caliber of churchmen, but without challenging the Church's traditional collaboration with kings and princes—a collaboration that had been sweetened by countless gifts of lands and privileges. The second group was much more radical. Its goal was to demolish the tradition of lay control and to rebuild society on the pattern of the papal monarchy theory. The radical reformers struggled to establish an ideal Christian commonwealth in which laymen no longer appointed churchmen—in which kings deferred to bishops and bishops were responsive to papal directives. The moderate reformers endeavored to heal society; the radicals were determined to transform it into an international spiritual monarchy centering on the pope.

The struggle between papal monarchy and royal-imperial authority is often described by historians as a "conflict between church and state," but this is misleading. Many lay lords supported the reform papacy and many churchmen opposed it. By and large, bishops had grown accustomed to their partnership with regional princes, to whom they were often connected by bonds of kinship or gratitude. They had no desire to become the pawns of some overmighty pope who would, as one German archbishop expressed it, "order bishops and abbots about as though they were servants on his estates." Eleventh-century bishops were inclined to regard themselves as a brotherhood of spiritual leaders, exercising much local autonomy and wide powers of jurisdiction, under a papacy that guided them only very gently, often falteringly, and always from a respectful distance.

Conversely, a number of princes were advocates of church reform, at least in its moderate form. These lay reformers—among whom were French counts and dukes, English kings, and German emperors—planted Cluniac and other reformed monasteries in their dominions and appointed staunch Christians to their bishoprics. One of eleventh-century Europe's most dedicated reformers was Emperor Henry III (1039–1056), who used his imperial authority to intervene decisively in the politics of papal Rome. Shocked by the antics of Pope Benedict IX and the three-way tug-of-war for the papal throne, Henry III marched into Italy in 1046. He arranged the deposition of

Chronology of the Papal-Imperial Conflict

1039–1056:	Reign of Henry III
1046:	Henry III deposes three rival popes, inaugurates papal reform movement
1049–1054:	Pontificate of Leo IX
1056–1106:	Reign of Henry IV
1059:	Papal Election Decree
1073–1085:	Pontificate of Gregory VII
1075:	Gregory VII bans lay investiture
1076:	Gregory VII excommunicates and deposes Henry IV
1077:	Henry IV humbles himself at Canossa
1080:	Second excommunication and deposition of Henry IV
1088–1099:	Pontificate of Urban II
1106–1125:	Reign of Henry V
1122:	Concordat of Worms
1152–1190:	Reign of Frederick I "Barbarossa"
1154–1159:	Pontificate of Hadrian IV
1155:	Execution of Arnold of Brescia
1159–1181:	Pontificate of Alexander III
1176:	Lombards defeat Barbarossa at Legnano
1180:	Barbarossa defeats Duke Henry the Lion of Saxony
1190–1197:	Reign of Henry VI
1194:	Henry VI becomes king of Sicily
1198–1216:	Pontificate of Innocent III
1211–1250:	Reign of Frederick II
1214:	Philip Augustus defeats Otto of Brunswick at Bouvines
1215:	Fourth Lateran Council
1227–1241:	Pontificate of Gregory IX
1243–1254:	Pontificate of Innocent IV
1245:	Council of Lyons
1254–1273:	Interregnum in Germany
1273–1291:	Reign of Rudolph of Hapsburg
1282–1302:	War of the Sicilian Vespers
1294–1303:	Pontificate of Boniface VIII
1302:	Boniface VIII issues *Unam Sanctam*
1303:	Boniface VIII humiliated at Anagni
1305–1314:	Pontificate of Clement V. Papacy moves to Avignon

Benedict and his two rivals and drastically improved the quality of the papal leadership by appointing the first of a series of reform popes.

The ablest of Henry's appointees, Pope Leo IX (1049–1054), carried on a vigorous campaign against simony and clerical marriage, holding yearly synods at Rome, sending papal legates far and wide to enforce reform, and traveling constantly himself to preside over local councils and depose guilty churchmen. Leo's reform pontificate opened dramatically when, at the Roman Synod of 1049, the bishop of Sutri was condemned for simony and promptly fell dead.

From Leo IX to Gregory VII

Leo IX labored tirelessly for reform. His vigorous assertion of papal authority aggravated the long and deepening hostility between the churches of Rome and Constantinople, and in 1054 two of his legates placed a papal bull on the high altar of Sancta Sophia excommunicating the Eastern patriarch. More than anything else, Leo struggled to enforce canon law and to purge the Church of simony and clerical marriage. In most of his enterprises, he could count on the support of Emperor Henry III, for in these early years empire and papacy worked hand in glove to raise the moral level of the European Church.

But whatever the success of Leo's reforms, there were those who felt that he was not going far enough. The real evil, in the view of the radical reformers, was lay supremacy over the Church. To them Henry III's domination of papal appointments, however well-intentioned, was the supreme example of that evil. A number of ardent reformers were to be found among the cardinals whom Pope Leo appointed and gathered around him. These newcomers, who dominated the reform papacy for the next several decades, came for the most part from monastic backgrounds. Many of them were influenced by the piety surging through the towns of eleventh-century northern Italy and Lorraine, a piety that was stimulating the widespread revival of hermit monasticism.

One such reformer was St. Peter Damiani, a leader of the northern-Italian hermit movement before he was brought to Rome by Leo IX and made a cardinal. Damiani was a man of many contrasting aspects: a forceful preacher and writer dedicated to the eradication of vices—some of which he described so graphically that a sixteenth-century editor felt constrained to tone down his language. He served the reform papacy tirelessly, traveling far and wide to enforce the prohibitions against simony and clerical marriage and to reform the clergy. Yet he drew back from what seemed to him the irresponsible efforts of his more radical associates to challenge and transform the social order.

The leaders of the radical group were Humbert of Silva Candida and Hildebrand. Both were papal officials under Leo IX; both had, like Damiani, left monastic lives to join the Roman curia. Humbert of Silva Candida was a German from Lorraine, probably of aristocratic background, who used his subtle, well-trained intellect to support papal reform in its most radical aspect. He was one of Pope Leo's legates to Constantinople during the dispute with the Eastern Church where his uncompromising attitudes on papal supremacy clashed with the equally intransigent views of the Eastern patriarch. Indeed, it was Humbert himself who precipitated the schism of 1054 by laying a bull excommunicating the patriarch on the high altar of Sancta Sophia. A few years later Humbert produced a bitter, closely reasoned attack against the lay-dominated social order in the West, *Three Books Against the Simoniacs*, in which he extended the meaning of simony to include not merely the buying or selling of ecclesiastical offices but any instance of lay interference in clerical appointments. In Humbert's view the Church ought to be utterly free of lay control and supreme in European society.

Hildebrand, an Italian, lacked the originality and intellectual depth of Humbert but had a remarkable ability to draw ideas from the minds of others and formulate them into a clearly articulated program. Intellectually, Hildebrand was a disciple of Humbert, but as a spellbinding leader and mover of events he stood alone. Contemporaries described Hildebrand as a small, ugly, pot-bellied man, but they also recognized that a fire burned inside him—a holy or unholy fire depending on one's point of view. Hildebrand was the most controversial figure of his age. He was thought to have the power to read minds and may well have believed so himself. Consumed by the ideal of a Christian society dominated by the Church and a Church dominated by the papacy, Hildebrand served with prodigious vigor and determination under Pope Leo IX and his successors. At length he became pope himself, taking the name Gregory VII (1073–1085). His pontificate was to be one of the most violent and tragic of the Middle Ages.

So long as Henry III lived, radicals such as Humbert of Silva Candida and Hildebrand remained in the background. But in 1056 the emperor died in the prime of life, leaving behind him a six-year-old heir, Henry IV, and a weak regency government. Henry III's death was a catastrophe for the Empire and a godsend to the radicals who longed to wrest the papacy from imperial control. At the death of Henry III's last papal appointee in 1057, the reform cardinals began electing popes on their own. In 1059, under the influence of Humbert and Hildebrand, they issued a daring declaration of independence known as the "Papal Election Decree," which stated that thenceforth the pope would be chosen by cardinals. The Emperor and the Roman laity would merely give formal approval. In the years that followed, this revolutionary proclamation was challenged by both the Empire and the Roman aristocracy, but in the end the reformers won out. The papacy had broken free of lay control; cardinals elected the pope, and the pope appointed the cardinals. The Decree of 1059 created at the apex of the ecclesiastical hierarchy a reform oligarchy of the most exclusive sort.

The next step in the program of the radical reformers was far more difficult. It involved nothing less than the annihilation of lay control over the Church and the strict subordination of bishops and archbishops to the pope. At a time when the Church possessed perhaps a third of the land in Europe, the full realization of this vision of papal monarchy would cripple secular power, destroy episcopal autonomy, and revolutionize the European political order. Yet only by its realization, so the radical reformers believed, could a justly ordered Christian commonwealth be achieved.

One of the first arenas of conflict was the city of Milan, with its proud archbishopric renowned since St. Ambrose's time. Milan was in the grip of the new commercial revival and, like many other Lombard towns of the eleventh century, was seething with activity. Most Lombard cities of this era were, as we have seen, dominated by their bishops, who were inclined to cooperate with the Holy Roman Empire and were supported by an elite group of landholding nobles. As a group, the Lombard bishops opposed the new wave of reform, and some were themselves guilty of simony. Throughout Lombardy, and in Milan in particular, their rule was being challenged by the growing class of merchants and artisans, backed by day workers and peasants. In

Milan and elsewhere, these dissidents were referred to by their enemies as *patarenes* (rag-pickers). Hostile to the domination of the traditional ruling group and fired by the new piety, the patarenes made common cause with the reform papacy against their bishops. The reformers in Rome had no sympathy for the archbishop of Milan who was, in effect, an imperial agent and who, by condoning simony and marriage among his clergy, symbolized the traditional Church at its worst.

In 1059 Cardinal Peter Damiani journeyed to Milan to enforce reform. Backed by the patarenes and the authority of Rome, he humbled the archbishop and the higher clergy, made them confess their sins publicly, and wrung promises of amendment from them. Thus, the Milanese church, despite its friendship with the Empire and its tradition of independence, was made to submit to the power of the papacy. Over the next fifteen years, the patarenes continued their struggle against the noble-ecclesiastical ruling group, and the city was torn by murder and mob violence. When in 1072 the young Emperor Henry IV ordered the consecration of an antireformer as archbishop of Milan, he was faced with the combined wrath of the patarenes and the papacy, and he lost. The patarenes rioted and the pope excommunicated Henry's counselors. The entire affair typifies the close alliance between radical urban piety and papal reform. Having placed themselves at the forefront of the new piety, the reformers were propelled by the revolutionary social-spiritual movement that was sweeping Europe. At odds with much of the traditional ecclesiastical establishment, they were in tune with the most vigorous forces of the age.

Gregory VII and Henry IV

The struggle over lay control of ecclesiastical appointments broke out in earnest in 1075 when Hildebrand, now Pope Gregory VII, issued a proclamation banning lay investiture. Traditionally, a newly chosen bishop or abbot was invested by a lay lord with a ring and a pastoral staff, symbolic of his marriage to the Church and his duty to be a good shepherd to his Christian flock. Gregory attacked this custom of lay investiture as the crucial symbol of lay authority over churchmen. Its prohibition was a challenge to the established social order. It threatened to compromise the authority of every ruler in Christendom, and none more than the Holy Roman emperor himself. For the imperial system of administration was particularly dependent on the German and Lombard bishops.

By Gregory VII's time, Henry IV had grown to vigorous manhood and was showing promise of becoming as strong a ruler as his father. When Gregory VII suspended a group of uncooperative, imperially appointed German bishops, Henry IV responded with a vehement letter of defiance. Backed by his bishops, he asserted his authority as a divinely appointed sovereign to lead the German Church without papal interference and challenged Gregory's very right to the papal throne. The letter was addressed to Gregory under his previous name, "Hildebrand, not pope but false monk." It concluded with the dramatic words, "I, Henry, king by grace of God, with all my bishops, say to you: 'Come down, come down, and be damned throughout the ages.'"

Henry's letter was in effect a defense of the traditional social order of divinely ordained priest-kings ruling over semiautonomous bishops. Gregory's view of society was vastly different: he denied the priestly qualities of kings and emperors, suggested that most of them were gangsters destined for hell, and repudiated their right to question his status or his decrees. Emperors had no power to appoint churchmen, much less depose popes. But the pope, as the ultimate authority in Christendom, had the power to depose not only bishops but kings and emperors as well. Accordingly, Gregory responded to the letter with a startling exercise of his spiritual authority: he excommunicated and deposed Henry IV. It was for the pope to judge whether or not the king was fit to rule, and Gregory had judged.

Radical though it was, the deposition was effective. Under the relatively placid surface of monarchical authority in Germany, aristocratic opposition had long been gathering force. Subdued during the reign of Henry III, local and regional princes asserted themselves during the long regency following his death, and Henry IV, on reaching maturity, had much ground to recover. In 1075 he succeeded in stifling a long, bitter rebellion in Saxony and seemed to be on his way toward reasserting his father's power when the controversy with Rome exploded. Gregory VII's excommunication and deposition—awesome spiritual sanctions to the minds of eleventh-century Christians—unleashed in Germany all the latent hostility that the centralizing policies of the Salian dynasty had evoked. Many Germans, churchmen and aristocrats alike, refused to serve an excommunicated sovereign. The German nobles took the revolutionary step of threatening to elect a new king in Henry's place, thereby challenging the ingrained German tradition of hereditary kingship with the counterdoctrine of elective monarchy. The elective principle, which crippled the later-medieval and early-modern German monarchy, had its real inception at this moment.

Desperate to keep his throne, Henry crossed the Alps into Italy to seek the pope's forgiveness. In January 1077, at the castle of Canossa in northern Italy, the two men met in what was perhaps medieval history's most dramatic encounter—Henry IV humble and barefoot in the snow, clothed in rough, penitential garments; Gregory VII torn between his conviction that Henry's change of heart was a mere political subterfuge and his priestly duty to forgive a repentant sinner. Finally Gregory lifted Henry's excommunication and the monarch, promising to amend his ways, returned to Germany to rebuild his authority.

Through the centuries Canossa has symbolized the ultimate royal degradation before the power of the Church. Perhaps it was—but in the immediate political context it was a victory, and a badly needed one, for Henry IV. It did not prevent a group of German nobles from electing a rival king, nor did it restore the powerful centralized monarchy of Henry III, but it did save

Henry IV's throne. Restored to communion, he was able to rally support, to check for a time the forces of princely particularism, and to defeat the rival king.

As his power waxed, Henry ignored his promises at Canossa. In 1080 Gregory excommunicated and deposed him a second time, only to find that Henry had consolidated his political position to such a degree that he could now withstand these papal weapons. In the early 1080s Henry returned to Italy, this time with an army. Gregory summoned his vassal and ally, the Norman Robert Guiscard, to rescue him from his situation, but Robert's boisterous Normans, although they frightened Henry away, became involved in a destructive riot against the Roman townspeople. The commoners of Rome had always supported Gregory, but now they turned furiously against him and he was obliged, for his own protection, to accompany the Normans when they withdrew to the south. In 1085 Gregory died at Salerno, consumed by bitterness and a conviction of failure. His last words were these: "I have loved justice and hated iniquity; therefore I die in exile."*

The Papal Recovery and the Investiture Settlement

Gregory VII failed to transform Europe. "When I look over the lands of the West," he wrote, "I find scarcely any bishops, whether to north or south, who conform to the law." But his vision of papal monarchy long outlived him. The papacy soon fell into the expert hands of Urban II (1088–1099), a former prior of Cluny who had afterward become one of Gregory VII's most faithful and effective cardinals. In calling the First Crusade in 1095, Urban wedded the papal reform movement to the moral fervor of Christian militancy. Ideologically, Urban was a Gregorian, but he was much more practical and diplomatic than his fiery predecessor. The papal administration, which had disintegrated during Gregory's final years, was rebuilt under Urban II into a smoothly functioning bureaucracy, suited to the needs of a centralized papal government in regular communication with the bishops and abbots of Western Christendom. Papal correspondence increased, financial management improved, and the papal tribunal became steadily more active and effective. In the long run, the papal monarchy of the High Middle Ages probably owed more to its administration than to its excommunications.

Urban II and his successors continued to harass the unlucky Henry IV, stirring up rebellions in Germany and eroding the power of the imperial government. At the emperor's death in 1106, his own son and heir, the future Henry V, was in rebellion against him. Henry V (1106–1025) enjoyed a happier reign than his father's, but only because he forsook his father's struggle to recover the fullness of imperial power as it had existed in the mid-eleventh century. The independence-minded aristocracy consolidated the gains it had made during the preceding era of chaos, and Henry V could do little about it.

*An ironic twist to Psalm 45, verse 7: "You have loved justice and hated iniquity; therefore God, your God, has anointed you with the oil of gladness, above all your rivals."

Toward the end of his reign, Henry V worked out a compromise settlement with the papacy that brought the "investiture contest" to an end at last. Already the issue had been resolved in England and France, where the struggle had been considerably less bitter than in Germany. As time progressed both papacy and Empire tended to draw back from the extreme positions they had taken during Gregory VII's pontificate, and in 1122 they reconciled their differences in the Concordat of Worms. Henry V agreed to give up lay investiture, while the pope conceded to the emperor the important privilege of bestowing on the new prelate the symbols of his *territorial* and *administrative* jurisdiction. Bishops and abbots were thenceforth to be elected according to the principles of canon law, by the monks of a monastery or the canons of a cathedral, but the emperor had the right to be present at such elections and to make the final decision in the event of a dispute. These reservations enabled the emperor to retain a considerable degree of *de facto* control over the appointment of important German churchmen. The exercise of royal control over a "canonical election" is illustrated in the later twelfth century by a command of King Henry II of England to the monks at Winchester: "I order you to hold a free election, but nevertheless I forbid you to elect anyone except Richard, my clerk, the archdeacon of Poitiers."

There was no real victor in the investiture controversy. The papacy had won its point—lay investiture was banned—but monarchs still exercised considerable control over their churches. The theory of papal monarchy over a reconstituted Christian society remained unrealized, and the old tradition of peaceful cooperation between kings and prelates was shaken but not destroyed. The papacy, however noble its intentions, had become politicized as never before. And by asserting its authority across Europe, it evoked hostile royalist propaganda and growing opposition.

Still, the papal-imperial balance of power had changed radically since the mid-eleventh century. The papacy was now a mighty force in Europe, and the power of the emperor had declined. During the chaotic half-century between the onset of the controversy in 1075 and Henry V's death in 1125, a powerful new aristocracy emerged. Ambitious landowners rose to great power, built castles, extended their estates, and usurped royal rights. They forced minor nobles to become their vassals and, in some instances, forced free peasants to become their serfs. The monarchy was helpless to curb this process of fragmentation.

The investiture controversy resulted in the crippling of imperial authority and episcopal autonomy in northern Italy. The fierce patarene struggle in Milan was repeated throughout Lombardy, and in the anarchy wrought by the papal-imperial conflict, the pro-imperial Lombard bishops lost the wide jurisdictional powers they had formerly exercised over their cities. Lombard burghers, under the banner of papal reform, rebelled against the control of nobles, bishops, and emperor alike, and established quasi-independent city states. By 1125, Milan and its sister cities were free urban communes, and imperial authority in Lombardy had become nominal.

In Germany and Italy alike, imperial power was receding before the whirl-wind of local particularism, invigorated by the investiture controversy, the rise of towns, and the soaring popular piety of the age. Well before the Concordat of Worms, the decline of the medieval Empire had begun.

THE SECOND PHASE: PAPAL MONARCHY

The Age of Frederick Barbarossa

The Salian dynasty died out with the passing of Henry V in 1125. During the next quarter century, Germany reaped the harvest of princely particularism. Disregarding the principle of direct hereditary succession, the nobles reverted to the elective principle that they had asserted at the time of Canossa. Their choice always fell to a man of royal blood but never to the most direct heir. In the decades between 1125 and 1152 a rivalry developed between two great families that had risen to power in the investiture era: the Welfs of Saxony and the Hohenstaufen of Swabia. In 1152 the princes elected as king a talented Hohenstaufen, Frederick I, Barbarossa ("Red-Beard"), duke of Swabia, who took as his mission the reconstruction of the German monarchy.

Emperor Frederick Babarossa recognized that the mighty imperial structure of Henry III was beyond recovery. His goal was to harness the new feudal forces of his age to the royal advantage. He deliberately encouraged the great princes of the realm to expand their power and privileges at the expense of lesser lords, but at the same time he forced them to recognize his own lordship over all the kingdom. In other words, he succeeded in establishing his authority over the leading magnates, making them his obedient vassals—his tenants-in-chief.

But as the sorry state of the early French monarchy well illustrates, overlordship was an ephemeral thing if the royal overlord lacked the resources to support his position. Therefore, Frederick Barbarossa set about to increase his revenues and extend the territories under his direct authority. A strong feudal monarchy required a substantial territorial core under exclusive royal control—an extensive royal demesne—to act as a counterweight to the great fiefs of the chief vassals. Frederick enlarged his demesne territories, most of which were concentrated in Swabia, by bringing many of the new monasteries and rising towns under imperial jurisdiction. The crux of his imaginative policy was the reassertion of imperial authority over the wealthy Lombard cities. With Lombardy under his control and its revenues pouring into the imperial treasury, no German lord could challenge him.

Barbarossa's Lombard policy earned him the hostility of the papacy, which had always feared the consolidation of imperial power in Italy, and of the intensely independent Lombard cities, which were determined to give up as little of their wealth and autonomy as they possibly could. And should he become too deeply involved in Italy, Barbarossa exposed himself to rebellion on the part of the German nobility—in particular, the Welf family, which was vigorously represented at the time by Duke Henry the Lion of Saxony.

The papacy of the mid-twelfth century was having problems of its own. Pope Hadrian IV (1154–1159), who was to become one of Frederick Barbarossa's most bitter foes, was faced at the beginning of his pontificate with the problem of maintaining the papacy's hold on Rome itself. A gifted man of humble origins, Hadrian IV was the one Englishman ever to occupy the papal throne. Rome was turbulent during his years, for the patarene movement had reached the Holy City and had turned violently antipapal. The revolutionary social forces that had earlier allied with the papacy in breaking the power of an archbishop in Milan were now challenging the pope's authority over Rome. In the 1140s the city was torn by a rebellion whose leaders struggled to drive out the pope and dreamed of reestablishing the ancient Roman Republic. Very quickly this antipapal communal movement spread to other cities in the Papal States, and for a time the pope himself was forced into exile.

Before long, the Roman rebellion fell under the leadership of Arnold of Brescia, a gifted scholar and spiritual revolutionary, whose goal it was to strip the Church of its wealth and secular authority. Suppressed by the Norman troops of Roger the Great in the 1140s, Arnold's revolution reasserted itself under Hadrian IV, and the pope was driven to the desperate expedient of placing Rome itself under interdict, ordering the suspension of church services throughout the city. The interdict proved an effective weapon. Among other things it afflicted Rome's economy by discouraging pilgrimages. The revolution collapsed and Arnold of Brescia was driven from the city. Hadrian and Barbarossa joined forces to hunt him down, and once he fell into their hands he was hanged, burned, and thrown in the Tiber (1155). Thus Arnold was emphatically eliminated, and his relics were put out of the reach of any future admirers. But his movement persisted as an anticlerical heresy—an early example of the opposition to ecclesiastical wealth and power that was soon to find expression among the Waldensians and Albigensians.

The growing hostility between the papacy and the Roman townspeople was an ominous indication that papal leadership over urban reform movements was at an end. The papacy was no longer able to make common cause with the explosive forces of urban piety, as it had under Gregory VII, but was now beginning to suppress them. This split between papal leadership and popular piety was a factor of decisive importance in the ultimate decline of the papacy in the late Middle Ages.

Hadrian IV and Frederick Barbarossa first met on the occasion of the imperial coronation in Rome in 1155. The two men had collaborated against Arnold of Brescia, but thereafter they became enemies. At their initial encounter, Hadrian insisted that Frederick follow ancient tradition and lead the papal mule.* At first Frederick refused to humble himself in such a manner, but

---

*The tradition of ceremonial mule-leading seems to have originated in the eighth-century forgery, the "Donation of Constantine" (see p. 90).

when it appeared that there would be no coronation at all, he grudgingly submitted. This small conflict was symbolic of far greater ones, for Hadrian and his successors proved to be implacable opponents of Frederick's drive to win control of the Lombard cities.

The Lombard struggle reached its height in the pontificate of Alexander III (1159–81), Hadrian's successor. Shrewd and learned, Alexander was Frederick Barbarossa's most formidable opponent. Whereas most of the early reform popes had been monks, Alexander and many of his successors were canon lawyers. Gregory VII and Urban II had both urged the study of canon law and the formulation of canonical collections in order to provide intellectual ammunition to support papal claims. During the later eleventh and twelfth centuries, the study of canon law was pursued vigorously in north Italian schools, particularly the great law school at Bologna, and a good number of twelfth- and thirteenth-century popes were products of these schools. Alexander III was the first of them, and one of the ablest.

Determined to prevent Frederick Barbarossa from establishing himself strongly in northern Italy, Alexander rallied the Lombard towns that had long been engaged in intercity warfare but now combined forces against the Empire. They formed an association called the "Lombard League" and organized an interurban army. Frederick had meanwhile thrown his support behind a rival claimant to the papal throne, and Alexander responded by excommunicating the emperor. There followed a prolonged struggle involving Alexander, Barbarossa, and the Lombard League, ending in the total victory of the Lombard army at the battle of Legnano in 1176.

Barbarossa submitted with as much good cheer as he could manage. He granted *de facto* independence to the Lombard cities in return for their admission of a vague imperial overlordship. Pope and emperor tearfully embraced. Barbarossa led Alexander's mule and promised to be a dutiful son of the Roman See.

But Barbarossa did not abandon his designs on Italy; he merely shifted his theater of operations. Leaving Lombardy severely alone, he redirected his efforts southward and succeeded in gaining control of Tuscany, the rich province just to the north of the Papal States. At about the same time he arranged a marriage between his son and the future heiress of the Norman kingdom of southern Italy and Sicily—a marriage that ultimately brought that opulent realm into the imperial fold. Outmaneuvered and outwitted, the papacy faced the chilling prospect of imperial encirclement. In 1180 Barbarossa tightened his hold on Germany by crushing the most formidable of his vassals, Henry the Lion, the Welf duke of Saxony. After Alexander III's death in 1181, the papacy ceased for a time to be a serious threat, and the far-sighted emperor was at the height of his power when he died in 1190 while leading his army toward the Holy Land on the Third Crusade.

Barbarossa had taken pains to circumvent the princely policy of elective monarchy by forcing the princes, prior to his death, to elect his eldest son, Henry VI. In 1190 Henry succeeded his father without difficulty, and in 1194

THE HOLY ROMAN EMPIRE IN 1190

North Sea

KINGDOM OF DENMARK

Baltic Sea

LITHUANIA

PRUSSIANS

Elbe R.

Lübeck

POMERANIA

SAXONY

BRANDENBURG

KINGDOM OF POLAND

R U S S I A

Rhine

Cologne

NASSAU

KINGDOM OF FRANCE

LORRAINE

FRANCONIA

Worms

BOHEMIA

MORAVIA

Danube

ALSACE

SWABIA

Augsburg

Constance

KINGDOM OF BURGUNDY

Legnano

Milan

BAVARIA

KINGDOM OF HUNGARY

LOMBARDY

Bologna

Venice

BULGARIANS

Danube

Florence

TUSCANY

Pisa

SERBIA

CORSICA

Sutri

Rome

Anagni

Adriatic Sea

BYZANTINE EMPIRE

SARDINIA

KINGDOM OF SICILY

Palermo

Mediterranean Sea

MILES
0   100   200   300   400

he made good his claim to Sicily. He was crowned king of Sicily on Christmas day, 1194, and on the next day his wife Constance, the Sicilian heiress, gave birth to their son, the future Frederick II. The Papal States were now encircled by the Holy Roman Empire, and the papacy was powerless to alter the situation. The revenues of southern Italy and Sicily fattened the imperial purse. The territories under imperial rule had never been so extensive.

But for an age in which the emperor had to remain always on the watch for regional rebellion, particularly among his vassals in Germany, the imperial frontiers had become dangerously overextended. To make matters worse, Henry VI died prematurely in 1197 leaving as his heir his infant son, Frederick II. The problems the Empire faced in 1197 would have taxed the ablest of leaders, yet at this moment imperial leadership failed. The papacy had its opportunity.

The High Noon of the Medieval Papacy: Innocent III

During the twelfth century, the papacy lost much of its former zealous reform spirit as it evolved into a huge, complex administrative institution. Taxes flowed into its treasury from all Western Christendom; bishops traveled vast distances to make their spiritual submission to the Roman pontiff; the papal curia served as a court of last appeal for an immense network of ecclesiastical courts across Christendom. Papal authority over the European Church had increased immeasurably since the mid-eleventh century. And as the dream of papal monarchy came nearer realization, the traditional theory of papal supremacy over Christian society was increasingly magnified by the canon lawyers. These subtle ecclesiastical scholars were beginning to dominate the papal curia and, like Alexander III, to occupy the papal throne itself.

Innocent III (1198–1216), the most powerful of all the lawyer popes, began his pontificate in the year following Emperor Henry VI's death. Although deeply pious, Innocent was an imperious, self-confident aristocrat who held aloof from the surging religious emotionalism of the humbler Christians of his age. He had the wisdom and sensitivity to support the Franciscans, and the ruthlessness to mount the Albigensian Crusade.

Animated by the theory of papal monarchy in its most uncompromising form, Innocent forced his will on the leading monarchs of Europe, playing off one ruler against another with consummate skill. In the course of a long struggle with King John of England over the appointment of an archbishop of Canterbury, Innocent laid John's kingdom under interdict, threatened to depose John himself, and urged King Philip Augustus of France to send an army against him. The struggle ended with John's complete submission. Innocent's man was installed as archbishop of Canterbury, and John consented to papal lordship over England.

Innocent had earlier clashed with Philip Augustus over the king's refusal to repudiate an uncanonical second marriage and return to his first wife (whom Philip had cast aside after their wedding night, supposedly because of her exceptionally bad breath). After laying France under interdict and excommunicating Philip, Innocent obtained his submission—though only after the death of Philip's second wife. It has already been shown how Innocent instigated the Fourth Crusade, which was aimed at Jerusalem but ended in Constantinople, and how he mounted crusades against the Albigensians and the Spanish Moors. These diverse activities illustrate the unprecedented political and moral authority that Innocent exercised over Christendom.

A mighty force in the secular politics of his age, Innocent also dominated the Church more completely than any of his predecessors had done. In 1215 he summoned a general Church council in Rome—the Fourth Lateran Council—which produced a remarkable quantity of significant ecclesiastical legislation: clerical dress was strictly regulated, a moratorium was declared on new religious orders, Jews were required to wear special badges, clerics were forbidden to participate in the ancient Germanic legal procedure of the ordeal,* fees for the administration of sacraments were forbidden, bishops were ordered to maintain schools and to provide sermons at their services, and all Catholics were bound to receive the sacraments of penance and the Eucharist at least once a year. The efficient organization of the Fourth Lateran Council and the degree to which Pope Innocent dominated and directed it are illustrated by the fact that the churchmen in attendance—more than twelve hundred bishops, abbots, and priests—produced their important new legislation in meetings that lasted a total of only three weeks. By contrast, the fifteenth-century Council of Basel met off and on for eighteen years and the Council of Trent for nineteen.

The range of Innocent III's activities was seemingly boundless. But throughout his pontificate one political issue took precedence over all others— that of the German imperial succession. It was a marvelously complex problem that taxed even Pope Innocent's diplomatic skill. Involved were the questions of whether or not the Kingdom of Sicily would remain in imperial hands, whether the imperial throne would pass to the Welfs or the Hohenstaufens, and whether an accommodation could be achieved between the traditionally hostile forces of papacy and empire. The German succession problem also touched the interests of the French and English monarchies: the Welf claimant, Otto of Brunswick, was a nephew and favorite of King John of England and could count on his support, whereas the Hohenstaufens enjoyed the friendship of the French king, Philip Augustus.

The direct Hohenstaufen heir was the infant Frederick, son of the late Henry VI. But since a child could hardly be expected to wage a successful fight for the throne in these anxious years, the Hohenstaufen claim was taken up by Frederick's uncle, Philip of Swabia, younger brother of the former emperor. The young Frederick remained in Sicily while Philip of Swabia and the Welf, Otto of Brunswick, battled for the imperial throne. Innocent recognized the German princes' right to elect their own monarch, but, as it happened, Philip and Otto had both been elected, each by a different group of nobles. In

*See pp. 27–28, and 144.

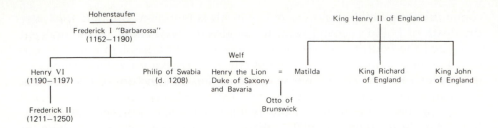

the case of a disputed election such as this, Innocent claimed the right to intervene by virtue of the traditional papal privilege of crowning the emperor. He delayed his decision considerably, and in the meantime civil war raged in Germany. At length he settled on Otto of Brunswick, who had promised to support the papal interests in Germany and to loosen imperial control of the German church. Since a Welf emperor would presumably have no claim on the Hohenstaufen kingdom of Sicily, Otto's coronation would realize the papal goal of separating the two realms.

Despite Innocent's decision, the civil war continued in Germany until Philip of Swabia's death in 1208. Otto was crowned emperor in 1209, but now, having no rival to oppose him, he repudiated his promises, asserted his mastery .over the German church, and even launched an invasion of southern Italy. Innocent responded to this breach of faith by deposing and anathematizing Otto and throwing his support behind the young Frederick of Hohenstaufen. From its inception, the Kingdom of Sicily had been, at least nominally, a papal vassal state, and Innocent claimed the overlord's privilege of being guardian of its underage king. But before undertaking to back Frederick, Innocent wrung promises from him: to abdicate as king of Sicily and sever the Sicilian kingdom from the Empire, to lead a crusade, to follow the spiritual direction of the papacy, and in general to confirm the pledges that Otto of Brunswick had made and then broken.

Innocent's decision revived the Hohenstaufen cause in Germany and renewed the civil war. The pope employed all his diplomatic skill and leverage to win over German nobles to Frederick's cause. He was supported in these maneuverings by King Philip Augustus of France, now on friendly terms with the papacy, traditionally sympathetic to the Hohenstaufens, and hostile to the English and their Welf allies.

The complex currents of international politics in Innocent's pontificate reached their climax and their resolution in 1214. King John invaded France from the west while Otto of Brunswick led a powerful army against Philip Augustus from the east—an army heavily subsidized by England and consisting of the combined forces of pro-Welf princes from Germany and the Low Countries. But John's invasion bogged down and accomplished nothing, while Otto's army was routed by Philip Augustus at the battle of Bouvines.

This decisive engagement changed the political face of Europe. As a result of Bouvines, Philip Augustus emerged as Europe's mightiest monarch, Otto's imperial dreams were dashed, and Frederick became emperor in fact as well as in theory. The battle of Bouvines was a triumph not only for Philip Augustus and Frederick but also for Innocent III. His ward was now emperor-elect and was pledged to sever the kingdom of Sicily from Germany and free the German Church of imperial control.

Germany itself was in a state of chaos. The solid achievements of Frederick Barbarossa, which might have served as the foundation for a revival of imperial power, were compromised by the subsequent imperial involvement in the affairs of the Sicilian kingdom and were demolished by long years of dynastic strife, during which the German princes usurped royal privileges and royal lands on a vast scale. By the time of Innocent's death the imperial authority that Barbarossa had achieved was almost beyond recovery.

The policies of Innocent III seemed everywhere triumphant. Yet even at its height, papal authority remained limited in many ways—by the growing power of the Western monarchies, by the fragility of royal promises of good behavior, and by the longstanding difficulties in enforcing papal reform measures throughout the length and breadth of Christendom. Innocent's Fourth Lateran Council had decreed that all Christians must go to confession at least once a year, yet a study of late-medieval Flanders has disclosed that a good many Flemings never confessed to a priest. Even in the area of international diplomacy, where Innocent achieved such conspicuous triumphs, his successors could hardly be expected to carry on his juggling act indefinitely.

At a deeper level, the ever-increasing involvement of the papal government in secular politics was making it steadily more difficult to view the papacy as a holy institution. Ultimately, papal power was based on spiritual prestige, and the thirteenth-century popes, despite their piety, their good intentions, and their continuing concern for ecclesiastical reform, were lawyers and diplomats rather than charismatic spiritual leaders. The papacy was a mighty force in the world of the thirteenth century, but it was failing more and more to satisfy the spiritual hunger of devoted Christians. Piety remained as strong as before, but many of the pious were coming to doubt that the papal government, with its money chests and bureaucratic machinery, was the true spiritual center of the apostolic Church and the citadel of Christ's kingdom on earth. Popes continued to dream of a regenerated Christian society led and inspired by the Roman Church. But as time went on they dreamed less and plotted more.

Frederick II (1211–1250)

Frederick II, whose Sicilian childhood had exposed him to several faiths, grew up to be a brilliant, anticlerical skeptic, more concerned with his harem and his exotic menagerie than with his soul. His dazzling career earned him the name *Stupor Mundi*, the "Wonder of the World." In the years after Innocent III's death in 1216, Frederick made it clear that he would ignore his promises as completely as Otto of Brunswick had earlier done. Refusing to relinquish his kingdom of Sicily, he sought instead to bring all Italy within his empire.

This policy won him the implacable hatred of the papacy and prompted some churchmen to view him quite literally as the incarnate Antichrist.

Frederick was a talented, many-sided man—perhaps the most flamboyant product of an intensely creative age. He was a writer of considerable skill and an amateur scientist, curious about the world around him, but in some matters deeply superstitious. After much delay he kept his promise to lead a Crusade (1228), but instead of fighting the Muslims, he negotiated with them, and with such success that Jerusalem itself came into his hands for a time. The amicable spirit of Frederick's Crusade against the infidel struck many churchmen as unholy, and its success infuriated them.

Frederick II ruled his kingdom of Sicily in the autocratic and systematic manner of a Renaissance despot. He established a uniform legal code; tightened and broadened the centralized administrative system of his Norman-Sicilian predecessors; encouraged agriculture, industry, and commerce; abolished interior tariffs and tolls; and founded a great university in Naples. Germany, however, he left largely to its princes. He had always preferred his urbane Sicilian homeland to the forests and gloomy castles of the German north. Like Frederick Barbarossa, he tried to expand the royal demesne in Germany and to enforce the feudal obligations of his great German vassals. But he did so halfheartedly. Germany was important to Frederick chiefly as a source of money and military strength with which to carry out his policy of bringing all Italy under his rule.

As it happened, this policy proved disastrous to the Holy Roman Empire. Frederick's aggressions in Italy evoked the opposition of a revived Lombard League and the bitter hostility of the papacy. He gave up lands and royal rights in Germany in order to keep peace with the German princes and win their support for his persistent but inconclusive Italian campaigns. In the end, he was obliged to tax his beloved Sicily to the point of impoverishment in order to support his wars. Astute lawyer-popes such as Gregory IX and Innocent IV devoted all their diplomatic talents and spiritual sanctions to blocking Frederick's enterprises, building alliances to oppose him and hurling anathemas against him. In 1245 Innocent IV presided over a universal council of the Church at Lyons, which condemned and excommunicated the emperor. Frederick was deposed, a rival emperor was elected in his place, and a crusade was called to rid the Empire of its ungodly tyrant. Revolts now broke out against Frederick throughout his dominions. The royal estates in Germany slipped more and more from his grasp, and his Italian holdings were riddled with rebellion. Against this unhappy background Frederick II died in 1250. In a very real sense, the hopes of the medieval Empire died with him.

THE OUTCOME OF THE PAPAL-IMPERIAL STRUGGLE

The Decline of the Medieval Empire

Frederick II's son succeeded him in Germany but died in 1254 after a brief and unsuccessful reign. For the next nineteen years, Germany suffered a crippling interregnum (1254–1273) during which no recognized emperor held the throne. Castles rose like mushrooms from the German soil as princes and nobles, lacking a royal referee, undertook to defend and advance their interests on their own. Finally, in 1273, a vastly weakened Holy Roman Empire reemerged with papal blessing under Rudolph of Hapsburg, the first emperor of a family that was destined to play a crucial role in modern European history.

Rudolph attempted to rebuild the shattered royal demesne and shore up the foundations of imperial rule, but it was much too late. The monarchy's one hope had been to strengthen and extend the crown lands to the point where they provided resources overwhelmingly superior to those of any magnate. This was the policy on which the medieval French monarchy had risen to a position of dominance in France; it was the policy that Frederick Barbarossa had pursued so promisingly in Germany. But it aroused the unremitting opposition of the German princes, who had no desire to see their own rights and territories eaten away by royal expansion and would much prefer to extend their own principalities at the expense of the crown.

The civil strife during Innocent's pontificate, the Italian involvements of Frederick II, and the interregnum of 1254–1273 gave the princes their opportunity, and by 1273 the crown lands were hopelessly shrunken and disorganized. Germany was now drifting irreversibly toward the loose confederation of principalities and the anemic elective monarchy that characterized its constitutional structure from the fourteenth to the later-nineteenth century. The tragic failure of the medieval Empire doomed Germany to six hundred years of disunity—a heritage that may well have contributed to its catastrophic career in the first half of the present century.

Italy, too, emerged from the struggles of the High Middle Ages hopelessly fragmented. The Papal States, straddling the peninsula, were torn with unrest and disaffection, and the papacy had trouble maintaining its authority over the inhabitants of Rome itself. North of the Papal States, Tuscany and Lombardy had become a mosaic of independent, warring city-states—Florence, Siena, Venice, Milan, and many others—whose rivalries would form the political backdrop of the Italian Renaissance.

Southern Italy and Sicily

The kingdom of Sicily, established by the Normans and cherished by the Hohenstaufens, passed shortly after Frederick II's death to his illegitimate son, Manfred. The papacy, determined to rid Italy of Hohenstaufen rule, bent all its energies toward securing Manfred's downfall. At length it offered the Sicilian crown to Charles of Anjou, a younger brother of King Louis IX of France (St. Louis). The pope's intention was that the power of France be used to drive Manfred out of the Sicilian kingdom. Charles of Anjou—dour, cruel, and ambitious—defeated and killed Manfred in 1266 and established a new French dynasty on the throne of the kingdom.

The inhabitants of the realm, particularly those on the island of Sicily, had become accustomed to Hohenstaufen rule and resented Charles of Anjou. They looked on his French soldiers as an army of occupation. When, on Easter Monday 1282, a French soldier molested a young married woman on her way to evening vesper services in Palermo, he was struck down, and on all sides was raised the cry, "Death to the French!" The incident resulted in a spontaneous uprising and a general massacre of Frenchmen, which spread swiftly throughout the island. When the French retaliated, the Sicilians offered the crown to Peter III of Aragon, Manfred's son-in-law, who claimed the Hohenstaufen inheritance and led an army to Sicily.

There ensued a long, bloody, indecisive struggle known by the romantic name, "the War of the Sicilian Vespers." For twenty years Charles of Anjou and his successors, backed by the French monarchy and the papacy, fought against the Sicilians and Aragonese. In the end, southern Italy remained under Charles of Anjou's heirs, who ruled it from Naples, while the island of Sicily passed under the control of the kings of Aragon. The dispute between France and Aragon over southern Italy and Sicily persisted for generations and was an important factor in the politics of modern Europe.

The strife of the thirteenth century destroyed Sicilian prosperity. Once the wealthiest and most enlightened state in Italy, the kingdom of Sicily became pauperized and divided—a victim of international politics and of the ruthless struggle between papacy and empire.

The Papacy After Innocent III

To judge by the disintegration of the Holy Roman Empire, one might conclude that the papacy had won an overwhelming victory. But as popes like Innocent III, Gregory IX, and Innocent IV became increasingly absorbed in power politics, the papacy was slowly losing its hold on the hearts of Christians. Papal excommunication, after several centuries of overuse, was no longer the terrifying weapon it once had been. To call a crusade against Frederick II was an effective means of harassment, but the crusading ideal was debased in the process.

As the papacy became a great political power and a big business, it found itself in need of ever-increasing revenues. By the end of the thirteenth century the papal tax system was admirably efficient, with the result that the papacy acquired an unsavory reputation for greed. As one contemporary complained, the supreme pastor was supposed to lead Christ's flock, not to fleece it. Ironically, the fiscal and political cast of the later medieval papacy came as a direct consequence of its earlier dream of becoming the spiritual dynamo of a reformed Christendom. Rising to prominence in the eleventh century on the floodtide of the new popular piety, the papacy became in the twelfth and thirteenth centuries increasingly insensitive to the deeper spiritual aspirations of Christians.

The papacy humbled the empire only to be humbled itself by the rising power of the new centralized monarchies of northern Europe. By the end of the thirteenth century a new concept of royal sovereignty was in the air. The kings of England and France were becoming less and less willing to tolerate the existence of a semi-independent, highly privileged, internationally controlled Church within their realms. By endeavoring to bring these ecclesiastical "states within states" under royal control, the two monarchies encountered vigorous papal opposition. The issue of papal versus royal control of the Church was an old one, but the ancient controversy now took a new form. The monarchies found themselves increasingly in need of money, particularly after 1294 when England and France became locked in a costly war. Both monarchies adopted the novel policy of systematically taxing the clergy of their realms, and Pope Boniface VIII (1294–1303) retaliated in 1296 with the papal bull *Clericis Laicos* that expressly forbade this practice. Once again, monarchy and papacy were at an impasse.

Boniface VIII was another lawyer-pope—proud, aged, and inflexible—whose visions of papal power transcended even Innocent III's. He made it known that the pope is the "emperor sent from heaven" and "can do whatever God can do." But Boniface failed to grasp the momentous implications of the new centralized monarchies. His great weakness was his inability to bend his stupendous concepts of papal authority to the realities of European politics.

In King Philip the Fair of France (1285–1314) Boniface had a dangerous antagonist. Ignoring *Clericis Laicos,* Philip continued to tax his clergy. At the same time he set his agents to work spreading scandalous rumors about the pope's morals and exerted financial pressure on Rome by cutting off all papal taxes from his French realm. Boniface was obliged to submit for the moment, but a vast influx of pilgrims into Rome in the Jubilee year of 1300 restored the pope's confidence. He withdrew his concession to Philip the Fair on clerical taxation and in 1302 issued the bull *Unam Sanctam,* which asserted the doctrine of papal monarchy in uncompromising terms: "We declare, announce, affirm and define that, for every human creature, to be subject to the Roman pontiff is absolutely necessary for salvation."

Philip the Fair now summoned a kingdom-wide assembly, and before it he accused Boniface of every imaginable crime from murder to black magic to sodomy to keeping a demon as a pet. A small French military force crossed into Italy in 1303 and took Boniface prisoner at his palace at Anagni with the intention of bringing him to France for trial. Anagni, the antithesis of Canossa, symbolized the humiliation of the medieval papacy. The French plan failed—Boniface was freed by local townspeople a couple of days later—but the proud old pope died shortly thereafter, outraged and chagrined that armed Frenchmen had dared to lay hands on his sacred person. Contemporaries found it significant that his burial was cut short by a furious electrical storm.

The high tide of papal monarchy now began to recede. In 1305 the cardinals elected the Frenchman Clement V (1305–1314), a native of Gascony, who pursued a policy of cautious accommodation to the French throne. Clement submitted on the question of clerical taxation and publicly burned *Unam Sanctam*, conceding that Philip the Fair, in accusing Pope Boniface, had shown "praiseworthy zeal." A few years after his election, Clement abandoned faction-ridden Rome for a new papal capital at Avignon on the Rhône river, in present-day southern France, where the papacy remained for several generations. At Avignon the papal administration continued to grow, and papal spiritual prestige continued to diminish. The town of Avignon belonged to the papacy, not to the French crown, yet France's enemies could never be confident of the Avignon papacy's political impartiality. The French kings were strong, and they were nearby.

It is easy to criticize Boniface VIII's inflexibility or Clement V's eagerness to please, but the waning of papal authority in the later Middle Ages did not result primarily from personal shortcomings. It stemmed from an ever-widening gulf between papal government and the spiritual thirst of ordinary Christians, combined with the hostility to Catholic internationalism on the part of increasingly powerful centralized states such as England and France. It would be grossly unfair to describe the high-medieval papacy as "corrupt." Between 1050 and 1300 men of high purposes sat on the papal throne. Not satisfied merely to chide the society of their day by innocuous moralizing from the sidelines, they plunged into the world and struggled to sanctify it. Tragically, perhaps inevitably, they soiled their hands.

CONCLUSION

The foregoing account of the high-medieval papacy has attempted to balance the ideal of ecclesiastical centralization against the untidy local realities of episcopal autonomy, noncompliance with papal commands, and disputes between archbishops, bishops, and abbots. Distances were too great and ecclesiastical egos too tender for the pope to become the great puppeteer of the European Church. And secular rulers were much too strong to permit anything resembling a papal theocracy.

Nevertheless, looking at the high-medieval Church from the broadest possible perspective we see a religious institution with a cohesion, independence, and political leverage unmatched in all history. Although popes were never able to dominate kingdoms, at crucial moments they could wrestle with kings on even terms. The papacy was thus able to play an historically unprecedented role in inhibiting the rise of royal absolutism. Unlike the patriarchs of Constantinople, the popes acted independently of imperial control. And they fought tooth and claw to retain their independence against the threat of imperial encirclement—as Frederick II discovered to his sorrow.

Beneath the dust clouds of battles and high politics, the Church sponsored the rise of universities, of schools and hospitals in vast number, of hostels for the poor and refuges for orphans and the physically handicapped.

Under papal direction, Church law and doctrine were developed and refined, and theological systems emerged that explored in rational terms the secrets of divine creation. In these and countless other ways the high-medieval Church served and shaped the civilization of Western Europe. Notwithstanding historical myths to the contrary, the Church did far more to stimulate European rationalism than to shackle it, to limit autocracy than to encourage it, to affirm human dignity than to diminish it. The impact of medieval Christianity on our modern world is too pervasive and complex to be precisely measured. But it may be more than coincidence that the civilization that has transformed the globe emerged from a society that possessed, in the words of Sir Richard Southern, "the most elaborate and thoroughly integrated system of religious thought and practice the world has ever known."

13

The Growth of the Kingdoms of England and France

ENGLAND AND ITS CONTINENTAL DOMINIONS

The Anglo-Norman Monarchy

While empire and papacy were engaged in their drawn-out struggle, England and France were evolving into centralized states. Strong monarchy came to England sooner than to France, yet in the long run it was the English who were the more successful in limiting royal power. French royal absolutism and English parliamentary monarchy are both rooted in the High Middle Ages.

More than that, the rise of effective royal law and administration was an early, crucial step in the evolution of the political environment that surrounds us today. The secret of writing entertaining administrative history has yet to be discovered, but the tedious details of medieval governance in England and France mark the genesis of the modern state and all that it implies. These details can be overlooked only at the peril of missing one of the most fundamental medieval contributions to modern civilization.

The Anglo-Saxon period of English history came to an end when Duke William of Normandy won the English crown with his victory at Hastings in 1066. Thereafter, William the Conqueror and his successors ruled wide dominions on both sides of the English Channel. As kings of England they were masterless, but the French monarchy claimed the overlordship of their possessions in France. England's continental involvement continued, with various ups and downs, from 1066 until the mid-fifteenth century. It led to generations of hostility between the two monarchies, but it was also a source of power and wealth to the kings of England. Throughout much of the period between 1066 and 1204, England was merely one important component of a great trans-channel realm that played a dominant part in twelfth-century politics. When the English monarchy lost the bulk of its French dominions in 1204, its power declined sharply, while the kings of France became the foremost monarchs of thirteenth-century Christendom.

230

The English kingdom that William the Conqueror won in 1066 was already centralized and well-governed by the standards of mid-eleventh-century Europe. Its kings had enjoyed the direct allegiance of all their subjects. Its army was subject only to the commands of the king or his representatives. An informal counsel of churchmen, nobles, and royal household officials known as the *witenagemot* advised the king on important matters and approved the succession of new kings. The chief officers in the royal household were coming to assume important administrative responsibilities: issuing writs that carried royal decisions and commands to local officials in the countryside, administering the royal finances, and performing other governmental functions. Although the pre-Conquest royal household was constantly on the move, traveling around England from one royal estate to another, the treasury had become fixed permanently at Winchester.

England in 1066 had long been divided into shires (or counties), each with its own shire court and its own royal officer—the "shire reeve," or sheriff. It was the sheriff's responsibility to collect royal taxes and the revenues of royal estates, and to assemble the shire's military contingent when the king summoned the army. The sheriff presided over the shire court, the membership of which was drawn from important landholders of the district. The customs and procedures of the shire court were rooted in local traditions, and the sheriff, too, was usually a local figure whose sympathies were apt to be divided between his native shire and the king. The interplay between local initiative and royal authority that characterized Anglo-Saxon government persisted over the post-Conquest centuries to give England a political balance lacking in most medieval states.

William the Conqueror came to England as a legitimate claimant to the throne, related (distantly) to Edward the Confessor who died childless early

Chronology of the English and French Monarchies in the High Middle Ages

England	France
1066: Norman Conquest of England	987–1328: Rule of the Capetian Dynasty
1066–1087: Reign of William the Conqueror	1060–1108: Reign of Philip I
1087–1100: Reign of William II	
1100–1135: Reign of Henry I	1108–1137: Reign of Louis VI, "the Fat"
1135–1154: Disputed succession: King Stephen	
1154–1189: Reign of Henry II	1137–1180: Reign of Louis VII
1189–1199: Reign of Richard I, "the Lion-Hearted"	1180–1223: Reign of Philip II, "Augustus"
1199–1216: Reign of John	
1203–1204: Loss of Normandy	1214: Battle of Bouvines
1215: Magna Carta	1223–1226: Reign of Louis VIII
1216–1272: Reign of Henry III	1226–1270: Reign of St. Louis IX
1264–1265: Simon de Montfort's rebellion	1270–1285: Reign of Philip III
1272–1307: Reign of Edward I	1285–1314: Reign of Philip IV, "the Fair"

in 1066. The *witenagemot* had chosen Edward's brother-in-law, Harold, earl of Wessex, to succeed him. But when Harold was killed at Hastings and his army routed, William maintained that he was assuming his rightful inheritance. He was crowned in London on Christmas Day, 1066, and turned at once to the task of governing his new realm.

William promised to preserve the laws and customs of Edward's day. Indeed, it was to his advantage to do so, since many of these customs were exceedingly beneficial to the monarchy—a smoothly functioning system of taxation, a configuration of shire courts unmatched elsewhere. But William added important new customs, many from his native Normandy, which made his government stronger than that of the Anglo-Saxon kings.

In the years immediately following the Conquest, William effected a revolutionary change in England's aristocratic power structure by dispossessing virtually all Anglo-Saxon landholders and replacing them with his own friends and military followers. The new aristocracy was French-speaking (as was William himself) and well-trained in the continental techniques of mounted combat. William established a feudal regime in England more or less on the Norman pattern but more systematically organized and more directly subordinate to the royal will. Most English estates, both lay and ecclesiastical, were transformed into fiefs, held by crown vassals in return for a specified number of mounted knights and certain other feudal obligations. The greatest of the new magnates tended to acquire their lands piecemeal as the kingdom passed progressively under William's control, with the result that their estates were scattered across various shires rather than coalescing into territorial blocs. This dispersion of great fiefs shaped England's political future, giving the baronage a kingdomwide perspective at a time when France and Germany—segmented into regional princedoms—remained politically provincial. And William was careful to reserve for his own royal demesne about a sixth of the lands of England (similarly scattered), so that he and his successors would not be mere nominal overlords like the early Capetian kings of France and the later Hohenstaufen emperors.

The English crown vassals, or tenants-in-chief, in order to raise the numerous knights required by the monarchy, subdivided portions of their fiefs into smaller fiefs and granted them to knightly subvassals. In other words, the process of subinfeudation in post-Conquest England followed the earlier continental pattern, except that it occurred much more swiftly and systematically. As a byproduct of the establishment of this new aristocracy, scores of castles were quickly erected across the land by the king and his barons. Most of these early castles were simply square wooden towers built on earthen mounds and encircled by wooden palisades. Only later did they become elaborate works of stone.

With the resources of their vast royal domain on which to draw, the Norman kings of England were generally successful in keeping their vassals under tight rein. Their authoritative position in the Anglo-Norman feudal structure owed much to the centralizing traditions of the Anglo-Saxon monarchy.

The new barons established feudal courts, as had been their custom in Normandy, but alongside these baronial courts there persisted the older shire courts. The new feudal army could be an effective force, but when it proved inadequate or unreliable, the monarchy would summon the Old English army or use the royal revenues to hire mercenary troops.

Feudal particularism was diminished by the Anglo-Saxon custom of general allegiance to the crown, which enabled the Norman kings to claim the direct and primary loyalty of every vassal and subvassal in England. A knight's allegiance to his lord was now secondary to his allegiance to the king. Private war between vassals was prohibited, and private castles could be built only by royal license. In brief, the newly imported system of fiefs and vassals was molded by the powerful Anglo-Saxon tradition of royal supremacy, and by William the Conqueror's authority, into a tightly centralized regime.

On the Conqueror's death, his kingdom passed in turn to his two sons, William II (1087–1100) and Henry I (1100–1135). Both were strong leaders, but Henry I was the abler of the two. A skillful diplomat and administrative innovator, Henry I rid England of rebellion and exploited the growing prosperity of his day through heavy taxes. By exiling troublemakers and winning baronial friends through his adroit use of royal patronage, Henry created a docile and strongly royalist aristocracy. In the words of one eyewitness observer, he gave his dominions "a peace such as no age remembers, such as his father himself was never able to achieve."

The reigns of William the Conqueror and his sons witnessed a significant growth in royal administrative institutions. A unique survey of landholdings known as *Domesday Book,* the product of William the Conqueror's kingdomwide census of 1086, bears witness to the administrative vigor of the new regime. Between 1066 and 1135 the royal administration became steadily more elaborate and efficient. By the close of Henry I's reign, royal justices were traveling about England hearing cases in the shire courts, extending the king's jurisdiction far and wide across the land. The baronial courts and ecclesiastical courts continued to function, as did the traditional shire courts (under tightening royal control), but royal justice was on the march, and Henry I's innovations mark the initial step in a long, significant process whereby folk and private courts were gradually overshadowed by the king's courts.

Administrative efficiency and royal centralization were the keynotes of Henry I's reign. Royal dues were collected systematically by the king's sheriffs, who delivered their revenues to a remarkable new central auditing board known as the "exchequer." An effective royal bureaucracy was gradually coming into being. The growing efficiency of the exchequer and the expansion of royal justice were both motivated in part by the king's desire for larger revenues. For the more cases the royal justices handled, the more fines went into the royal treasury; the more closely the sheriffs were supervised, the less likely it was that royal taxes would stick to their fingers. The Norman kings discovered that strong government was good business.

The Anglo-Norman Church was ornamented by two exceptionally able archbishops of Canterbury: Lanfranc (d. 1089) and St. Anselm (d. 1109). Both were theologians; both, in different ways, were deeply involved in the politics of their day; and both were Italians who had migrated to the Benedictine monastery of Bec in Normandy.

William the Conqueror drew Lanfranc from Normandy in 1070 to become archbishop of Canterbury and primate of the English Church. William and Lanfranc were contemporaries of Hildebrand and could not help becoming involved in the raging controversy over ecclesiastical reform. The king and archbishop were both sympathetic to reform, but neither was receptive to the Gregorian notion of an independent Church under tight papal control. William and Lanfranc were more than willing to work toward the abolition of simony and clerical marriage. But when Gregory insisted on becoming William's overlord, the Conqueror flatly refused: "I have not consented to pay fealty nor will I now, because I never promised it, nor do I find that my predecessors ever paid it to your predecessors."

Gregory VII, preoccupied with his struggle against the Holy Roman emperor, could not afford to alienate William, who was, after all, friendly toward reform. Accordingly, the specific issue of lay investiture did not emerge in England until after Gregory's death. It was raised by St. Anselm, who had followed Lanfranc to Bec and was chosen in 1093 to succeed him as archbishop of Canterbury. Lanfranc and William the Conqueror had worked in close cooperation with one another, but St. Anselm's relations with the Norman monarchy were stormy. Already advanced in years when he became archbishop, Anselm was the foremost theologian of his age. He was also devoted to the notion of ecclesiastical independence.

This notion no Norman king could accept, and Anselm came into conflict with both William II and Henry I. He spent much of his time in exile, and it was not until 1107 that a compromise on the investiture issue was ratified between Henry, Anselm, and the papacy. As in the later Concordat of Worms, the agreement of 1107 banned lay investiture as such but permitted the king to retain much control over Church appointments. And ecclesiastical tenants-in-chief were to continue their traditional practice of rendering homage to the king. Two years thereafter Anselm died, and Henry, rid at last of his troublesome saint, dominated the English Church through pressure and patronage. He continued to support decrees prohibiting simony and enforcing priestly chastity. But as the father of no less than twenty-two bastards, by a parade of mistresses, Henry was thought by some to have questionable credentials as a moral reformer.

Henry I's death in 1135 was followed by a period of unrest brought on by a disputed royal succession. Ironically, Henry's record-breaking romantic exploits resulted in only a single surviving legitimate offspring—a daughter named Matilda, who was wed to Geoffrey Plantagenet, count of Anjou. Henry had arranged the marriage with the hope of healing the longstanding rivalry between the two great powers of northern France, Normandy and Anjou.

Two years before Henry died, Matilda bore him a grandson, Henry Plantagenet, who would ultimately rule widespread dominions including Anjou, Aquitaine, Normandy, and England. But when the old king died, Henry Plantagenet was only two years old, and the crown was seized by Henry I's nephew, Stephen of Blois (1135–1154). For nineteen troubled years Stephen struggled with Matilda, her husband Geoffrey, and their growing son for control of the Anglo-Norman realm, while the barons, some supporting one side and some the other, built unlicensed castles and fought for their own interests. Tormented by warfare, people looked back longingly toward the peaceful days of Henry I. As one chronicler stated, "Whatever King Henry had done, either despotically or in the proper exercise of his royal authority, seemed in comparison most excellent."

Henry II (1154–1189)

Toward the end of Stephen's embattled reign, Henry Plantagenet was growing into vigorous manhood, and his prospects were brightening year by year. He became duke of Normandy in 1150 and inherited Anjou on the death of his father Geoffrey in 1151. In 1152 he extended his dominion still further by marrying Eleanor, heiress of the large southern French duchy of Aquitaine. In 1153 King Stephen was forced by his declining military fortunes to name Henry as his heir, and when Stephen died the following year, Henry peacefully assumed the throne as King Henry II of England (1154–1189).

Henry Plantagenet now ruled an immense constellation of territories north and south of the English Channel, which historians have termed the "Angevin Empire"—Angevin because Henry II and his heirs descended in the male line from counts of Anjou. On the map, these Angevin dominions dwarf the modest territory controlled by the king of France. But Henry II, and his sons who succeeded him, had difficulty in keeping order throughout

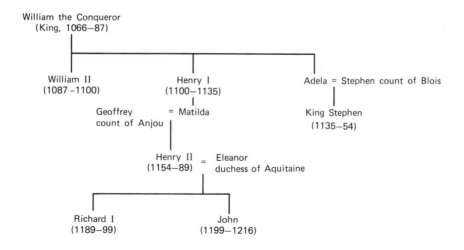

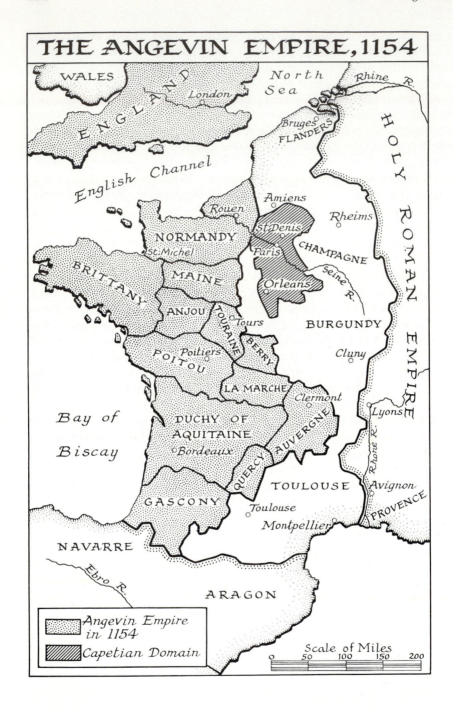

THE ANGEVIN EMPIRE, 1154

WALES

ENGLAND

London

North
Sea

Rhine R.

English Channel

Bruges
FLANDERS

HOLY ROMAN EMPIRE

Rouen

Amiens

Rheims

NORMANDY

St.Denis

St.Michel

Paris

CHAMPAGNE

Orleans

Seine R.

BRITTANY

MAINE

ANJOU

TOURAINE

Tours

BERRY

BURGUNDY

POITOU

Poitiers

Cluny

LA MARCHE

Clermont

Lyons

Bay of

Biscay

DUCHY OF
AQUITAINE

AUVERGNE

Rhone R.

Bordeaux

QUERCY

TOULOUSE

Avignon

GASCONY

Toulouse

PROVENCE

Montpellier

NAVARRE

Ebro R.

ARAGON

Angevin Empire
in 1154

Capetian Domain

Scale of Miles

0   50   100   150   200

these vast, diverse territories. They were a source of wealth, power, and prestige to their rulers, but a burden as well. And the passing of all these districts into the control of one man destroyed for all time the system of medium-sized principalities that had previously shaped the political development of France.

Henry was an energetic, brilliant, exuberant man—short, burly, and redheaded. Named after his grandfather, he was more flamboyant than Henry I yet ruled in his imperious tradition and consciously imitated him. In many respects he was a creature of his age—a product of the intellectual and cultural outburst of twelfth-century Europe. He was a literate monarch who consorted with scholars, encouraged the growth of towns, and presided over an age of economic boom. A chaos of feverish activity pervaded his court, which was constantly on the move and, in the opinion of one court scholar, "a perfect portrait of hell."

Henry pursued the interdependent goals of preserving his Angevin dominions, strengthening his royal authority, and increasing his revenues. He began his reign by ordering the destruction of unlicensed castles that English barons had thrown up during the previous anarchic period and was cautious thereafter in permitting new private castles to be built. At once he began to recover the royal privileges that had been eroding during Stephen's reign and, in some cases, to expand them. During the thirty-five years of his rule in England, the royal administration grew in complexity and effectiveness. The maturity of Henry's exchequer is illustrated not only by a series of annual financial accounts—known as "Pipe Rolls"—but also by a comprehensive, detailed treatise on the exchequer's organization and methods—the *Dialogue of the Exchequer*—written by one of the king's financial officers. The royal secretarial office—the chancery—was similarly increasing in efficiency and scope. Indeed, the entire royal administration was growing more specialized, more professional, and more self-conscious. Separate administrative departments were evolving, and public records became fuller and more extensive. Many were delighted at the return of peace and order; others were uneasy over the steady rise of "big government."

Throughout the twelfth century, commerce was becoming ever more vigorous, and the circulation of money was rapidly increasing. Under the pressure of royal ambition and the growing money economy, the older feudal relationship of service in return for land was giving way to wage service. By the time of Henry II it had become commonplace for feudal tenants-in-chief to pay scutage to the crown in lieu of their military-service obligation. Dues from the royal demesne estates were being collected in coin rather than in kind, and royal troops, servants, and administrators customarily served for wages. These trends can be traced back to the reign of Henry I and beyond, but under Henry II they were accelerating. The baronage remained powerful, but feudal obligations were being translated into fiscal terms. Both the economy and the administration were steadily increasing in complexity and sophistication.

Henry II has been called the father of the English common law. Like his predecessors he favored the extension of royal jurisdiction, partly for its financial rewards to the crown. In his quest for ever-greater judicial revenues he was able to advance the powers of the royal courts and the activities of the itinerant royal justices well beyond their former limits. His "Assize of Clarendon" of 1166 widened the scope of royal justice to include the indictment and prosecution of local criminals. It provided that regional inquest juries should meet periodically under royal auspices to identify and denounce neighborhood criminals, whose guilt or innocence was then to be determined by the ordeal of cold water.* Henry's skepticism toward this ancient procedure is suggested by his provision that if the accused person was of notorious reputation, he should be exiled even if he passed the ordeal.

The inquest juries set up by the Assize of Clarendon were more akin to the modern grand jury than to the modern trial jury, for their duty was to investigate and indict rather than to judge guilt. Inquest juries had been used before: they were assembled under William the Conqueror to provide information for the Domesday survey; there is a reference to one such jury in the records of late Anglo-Saxon times; and bodies of a similar nature were employed in the administration of Carolingian Francia. Never before, however, had they been used in such a systematic fashion.

Henry also extended royal jurisdiction over the tangled jungle of land disputes. Here again local juries were employed to determine the rightful possessors or heirs of disputed estates. The most important of Henry's "possessory assizes," the "Assize of Novel Disseisin," was designed to protect property rights by providing a legal action for anyone who was wrongfully dispossessed of an estate. Regardless of whether the plaintiff had a just claim to the estate in question, if he had been dispossessed without legal judgment he was entitled to purchase a royal writ commanding the sheriff to assemble a jury to determine the facts of the case. If the jury concluded that the plaintiff had indeed been wrongfully dispossessed, the sheriff, acting with full royal authority, would see that the estate was restored. Another of the new legal actions provided by Henry II—the "Grand Assize"—used a similar procedure of purchased writ and jury to determine not whether the plaintiff had been improperly dispossessed, but whether he had, in fact, the best title to the land in question.

These and similar assizes carried the king's justice into an area that had once been dominated by the baronial courts, which often settled questions of land possession by the crude procedure of trial by combat. Previous kings had intervened in quarrels over property, but only on an *ad hoc* basis, never in such a consistent, systematic way. Now, English landholders turned *en masse* to Henry II's courts for quick, rational justice. The baronial courts, with their leisurely procedures, lost out in the competition. Gradually the patchwork of local laws and customs that had so long divided England was giving way to a uniform royal law—a "common law" by which all free subjects were ruled. The *political* unification of the tenth-century kings of Wessex was con-

*See p. 27.

summated by a process of *legal* unification that advanced significantly under the early Angevin kings.

Henry II also sought to expand royal justice at the expense of the ecclesiastical courts. A separate system of ecclesiastical jurisdiction had long been in effect, distinct from the various secular courts—local, baronial, and royal. The ecclesiastical court system can be regarded as one manifestation of the complex government of the international Church, which, as it became more and more elaborate, came increasingly into conflict with the growing governmental structures of England and other secular states. The two governments, royal and ecclesiastical, were both expanding in the twelfth century, and conflicts between them were bound to occur. The first great conflict centered on Anselm, the second on Becket.

In 1162 Henry sought to bring the English Church under strict royal control by appointing to the archbishopric of Canterbury his chancellor and good friend, Thomas Becket. But in raising Becket to the primacy, Henry had misjudged his man. As chancellor Becket had been a devoted royal servant, but as archbishop of Canterbury he became a fervent defender of ecclesiastical independence and an implacable enemy of the king. Henry and Becket became locked in a furious quarrel over the issue of royal control of the English Church. In 1164 Henry issued a list of pro-royal provisions relating to church-state relations known as the "Constitutions of Clarendon," which, among other things, prohibited appeals to Rome without royal license and established a degree of royal control over the Church courts. Henry maintained that the Constitutions of Clarendon represented ancient custom; Becket regarded them as unacceptable infringements of the freedom of the Church.

At the heart of the quarrel was the issue of whether churchmen accused of crimes should be subject to royal jurisdiction after being found guilty and punished by Church courts. The king complained that "criminous clerks" were often given absurdly light sentences by the ecclesiastical tribunals. A murderer, for example, might simply be defrocked and released, whereas in the royal courts the penalty was execution or mutilation. The Constitutions of Clarendon provided that once a cleric was tried, convicted, and defrocked by an ecclesiastical court, the Church should no longer prevent his being brought to a royal court for further punishment. Becket replied that nobody ought to be put in double jeopardy. In essence, Henry was challenging the competence of an agency of the international Church, whereas Becket, as primate of England, felt bound to defend the ecclesiastical system of justice and the privileges of churchmen. Two worlds were in collision.

Henry turned on his archbishop, accusing him of various crimes against the kingdom, and Becket, denying the king's right to try an archbishop, fled England to seek papal support. Pope Alexander III, who was in the midst of his struggle with Frederick Barbarossa, could not afford to alienate Henry; yet neither could he turn against such an ardent ecclesiastical champion as Becket. The great lawyer-pope was forced to equivocate—to encourage Becket without breaking with Henry—and Becket remained in exile for the next six years. At length, in 1170, the king and his archbishop agreed to a truce. Most of the outstanding issues between them remained unsettled, but Becket was permitted to return peacefully to England and resume the archbishopric. At once, however, the two antagonists had another falling out. Becket excommunicated a number of Henry's supporters; the king flew into a rage, and four overenthusiastic barons of the royal household went to Canterbury cathedral and murdered Becket at the high altar.

This dramatic crime made a deep impact on the age. Becket was regarded as a martyr; miracles were alleged to have occurred at his tomb, and he was quickly canonized. For the remainder of the Middle Ages, Canterbury was a major pilgrimage center, and the cult of St. Thomas enjoyed immense popularity. Henry, who had not ordered the killing but whose anger had prompted it, suffered acute embarrassment. He was obliged to do penance by walking barefoot through the streets of Canterbury and submitting to a flogging by the Canterbury monks. But his campaign against the ecclesiastical courts was delayed only momentarily. Although forced to give in on specific matters such as royal jurisdiction over criminous clerks and unlicensed appeals to Rome, he obtained through indirection and maneuvering what he had failed to win through open conflict. He succeeded generally in arranging the appointment to high ecclesiastical offices of men friendly to the crown, and by the end of his reign royal justice had made significant inroads on the authority of the Church courts. Here, as elsewhere, Henry was remarkably successful in steering England toward administrative and legal centralization.

Throughout his reign Henry divided his time between England and the other territories of his "Angevin Empire." Strictly speaking, these trans-channel dominions did not constitute an empire in any real sense, nor were they called an empire at the time. They were, instead, a multiplicity of individual political units, each with its own customs and administrative structure, bound together by their allegiance to Henry Plantagenet. The French monarchy did what it could to break up this threatening configuration, encouraging rebellions on the part of Henry's sons and his estranged wife, Eleanor of Aquitaine. Henry put down the rebellions one by one, relegated Eleanor to comfortable imprisonment in a royal castle, and sought to placate his sons. It did little good. The rebellions persisted, and as Henry neared death in 1189 his two surviving sons, Richard and John, were both in arms against him. In the end the aged monarch was outmaneuvered and defeated by his offspring and their French allies; he died with the statement, "Shame, shame on a conquered king."

Richard and John

Although Henry's final days were saddened by defeat, his Angevin dominions remained intact, passing into the hands of his eldest surviving son, Richard I, "the Lion-Hearted" (1189–1199). This warrior-king devoted himself chiefly to two projects: defending his possessions in France against the French crown and crusading against the Muslims. He was a skillful general who not only won renown on the Third Crusade but also foiled every attempt of the French monarchy to reduce his continental territories. He spent less than six months of his ten-year reign in England, and during his protracted absences, the administrative system of Henry II proved its worth. It governed England more or less satisfactorily for ten kingless years and even produced the huge ransom demanded by Emperor Henry VI, who had imprisoned Richard on his homeward journey from the Holy Land.

The fortunes of the Angevin dominions veered sharply with the accession of King John (1199–1216), Richard the Lion-Hearted's younger brother. John is an enigmatic figure—brilliant in certain respects, a master of administrative detail, but suspicious, unscrupulous, and mistrusted. His crisis-prone career was sabotaged repeatedly by the half-heartedness with which his vassals supported him—and the energy with which some of them opposed him.

In Philip Augustus of France (1180–1223) John had a shrewd, unremitting antagonist. Philip took full advantage of his position as overlord of John's continental possessions. In 1202 John was summoned to the French royal court to answer charges brought against him by one of his own Aquitainian vassals. When John refused to come, Philip Augustus declared his French lands forfeited and proceeded to invade Normandy. The duchy quickly fell into Philip's hands (1203–1204). John's demoralized Norman vassals began to defect, one after another, and John himself fled to England—leaving his remaining loyalists twisting in the wind. In the chaos that followed, Philip Augustus was able to wrest Anjou and other French dominions from John's control. Only portions of distant Aquitaine retained their connection with the English monarchy. King John had sustained a monstrous political and military disaster.

For the next ten years John wove a dextrous web of alliances against King Philip in hopes of regaining his lost possessions. His careful plans were shattered by Philip's decisive victory over John's Flemish and German allies at the battle of Bouvines in 1214.* With Bouvines went John's last hope of recovering Normandy and Anjou.

In the decade between the loss of Normandy and the catastrophe at Bouvines, John engaged in a bitter quarrel with Pope Innocent III. At stake was royal control over the appointment of an archbishop of Canterbury. According to canon law and established custom, a bishop or archbishop was to be elected by the canons or monks of the cathedral chapter. The investiture controversy notwithstanding, such elections were commonly controlled by the king, who would overawe the chapter into electing the candidate of his choice. In 1205, however, the monks of Canterbury, declining to wait for royal instructions, elected one of their own number as archbishop and sent a delegation to Rome to obtain Pope Innocent's confirmation. Going personally to Canterbury, John forced the monks to hold another election and to select his own nominee. In the course of events several delegations went from England to Rome, and Innocent, keenly interested in the enforcement of proper canonical procedures, quashed both elections. He ordered those Canterbury

*See pp. 222–223.

monks who were then in Rome—quite a number by this time—to hold yet another election, and under papal influence they elected Stephen Langton, a learned Englishman who had spent some years as a scholar in Paris.

Furious that his own candidate should have been passed over, John refused to confirm Langton's appointment or admit him into England. For the next six years, 1207–1213, John held to his position, while Innocent used every weapon at his disposal to make the king submit. England was laid under interdict; John retaliated by confiscating all ecclesiastical revenues. John was excommunicated, and Innocent even threatened to depose him. This threat, together with the danger of a projected French invasion of England with full papal backing, forced John to submit at last. In 1213 he accepted Stephen Langton as archbishop of Canterbury. Going still further, John conceded to Innocent the overlordship of England that Gregory VII had fruitlessly demanded of William the Conqueror long before. John agreed to hold his kingdom thenceforth as a papal fief and render a substantial annual tribute to Rome. Having lost the struggle over the archbishopric, John was anxious to transform his papal antagonist into a devoted friend, and his concession of the overlordship had precisely that effect.

John had won the papal friendship, but many of his own barons were regarding him with increasing hostility. The Bouvines disaster of 1214, coming at the end of a long series of expensive and humiliating diplomatic failures, diminished John's prestige still further. It paved the way for the uprising of English barons that ended on the field of Runnymede in 1215, where they forced John to issue *Magna Carta* ("the Great Charter"). John had been taxing his subjects with grim efficiency to support his luckless military and diplomatic maneuvers, and he had proven himself much less adroit than his royal predecessors in winning the support of great magnates through favoritism and patronage. His baronial enemies had good reason to oppose him.

Magna Carta has been interpreted in contradictory ways: as the foundation stone of England's later constitutional monarchy, and as a backward-looking document designed to favor the old aristocracy at the expense of the enlightened Angevin regime. But in historical perspective, Magna Carta was both feudal and constitutional, both backward-looking and forward-looking. Still more to the point, its authors were looking neither forward nor backward but were contending with problems of the moment. Magna Carta's more important clauses were designed to keep the king within the bounds of popular and feudal custom. Royal taxes not sanctioned by custom, for example, were to be levied only by the common counsel of the kingdom. But implicit in the traditional doctrine that the lord had to respect the rights of his vassals and rule according to good customs was the constitutional principle of government under the law. In striving to make King John a good feudal lord, the barons in 1215 were moving uncertainly and unconsciously toward constitutional monarchy. Thus, Magna Carta expresses the notion that the king is bound by traditional legal limitations in his relations with all classes of free Englishmen. One must not lay too much stress on the underlying principles of this intensely practical document, which was concerned primarily with correcting specific royal abuses. But it would be equally misleading to ignore the implication in Magna Carta, derived from feudal ideology, of an overarching body of law which limited and circumscribed royal authority. It was not only the international Church but the feudal nobility as well that set limits to royal absolutism in the High Middle Ages.

The chief constitutional problem in the years following Magna Carta was the question of how an unwilling king might be forced to stay within the bounds of law. A series of royal promises was obviously insufficient to control an ambitious monarch who held all the machinery of the central government in his grasp. Magna Carta itself relied on a watchdog committee of twenty-five barons who were empowered, should the king violate the charter, to call upon the English people "to distrain and distress him in every possible way." The committee was not long idle, for John had no intention of carrying out his promises. He repudiated Magna Carta at the first opportunity, with the full backing of his papal overlord. The result was a full-scale revolt that ended only with John's death in 1216.

The crown now passed, with little objection, to John's nine-year-old son, Henry III (1216–1272), who was supervised during his minority by a baronial council and a papal legate. In the decades that followed, Magna Carta was reissued many times, but the great task of the new age was to create political institutions capable of uniting king, bureaucracy, and baronage in the governance of England. The ultimate solution to this problem was found in Parliament.

Henry III

Henry III was a petulant, erratic monarch, pious without being holy, bookish without being wise. Surrounding himself with foreign favorites and intoxicated by grandiose, impractical foreign projects, he ignored the advice of his barons and gradually lost their confidence.

Ever since its beginning, the English monarchy had customarily arrived at important decisions of policy with the advice of a royal council of nobles, prelates, and officials. In Anglo-Saxon times, this council was called the *witenagemot;* after 1066 it was known as the *curia regis*—the "king's court." Its composition had always been vague, and it had never possessed anything resembling a veto power over royal decisions. But many of the king's aristocratic subjects valued the tradition of royal policy being framed in consultation with lay and ecclesiastical lords.

Traditionally, English royal councils were of two types. Ordinary royal business was conducted in a small council that perambulated with the king, consisting of household officials along with royal favorites and others who happened to be at court at the time. But on great ceremonial occasions such as Christmas and Easter, or at other times when some important decision was pending, the kings supplemented their normal coterie of advisors by assembling around them all the important noblemen and churchmen of the realm. These great councils eventually evolved into Parliament.

Accompanying the evolution from great council to Parliament was a gradual trend, beginning in the thirteenth century, toward including representatives of the country gentry and the burghers alongside the great barons, prelates, and royal officials. This development resulted from the royal policy, particularly common after Magna Carta, of summoning great councils for the purpose of winning approval of some uncustomary tax. As royal justice and royal taxation gradually expanded to include all free persons of the realm, the magnates lost the power and confidence to commit social inferiors to the payment of a royal tax. Hence, the king found it expedient on occasion to obtain the consent of these lesser orders by summoning their representatives to great councils.

The baronial opposition to Henry III arose primarily from his habit of summoning great councils not for the purpose of consulting his magnates but chiefly to seek their consent to new taxes. For advice he depended heavily on his wife's relatives from southern France. His barons resented being asked to finance foreign schemes on which they had not been consulted and of which they disapproved. They resisted Henry's fiscal demands from the first, and by 1258 the monarch's diplomatic initiatives, military blunders, and soaring debts had brought on a financial crisis of major proportions. To obtain desperately needed monetary support, Henry submitted to a set of baronial limitations on royal power known as the "Provisions of Oxford."

These provisions of 1258 went far beyond Magna Carta in creating machinery to force the king to govern in accordance with good custom and in consultation with his magnates. Great councils, now called "parliaments," were to be assembled three times a year.* They were to include, along with their usual membership, twelve men "elected" by the "community"—in other words, chosen by the barons. These twelve were empowered to speak for all the magnates, so that even if heavily outnumbered in a parliament, their authority would be great. The Provisions of Oxford also established a "Council of Fifteen," chiefly barons, which shared with the king control over the royal administration. Specifically, this council was given authority over the exchequer and the power to appoint the chancellor and other high officers of state.

The Provisions of Oxford proved premature, and the governmental system they established turned out to be unworkable because of baronial factionalism. But they do cast precious light on the attitude of many midthirteenth-century barons toward the royal administration. These magnates had no thought of abolishing the administrative and legal advances of the past two centuries or of weakening the central government. Their interests were national rather than provincial; they sought to exert a degree of control over the royal administration rather than dismantle it. They were motivated

---

*"Parliament" is derived from the French word *parler*, "to talk," from which comes our word "parley."

not by constitutional abstractions but by the need, as they saw it, to curb an incompetent, arbitrary, spendthrift king.

With the failure of the Provisions of Oxford, Henry III resumed exclusive control of his administration and returned to the arbitrary and inept governance that his barons found so distasteful. At length, discontent exploded into open rebellion. A group of dissidents led by Simon de Montfort, earl of Leicester, defeated the royal army at Lewes in 1264 and captured King Henry himself.

For the next fifteen months Simon de Montfort ruled England in the king's name. He shared his authority with two baronial colleagues and a committee of magnates, augmented periodically by parliaments. Simon's government was a product of the same impulse toward baronial participation that had evoked the Provisions of Oxford. But Simon was supported by only a portion of the baronage, along with townspeople and lesser landholders. Many barons remained royalists, as was usually the case in such crises. And with their backing the monarchy rallied under the leadership of the Lord Edward, Henry III's talented son. Edward defeated Simon's army at Evesham in 1265, and the rebellion dissolved.

The Evolution of Parliament

Earlier in 1265 Simon de Montfort had summoned a parliament that included, for the first time, all the classes that were to characterize the parliaments of the late Middle Ages. It included, in addition to great lords and royal officials, two knights from every shire and two burghers from every town. Shire knights and burghers had been called to earlier great councils, but only rarely and for some specific purpose—and never jointly. Simon's chief motive for summoning them was probably to broaden the base of his rebellion, but they continued to be included, from time to time, in the parliaments of subsequent years.

The barons, burghers, and shire knights all brought with them a wealth of local political experience. The burghers in parliament were usually veterans of town government. The shire knights had long been involved in the administration of the counties and county courts. Intermediate between the barons and the peasantry, these men represented a separate, emerging class of country gentry, rooted to their shires and their ancestral estates, experienced in local government. But for several generations, burghers and shire knights were summoned only on occasion. Through the thirteenth century and beyond, parliaments consisted primarily of great lords, royal judges and administrators, and, of course, the king himself.

In 1272 Henry III was succeeded by his son, Edward I, a strong-willed monarch who had the sagacity to take the barons into his confidence. Edward summoned parliaments often and experimented endlessly in their composition. Like Simon de Montfort, he sometimes included shire knights and townsmen, particularly in the later years of his reign. But it was not until well into

the fourteenth century that the knights and burghers began meeting separately from the barons, giving birth to the great parliamentary division into
Lords and Commons.

As the thirteenth century closed, the powers of parliaments remained
vague and their composition was still fluid. Barons might bargain discreetly
with the king in parliament for concessions in return for the granting of a
special tax. But parliaments remained primarily instruments to serve the king's
purposes and to assist him in the governance of the realm. They did so in
many ways: by sitting as a high court of law, by settling thorny issues of law
and administration, by hearing petitions of complaint from subjects seeking
the redress of grievances (particularly those arising from the misconduct of
royal officials), by giving counsel on important matters of state, and by declaring their support in moments of crisis.

Edward I, backed by his officials and usually by a sympathetic baronial
majority, was the controlling figure in all his parliaments. There was nothing
remotely democratic about them. Edward regarded these assemblies as tools
of royal policy and used them to aid and strengthen the monarchy rather than
limit it. He would have been appalled to learn that his royal descendants would
one day be figurehead monarchs and that Parliament was destined to rule
England. Only then would it become evident that Parliament was the crucial
institutional bridge spanning the chasm between medieval feudalism and modern democracy.

Edward I (1272–1307)

The reign of Edward I witnessed the culmination of many trends in English
law and administration that had been developing throughout the High Middle Ages. Edward was a great systematizer, and in his hands the royal administrative structure and the common law acquired the shape and coherence that they were to retain through future centuries.

The four chief agencies of royal government under Edward I were the
chancery, the exchequer, the council, and the household. Chancery and exchequer were by now both permanently established at Westminster, just outside London. The chancery remained the royal secretarial office, and its chief
officer, the chancellor, was the custodian of the great seal by which royal documents were authenticated. A staff of professional chancery clerks prepared
the numerous letters and charters by which the king made his will known
and preserved copies of them for future reference. The exchequer, headed by
a royal official known as the "treasurer," continued to serve, as it long had,
as the king's accounting agency. By now it supervised the accounts not only
of sheriffs but of many other local officials who were charged with collecting
royal revenues.

Unlike the chancery and exchequer, the council and household accompanied the king on his endless travels. Since meetings of the great council
were coming more and more to be referred to as "parliaments," the "council"

in Edward's government is to be identified with the earlier "small council." It was a permanent royal entourage of varied and changing membership, consisting of judges, administrators, magnates, and prelates, who advised the king on routine matters. In the Provisions of Oxford the barons had tried to wrest control of the council from the king, but in Edward's reign it was firmly under royal authority. Traveling with the king, the household became a royal government in miniature. It had its own writing clerks, supervised by the keeper of the privy seal, and its own financial office known as the "wardrobe." By means of his household administration the king could govern on the move, without the necessity of routing all his business through Westminster.

Royal government in the countryside continued to depend on sheriffs and itinerant justices, whose duties and responsibilities were defined and regularized as never before. But now other royal servants were working alongside them: coroners, who were charged with investigating felonies; keepers of the peace, whose duty it was to apprehend criminals; assessors, tax collectors, customs officials, and others—local men, for the most part, who were responsible for serving the king in their native districts.

The royal legal system was also taking permanent form. Cases of singular importance were brought before the king himself, sitting in Parliament or surrounded by his council. Less important cases were handled by the king's itinerant justices or by one of the three royal courts sitting at Westminster: (1) the "king's bench," which heard cases of particular royal concern; (2) the "exchequer court," which, besides its accounting duties, heard cases touching on the royal revenues; and (3) the "court of common pleas," which had jurisdiction over most remaining types of cases. These courts were all staffed with trained professionals— lawyers or, in the case of the exchequer, experienced accountants.

Like his predecessors, Edward worked toward the expansion of royal justice over private justice. From the beginning of his reign he issued numerous writs of *quo warranto* ("by what warrant?"), which obliged lords who claimed the right of private legal jurisdiction to prove their claim by producing a royal charter to that effect. In 1290 Edward issued the statute of *Quo Warranto*, which quashed all private jurisdictions unsupported by royal charter or ancient custom. By means of these policies, Edward eliminated a good number of private jurisdictional franchises and asserted his right to exercise some supervision over those that remained. If a lord seriously abused his jurisdictional authority, Edward was prepared to seize his lands. The ultimate supremacy of the king's jurisdiction was thus established beyond question.

Edward's reign was marked by the appearance of a great many royal statutes that elaborated and systematized royal administrative and legal procedures in many different ways. Law had formerly been regarded as a matter of custom; the king might interpret or clarify it, but he seldom made a new law. As ancient Germanic tradition had it, the king was bound by the customs of his people. It is not always possible to distinguish between the act of clarifying or elaborating old law and making new law, and many of Edward's predecessors had been lawmakers in fact, if not in theory. But in the later thirteenth century the English government began to legislate on a larger scale than before. Even in Edward's day, original legislation was such a solemn affair that the king issued his statutes only with the approval of the "community of the realm" as expressed in his parliaments. Edward dominated his parliaments, and his statutes were unquestionably products of the royal initiative, but it is nevertheless significant that he recognized the role of parliaments in the making of law. In the course of the fourteenth century, Parliament employed its power of approving royal taxes to win control of the legislative process itself.

Thus Edward I completed the work of his predecessors in creating an effective and complex royal administrative system, bringing feudal justice under royal control, and building a comprehensive body of common law. More than that, he solidified the concept of original legislation and nurtured the developing institution of Parliament, setting into motion forces that would have an immense impact on the future of England and the world.

Edward was also a skillful and ambitious warrior. He brought to a decisive end the centuries-long military struggle along the Welsh frontier by conquering Wales altogether in a whirlwind campaign during 1282 and 1283. He granted his eldest son the title "Prince of Wales," which male heirs-apparent to the English throne have held ever since. By a ruthless exploitation of the traditional English overlordship over the Scottish realm he came very near to conquering Scotland and was foiled only by the dogged determination of the Scottish hero-king, Robert Bruce. His war with Philip IV of France was expensive and inconclusive, but it did succeed in preserving English lordship over Gascony (southwestern Aquitaine) which had been seriously threatened. These wars gradually exhausted the royal treasury, and during the latter portion of his reign, Edward was faced with growing baronial and popular opposition to his expensive policies. But the king was able to ride out this opposition by making timely concessions—reissuing Magna Carta and recognizing Parliament's right to approve all extraordinary taxation.

At his death in 1307, Edward left behind him a realm exhausted by his wars but firmly under his control. Edward's England was still, in spirit, a feudal kingdom rather than a modern nation, but the initial steps toward nationhood had been taken.

FRANCE: THE CAPETIAN KINGS

The Early Capetians

When William of Normandy conquered England in 1066, the king of France exerted unsteady control over a modest territory around Paris and Orléans known as the "Île de France" and was virtually powerless in the lands beyond.* Although the French monarchy claimed the overlordship of great princes such as the dukes of Normandy and Aquitaine and the counts of

*See map. p. 236.

Anjou, Flanders, and Champagne, only gradually did it acquire the power and respect to make good this claim. In theory the anointed king of the French was a mighty figure—with his royal charisma, with the sovereign power traditionally associated with monarchy, and with the supreme overlordship. But in reality he was impotent to control the princes and hard-pressed to keep order in the Île de France itself.

Since 987 the French crown had been held by the Capetian dynasty. The achievement of the Capetians in the first century or so of their rule was modest enough. Their one success was in keeping the crown within their own family. The Capetians had gained the throne originally by virtue of being elected by the magnates of the realm, but from the first they sought to purge the monarchy of its elective character and make it hereditary. This they accomplished by managing to produce male heirs at the right moment and by arranging for the new heir to be crowned before the old king died.

In the early twelfth century the Capetians remained no stronger than several of their own vassals. While principalities like Normandy and Anjou were becoming increasingly centralized, the Capetian Île de France, a fertile grain and wine producing district of great potential value to the monarchy, was still ridden with insubordinate barons. If the Capetians were to realize the potential of their royal title they had three great tasks before them: (1) to master and pacify the Île de France; (2) to expand their political and economic base by bringing additional territories under direct royal authority; and (3) to make their lordship over the great feudal principalities real rather than merely theoretical.

During the twelfth and thirteenth centuries a series of able Capetian kings pursued and achieved these goals. Their success was so complete that by the opening of the fourteenth century the Capetians controlled all France, either directly or indirectly, and had developed an efficient, sophisticated royal bureaucracy. They followed no hard and fast formula. Their success depended instead on a combination of luck and ingenuity—on their clever exploitation of the powers which, potentially, they had always possessed as kings and overlords. They were successful in avoiding the family squabbles that had at times paralyzed Germany and the Anglo-Norman dominions. Unlike the German monarchs, they maintained comparatively good relations with the papacy. They had the enormous good fortune of an unbroken sequence of direct male heirs from 987 to 1328. Above all, they seldom overreached themselves: they avoided grandiose schemes, preferring to extend their power gradually and cautiously by favorable marriages, by confiscating the fiefs of vassals who died without heirs, and by dispossessing vassals who violated their feudal obligations toward the monarchy. Yet the majority of the Capetians had no desire to absorb the territories of all their vassals; rather they sought to build a kingdom with a substantial core of royal domain lands surrounded by the fiefs of loyal, obedient magnates.

Philip I, Louis VI, and Louis VII

The first Capetian to work seriously toward the consolidation of royal control in the Île de France was King Philip I (1060–1108), a bloated hedonist who grasped the essential fact that the Capetian monarchy had to make its home base secure before turning to loftier goals. Philip's realistic policy was pursued far more vigorously by his son, Louis VI, "the Fat" (1108–1137)— gluttonous and mediocre, but blessed with an intelligent wife, Adelaide of Murienne. Encouraged by Queen Adelaide, Louis the Fat battled dissident barons of the Île de France year after year, until he could no longer find a horse with the strength to carry him. Besieging baronial castles one by one, he gradually reduced the Île de France to obedience. By his death in 1137 it was orderly and prosperous, and the French monarchy was stronger than it had been since Carolingian times.

Louis the Fat received invaluable assistance in the later part of his reign from Abbot Suger of the great royal monastery of Saint-Denis. This talented statesman served as chief royal adviser from 1130 to 1151 and labored hard and effectively to extend the king's sway, to systematize the royal administration, and, incidentally, to augment the wealth and prestige of Saint-Denis.

Suger provided an invaluable element of continuity between the reigns of Louis the Fat and his son, Louis VII (1137–1180). Pious and gentle, Louis VII was, in the words of one contemporary observer, "a very Christian king, if somewhat simple-minded." When Abbot Suger died in 1151, Louis was left to face unaided a new and formidable threat to the French monarchy. The Angevin dominions were just then in the process of formation, and in 1154 the ominous configuration was completed when Henry Plantagenet, count of Anjou and duke of Normandy and Aquitaine, acceded to the English throne as King Henry II. Louis VII sought to embarrass his mighty vassal by encouraging Henry's sons to rebel, but his efforts were too halfhearted to be successful.

Still, Louis' reign witnessed a significant extension of royal power. Indeed, as one historian has aptly said, it was under Louis VII that "the prestige of the French monarchy was decisively established."* The great vassals of the crown, fearful of their powerful Angevin colleague and respectful of Louis' piety and impartiality, began for the first time to bring cases to the court of their royal overlord and submit their disputes to his judgment. Churchmen and townspeople alike sought his support in struggles with the nobility. These developments resulted not so much from royal initiative as from the fundamental trends of the age toward peace, order, and growing commercial activity. The French were turning in increasing numbers to their genial, unassuming monarch for succor and justice. And the fertile Île de France, now well pacified, was providing more and more revenue for the Capetian treasury.

Philip Augustus: 1180–1223

The French monarchy came of age under Louis VII's talented son, Philip II, "Augustus." Following a policy of dextrous opportunism, Philip Augustus enlarged the royal territories enormously and tightened his overlordship of the remaining principalities.

*Robert Fawtier, *The Capetian Kings of France* (London: Macmillan & Co., 1960), p. 23.

Philip Augustus's great achievement was the destruction of the Angevin configuration and the establishment of royal jurisdiction over Normandy, Anjou, and their dependencies. For two decades he plotted with dissatisfied members of the Angevin family against Henry II and Richard the Lion-Hearted, but it was not until the reign of King John (1199–1216) that Philip's efforts bore fruit. Against John's faithlessness, Philip was able to play the role of the just lord rightfully punishing a disobedient vassal. And when Philip Augustus moved against Normandy in 1203–1204, John's unpopularity played into his hands. The prize that Philip had sought so long was now won with surprising ease. And once Normandy was conquered, John's remaining fiefs in northern France fell quickly. Ten years later, in 1214, Philip extinguished John's last hope of recovering the lost territories by winning his decisive victory over John's German allies at Bouvines.* Settling for good the question of Normandy and Anjou, Bouvines was also a turning point in the power balance between France and Germany in the High Middle Ages. Thereafter the Capetian monarchy overshadowed the faltering kingdom of Germany and the much reduced territories of the kings of England. France became the great power in thirteenth-century Christendom.

Under Philip Augustus and his predecessors significant developments were occurring in the royal administrative system. The *curia regis* had assumed its place as the high feudal court of France and was proving an effective instrument for the assertion of royal rights over the dukes and counts. Hereditary noblemen who had traditionally served as local administrators in the royal territories were gradually replaced by salaried officials known as "baillis." These new officials, whose functions were at once financial, judicial, military, and administrative, owed their positions to royal favor and were fervently devoted to the interests of the crown. Throughout the thirteenth century the baillis worked tirelessly and often unscrupulously to erode the privileges of the aristocracy and extend the royal sway. This loyal and highly mobile bureaucracy, without local roots and without respect for local traditions, became in time a powerful instrument of royal absolutism. The baillis stood in sharp contrast to the local officials in England—the sheriffs and shire knights—who were customarily drawn from the local gentry and whose loyalties were divided between the monarch whom they served and the region and class from which they sprang.

Louis VIII: 1223–1226

The closing years of Philip Augustus's reign were concurrent with the Albigensian crusade, called by Innocent III against the dualist heretics of southern France.† Philip Augustus declined to participate personally in the crusade, but his son, Prince Louis, took an active part in it. And when the prince

*See pp. 222–223, 241.
†See pp. 196–197.

succeeded to his father's throne in 1223 as Louis VIII, he threw all the resources of the monarchy behind the southern campaign. The crusade succeeded in breaking the power of the Albigensians and extending Capetian royal authority southward to the Mediterranean.

It may perhaps be surprising to discover that Louis VIII, who inherited from his father a vastly expanded royal jurisdiction and extended it still further himself, gave out about a third of the hard-won royal territories as fiefs to junior members of the Capetian family. These family fiefs, carved out of the royal domain, are known as *apanages*. Their creation should serve as a warning that the growth of the Capetian monarchy cannot be understood simply as a linear process of expanding the royal territories. The Capetians had no objection to governing through vassals so long as they were obedient and subject to royal control. Indeed, given the limited transportation and communication facilities of twelfth- and thirteenth-century France, the kingdom was too large to be controlled directly by the monarchy. At least for the time being the new vassals, bound to the crown by strong family ties, strengthened rather than weakened the effectiveness of Capetian rule.

St. Louis: 1226–1270

Louis VIII died prematurely in 1226, leaving the kingdom in the skillful hands of his pious Spanish widow, Blanche of Castile, who acted as regent for the boy-king Louis IX (1226–1270), later St. Louis. Even after St. Louis came of age in 1234 he remained devoted to his mother, and Queen Blanche continued for years to play a dominant and highly capable role in the royal government.

St. Louis possessed both his mother's sanctity and his mother's firmness. He was a strong monarch, determined to rule justly and to promote moral rectitude throughout the kingdom of France. His policy was to pursue peace at home while devoting every resource to crusading against the Muslims. Like earlier Crusaders, he hated Judaism: he launched a major effort to persuade Jewish children to become Christians, yet he protected his Jewish subjects from grassroots violence much more effectively than, for example, King Henry III was protecting the Jews in England.

St. Louis was content, in general, to maintain the royal rights established by his predecessors. His baillis and other officials were actually far more aggressive than he in extending the royal power. As one historian put it, "in this reign monarchical progress was the complex result of the sanctity of a revered ruler, and the patient and obstinately aggressive policy of the king's servants." Indeed, St. Louis went to the length of establishing a system of itinerant royal inspectors known as *ênqueteurs*, who reported local grievances and helped keep ambitious officials in check. Originally instituted to keep order in France during Louis' absence on the Sixth Crusade, the *ênqueteurs* labored through the remainder of the reign to restrain the abuses of other royal agents.

Sculpture of St. Louis, Manneville, Normandy.

Louis interpreted the failure of the crusade as a divine punishment for his sins, and from his return in 1254 until his death in 1270 he dedicated himself to creating the ideal Christian monarchy. He opened the royal courts to all freemen and did everything in his power to ensure that royal justice was fair and compassionate. He sponsored charitable works on an unprecedented scale. He instituted a new gold coinage of high quality, to the great benefit of French commerce. And he labored to achieve peace throughout Christendom, arranging treaties with Henry III of England and with the king of Aragon that settled all outstanding disputes. He came to be venerated as a peacemaker among Christians and was even called on to arbitrate between Henry III and his barons (who were chagrined when he decided solidly in favor of the royal authority).

In St. Louis' France, medieval culture blossomed as never before. Towns and commerce flourished, and in the towns magnificent Gothic churches were rising. The University of Paris became Europe's foremost intellectual center, where some of the keenest minds of the age—Bonaventure, Albertus Magnus, Thomas Aquinas—were assembled concurrently. Amidst these developments

THE EXPANSION OF
THE FRENCH ROYAL DOMAIN

St. Louis planned his final Crusade. He died while campaigning in Tunisia in 1270, with victory still eluding him. His most cherished goal was never to be realized, but his policies at home won him the hearts of his Christian subjects. His reign brought enduring prestige to the Capetian family and the French monarchy.

Philip IV, "the Fair": 1285–1314

St. Louis was loved and admired for keeping his ambitious officials in check. Under his successors the royal bureaucracy pursued its centralizing policies with little restraint. The saint-king was succeeded first by his son, Philip III (1270–1285), then by his grandson, Philip IV, "the Fair" or "the Handsome" (1285–1314). Philip the Fair was a silent, enigmatic figure who fails to emerge from the records of his reign as a rounded personality. Lacking St. Louis' infectious charm, he said little and listened much. One of his bishops observed, "He is neither a man nor a beast; he is a statue." Yet Philip was genuinely pious, intensely so after the death of his wife in 1305, and he was by no means lacking in intelligence. He had a flair for choosing skillful ministers who devoted themselves to the exaltation of the French crown.

Philip and his ministers had a lofty view of the rightful authority of the monarchy, a conception derived in part from Roman law. They sought to advance royal power at the expense of the papacy, the nobility, and neighboring states. Philip waged an indecisive war against King Edward I of England over Edward's remaining fiefs in western Aquitaine. He made a serious effort to absorb Flanders, imprisoning the Flemish count and ruling the county directly through a royal agent, but he was thwarted by a bloody uprising of Flemish nobles and townspeople who routed his army at the battle of Courtrai in 1302. More successful was his policy of nibbling aggression to the east against the faltering Holy Roman Empire.

Like Edward I, Philip the Fair was constantly in need of money for his wars. And he was prepared to raise it by almost any means. In 1306 he arrested all the Jews in his dominions, and after seizing their property and loan accounts, he had them expelled from France. Edward I had treated English Jews in the same cruel fashion, and for similar reasons. Philip likewise despoiled his Lombard bankers. Another of his targets was the rich crusading order of Knights Templars, from whom he had been borrowing heavily. He darkened their reputation by a campaign of vituperative propaganda, much of which he may actually have believed. His charge that the Templars venerated the devil was repeated by Edward II of England, and even by the papacy. Philip had more than fifty Templars burned at the stake as heretics, and their wealth found its way into the royal treasury. He launched a similar propaganda campaign, as we have seen, against Pope Boniface VIII, and sent his agents to arrest the proud old pope at Anagni.*

Against his nobles, Philip pursued a strongly royalist policy, demanding direct allegiance and obedience from all the French. All these activities were manifestations of the prevailing political philosophy of his reign: that the French king was by rights the secular and spiritual master of France and the dominating political figure in Western Christendom.

*See p. 227.

Throughout the thirteenth century the French royal bureaucracy had been developing steadily. The royal revenues came to be handled by a special accounting bureau, roughly parallel to the English exchequer, called the *chambre des comptes*. The King's judicial business became the responsibility of a high court known as the "Parlement of Paris," which was to play a significant political role in later centuries. Under Philip the Fair the bureaucracy became a refined and supple tool of the royal interest; its middle-class background and tenacious royalism gave the king a degree of independence from the nobility that was quite unknown in contemporary England.

Still, the king could not rule without support from his subjects. Philip's victory over the papacy on the issue of royal taxation of the clergy and his attacks against the Jews and Knights Templars brought additional money into his treasury. But the soaring expenses of government and warfare forced him to seek ever-new sources of revenue and, as in England, to secure his subjects' approval of extraordinary taxation. Instead of summoning a great assembly—a parliament—for this purpose, he usually negotiated individually with various tax-paying groups.

Nevertheless, it was under Philip the Fair that France's first kingdomwide representative assemblies were summoned. Beginning in 1302, the "Estates General" was assembled from time to time, primarily for the purpose of giving formal support to the monarchy in moments of crisis—during the struggle with Pope Boniface VIII, for example, or in the midst of the Knights Templars controversy. The assembly included members of the three great social classes or "estates": the clergy, the nobility, and the townspeople. It continued to meet occasionally over the succeeding centuries, but it never became an integral organ of government as did Parliament in England. Its failure resulted in part from the fact that it had no real voice in royal taxation and was therefore not in a position to bargain with the king through increasing control of the purse strings. It was not, as in England, an evolutionary outgrowth of the royal council, but rather an entirely separate body. There was no real opportunity for the burghers and gentry to join ranks as in the English House of Commons; lacking the important responsibilities in local government that fell on English shire knights, the knights of France remained a subordinate part of the aristocratic class. Above all, the French nobility and bourgeoisie lagged far behind the English in developing a national consciousness. Late-thirteenth-century France was too large, too segmented into cohesive principalities, and too recently brought under royal authority for its inhabitants to have acquired a strong sense of identification as a people. Their outlook remained provincial.

Yet despite the significant differences between the English Parliament and the French Estates General, the two institutions were kindred offspring of feudal monarchy. Both expressed the developing medieval concept of government by the consent of the realm. Similar representative institutions were emerging concurrently all over Western Christendom: in the Christian kingdoms of Spain, in Italy under Frederick II, in the principalities of Germany, and in innumerable counties, duchies, and communes across Europe. Of these many experiments only the English Parliament survives today. But Parliament was merely one particular expression of a broad and fundamental trend in medieval civilization.

CONCLUSION

In the opening years of the fourteenth century, the English Parliament was meeting regularly but the French Estates General only occasionally. The thirteenth-century conflicts between the English kings and nobility had resulted in a monarchy that routinely transacted its most important business in Parliament, with the assent of a nobility that was national in perspective. The outlines of modern England's parliamentary monarchy were already faintly visible in the thirteenth-century idea of a community of the realm.

In France, on the other hand, the crown had become the one great unifying concept. Originating in the cautious efforts of the twelfth-century Capetians, the concept was strengthened by Philip Augustus's military triumphs, strengthened still more by St. Louis' determination to create an ideal Christian monarchy, and given final shape by the royalist policy and ideology of Philip the Fair.

In the course of the High Middle Ages, both monarchies developed effective royal bureaucracies. Both tightened their control over baronial and ecclesiastical jurisdictions, although for centuries to come both would continue to share their sovereign authority—to tax, prosecute criminals, and adjudicate civil disputes—with others within their kingdoms: nobles, bishops, abbots, chartered towns, and rural communes. In 1300 the two regimes as yet had much in common. But with respect to the relationship between crown and community, their paths had clearly forked.

14

Literature, Art, and Thought

Europe in the High Middle Ages underwent an artistic and intellectual awakening that affected every imaginable form of expression. Revolutionary changes in economic, religious, and political institutions were paralleled by developments in literature, architecture, sculpture, drama, law, philosophy, political theory, and science. By the close of the period, the foundations of the Western cultural tradition were firmly established. The following discussion will provide only a glimpse at these achievements.

LITERATURE

The literature of the High Middle Ages was abundant and richly varied. Poetry was written both in the traditional Latin, the universal scholarly language of medieval Europe, and in the vernacular languages of ordinary speech that had long been evolving in the various regions of Christendom. Christian piety found expression in a series of somber and majestic Latin hymns. But one also encounters Latin poetry of quite a different sort, composed by young, wandering scholars and older "nonstudents":

For on this my heart is set, when the hour is nigh me
Let me in the tavern die, with my ale cup by me,
While the angels, looking down, joyously sing o'er me...etc.

One of these wandering-scholar poems is an elaborate and impudent parody of the Apostles' Creed. The phrase from the Creed, "I believe in the Holy Ghost, the Holy [Catholic] Church..." is embroidered as follows:

I believe in wine that's fair to see,
And in the tavern of my host
More than *in the Holy Ghost*
The tavern will my sweetheart be,
And *the Holy Church* is not for me.

These sentiments do not betoken a sweeping trend toward agnosticism but simply reflect the perennial student irreverence toward established institutions.

258

For all its originality, the Latin poetry of the High Middle Ages was out-stripped both in quantity and in variety of expression by vernacular poetry. The drift toward emotionalism, which we have already noted in medieval piety, was closely paralleled by the evolution of vernacular literature from the martial epics of the eleventh century to the delicate, sensitive romances of the thirteenth.

The Epic

In the eleventh and early twelfth centuries, vernacular epics known as *chansons de geste* ("songs of great deeds") were enormously popular among the northern French aristocracy. Sung aloud by minstrels in the halls of castles, these chansons were rooted in the earlier heroic tradition of the Teutonic north that had produced moody and violent masterpieces such as *Beowulf*. The hero Beowulf is a lonely figure who fights monsters, slays dragons, and pits his strength and courage against a wild, windswept wilderness. The chansons de geste were equally heroic in mood. Like old-fashioned Westerns, they were packed with action, and their heroes tended to steer clear of sentimental entanglements with women. The battle descriptions, often characterized by gory realism, tell of Christian knights fighting with almost superhuman strength against fantastic odds. The heroes of the chansons are not only proud and loyal to their lords but also capable of experiencing deep emotions—weeping at the deaths of their comrades and appealing to God to receive the souls of the fallen. In short, the chansons de geste mirror the warlike spirit and sense of military brotherhood that characterized the knighthood of eleventh-century Europe. These qualities find vivid expression in the most famous chanson de geste, the *Song of Roland*, which tells of a bloody battle between a horde of Muslims and the detached rearguard of Charlemagne's army as it was withdrawing from Spain:

Turpin of Reims, his horse beneath him slain,
And with four lance wounds he himself in pain,
Hastens to rise, brave lord, and stand erect.
He looks on Roland, runs to him, and says
Only one thing: "I am not beaten yet!
True man fails not, while life in him is left."
He draws Almace, his keen-edged steel-bright sword,
And strikes a thousand strokes amid the press.

Count Roland never loved a recreant,
Nor a false heart, nor yet a braggart jack,
Nor knight that was not faithful to his lord.
He cried to Turpin—churchman militant—
"Sir, you're on foot, I'm on my horse's back.
For love of you, here will I make my stand,
And side by side we'll take both good and bad.
I'll not leave you for any mortal man."

Now Roland feels that he is nearing death;
Out of his ears the brain is running forth.
So for his peers he prays God call them all,
And for himself St. Gabriel's aid implores.

Roland and his rearguard are slain to a man, but the Lord Charlemagne returns to avenge them, and a furious battle ensues:

Both French and Moors are fighting with a will.
How many spears are shattered! lances split!
Whoever saw those shields smashed all to bits,
Heard the bright hauberks grind, the mail rings rip,
Heard the harsh spear upon the helmet ring,
Seen countless knights out of the saddle spilled,
And all the earth with death and deathcries filled,
Would long recall the face of suffering!

The French are victorious. Charlemagne himself defeats the Moorish emir in single combat, and Roland is avenged:

The Muslims fly, God will not have them stay.
All's done, all's won, the French have gained the day.

It should not be supposed that any such battle actually occurred. By and large, Charlemagne's Spanish campaign was a fiasco, and it was left to the *Song of Roland* to supply the happy ending.

The Lyric

During the middle and later twelfth century the martial spirit of northern French literature was gradually transformed by the influx of the romantic troubadour tradition of southern France. In Provence, Toulouse, and Aquitaine a rich, colorful culture had been developing in the eleventh and twelfth centuries, and out of it came a lyric poetry of remarkable sensitivity and enduring value. The lyric poets of the south were known as "troubadours." Many of them were court minstrels, but some, including Duke William IX of Aquitaine (Eleanor's grandfather), were members of the upper nobility. The wit, delicacy, and romanticism of the troubadour lyrics disclose a more genteel and sophisticated nobility than that of the north—a nobility that preferred songs of love to songs of war. Indeed, medieval southern France was the source of the romantic-love tradition of Western civilization. It was from there that Europe derived such concepts as the idealization of women, the importance of male gallantry and courtesy, and the impulse to embroider relations between man and woman with emotions of eternal oneness, undying devotion, agony, and ecstasy. One of the favorite themes of the lyric poets was the hopeless love—the unrequited love from afar:

I die of wounds from blissful blows,
And love's cruel stings dry out my flesh,

My health is lost, my vigor goes,
And nothing can my soul refresh.
I never knew so sad a plight,
It should not be, it is not right.

I'll never hold her near to me,
My ardent joy she'll ever spurn,
In her good grace I cannot be,
Nor even hope, but only yearn.
She tells me nothing, false or true,
And neither will she ever do.

The author of these lines, Jaufré Rudel (fl. 1148), unhappily and hopelessly in love, finds consolation in his talents as a poet, of which he has an exceedingly high opinion. The poem concludes on a much more optimistic note:

Make no mistake, my song is fair,
With fitting words and apt design.
My messenger would never dare
To cut it short or change a line.

My song is fair, my song is good,
'Twill bring delight, as well it should.

Many such poems were written in twelfth-century southern France. Their recurring theme is the poet's passionate love for a woman. Occasionally, however, the pattern is reversed, as in this mid-twelfth-century lyric poem by Beatritz, countess of Dia, one of twenty known female troubadours:

I live in grave anxiety
For one fair knight who loved me so.
It would have made him glad to know
I loved him too—but silently.
I was mistaken, now I'm sure,
When I withheld myself from him.
My grief is deep, my days are dim,
And life itself has no allure.

I wish my knight might sleep with me
And hold me naked to his breast,
And on my body take his rest,
And grieve no more, but joyous be.
My love for him surpasses all
The loves that famous lovers knew.
My soul is his, my body, too,
My heart, my life, are at his call.

My most beloved, dearest friend,
When will you fall into my power?
That I might lie with you an hour,
And love you 'till my life should end.

My heart is filled with passion's fire.
My well-loved knight, I grant thee grace
To hold me in my husband's place,
And do the things I so desire.

The reversal of roles disclosed in Beatritz of Dia's poem was by no means unusual. Indeed, the idealized qualities of the beloved are often presented with such sexual ambiguity that one cannot tell whether the poet is referring to a man or a woman.

Not every lyric poet took love or life as seriously as Jaufré Rudel or Beatritz of Dia. The following verses by William IX, duke of Aquitaine (1071–1127), parody both the passionate seriousness of the love lyric and the heroic mood of the chanson de geste:

I'll make some verses just for fun, not for myself or anyone,
Nor of great deeds that knights have done, nor lovers true.
I made them riding in the sun, my horse helped, too.

When I was born I'm not aware; I'm neither glad nor in despair,
Nor stiff, nor loose, nor do I care, nor wonder why.
Since meeting an enchantress fair, bewitched am I.

Living for dreaming I mistake, I must be told when I'm awake.
My mood is sad, my heart may break, such grief I bear!
But never mind, for heaven's sake, I just don't care.

I'm sick to death, or so I fear; I cannot see but only hear.
I hope that there's a doctor near, no matter who.
If he can heal me I'll pay dear; if not, he's through.

My lady fair is far away, just who or where I cannot say,
She tells me neither yea nor nay, yet I'm not blue,
So long as all those Normans stay far from Poitou.

My distant love I so adore, though me she has no longing for;
We've never met, and furthermore—to my disgrace—
I've other loves, some three or four, to fill her place.

This verse is done, as you can see, and by your leave, dispatched 'twill be
To one who'll read it carefully in far Anjou.
Its meaning he'd explain to me if he but knew.

The Romance

Midway through the twelfth century, the southern troubadour tradition began to filter into northern France, England, and Germany. It brought with it a new aristocratic ideology of courtly manners, urbane speech, and romantic idealization. These, briefly, were the ideals of what has been called "courtly love." Their impact on the actual behavior of knights was limited, but their effect on the literature of northern Europe was revolutionary. Out of the convergence of vernacular epic and vernacular lyric there emerged a new poetic form known as the "romance."

Like the chanson de geste, the romance was a long narrative; like the southern lyric, it was sentimental and concerned with love. It was commonly based on some theme from the remote past: the Trojan War, Alexander the Great, and above all, King Arthur—the half-legendary sixth-century British king. Arthur was transformed into an idealized twelfth-century monarch surrounded by charming ladies and chivalrous knights. His court at Camelot, as described by the late-twelfth-century French poet, Chrétien de Troyes, was a center of romantic love and refined religious sensibilities where knights worshiped their ladies and went on daring quests in a world of magic and fantasy.

In the chanson de geste the great virtue was loyalty to one's lord; in the romance it was love for one's lady. Several romances portray the old and new values in conflict. An important theme in both the Arthurian romances and the twelfth-century romance of *Tristan and Iseult* is a love affair between a vassal and his lord's wife. Love and feudal loyalty stand face to face, and love wins out. Tristan loves Iseult, the wife of his lord, King Mark of Cornwall. King Arthur's beloved knight Lancelot loves Arthur's wife, Guinevere. In both stories the lovers are ruined by their love, yet love they must—they have no choice—and although the conduct of Tristan and Lancelot would have been regarded by earlier standards as nothing less than treasonable, both men are presented sympathetically in the romances. Love destroys the lovers in the end, yet their destruction is romantic—even glorious. Tristan and Iseult lie dead together, side by side, and in their very death their love achieves its deepest consummation.

Alongside the theme of love in the romances is the theme of Christian purity and dedication. The rough-hewn knight of old, having been instructed to be courteous and loving, was now instructed to be holy. Lancelot was trapped in the meshes of a lawless love, but his son, Galahad, became the prototype of the Christian knight—worshipful and chaste. And Perceval, another knight of the Arthurian circle, quested not for a lost loved one but for the Holy Grail of the Last Supper.

The romance flourished in twelfth- and thirteenth-century France and among the French-speaking nobility of England. It spread also into Italy and Spain and became a crucial factor in the evolution of vernacular literature in Germany. The German poets, known as "Minnesingers," were influenced by the French lyric and romance but developed these literary forms along highly original lines. The Minnesingers produced their own deeply sensitive and mystical versions of the Arthurian stories that, in their exalted symbolism and deep emotion, rival even the works of Chrétien de Troyes and his French contemporaries.

As the thirteenth century drew toward its close, the romance was becoming conventionalized and drained of inspiration. The love story of *Aucassin et Nicolette*, which achieved a degree of popularity, was actually a satirical ro-

mance in which the hero is much less heroic than heroes usually are, and a
battle is depicted in which the opponents cast pieces of cheese at each other.
Based on earlier Byzantine material, *Aucassin et Nicolette* makes mortal love
take priority over salvation itself. Indeed, Aucassin is scornful of Heaven:

> For into Paradise go only such people as these: There go those aged
> priests and elderly cripples and maimed ones who day and night stoop
> before altars and in the crypts beneath the churches; those who go
> around in worn-out cloaks and shabby old habits; who are naked and
> shoeless and full of sores; who are dying of hunger and thirst, of cold
> and misery. Such folks as these enter Paradise, and I will have nothing
> to do with them. I will go to hell. For to hell go the fair clerics and
> comely knights who are killed in tournaments and great wars, and the
> sturdy archer and the loyal vassal. I will go with them. There also go
> the fair and courteous ladies who have loving friends, two or three,
> together with their wedded lords. And there go the gold and silver, the
> ermine and all rich furs, the harpers and the minstrels, and the happy
> folk of the world. I will go with these, so long as I have Nicolette, my
> very sweet friend, at my side.

Another important product of thirteenth-century vernacular literature,
the *Romance of the Rose*, was in fact not a romance in the ordinary sense but an
allegory of the whole courtly love tradition in which the thoughts and emotions of the lover and his lady are personified in actual characters such as
Love, Reason, Jealousy, and Fair-Welcome. Begun by William of Lorris as an
idealization of courtly love, the *Romance of the Rose* was completed after
William's death by Jean de Meun, a man of limited talent and bourgeois origin. Jean's contribution was long-winded and encyclopedic, and the poem
as a whole lacks high literary distinction; yet it appealed to contemporaries
and enjoyed a great vogue.

Fabliaux and Fables

Neither epic, lyric, nor romance had much appeal below the level of the
landed aristocracy. The inhabitants of the rising towns had a vernacular
literature all their own. From the bourgeoisie came the high medieval
fabliaux, short satirical poems filled with vigor and crude humor, which
devoted themselves chiefly to ridiculing conventional morality. Priests and
monks were portrayed as lechers, merchants' wives were easily and frequently seduced, and clever young men perpetually made fools of sober
and stuffy merchants.

Medieval urban culture also produced the fable, or animal story, an allegory in the ancient Greek tradition of *Aesop's Fables*, in which various stock
characters in medieval society were presented as animals—thinly disguised.
Most of the more popular fables dealt with Renard the Fox and were known
collectively as the *Romance of Renard*. These tales constituted a ruthless par-

ody of chivalric ideals in which the clever, unscrupulous Renard persistently outwitted King Lion and his loyal but stupid vassals.

Dante

Vernacular poetry matured late in Italy, but in the works of Dante (1265–1321) it achieved its loftiest expression. Dante wrote on a wide variety of subjects, sometimes in Latin, more often in the Tuscan vernacular. He composed a series of lyric poems celebrating his unconsummated love for the lady Beatrice, which are assembled, with prose commentaries, in his *Vita Nuova* ("the New Life"). Dante's lyrics reflect a more mystical and idealized love than that of the troubadours:

A shining love comes from my lady's eyes,
All that she looks on is made lovelier,
And as she walks, men turn to gaze at her,
Whoever meets her feels his heart arise.

Humility, and hope that hopeth well,
Come to the mind of one who hears her voice,
And blessed is he who looks on her awhile.
Her beauty, when she gives her slightest smile,
One cannot paint in words, yet must rejoice
In such a new and gracious miracle.

Firmly convinced of the literary potential of the Tuscan vernacular, Dante urged its use in his *De Vulgari Eloquentia*, which he wrote in Latin so as to appeal to scholars and writers who scorned the vulgar tongue. And he filled his own vernacular works with such grace and beauty as to convince by example those whom he could not persuade by argument. In his hands the Tuscan vernacular became the literary language of Italy.

Dante's masterpiece, the *Divine Comedy*, was written in the Tuscan vernacular. Abounding in allegory and symbolism, it encompasses in one majestic vision the entire medieval universe. Dante tells of his own journey through hell, purgatory, and paradise to the very presence of God. This device permitted the poet to make devastating comments on past and contemporary history by placing all those of whom he disapproved—from local politicians to popes—in various levels of hell. Virgil, the archetype of ancient rationalism, is Dante's guide through hell and purgatory; the lady Beatrice, a symbol of purified love, guides him through the celestial spheres of paradise; and St. Bernard, the epitome of medieval sanctity, leads him to the threshold of God. The poem closes with Dante alone in the divine presence:

Eternal Light, thou in thyself alone
Abidest, and alone thine essence knows,
And loves, and smiles, self-knowing and self-known....

Here power gave way to high sublimnity,
But my desire and will were turned—as one—

And as a wheel that turneth evenly,
By Holy Love, that moves the stars and sun.

ARCHITECTURE AND SCULPTURE

The Romanesque Style

During the High Middle Ages, stone churches, abbeys, castles, hospitals, and town halls were built in prodigious numbers. More stone was quarried in high-medieval France alone than by the pyramid and temple builders across the 3000-year history of ancient Egypt. The most celebrated buildings of the High Middle Ages are the great cathedrals and abbeys: Chartres, Mont-St-Michel, Westminster Abbey, Notre Dame of Paris, and many more. But it is nearly as impressive, driving through the European countryside, to see stone churches of the twelfth and thirteenth centuries still in use in town after town.

Two great architectural styles dominated the age: the Romanesque style flourished in the eleventh century and early twelfth; during the middle decades of the twelfth century it gave way gradually to the Gothic style. From about 1150 to the early 1300s the most famous of the Gothic cathedrals were built. Thereafter the Gothic builders, having exhausted the structural possibilities of their style, turned to decorative elaboration. At its height, Gothic architecture constituted one of humanity's most audacious and successful architectural experiments.

The cathedrals were designed by master architects, some of whose names have come down to us. Cathedral-building represented an enormous investment of money and effort: Chartres alone would cost about one hundred million dollars to reproduce today. Revenues were raised in a variety of ways—through episcopal taxes and fund drives, through donations by townspeople, guilds, regional lords, and great princes and kings. One of the rose windows of Chartres displays the coats of arms of two of its benefactors—St. Louis and his mother, Blanche of Castile. Other Chartres windows depict the symbols of various contributing guilds—tailors, bakers, shoemakers, wheelwrights. Sometimes townspeople and even noble men and women would perform volunteer labor, pulling carts from the stone quarry to the building site, or carrying food and wine to the workers. At other times people objected violently to heavy episcopal taxes, and construction might be long delayed for want of funds. The building of a cathedral could drag on for a century or more, not because of slow work but because of periodic shortages of money necessary to support a construction of such scope. St. Louis' stunning palace church, La Sainte-Chapelle, was well financed and completed in half a decade.

The evolution of high-medieval architecture was shaped by two fundamental trends in medieval civilization. First, the great cathedrals were products of the urban revolution—of rising wealth, civic pride, and intense urban piety. Second, the change from Romanesque to Gothic mirrors the shift in

Romanesque interior: Saint-Etienne in Nevers (*c.* 1083–1097).

Romanesque tympanum: Sainte-Foy in Conques (*c.* 1130).

Nave capital, Anzy-le-Duc (late eleventh century).

Detail of right portal, Vézelay (begun 1120).

literature, piety, and aristocratic life-style toward emotional intensity and re-finement. Romanesque architecture, though characterized by an exceeding di-versity of expression, tended toward the solemnity of earlier Christian piety and the rough-hewn power of the *chansons de geste*. The Gothic style, on the other hand, is dramatic, upward-reaching, aspiring. It embodies the height-ened sensitivity that one finds in the romance.

The development from Romanesque to Gothic can be understood, too, as an evolution in the principles of structural engineering. The key architec-tural ingredient in the Romanesque churches was the round arch, which ap-pears in their portals, their windows, their arcades, and the massive stone vaulting of their roofs. The immense downward and outward thrusts of these heavy stone roofs required massive pillars and thick supporting walls.

The great engineering achievement of the Romanesque architects was to replace flat wooden ceilings with stone vaulting, thereby creating build-ings less susceptible to fire and more artistically unified. In achieving this goal, the Romanesque builders constructed stone vaults far larger than ever before. The glittering mosaics and wooden roofs that characterized the churches of late-Roman, Byzantine, and Carolingian times gave way to the domination of stone as the key material in both Romanesque architecture and Romanesque sculpture. Indeed, the inventive religious sculpture of the age—ornamenting the capitals of Romanesque columns and the semicircular area between the lintel and round arch of the portal (the "tympanum")—were totally architectonic, completely fused into the structure of the church itself.

The Romanesque interior is characterized by heavy masses and relatively small windows. Graceful and richly decorated in southern Europe, the style tends to become increasingly severe as one moves northward. A church in the fully developed Romanesque style conveys a feeling of organic unity and solidity. Its sturdy arches, vaults, and walls, and its somber, shadowy inte-

Nave looking east (showing vault ribs), Notre Dame of Paris (begun 1163).

rior give the illusion of mystery and otherworldliness, yet suggest at the same time the steadfast power of the universal Church.

The Gothic Style

During the first half of the twelfth century, new structural elements began to be employed in the building of Romanesque churches: first, ribs of stone that crisscrossed the vaulting; next, pointed arches that permitted greater height in the vaults and arcades. By the middle of the century these novel features— vault rib and pointed arch—were providing the basis for an entirely new style of architecture. They were employed with such effect by Abbot Suger in his new abbey church of Saint-Denis near Paris around 1140 that Saint-Denis is regarded as the first true Gothic church.

French Gothic churches of the late twelfth century such as Notre Dame of Paris disclose the development of vault rib and pointed arch into a powerful, coherent style. During these exciting years, every decade brought new experiments and opened new possibilities in church building; yet Notre Dame of Paris and the churches of its period and region retain some of the heaviness and solidity of the earlier Romanesque. Not until the 1190s were the full potentialities of Gothic architecture realized. The use of the vault rib and pointed arch, and of a third Gothic structural element—the flying buttress— made it possible to support weights and stresses in a new way. The tradi-

High Gothic exterior: Reims Cathedral (showing the great clerestory windows around the rounded east end and the decorated flying buttresses: thirteenth century).

tional building, of roof supported by walls, was transformed into a radically new kind of building—a skeleton—in which the stone vault rested not on walls but on slender columns and graceful exterior supports. The walls became mere screens—structurally unnecessary. With the passage of time, they were replaced increasingly by huge windows of stained glass that flooded the church interior with light and color. For concurrent with the Gothic architectural revolution was the development, in twelfth-century Europe, of the new art of stained-glass making. The glowing windows created in the twelfth and thirteenth centuries, with episodes from the Bible and religious legend depicted in shimmering blues and reds, have never been equalled.

The Gothic innovations of vault rib, pointed arch, and flying buttress created the breathtaking illusion of stone vaulting resting on walls of glass. The new churches rose upward in seeming defiance of gravity, losing their earth-bound quality and reaching toward the heavens. By about the mid-thirteenth century

High Gothic facade: Amiens Cathedral, showing
the three west portals decorated with sculpture
(thirteenth century).

High Gothic interior: Amiens Cathedral looking east
toward the rounded apse (thirteenth century).

all the structural possibilities of the Gothic skeleton design were fully realized,
and in the towns of central and northern France there now rose churches of delicate, soaring stone with walls of lustrous glass. Never before in history had windows been so immense or buildings so lofty, and seldom since has European
architecture been at once so daring and so assured.

Gothic sculpture, like Romanesque, was intimately related to architecture, yet the two styles differed markedly. Romanesque fantasy, exuberance,
and distortion gave way to a serene, self-confident naturalism. Human figures were no longer crowded together on the capitals of pillars; often they
stood as statues—great rows of them—in niches on the cathedral exteriors:
saints, prophets, kings, and angels, Christ and the Virgin Mary, depicted as
tall, slender figures, calm yet warmly human, often young and sometimes
smiling. The greatest Gothic churches of thirteenth-century France—Bourges,
Chartres, Amiens, Reims, Sainte-Chapelle—are among the most impressive
buildings on earth. They bring together many separate arts: architecture, sculpture, stained glass, liturgical music—all directed to the single end of providing a majestic background for the central act of Christian worship, the Mass.

High Gothic sculpture: Apostle's head, from Sens Cathedral (central France, *c.* 1190–1200).

Cathedral Life in the Middle Ages

Stepping inside a medieval cathedral today, one finds an atmosphere of awesome quiet that contrasts sharply with the bustle of the surrounding city. But in the Middle Ages, cathedrals were centers of urban life rather than refuges from it. The cathedral bells announced the hours of the business day, called university students to their studies, and proclaimed great public events—a

Head of the Virgin Mary, from the west facade of Reims Cathedral
(first half of the thirteenth century).

victory in battle, the death of a famous person, the birth of a prince or princess. Townspeople flocked to their cathedral not for the Mass alone, but for marriages, baptisms, funerals, civic and religious festivals, excommunications, and victory celebrations. Famous traveling preachers addressed huge crowds from cathedral pulpits and sometimes stirred them into frenzied enthusiasm.

Often a cathedral was the site of a great assembly of nobles and princes or of a public meeting of the town council. On major feast days—Easter, Christmas, Pentecost, and others—the cathedral would be ablaze with candles. Colorful processions would march noisily along its aisles and then out through its portals into the narrow streets of the city.

A cathedral's relics might attract pilgrims from far and wide—many of them crippled or ill, desperate for a miraculous cure. At night, pilgrims might be found sleeping on the cathedral's straw-covered floor in company with local beggars and drunks. On great feast days, the church would be swarming with pilgrims and local worshipers. Abbot Suger, describing a boisterous multitude that pressed into his abbey church of St. Denis, complained of "howling men" and of women who screamed "as though they were giving birth." The crowd of visitors, shoving and struggling to see the relics of St. Denis, forced the abbey's monks "to flee through the windows, carrying the relics with them."

Even larger crowds were drawn to Canterbury Cathedral to visit the wonder-working tomb of St. Thomas Becket. If we could travel backwards in time to witness the scene, we would be appalled at the sight of cripples crawling on the floor near the tomb, the ear-shattering cries of the mentally handicapped, the suffocating odor of poverty and disease. We would hear people shouting out their prayers in the half-darkness or see them offering their pennies and homemade candles in desperate appeal for the saint's help. Someone is loudly explaining his miraculous cure to a monk; someone else is vomiting in a corner. Well-dressed nobles are there, too, along with some high officials of the Church; they ignore the crowds of poor and diseased as they await their opportunity to present offerings of silver or gems.

Canterbury Cathedral was a singularly popular pilgrimage center. Few holy relics were as famed for miraculous cures as those of St. Thomas Becket. But all across medieval Europe the cathedrals teemed with women and men from all social levels. One would encounter there the commotion and stench, the hopes and griefs, of a turbulent cross section of humanity.

THE NEW SCHOOLS

One of the most significant developments in the High Middle Ages was a vast increase in the use of the written word. There was an enormous proliferation of government documents—written commands, property deeds, financial accounts, judicial transcripts—along with records of individual transactions (wills, business records, property transfers) and systematic treatises on philosophy, theology, law, and medicine. Works of literature were committed to writing rather than transmitted by oral tradition. Law came to be based less on local, long-remembered custom, and more on coherent systems of secular and ecclesiastical jurisprudence. This entire process, which has been described as a shift "from memory to written record," resulted in basic changes in attitude and social organization. It encouraged a much more logical and systematic approach to every side of human experience, from the management of a business, farm, or kingdom to philosophical investigation. The ability to reason, read, and compute provided a direct avenue into the governmental institutions of church and state; it was becoming increasingly evident to young people of ambition that knowledge was power.

Accordingly, schools sprang up everywhere, and skilled teachers found themselves in great demand. The abbot Guibert of Nogent looked back from the early twelfth century to the earlier days of his youth, when "scarcely any teachers could be found in the towns and very few in the cities, and those who by good luck could be found didn't know much: they couldn't be compared with the traveling teachers of these days."

The Rise of Universities

The greatest of the new schools, the universities, were products of the growing cities. The urban revolution brought about the decline of the old monastic schools, which had done so much to preserve and enrich culture over the previous centuries. They were superseded north of the Alps by schools centering on non-monastic churches, often cathedrals, and in Italy by semi-secular municipal schools. Both the cathedral schools and municipal schools had long existed, but only in the eleventh and twelfth centuries did they rise to prominence. Many now became centers of higher learning of a sort that Europe had not known for centuries. Their enrollments increased and their faculties grew until, in the twelfth century, some of them evolved into universities.

In the Middle Ages, "university" was a vague term denoting nothing more than a group of persons associated for any purpose. The word was commonly applied to the merchant and craft guilds of the rising towns. A "guild" or "university" of students and scholars engaged in the pursuit of higher learning was given the more specific name, *studium generale*. When we speak of the medieval university, therefore, we are referring to an institution that would have been called a *studium generale* at the time. It differed from lesser schools in that students drawn from many lands received instruction from a number of specialized scholars in a variety of disciplines. The *studium generale* offered a basic program of instruction in the traditional "seven liberal arts": astronomy, geometry, arithmetic, music, grammar, rhetoric, and logic; and also instruction in one or more of the "higher" disciplines: theology, law, and medicine. On the successful completion of the liberal arts curriculum, the student could apply for a license to teach but might also wish to continue his studies by specializing in medicine, theology, or civil or canon law.

Fundamentally, the medieval university was neither a campus nor a complex of buildings, but a guild—a privileged corporation of teachers, or sometimes of students. With its classes normally held in rented rooms, it was a highly mobile institution, and, on more than one occasion, when a university was dissatisfied with local conditions it won important concessions from the townspeople simply by threatening to move elsewhere.

In the thirteenth century, universities flourished at Paris, Bologna, Naples, Montpellier, Oxford, Cambridge, and elsewhere. Paris, Oxford, and a number of others were dominated by guilds of instructors in the liberal arts. Bologna, whose pattern was followed by other universities of southern Europe, was governed by a guild of students. The Bologna student guild managed to reduce the exorbitant local prices of food and lodgings by threatening to move collectively to another town and established strict rules of conduct for the instructors. Professors, for example, were placed under the outrageous obligation to begin and end their classes on time and to cover the prescribed curriculum. Since Bologna specialized in legal studies, its pupils were older professional students for the most part—students who had completed their liberal arts curriculum and were determined to secure sufficient training for successful careers in law.

Notwithstanding the enormous differences between medieval and modern university life, the modern university is a direct outgrowth of its high-medieval predecessor. We owe to the medieval university such customs as the formal teaching license, the practice—unknown to antiquity—of group instruction, the awarding of academic degrees, the notion of a liberal arts curriculum, and the tradition of honoring commencement day by dressing in clerical garb (caps and gowns).

Student Life at the University of Paris

Let us imagine ourselves at the University of Paris in the days of St. Louis. Here the intellectual environment was alive with philosophical disputes and passionate intellectual rivalries. And besides these battles of words, there were frequent tavern brawls, sometimes exploding into full-scale battles between students and townspeople, or among rival student gangs. New students were hazed unmercifully and imaginatively, while unpopular professors were hissed, shouted down, or, as a last resort, pelted with stones.

Students flocked to the University of Paris from all over Western Christendom. Most of them were about seventeen when they began their studies, and they tended to come from the middle social stratum of town dwellers and lesser landholders. Poor boys occasionally made it, but the sons of the high aristocracy did not pour in until a later era; university educations did not become fashionable in high society until the fourteenth century. And there were no female students at all. (Until recent years women were excluded from most Oxford and Cambridge colleges and denied admission to some of America's foremost private universities.)

The letters of medieval students to their parents or guardians have a curiously modern ring:

> The city is expensive and makes many demands: I have to rent
> lodgings, buy necessities, and provide for many other things that I
> cannot specify. Therefore I beg your paternity that by the prompting of
> divine pity you may assist me, so that I may be able to complete what I
> have so well begun.

A father replies to his son:

> I have recently learned that you live dissolutely, preferring play to
> work, and strumming your guitar while others are at their studies.

In the course of the thirteenth century, wealthy benefactors founded residential colleges at Paris where poor students could receive room and board. Some students were monks or friars and lived in houses built and supported by their orders. But most students found whatever rented rooms they could afford, and more than one student riot was inspired by the high cost of food and housing.

Students in thirteenth-century Paris began their day at five or six in the morning, when the bells of Notre Dame Cathedral summoned them to work. They would flock out of their rooms and boarding houses into the narrow, noisy streets and on to the lecture halls, which were scattered about the university quarter of the city. These halls were bare and bitterly cold in the winter. Some of them had rough benches; in others students had to sit on a straw-covered floor, using their knees to support the wax tablets on which they took their lecture notes. The teacher mounted a platform at one end of the room and sat down to deliver a lecture that might run on all morning, unenlivened by audiovisual aids.

In the afternoon, students would congregate in the meadows outside the city walls to join in various sports: races, long-jump contests, lawn bowling, swimming, ball games of different sorts, and free-for-all fights pitting students from one region of Europe against those from another. In the evenings, serious students retired to their rooms for study, while others gathered in Paris's numerous taverns and brothels. One observer complained that in one and the same house there might be classrooms above and brothels below.

THE HIGHER DISCIPLINES: MEDICINE, LAW, PHILOSOPHY

Medicine

The chief medical school of medieval Europe was the University of Salerno in southern Italy. Here, in a land of vigorous cultural intermingling, scholars were able to draw from the medical heritage of Islam and Byzantium. In general, medieval medical scholarship was a bizarre medley of observation, common sense, and superstition. We encounter the good advice that a person should eat and drink in moderation. But we are also instructed that onions will cure baldness, that the urine of a dog is an admirable cure for warts, and that all one must do to prevent a woman from conceiving is to bind her head with a red ribbon.

Yet in the midst of all this, important progress was being made in medical science. The comprehensive medical writings of the Greek scientist Galen were studied and digested, along with the works of Arab medical scholars. And to this invaluable body of knowledge Europeans were now making their own original contributions on such subjects as the curative properties of plants and the anatomy of the human body. It is probable that both animal and human dissections were performed by the scholars of twelfth-century Salerno. These doctors, primitive though their methods were, laid the foundations on which Western European medical science was to rise.

Civil and Canon Law

Medieval legal scholarship addressed itself to two distinct bodies of material: civil law and canon law. The legal structure of early medieval society was largely Germanic in inspiration and custom-based, particularly in northern Europe where Roman law had virtually disappeared. Customary law remained strong throughout the High Middle Ages: it governed the relationships among the aristocracy and determined the obligations of the peasantry. It limited the prerogatives of kings and underlay Magna Carta. But from the late eleventh century on, Roman law was studied in Bologna and other European universities. Christendom was now exposed to a distinctly different legal tradition— coherent and logical—that began to compete with Germanic law, to rationalize it, and in some instances to replace it.

The foundation of medieval Roman law was the *Corpus Juris Civilis* of Justinian, which was all but unknown in the West throughout most of the early Middle Ages but reappeared at Bologna in the last quarter of the eleventh century. Italy remained the center of Roman legal studies throughout the High Middle Ages. The traditions of Roman law had never entirely disappeared there, and the Italian peninsula therefore provided the most fertile soil for their revival.

From Italy the study of Roman law spread northward. A great school of law emerged at Montpellier in southern France, and others flourished at Orléans, Paris, and Oxford. But Bologna remained the foremost center of Roman legal studies. There, scholars known as "glossators" wrote analytical commentaries on the *Corpus Juris,* clarifying difficult points and reconciling apparent contradictions. Later on they began to produce textbooks and important original treatises on the *Corpus* and to reorganize it into a coherent sequence of topics. Eventually such an extensive body of supplementary material existed that the glossators turned to the task of glossing the glosses—clarifying the clarifications. Around the mid-thirteenth century the work of the earlier glossators was brought to culmination with a comprehensive work by the Bolognese scholar Accursius—the *Glossa Ordinaria*—which synthesized all previous commentaries on the *Corpus Juris*. Thereafter, Accursius' *Glossa Ordinaria* became the authoritative supplement to the *Corpus Juris* in courts of Roman law.

The impact of the glossators was particularly strong in Italy and southern France where elements of Roman law had survived as local custom. By the thirteenth century Roman law was beginning to make a significant impact in the north as well, for by then civil lawyers trained in the Roman tradition were achieving an increasingly dominant role in the courts of France, Germany, and Spain. These lawyers devoted themselves to the royal service and used their legal training to exalt their monarchs. Although the Roman legal tradition had originally contained a strong element of constitutionalism, it inherited from Justinian's age an autocratic cast that the court lawyers of the rising monarchies put to effective use. Thus as Roman law gained an increasingly firm hold in the states of continental Europe it tended to make their governments at once more systematic and more autocratic. The development and durability of the parliamentary regime in England owed much to the fact that a strong monarchy, founded on the principles of Germanic law with its custom-based limitations on royal authority, was already well established before northern Europe felt the full impact of the Roman law revival.

Canon law developed alongside Roman law and derived a great deal from it. Methods of scholarship were similar in the two fields—commentaries and glosses were common to both—and the ecclesiastical courts borrowed much from the principles and procedures of Roman law. But whereas Roman law was based on the single authority of Justinian's *Corpus Juris,* canon law drew from many sources: the Bible, the writings of the ancient Church Fathers, the canons of Church councils, and the decrees of popes. The *Corpus Juris,* although susceptible to endless commentary, was fundamentally complete in itself; popes and councils, on the other hand, continued to issue decrees, and canon law was therefore capable of unlimited development.

Canon law, like civil law, first became a serious scholarly discipline in eleventh-century Bologna and later spread to other major centers of learning. The study of canon law was strongly stimulated by the investiture controversy and subsequent church-state struggles, for the papacy looked to canon lawyers to support its claims with cogent, documented arguments and apt precedents. But the medieval scholars of canon law were more than mere papal propagandists. They were grappling with the formidable problem of systematizing their sources, explaining what was unclear, reconciling what seemed contradictory—in other words, imposing order on the immense variety of dicta, opinions, and precedents on which their discipline was based.

The essential goal of the canon lawyers was to assemble their diverse sources—their canons—into a single coherent work. It was up to them, in short, to accomplish the task that Justinian had performed for Roman law back in the sixth century. The civil lawyers had their *Corpus Juris Civilis;* it was up to the canon lawyers to create their own "Corpus Juris Canonici." The first attempts to produce comprehensive canonical collections date from the early Middle Ages, but it was not until the eleventh-century revival at Bologna that serious scholarly standards were applied to the task. The definitive collection was completed around 1140 by the great Bolognese canon lawyer Gratian. Originally entitled *The Concordance of Discordant Canons*, Gratian's work is known to posterity as the *Decretum*.

Gratian not only brought together an immense body of canons from a wide variety of sources; he also framed them in a logical, topically organized scheme. Using methods that were just beginning to be employed by scholastic philosophers, he raised questions in logical sequence, quoted the relevant canons, and endeavored to reconcile contradictions. The result was an ordered body of general legal principles validated by passages from the Bible, the Fathers, and papal and conciliar decrees. The *Decretum* became the authoritative text in ecclesiastical tribunals and the basis of all future study in canon law.

As time passed, and new decrees were issued, it became necessary to supplement Gratian's *Decretum* by collecting the canons issued after 1140. One such collection was made in 1234 under the direction of the lawyer-pope Gregory IX, another in the pontificate of Boniface VIII, and still others in later generations. Together, the *Decretum* and the supplementary collections were given the title, *Corpus Juris Canonici*, and became the ecclesiastical equivalent of Justinian's *Corpus*. These two great compilations, ecclesiastical and civil, reflect the parallel growth of medieval Europe's two supreme sources of administrative and jurisdictional authority: church and monarchy. They further reflect the high-medieval shift toward elaborate intellectual systems, expressed in writing and shaped by rational analysis.

The Background of High-Medieval Philosophy

Medieval philosophy, too, is marked by analytical system-building. Although every important philosopher in the High Middle Ages was a churchman of one sort or another, ecclesiastical authority did not stifle speculation or limit controversy. Catholic orthodoxy, which would harden noticeably at the time of the Protestant Reformation, was still relatively flexible in the twelfth and thirteenth centuries, and philosophers were by no means timid apologists for official dogmas. If some of them were impelled to provide the Catholic faith with a logical substructure, others asserted that reason does not lead to the truth of Christian revelation. And among those who sought to harmonize faith and reason there was sharp disagreement as to how it should be done. Their shared faith did not limit their diversity or curb their spirit of intellectual adventure.

The high-medieval philosophers drew nourishment from five earlier sources: (1) From the Greeks they inherited the philosophical systems of Plato and Aristotle. At first these two Greek masters were known in the West only through a handful of translations and commentaries dating from late Roman times. By the thirteenth century, however, new and far more complete translations were coming into Christendom from Spain and Sicily, and Aristotelian philosophy became a matter of intense interest and controversy in Europe's universities. (2) From the Islamic world came a flood of Greek scientific and philosophical works that had long before been translated into Arabic and were now retranslated from Arabic into Latin. These works entered Europe accompanied by extensive commentaries and original writings of Arab philosophers and scientists, for the Arabs came to grips with Greek learning long before the West did. Islamic thought made a particularly vital contribution to European science. In philosophy it was enriched by the work of Jewish scholars such as Moses Maimonides (1135–1204), whose *Guide for the Perplexed*—a penetrating reconciliation of Aristotle and Scripture—influenced the work of thirteenth-century Christian philosophers and theologians. (3) The early Church Fathers, particularly Ambrose, Jerome, and Augustine, had been a dominant intellectual force throughout the early Middle Ages and their authority remained strong in the twelfth and thirteenth centuries. St. Augustine retained his singular significance and was, indeed, the chief vessel of Platonic and Neoplatonic thought in the medieval universities. (4) The early medieval scholars themselves contributed significantly to the high-medieval intellectual revival. Gregory the Great, Isidore of Seville, Bede, Alcuin, Raban Maur, John the Scot, and Gerbert of Aurillac were all studied in the new universities. The original intellectual contributions of these men were less important, however, than the fact that they and their contemporaries had kept classical learning alive, thus creating the intellectual climate that made possible the reawakening of philosophical speculation in the eleventh century. (5) The high-medieval philosophers looked back beyond the scholars of the early Middle Ages, beyond the Fathers of the early Church, to the Hebrew and early Christian religious traditions as recorded in Scripture. Among medieval theologians the Bible, the chief written source of divine revelation, was the fundamental text and the ultimate authority.

Such were the chief elements—Greek, Islamic-Jewish, Patristic, early medieval, and scriptural—that underlay the thought of the scholastic philosophers. Strictly defined, "Scholasticism" is simply the philosophical movement associated with the high-medieval schools—the cathedral and monastic schools and later the universities. More interestingly, it was a movement concerned above all with exploring the relationship between reason and revelation. All medieval scholastics believed in God; all were committed, to some degree, to the life of reason. Many of them were immensely enthusiastic over the intellectual possibilities inherent in the careful application of Aristotelian logic to basic human and religious problems. Some believed that logic was the master key to a thousand doors and that with sufficient methodological rigor, with sufficient exactness in the use of words, the potentialities of human reason were all but limitless.

The Scholastics applied their logical method to a multitude of problems. They were concerned chiefly, however, with matters of basic significance to human existence: the nature of human beings, the purpose of human life, the existence and attributes of God, the fundamentals of human morality, the ethical imperatives of social and political life, the relationship between God and humanity. It would be hard to deny that these are the most profound sorts of questions that one can ask. Many philosophers of our own day are inclined to reject them as unanswerable, but the scholastics, lacking the modern sense of disillusionment, were determined to make the attempt.

The Relationship of Faith and Reason

Among the diverse investigations and conflicting opinions of the medieval philosophers, two central issues deserve particular attention: the degree of interrelationship between faith and reason, and the relative merits of the Platonic-Augustinian and the Aristotelian intellectual traditions. The issue of faith versus reason was perhaps the more far-reaching. Ever since Tertullian in the third century, there had been Christian writers who insisted that God so transcended reason that any attempt to approach him intellectually was useless and, indeed, blasphemous. Tertullian had posed the rhetorical questions:

> What has Athens to do with Jerusalem? What concord is there between the Academy and the Church?...Let us have done with all attempts to produce a bastard Christianity of Stoic, Platonic, and dialectic composition! We desire no curious disputation after possessing Christ Jesus, no logical analyses after enjoying the Gospel!

Tertullian had many followers in the Middle Ages. St. Peter Damiani rejected the intellectual road to God in favor of the mystical, insisting that God, whose power is limitless, cannot be bound or even approached by logic. He was followed in this view by such later mystics as St. Bernard, who denounced his rationalist contemporary Peter Abelard, and St. Francis, who regarded intellectual speculation as irrelevant to salvation. A later spiritual Franciscan, Jacopone da Todi, expressed the position in verse:

Plato and Socrates may oft contend,
And all the breath within their bodies spend,
Engaged in disputations without end.
What's that to me?
For only with a pure and simple mind
Can one the narrow path to heaven find,
And greet the King; while lingers far behind,
Philosophy.

The contrary view was just as old. Third-century theologians such as Clement and Origen in the school of Alexandria had labored to provide Christianity with a sturdy philosophical foundation and did not hesitate to explain the faith by means of Greek—and particularly Platonic—thought. The fourth-century Latin Doctors, Ambrose, Jerome, and Augustine, had wrestled with the problem of whether a Christian might properly use elements from the pagan classical tradition in the service of the faith, and all three ended with affirmative answers. As Augustine expressed it,

> If those who are called philosophers, and especially the Platonists, have
> said anything that is true and in harmony with our faith, we must not
> only not shrink from it, but claim it for our own use from those who
> have unlawful possession of it.

This is the viewpoint that underlies most of high-medieval philosophy—
that reason has a valuable role to play as a servant of revelation. St. Anselm,
following Augustine, declared, "I believe so that I may know." Faith comes
first, reason second; faith rules reason, but reason can perform the useful service of illuminating faith. Indeed, faith and reason are separate avenues to a
single body of truth. By their very nature they cannot lead to contradictory
conclusions, for truth is one. Should their conclusions ever *appear* to be contradictory, the philosopher can be assured that some flaw exists in his logic.
Reason cannot err, but our use of it can, and revelation must therefore be the
criterion against which reason is measured.

This, in general, became the position of later Scholastic philosophers.
The intellectual system of St. Thomas Aquinas was built on the conviction
that reason and faith were harmonious. Even the arch-rationalist of the twelfth
century, Peter Abelard, wrote: "I do not wish to be Aristotle if it must separate me from Christ." Abelard believed that he could at once be a philosopher and a Christian, but his faith took priority.

Among some medieval philosophers the priorities were reversed. Averroës, an astute Aristotelian Muslim of twelfth-century Spain, boldly asserted
the superiority of reason over faith. He affirmed the truth of several of Aristotle's conclusions that were directly contrary to Islamic and Christian doctrine: that the world had always existed and was therefore uncreated; that all
human actions were determined; that there was no personal salvation but only
the return of human raindrops to the divine ocean. In the fourteenth century
there emerged a Christian philosophical school known as "Latin Averroism,"
based in part on the writings of the thirteenth-century Paris theologian, Siger
of Brabant. Like Averroës, Siger of Brabant accepted Aristotle's eternally existing world as "logically necessary" yet nevertheless believed firmly in the
Christian doctrine of the creation. Expanding on this dilemma, Latin Averroists
of the fourteenth century held that reason and revelation produced radically
different conclusions. Their position came to be called the doctrine of the
"twofold truth."

Platonism-Augustinianism versus Aristotelianism

The conflict between the intellectual systems of Plato-Augustine and Aristotle
did not emerge clearly until the thirteenth century when the full body of
Aristotle's writings came into the West in Latin translations from Greek and
Arabic. Until then, most efforts at applying reason to faith were based on the
Platonic tradition transmuted and transmitted by Augustine to medieval
Europe. St. Anselm, for example, was a dedicated Augustinian, as were many
of his twelfth-century successors. The tradition was carried on in the thirteenth
century by the Franciscan St. Bonaventure. Many thoughtful Christians were

deeply suspicious of the newly recovered writings of Aristotle. They regarded his work as pagan in viewpoint and dangerous to the faith. Other thirteenth-century philosophers, such as St. Thomas Aquinas, were much too devoted to the goal of reconciling faith and reason to reject the works of a man whom they regarded as antiquity's greatest philosopher. St. Thomas sought to Christianize Aristotle much as Augustine had Christianized Plato and the Neoplatonists. In the middle decades of the thirteenth century, the Platonic and Aristotelian traditions flourished side by side, and in the works of certain English scientific thinkers of the age they achieved a singularly fruitful synthesis.

The contest between Plato and Aristotle gave rise to a serious philosophical debate over the nature of the Platonic archetypes or, as they were called in the Middle Ages, "universals." Plato had taught that terms such as "dog" or "cat" not only describe particular creatures but also are language-symbols for things that have reality in themselves—that individual cats are imperfect reflections of a model cat, an archetypal or universal cat. Similarly, there are many examples of circles, squares, or triangles. Were we to measure these individual figures with sufficiently refined instruments we would discover that they were imperfect in one respect or another. No circle in this world is absolutely round. No square or triangle has perfectly straight sides. They are merely approximations of a perfect "idea." In "heaven," Plato would say, the perfect triangle exists. It is the source of the concept of triangularity that lurks in our minds and of all the imperfect triangles that we see in the physical world. The heavenly triangle is not only perfect but *real.* The earthly triangles are less real, and less worthy of our attention. Or, to take still another example, we call certain acts "good" because they partake, imperfectly, of a universal good that exists in heaven. In short, these universals—cat, dog, circle, triangle, beauty, goodness, etc.—exist apart from the multitude of individual dogs, cats, circles, triangles, and beautiful and good things in this world. And the person who seeks knowledge ought to meditate on these universals rather than study the world of phenomena in which they are only imperfectly reflected.

St. Augustine accepted Plato's theory of universals but not without amendment. Augustine taught that the archetypes existed in the mind of God instead of in Plato's abstract "heaven." And whereas Plato has ascribed our knowledge of the universals to dim memories from a prenatal existence, Augustine maintained that God puts a knowledge of universals directly into our minds by a process of "divine illumination." Plato and Augustine agreed, however, that the universal existed apart from the particular and, indeed, was *more real* than the particular. In the High Middle Ages, those who followed the Platonic-Augustinian approach to universals were known as "Realists"; they believed that universals were real.

The Aristotelian tradition brought with it another viewpoint on universals: they existed, to be sure, but only in the particular. Only by studying particular things in the world of phenomena could one gain a knowledge of universals. The human mind drew its knowledge of the universal from its observation of the particular by a process of abstraction. The universals were real, but in a sense less real—or less independently real—than Plato and Augustine believed. Accordingly, philosophers who inclined toward the Aristotelian position have been called "Moderate Realists."

As early as the eleventh century the philosopher Roscellinus rejected both these views, declaring that universals were not real at all. "Dog," "cat," and "triangle" are mere words—names that we have concocted for bunches of individual things that we have lumped into arbitrary categories. These categories, or "universals," have no objective existence whatever. Reality is not to be found in them, but rather in the multiplicity and variety of individual objects which we can see, touch, and smell in the world around us. Those who followed Roscellinus in this view were known as "Nominalists": for them, the universals had no reality apart from their *nomina*—"names." Nominalism remained in the intellectual background during the twelfth and thirteenth centuries but was revived in the fourteenth. Many churchmen regarded it as a dangerous doctrine, since its emphasis on the particular over the universal seemed to suggest that the Church was not, as Catholics believed, a single universal body but rather a vast accumulation of individual Christians.

THE MAJOR PHILOSOPHERS

St. Anselm

The Scholastic philosophers first made their appearance in the later eleventh century as an aspect of Europe's intellectual reawakening. The earliest important figure was St. Anselm (*c.* 1033–1109), the Italian philosopher who became abbot of Bec in Normandy and later, as archbishop of Canterbury, brought the investiture controversy into England.

As an Augustinian, Anselm took the Realist position on the problem of universals. It was from Augustine, too, that he derived his attitude on the relationship of faith and reason. He taught that faith must precede reason, but that reason could serve to illuminate faith. His conviction that reason and faith were compatible made him a singularly important pioneer in the development of high-medieval rationalism. He worked out several proofs of God, based on abstract reasoning rather than observation. And in his important theological treatise, *Cur Deus Homo* ("Why God Became Man"), he subjected the doctrines of the incarnation and atonement to rigorous logical analysis.

Anselm's emphasis on reason, employed within the framework of a firm Christian conviction, set the stage for the significant philosophical developments of the following generations. With Anselm, Western Christendom regained at last the intellectual level of the fourth-century Latin Doctors.

Abelard

The twelfth-century philosophers were intoxicated by the seemingly limitless possibilities of reason and logic. The most audacious of them all was Peter Abelard (1079–1142), whose dazzling career ended in tragedy and defeat.

Abelard is perhaps best known for his love affair with the young Heloise, a relationship that ended with Abelard's castration at the hands of thugs hired by Heloise's enraged uncle. The lovers separated permanently, both taking monastic vows, and in later years Abelard wrote regretfully of the affair in his autobiographical *History of My Calamities*. There followed a touching correspondence in which Heloise, now an abbess, confessed her enduring love— "I am tortured by passion and the fires of memory." In reply, Abelard offered her spiritual consolation but nothing more.

Abelard was the supreme logician of the twelfth century. Writing several decades before the great influx of Aristotelian thought in Latin translation, he anticipated Aristotle's position on the question of universals by advocating a theory rather similar to Aristotle's Moderate Realism. Universals, Abelard believed, have no separate existence; our knowledge of them is derived from particular things by a process of abstraction. In a famous work entitled *Sic et Non* ("Yes and No"), Abelard collected opinions from the Bible, the Latin Fathers, the councils of the Church, and the decrees of the papacy on a great variety of theological issues, demonstrating that these authorities disagreed on such issues as whether it is ever permissible to lie, whether anything happens by chance, and whether sin is pleasing to God. Others before him had collected authoritative opinions on theological and legal issues, but never so systematically. Abelard, in his *Sic et Non*, employed a method of inquiry that was developed and perfected by canon lawyers and philosophers over the next several generations. We have already seen how the canonist Gratian, in his *Decretum*, used the device of lining up conflicting authorities and reconciling them. Similarly, Abelard's successors in theology sought to reconcile contradictions and arrive at conclusions, whereas Abelard had earned the enmity of his conservative contemporaries by leaving the issues unresolved (arguing that students should reason them out for themselves). Abelard was a devoted Christian, if something of an intellectual show-off, but many regarded him as a budding skeptic. Thus he left himself open to attacks by St. Bernard, who was hostile to the Christian rationalist movement and called Abelard's theology a "fool-ology." The brilliant teacher was driven from one place to another until at length his opinions were condemned by an ecclesiastical council in 1141. Retiring to Cluny, he died in 1142. The abbot of Cluny wrote Heloise a touching letter praising Abelard's late-blooming humility and assuring her that they would be reunited on the day of the Lord's coming.

Twelfth-century rationalism was far more than a one-man affair, and the attacks on Abelard failed to halt its growth. His student Peter Lombard (c. 1100–1160) produced an important theological text, the *Books of Sentences*, which set off conflicting opinions on the pattern of the *Sic et Non*, but which, like Gratian's *Decretum*, took the further step of reconciling the contradictory authorities. Lombard's *Books of Sentences* remained for centuries a fundamental text in schools of theology.

John of Salisbury

As scholars grew increasingly excited at the possibilities of logic, the remaining liberal arts began to lose out in the competition. The urban schools of northern France—at Chartres, Paris, Laon, and elsewhere—had been important centers of Latin literary studies in the eleventh century and remained so through much of the twelfth. But as the century progressed, as more and more Aristotelian texts became available, and as the vision of rational solutions to the great questions became ever more captivating, the interest of students and scholars shifted increasingly from literature to logic. The accomplished twelfth-century English scholar, John of Salisbury (*c.* 1115–1180), was a pupil of Abelard's, a student of Greek, and a well-trained logician, but he was above all a humanist—a devotee of classical literature. He approved of logic but regretted that it was growing at the expense of other studies; he complained that the schools were tending to produce narrow logicians rather than broadly educated scholars.

In his *Policraticus* (1159), John of Salisbury made a major contribution to medieval political philosophy. Drawing on the thought of Classical Antiquity and the early Middle Ages, he stressed the divine nature of kingship but emphasized equally its responsibilities and limitations. The king drew his authority from God but was commissioned to rule for the good of his subjects rather than himself. He was bound to give his subjects peace and justice and to protect the Church. If he abused his commission and neglected his responsibilities, he lost his divine authority, ceased to be a king, and became a tyrant. As such, he forfeited his subjects' allegiance and was no longer their lawful ruler. Under extreme circumstances, and if all else failed, John of Salisbury recommended tyrannicide. A good Christian subject, although obliged to obey his king, might kill a tyrant. Apart from the highly original doctrine of tyrannicide, the views expressed in the *Policraticus* mirror the general political attitudes of the twelfth century—responsible limited monarchy and government in behalf of the governed. These theories, in turn, were idealized reflections of the actual monarchies of the day whose power was held in check by the nobility, the Church, and ancient custom.

Translation and System-Building

In the later twelfth and early thirteenth centuries the movement of Christian rationalism was powerfully reinforced by the arrival of vast quantities of Greek and Arabic writings in Latin translation. For the first time, significant portions of the philosophical and scientific legacy of ancient Greece became available to European scholars. Above all, the full Aristotelian corpus now came into the West through the labors of translators in Spain, Sicily, and the Latin Empire of Constantinople.

These translations came in answer to a deep hunger on the part of Western thinkers for a fuller knowledge of the Classical heritage in philosophy and science. The introduction of certain new Aristotelian works provoked a crisis in Western Christendom, for they contained implications that seemed hostile to the faith. And with them, as we have seen, came the skeptical and intellectually impressive works of the Islamic Spaniard Averroës, which gave rise to the doctrine of the "twofold truth." For a time it seemed as though reason and revelation were sundered, and the Church reacted in panic by condemning certain of Aristotle's writings. It was one of the major goals of thirteenth-century thought to rescue Aristotle and, indeed, reason itself for Western Christianity.

The thirteenth century was preeminently an age of consolidation and synthesis. Its scholars digested the insights and conclusions of the past and cast them into comprehensive systems of thought. Theologians such as Alexander of Hales (d. 1245), Albertus Magnus (1193–1280), and Thomas Aquinas (1225–1274) produced great systematic treatises known as "summas," which provided structure and unity to the theological speculations of theirs and past ages.

The thought of Aristotle loomed large in the thirteenth-century schools, but the Platonic-Augustinian tradition was well represented, too. There was a tendency for the Dominican scholars to espouse Aristotle, and the Franciscans to follow Plato and Augustine. Thus the outstanding thirteenth-century exponent of Platonism-Augustinianism was the Franciscan St. Bonaventure (1221–1274), an Italian of humble origin who rose to become a cardinal of the Church and minister-general of the Franciscan order.

Bonaventure was at once a philosopher and a mystic. Following in the Augustinian tradition, he was a realist on the matter of universals and a rationalist who stressed the subordination of reason to faith. He visualized the whole physical universe as a multitude of symbols pointing to God and glorifying him, eternally striving upward toward the Divine Presence. Human beings, he believed, stand at the fulcrum of creation. Our bodies make us the kin of beasts; our souls give us kinship with the angels. We perceive the physical universe through our senses, but we know the spiritual world—the world of universals—through the grace of divine illumination. The road to God and to truth, therefore, lies in introspection and worship, not in observation and experiment. Indeed, in Bonaventure's philosophy rational speculation is scarcely distinguishable from worship. His entire system of thought is a kind of prayer in praise of God.

While Bonaventure was bringing new dimensions to traditional Platonism-Augustinianism, two great Dominican scholars, Albertus Magnus and Thomas Aquinas, worked toward reconciling Aristotle's philosophy with Christianity. Albertus Magnus, a native of Germany, was a scholar of widely ranging interests who made important contributions to natural science—especially biology—

as well as to philosophy and theology. He was a master of Aristotelian thought and a summa writer, whose goal was to purge Aristotle of the heretical taint of Averroism and transform his philosophy into the intellectual foundation of Christian orthodoxy. But the full achievement of this goal was left to his gifted student, Thomas Aquinas.

St. Thomas Aquinas

St. Thomas was born of a Norman-Italian noble family in 1225. His parents intended him to become a Benedictine monk and to rise in due course to an influential abbacy. But in 1244 he shocked them by choosing a life of poverty in the new Dominican Order. He went to the University of Paris shortly thereafter and spent his ensuing years traveling, teaching, and writing. Unlike Augustine he had no youthful follies to regret. Unlike Anselm and Bernard, he played no great role in the political affairs of his day. He persevered in his academic tasks until, late in life, he suddenly declared that all his books were rubbish and devoted his remaining days to mysticism. At his death, the priest who heard his last confession described it as being as innocent as that of a five-year-old.

In his copious writings—particularly his *Summa Theologica*—Aquinas explored all the great questions of philosophy and theology, political theory and morality. He used Aristotle's logical method and Aristotle's categories of thought but arrived at conclusions that were in harmony with the Christian faith. Like Abelard, St. Thomas assembled every possible argument, pro and con, on every subject that he discussed, but unlike Abelard he drew conclusions and defended them with cogent arguments. Few philosophers before or since have been so generous in presenting and exploring opinions contrary to their own, and none has been so systematic and exhaustive.

St. Thomas created a vast, unified intellectual system, ranging from God to the natural world, logically supported at every step. His theological writings have none of the passion of St. Augustine, none of the literary elegance of Plato; rather, they have an *intellectual* elegance, an elegance of system and organization akin to that of Euclid's geometry. His *Summa Theologica* is organized into an immense series of separate sections, each dealing with a particular philosophical question. In Part I of the *Summa*, for example, Question 2 takes up the problem of God's existence. The *Question* is subdivided into three *Articles:* (1) "Whether God's existence is self-evident" (St. Thomas concludes that it is not); (2) "Whether it can be demonstrated that God exists" (St. Thomas concludes that it can be logically demonstrated); and (3) "Whether God exists" (here St. Thomas endeavors to prove God's existence).

In each *Article*, St. Thomas takes up a specific problem and subjects it to rigorous formal analysis. He always begins with a series of *Objections (Objection 1, Objection 2,* etc.) in which he sets forth as effectively as he possibly can all the arguments *contrary* to his final conclusion. For example, *Question 2, Article 3,* "Whether God exists," begins with two *Objections* purporting to demonstrate that God does not exist. One of them runs as follows:

Objection 1. It seems that God does not exist, because if one of two contraries can be infinite, the other would be altogether destroyed. But the name "God" means that He is infinite goodness. Therefore, if God existed there would be no evil discoverable; but there is evil in the world. Therefore God does not exist.

Leaving the objections for the time being, St. Thomas subjects the problem to his own logical scrutiny and concludes that "the existence of God can be proved in five ways." Here is one of them:

The fifth way is taken from the governance of the world. We see that things which lack knowledge, such as natural bodies, act for an end, and this is evident from their acting always or nearly always in the same way, so as to obtain the best result. Hence it is clear that they achieve their end not only by chance but by design. Now whatever lacks knowledge cannot move toward an end unless it be directed by some being endowed with knowledge and intelligence, as the arrow is directed by the archer. Therefore some intelligent being exists by whom all natural things are directed to their end; and this being we call God.

The analysis concludes with refutations of the earlier *Objections:*

Reply to Objection 1. As Augustine says, "Since God is the highest good, He would not allow an evil to exist in His works unless His omnipotence and goodness were such as to bring good even out of evil." This is part of the infinite goodness of God, that He should allow evil to exist, and out of it to produce good.

Having completed his analysis, St. Thomas then turns to the next *Article* or the next *Question* and subjects it to precisely the same process of inquiry. As in Euclidian geometry so in Thomistic theology, once a problem is settled, the conclusion can be used in solving subsequent problems. Thus the system grows, problem by problem, step by step, as St. Thomas's wide-ranging mind takes up such matters as the nature of God, the attributes of God, the nature and destiny of humanity, human morality, law, and political theory. The result is an imposing, comprehensive edifice of thought, embracing all major theological issues.

As the Gothic cathedral was the artistic embodiment of the high-medieval world, so the philosophy of Aquinas was its supreme intellectual expression. Both were based on clear and obvious principles of structure. St. Thomas shared with the cathedral builders the impulse to display rather than disguise the structural framework of his edifice. Like the boldly executed Gothic flying buttress, the Thomistic *Questions, Articles,* and *Objections* allowed no doubt as to what the builder was doing or how he was achieving his effects.

St. Thomas distinguished carefully between revelation and reason but endeavored to prove that they could never contradict one another. Since human reason was a valid avenue to truth, since Christian revelation was authoritative, and since truth was one, then philosophy and Christian doctrine had to be compatible and complementary. "For faith rests upon infallible truth, and therefore its contrary cannot be demonstrated." This was the essence of St. Thomas's philosophical position.

As against the Augustinianism of Anselm and Bonaventure, Aquinas emphasized the reality of the physical world as a world of things rather than symbols. Embracing the moderate realism of Aristotle, he declared that universals were to be found in the world of phenomena and nowhere else—that knowledge came from observation and analysis, not from divine illumination. He shared with St. Francis and others the notion that the physical world was deeply significant in itself.

Similarly, the state, which previous Christian thinkers had commonly regarded as a necessary evil—an unfortunate but indispensable consequence of the Fall of Adam—was accepted by Aquinas as a good and natural outgrowth of humanity's social impulse. He echoed Aristotle's dictum that "Man is a political creature" and regarded the justly governed state as a fitting part of the divine order. Like John of Salisbury, St. Thomas insisted that kings must govern in their subjects' behalf and that a willful, unrestrained ruler who ignored God's moral imperatives was no king but a tyrant. Just as the human body could be corrupted by sin, the body politic could be corrupted by tyranny. But although the Christian must reject both sin and tyranny, he should nevertheless revere the body, the state, and indeed all physical creation as worthy products of God's will, inseparable from the world of spirit, and essential ingredients in the unity of existence.

Aquinas sought to encompass the totality of being in a vast existential unity. At the center was God, the author of physical and spiritual creation, the maker of heaven and earth, who himself had assumed human form and redeemed all humanity on the cross, who discloses portions of the truth to his followers through revelation, permits them to discover other portions through the operation of the intellect, and will lead them into all truth through salvation. Ultimately, God *is* truth, and it is our destiny, on reaching heaven, to stand unshielded in the divine presence—to love and to know. Thus the roads of St. Thomas, St. Bonaventure, St. Bernard, and Dante, although passing over very different terrain, arrive finally at the same destination. It is not so surprising, after all, that in the end St. Thomas rejected theology for mysticism.

Although Aquinas's thought has been studied across the centuries, many of his own contemporaries rejected it in whole or in part. Franciscans such as Bonaventure were suspicious of the intellectual *tour de force* of this gifted Dominican. Bonaventure was a rationalist, but a cautious one, and his Franciscan successors came increasingly to the opinion that reason was of little or no use in probing metaphysical problems. The Scottish Franciscan Duns Scotus (d. 1308) undertook a subtle critique of St. Thomas's theory of knowledge. And in the philosophy of the astute English Franciscan, William of Ockham (*c.* 1300–1349), reason and revelation were divorced altogether.* Christian doctrine, Ockham said, could not be approached by reason at all but had to be

*See pp. 335–336.

accepted on faith. The Thomist synthesis was a mirage; reason's province was the natural world and that alone.

Science

By severing the bonds between revelation and reason, William of Ockham blazed two paths into the future: mysticism uninhibited by logic and science uninhibited by faith. In Ockham's time Western science was already well evolved. As far back as the later decades of the tenth century, Gerbert of Aurillac had visited Moorish Spain, familiarized himself with Islamic thought, and made his own modest contribution to scientific knowledge.* Gerbert built a simple "planetarium" of balls, rods, and bands to illustrate the rotation of the stellar sphere and the motions of the planets. He introduced the abacus and Arabic numerals into the West, and following the Greeks and Arabs, he taught that the earth was round.

Islamic science continued thereafter to inspire Western scholars, particularly in the late-eleventh and twelfth centuries. Men such as Adelard of Bath (d. 1144) retraced Gerbert's pilgrimage into Islamic lands and returned with a new respect for scientific inquiry—as well as an abundance of astrological texts. Among the works that Adelard translated from Arabic into Latin were Euclid's *Elements* and an important Muslim work on arithmetic that used Arabic numerals. Through the labors of the twelfth-century translators, the great scientific works of Greece and Islam were made known in the West—Aristotle's *Physics*, Ptolemy's *Almagest*, Arabic books on algebra, astrology, and medicine, and many others. And now Western scholars began to write scientific books of their own, such as Adelard of Bath's *Natural Questions*. Such works, however, were mere summaries of Greek and Arabic knowledge. The purely assimilative phrase of Western science continued until the thirteenth century when, particularly among the Franciscans, the first serious original work began.

Thirteenth-century Franciscans, anticipating Ockham, were inclined toward both pietism and the investigation of nature. The mysticism of St. Bonaventure represents one pole of Franciscan thought; at the other stands a group of scientific thinkers, who, inspired perhaps by St. Francis's love of nature, applied their logical tools to the task of investigating the physical world. Thirteenth-century Oxford became Europe's chief scientific center; it was there that Western science began to be creative.

The key figure in the development of medieval science was the English scholar Robert Grosseteste (c. 1170–1253), who, although not a Franciscan himself, was chief lecturer to the Franciscans at Oxford. Grosseteste was on intimate terms with Platonic and Neoplatonic philosophy, Aristotelian physics, and the scientific legacy of Islam. At bottom, he was a Platonist and an Augustinian, but he wrote important commentaries on the scientific works of

*See p. 124.

Aristotle and was able to draw on both traditions. From Plato Grosseteste derived the notion that mathematics is a basic key to understanding the physical universe; the fundamental importance of numbers is very much in keeping with the Platonic realist interpretation of universals, and Plato himself had once asserted that "God is a mathematician." From Aristotle Grosseteste learned the importance of abstracting knowledge from the world of phenomena by means of observation and experiment. Thus, bridging the two traditions, Grosseteste brought together the mathematical and experimental components that together underlie the rise of modern science. More than that, drawing on the suggestive work of his Islamic predecessors, he worked out a far more rigorous experimental procedure than is to be found in the pages of Aristotle. A pioneer in the development of scientific method, he outlined a system of observation, hypothesis, and experimental verification that was elaborated by his successors into the methodology that modern physical scientists still employ.

Like other pioneers, Grosseteste followed many false paths. He was better at formulating a scientific methodology than in applying it to specific problems, and his explanations of such phenomena as heat, light, color, comets, and rainbows were rejected in later centuries. But the experimental method that he formulated was to become in time a powerful intellectual tool. The problem of the rainbow, for example, was largely solved by the fourteenth-century scientist Theodoric of Freiburg, who employed a refined version of Grosseteste's experimental methodology. The great triumphs of European science lay far in the future, but with the work of Robert Grosseteste the basic instrument had been forged.

Grosseteste's work was carried further by his disciple, the Oxford Franciscan Roger Bacon (c. 1214–1294). The author of a fascinating body of scientific sense and nonsense, Roger Bacon dabbled in the mysteries of alchemy, and his curiosity carried him along strange roads. He was critical of the deductive logic and metaphysical speculations that so fascinated his Scholastic contemporaries: "Reasoning," he wrote, "does not illuminate these matters; experiments are required, conducted on a large scale, performed with instruments and by various necessary means."

At his best, Roger Bacon was almost prophetic:

> Experimental science controls the conclusions of all other sciences. It reveals truths which reasoning from general principles would never have discovered. Finally, it starts us on the way to marvelous inventions which will change the face of the world.

CONCLUSION

Underlying the achievements of the high-medieval logicians, scientists, and system-builders was a basic change in attitude toward the world. The best minds of the twelfth and thirteenth centuries were coming to view God's created universe as a natural order, functioning according to consistent, divinely constituted laws and therefore open to rational inspection. Abelard was an early exponent of this new naturalism, but it is also to be found in the writings of many others. The collapse of the central tower of Winchester Cathedral in 1107 was attributed by some to the fact that the blaspheming King William II lay entombed beneath it, but the historian William of Malmesbury had his doubts—"since the structure might have fallen because of faulty construction, even if the king had never been buried there." Similarly, a passage from the thirteenth-century *Romance of the Rose* ridicules the notion that storm damage is the work of demons,

With their hooks and cables, or their teeth and nails;
Such an explanation isn't worth
Two turnips; those accepting it are wrong.
For nothing but the tempest and the wind
Are needed to explain the havoc wrought.
These are the things that cause the injury.

In the view of the Scholastics, a rational, loving God had created a world that was both intelligible and good. The goodness of nature found its most eloquent expression in St. Francis's "Song of Brother Sun"; it also inspired the idealized naturalism of the Gothic sculptors, the poems of Dante in praise of Beatrice, and the philosophy of Thomas Aquinas. Many people would long continue to regard the world as threatening and unpredictable, governed by supernatural forces and possessed by the Devil. In the words of a twelfth-century hymn:

The world is very evil, the times are waxing late;
Be sober and keep vigil, the Judge is at the gate.

Such was the traditional view, and some might agree with it even today. But during the cultural awakening of the High Middle Ages it was gradually diminishing. A poet of the thirteenth century celebrated both the beauty of nature and the high-medieval awakening in his ovation to springtime:

The earth's ablaze again with lustrous flowers.
The fields are green again, the shadows deep.
Woods are in leaf again, and all the world
Is filled with joy again; this long-dead land
Now flames with life again: the passions surge,
Love is reborn, and beauty wakes from sleep.

Suggested Readings

GENERAL WORKS

The High Middle Ages are covered skillfully in two sequential textbooks, both in paperback: Christopher Brooke, *Europe in the Central Middle Ages, 962–1154* (2d ed., 1987); and John H. Mundy, *Europe in the High Middle Ages, 1150–1309* (1973).

John W. Baldwin, *The Scholastic Culture of the Middle Ages: 1000–1300* (1971). Universities, thought, and Gothic architecture are placed in their urban setting.

Caroline Walker Bynum, *Holy Feast and Holy Fast: The Religious Significance of Food to Medieval Women* (1987). This path-breaking study uses anthropological methods and feminist theory to demonstrate the central role of food and fasting in medieval women's religiosity.

Philippe Contamine, *War in the Middle Ages* (1984). A political, institutional, and intellectual history of warfare and military organization covering the entire Middle Ages, stressing the period 900–1500.

Carolly Erickson, *The Medieval Vision* (1976). A sensitively written account of how medieval people perceived their "enchanted world."

Jacques Le Goff, *The Medieval Imagination* (1988). A model of the "new history," with essays on dreams, conception of time, space, the body, devils, and marvels across the medieval centuries.

Lester K. Little, *Religious Poverty and the Profit Economy* (1978). A skillful and highly original study of the relationship between the urban mendicants and the development of a distinctive ideology and spirituality among the merchant class.

R. I. Moore, *The Formation of a Persecuting Society: Power and Deviance in Western Europe, 950–1250* (1987). The author makes a strong case for an intriguingly somber reappraisal of the High Middle Ages and its impact on the future.

Alexander Murray, *Reason and Society in the Middle Ages* (1978). Argues that a major increase in the circulation of money was accompanied by a shift in mental outlook and brought into power men skilled at reasoning and accounting.

Susan Reynolds, *Kingdoms and Communities in Western Europe, 900–1300* (1984). A perceptive, highly original work stressing the horizontal bonds of association in medieval lay society.

R. W. Southern, *The Making of the Middle Ages* (1953). A brilliant, sympathetic interpretation of the eleventh and twelfth centuries.

TOWN AND COUNTRYSIDE

Several recent books deal in whole or in part with medieval women or medieval families. The following are particularly recommended: Susan G. Bell, ed., *Women*

from the Greeks to the French Revolution (1973); Brenda M. Bolton and others, eds.,
Women in Medieval Society (1976); Vern L. Bullough, *The Subordinate Sex, a History
of Attitudes Toward Women* (1973); Frances and Joseph Gies, *Marriage and the Fam-
ily in the Middle Ages* (1987); Penny Schine Gold, *The Lady and the Virgin: Image,
Attitude, and Experience in Twelfth-Century France* (1985); Margaret Wade Labarge,
A Small Sound of the Trumpet: Women in Medieval Life (1986); Angela M. Lucas,
Women in the Middle Ages: Religion, Marriage and Letters (1984); and Eileen Power,
Medieval Women, ed. M. M. Postan (1975).

Robert Henri Bautier, *The Economic Development of Medieval Europe* (1971). A valuable,
superbly illustrated work that spans the entire Middle Ages.

Christopher Brooke, *The Medieval Idea of Marriage* (1989). An intriguing, multidisciplinary study of marriage across the period 1000–1500, focusing on the High Middle Ages.

Georges Duby, *The Knight, the Lady and the Priest: The Making of Modern Marriage in
Medieval France* (1983). Clarifies the importance of marriage to the survival and
advancement of aristocratic families and traces the conflict and reconciliation of
the aristocratic and ecclesiastical models of marriage.

——, *Rural Economy and Country Life in the Medieval West* (1968). A highly innovative
work, translated from the French.

Edith Ennen, *The Medieval Town* (1979). An excellent survey, originally published in
German in 1972.

Robert Fossier, *Peasant Life in the Medieval West* (1988). This engrossing study, translated from the French by Juliet Vale, uses historical, archaeological, and anthropological methods to investigate the high-medieval peasantry.

J. K. Hyde, *Society and Politics in Medieval Italy, 1000–1350* (1973). A study of socioeconomic and cultural changes among the urban governing classes.

C. Stephen Jaeger, *The Origins of Courtliness: Civilizing Trends and the Formation of Courtly
Ideals, 939–1210* (1985). This book brilliantly traces ideals of courtly behavior to
the training of future bishops at tenth-century German cathedral schools and
the royal chapel on principles derived from Cicero and other classical writers.

William C. Jordan, *From Servitude to Freedom: Manumission in the Senonais in the Thirteenth Century* (1986). A deft use of a case study to illuminate a fundamental trend
in high-medieval society.

Robert S. Lopez, *The Commercial Revolution of the Middle Ages, 950–1350* (1971). Advances
the thesis that the medieval commercial revolution was unique in world history
and an essential precondition to later industrialization.

Michel Mollat, *The Poor in the Middle Ages: An Essay in Social History* (1986). Translated
from the French, this pioneering study of poverty and charity spans the whole
of the Middle Ages.

Colin Platt, *The English Medieval Town* (1976). A masterful, well-illustrated survey running to 1600 that makes skillful use of archaeological evidence.

N. J. C. Pounds, *An Economic History of Medieval Europe* (1974). A good, analytical account, written for students.

TERRITORIAL EXPANSION

David Douglas, *The Norman Achievement* (1969) and *The Norman Fate* (1976). Expert,
readable studies of Norman activities in Normandy, Syria, Italy-Sicily, and England, 1050–1154.

John Godfrey, *The Unholy Crusade* (1980). A careful study of the Fourth Crusade in its full historical context.

Norman Housley, *The Italian Crusades: The Papal-Angevin Alliance and the Crusades against Christian Lay Powers, 1254–1343* (1982). Housley argues that these were proper Crusades with useful and significant consequences.

Benjamin Z. Kedar, *Crusade and Mission: European Approaches toward the Muslims* (1984). Argues persuasively that, because Christian preaching was forbidden in Muslim lands, missions and Crusades were seen as compatable; conquest must precede mission.

Derek W. Lomax, *The Reconquest of Spain* (1978). A detailed military-political narrative that portrays the reconquest as a conscious effort to reclaim for Christianity the lands lost to Islam in the early eighth century.

Lord John Julius Norwich, *The Normans in the South* (1966) and *The Kingdom in the Sun* (1970). A lively, two-volume account of the Normans in Southern Italy and Sicily.

J. R. S. Phillips, *The Medieval Expansion of Europe* (1988). Demonstrates that the expansion of Europe in the High and Late Middle Ages was built on Classical geographical knowledge and was a precondition for the voyages of discovery.

Donald E. Queller, *The Fourth Crusade: The Conquest of Constantinople, 1201–1204* (1977). A detailed, well-written study, sympathetic to the Venetians.

Jonathan Reilly-Smith, *The Crusades: A Short History* (1987). Concise, lively, authoritative, and aptly subtitled.

Steven Runciman, *A History of the Crusades* (3 vols., 1964–1967). Comprehensive and stylishly written.

William H. Te Brake, *Medieval Frontier: Culture and Ecology in Rijnland* (1985). An important study of land use and land reclamation in the western Netherlands from the Neolithic era to the mid-fourteenth century, showing the social and economic effects of reclamation.

CHRISTIANITY

Jeffrey Burton Russell's *History of Medieval Christianity* (p. 136) remains useful throughout the medieval period.

Edward A. Armstrong, *St. Francis: Nature Mystic* (1973). A graceful, sophisticated study of St. Francis's perceptions of God's creation.

Rosilind and Christopher Brooke, *Popular Religion in the Middle Ages* (1985). A succinct, erudite, well-illustrated survey of popular religious practices and customs from the early eleventh to the early fourteenth centuries, intended for nonspecialists.

Bernard Hamilton, *The Medieval Inquisition* (1981). Brief, clear, and balanced.

David Knowles, *The Monastic Order in England* (2d ed., 1963) and *The Religious Orders in England* (3 vols., 1948–1959). These volumes constitute the definitive study of English medieval monasticism.

Malcolm Lambert, *Medieval Heresy: Popular Movements from Bogomil to Hus* (1977). A learned, readable, thoughtfully original study of high-medieval and late-medieval heresy.

Kenneth Pennington, *Popes and Bishops: The Papal Monarchy in the Twelfth and Thirteenth Centuries* (1984). A study of the writings of canon lawyers between 1180 and 1270, showing that papal monarchy was limited, not absolute, and that bishops enjoyed significant rights within the ecclesiastical system.

R. W. Southern, *Western Society and the Church in the Middle Ages* (1970). A masterful survey and interpretation showing the interactions between the Church and the secular world.

Benedicta Ward, *Miracles and the Medieval Mind* (1982). Meticulous studies of miracle accounts at Canterbury, Compostela, Rome, and Jerusalem demonstrate both change and continuity in attitudes toward miracles during the High Middle Ages.

EMPIRE AND PAPACY

David Abulafia, *Frederick II: A Medieval Emperor* (1988). This comprehensive study, which is now the best of several accounts of Frederick II, portrays him as a ruler with traditional goals, less spectacularly innovative than previous historians have viewed him.

Geoffrey Barraclough, *The Medieval Papacy* (1968). A thoughtful interpretive survey, beautifully illustrated.

Uta-Renate Blumenthal, *The Investiture Controversy: Church and Monarchy from the Ninth to the Twelfth Century* (1988). The best account of the investiture controversy in English.

Horst Fuhrmann, *Germany in the High Middle Ages,* trans. Timothy Reuter (1986). This work, together with Haverkamp (below), replaces all earlier surveys of medieval Germany.

Alfred Haverkamp, *Medieval Germany, 1056–1273,* trans. Helga Braun and Richard Mortimer (1988). A multidisciplinary account, providing particularly sympathetic treatments of Frederick Barbarossa and Rudolf of Hapsburg.

Colin Morris, *The Papal Monarchy: The Western Church from 1050 to 1250* (1989). A stylishly written account that places the growth of the papal monarchy in a broad political and social setting.

Marcel Pacaut, *Frederick Barbarossa* (1970). An "unashamed work of popularization" by an able scholar who argues that Barbarossa, "better than anyone else, expressed the imperial ideal."

I. S. Robinson, *Authority and Resistance in the Investiture Contest: The Polemical Literature of the Late Eleventh Century* (1978). A study of Europe's first great war of propaganda, between Gregorians and supporters of the empire and traditional episcopacy.

Gerd Tellenbach, *Church, State, and Christian Society at the Time of the Investiture Contest* (1940). A brilliant, pioneering interpretation of the investiture controversy.

Helene Tillmann, *Pope Innocent III* (1980). An extremely sympathetic scholarly biography originally published in 1954 and revised by the author for this first translation into English.

ENGLAND AND FRANCE

For a comprehensive general treatment of medieval England, see C. Warren Hollister, *The Making of England, 55 B.C. to 1399* (5th ed., 1988).

Frank Barlow, *Thomas Becket* (1986). An astute, well-balanced biography.

David Bates, *William the Conqueror* (1989). Although written in an attractive style aimed at the general reader, and naked of footnotes, this work rests on an impressive body of scholarship and embodies important new interpretations.

R. Allen Brown, *The Normans and the Norman Conquest* (2d ed., 1986). A well-written, pro-Norman account of the Conquest and its background and aftermath.

Michael T. Clanchy, *England and Its Rulers, 1066–1272: Foreign Lordship and National Identity* (1983). A stimulating interpretation of high-medieval England under Norman, then Angevin, and finally Poitevin and Savoyard influence.

David Douglas, *William the Conqueror* (1964). The classic account of the Conqueror's career, giving due attention to his activities in Normandy.

Jean Dunbabin, *France in the Making, 843–1180* (1985). An excellent survey giving due attention to historical sources and to regional history.

Robert Fawtier, *The Capetian Kings of France* (1960). A short, masterful treatment.

John Gillingham, *Richard the Lionheart* (1978). An engagingly written biography portraying Richard not as an absentee king of England but as the effective ruler of his Anglo-Continental dominions.

———, *The Angevin Empire* (1984). This brief, elegantly written work covers the period from 1144 to the early years of Henry III.

Elizabeth M. Hallam, *Capetian France, 987–1328* (1980). More comprehensive and up-to-date than Fawtier's classic work (above), this study portrays the Capetian kings in their economic, social, religious, and cultural setting.

James C. Holt, *Magna Carta* (1965). The definitive study.

William C. Jordan, *Louis IX and the Challenge of the Crusade* (1979). Shows how St. Louis' crusading zeal shaped his administrative policies and social reforms.

Edmund King, *England, 1175–1425* (1979). A skillfully presented survey incorporating social and economic history.

———, *Medieval England, 1066–1485* (1988). A multidisciplinary history, gracefully written and lavishly illustrated.

John Le Patourel, *The Norman Empire* (1976). Stresses the unity of Norman politics in England and northern France to 1154.

Michael Prestwich, *Edward I* (1988). The definitive biography of one of medieval England's most notable kings.

G. O. Sayles, *The King's Parliament of England* (1974). A brief but important interpretation of the development of Parliament as a response to contemporary problems.

Joseph R. Strayer, *The Reign of Philip the Fair* (1980). A model biography reflecting a lifetime of scholarship.

LITERATURE, ART, AND THOUGHT

Harold J. Berman, *Law and Revolution: The Formation of the Western Legal Tradition* (1983). This important and challenging work of reinterpretation places the roots of the Western legal tradition in the investiture controversy of the later eleventh century.

Christopher Brooke, *The Twelfth-Century Renaissance* (1969). A well-illustrated, sensitively written essay on cultural figures of twelfth-century Europe.

Jean Bony, *French Gothic Architecture of the Twelfth and Thirteenth Centuries* (1983). A masterful, highly original, and beautifully illustrated study.

M. D. Chenu, *Nature, Man and Society in the Twelfth Century* (1968). Translated essays exploring basic changes in mental outlook in twelfth-century theology.

M. T. Clanchy, *From Memory to Written Record: England, 1066–1307* (1979). A challenging study of the emergence of a literate mentality in high-medieval England.

Stephen C. Ferruolo, *The Origins of the University: The Schools of Paris and Their Critics, 1100–1215* (1985). A deft work of scholarship, the best on the subject.

Edward Grant, *Physical Science in the Middle Ages* (1971). Stresses the impact of Aristotelian physical science on the medieval mind.

Michael Haren, *Medieval Thought: The Western Intellectual Tradition from Antiquity to the Thirteenth Century* (1985). A clear, concise, well-organized survey from Plato to Aquinas and Siger of Brabant stressing the Greek roots of medieval philosophy.

Charles Homer Haskins, *The Renaissance of the Twelfth Century* (1927). A pioneering book, particularly strong on Latin literature.

David Knowles, *The Evolution of Medieval Thought* (rev. ed., 1988). A short, lucid survey.

Henry Kraus, *Gold Was Their Mortar: The Economics of Cathedral Building* (1979). A readable study of the various funding techniques of eight cathedral cities.

Bernard McGinn, *The Calabrian Abbot: Joachim of Fiore in the History of Western Thought* (1985). The best English-language treatment of Joachim.

John C. Moore, *Love in Twelfth-Century France* (1972). Short, learned, and gracefully written.

Colin Morris, *The Discovery of the Individual, 1050–1200* (1972). The controversial and much-discussed thesis of this book is nicely embedded in its title.

Nancy Partner, *Serious Entertainments: The Writing of History in Twelfth-Century England* (1977). An extremely gifted writer and scholar explores the spiritual and intellectual qualities of three important twelfth-century historians and, in the process, casts fresh light on the mentalities of their era.

Brian Stock, *The Implications of Literacy: Written Language and Models of Interpretation in the Eleventh and Twelfth Centuries* (1983). A work of major importance: the concept of emerging "textual communities" illuminates the changing intellectual order of the High Middle Ages.

R. W. Southern, *Medieval Humanism and Other Studies* (1970). Related essays on medieval thought and life, including an important reinterpretation of humanism in Western culture and a trashing of the "school of Chartres."

James A. Weisheipl, *Friar Thomas d'Aquino* (1975). A sympathetic scholarly treatment of Aquinas's life in its historical setting.

SOURCES

Dante Alighieri, *The Divine Comedy*. Many translations.

Angel Flores, *An Anthology of Medieval Lyrics*. English translations of medieval lyric poems from France, Italy, Germany, and Spain.

The Correspondence of Pope Gregory VII, ed. and trans. Ephraim Emerton.

Guibert of Nogent, *Self and Society in Medieval France*, trans. John F. Benton. The fascinating autobiography of a twelfth-century abbot and scholar, to which Benton gives a Freudian twist in his playful introduction.

Otto of Freising, *The Deeds of Frederick Barbarossa*, trans. C. C. Mierow and Richard Emery.

Anton C. Pegis, ed., *Introduction to St. Thomas Aquinas*. Intelligently chosen selections with a stimulating introduction.

The Song of Roland, trans. Frederick Golden.

Villehardouin and de Joinville, *Memoirs of the Crusades*, trans. Sir Frank Marzials.

PART THREE

The Late Middle Ages
The Ordeal of Transition

THE LATE MIDDLE AGES (c. 1300–1500): AN OVERVIEW

Even more than most eras of human history, the fourteenth and fifteenth centuries were violent and unsettled. They were marked by a gradual ebbing of confidence in the values on which high-medieval civilization had rested. General prosperity gave way to sporadic depression, optimism to disillusionment, and the thirteenth-century dream of fusing the worlds of matter and spirit faded. Social behavior ran to extremes—to rebellion, hedonism, flagellation, cynicism, and witch-hunting. People might lead quiet, happy lives during these centuries but, as in other times, such lives did not attract much public notice. Powerful creative forces were at work, but they were less evident to many observers than the forces of disintegration and decay.

The shrinking of Europe's economy, population, and territorial frontiers was accompanied by a mood of pessimism and claustrophobia, erupting periodically into rage or frenzy. Writers and artists were often preoccupied with fantasy, eccentricity, and death. England and France were tormented by war, and both were ruled for a time by madmen. The Black Death struck in the mid-fourteenth century and returned periodically for many generations thereafter, carrying off millions of victims and darkening the spirits of those who survived.

These varied symptoms of social and psychological disorder were associated with a gradual shift in Western Europe's political orientation—from a Christian commonwealth, linked together by a strong papacy, to a constellation of virtually autonomous kingdoms and principalities. The Roman Catholic Church fared badly during the late Middle Ages. For a time the Great Schism split the papacy into contending factions, one in Avignon, the other in Rome. The Western kingdoms were racked by civil and external war and, at times, by a near breakdown of royal government. Town and countryside alike were afflicted by crime and violence, murders and assaults. Gangs of armed outlaws pillaged and terrorized portions of England (one such gang ruled for a time the bustling port of Bristol), while in France bands of unemployed mercenary troops roamed almost at will, plundering and killing.

Yet during the final half-century of the period (c. 1450–1500) strong monarchies reemerged in England, France, and Spain. These three states were to dominate Western European politics far into the future and to send their explorers, warriors, and settlers across the globe. By 1500 the monarchies were replacing the international Church as the object of their inhabitants' highest allegiance. The pope had become mired in local Italian politics, and medieval Christendom was breaking into sovereign fragments.

In a presidential address to the American Historical Association some years ago, Professor Joseph R. Strayer contrasted the crises of the fourth and fourteenth centuries. The fourth-century crisis resulted ultimately in the disintegration of Roman imperial government in the West. The

fourteenth-century crisis, on the other hand, left Europe's political and social institutions battered but intact. One might attribute their survival to
the greater ingenuity and tenacity of late-medieval Europeans, but the like-
lier explanation is to be found in the tremendous changes that Europe had
experienced between Roman and high-medieval times. Its towns and commerce were far more vigorous in 1300 than in 300, and its agricultural productivity far greater. During the High Middle Ages, Western civilization
had become much more deeply rooted than ever before, and throughout
the late-medieval crisis Europe remained a land of towns, cities, and cultivated fields, a land where governments, guilds, hospitals, and universities
continued to function. Whereas Roman Europe north of the Alps had
lacked a vigorous urban and commercial life, the civilization that emerged
in the High Middle Ages, although capable of enormous future development, proved indestructible.

15

The Troubles of Church and State

THE CHURCH

The late-medieval evolution from Christendom toward nationhood was not so much a transformation as a shift in balance. Even during the High Middle Ages the ideal of a Christian commonwealth, guided by pope and clergy, had never been fulfilled. At best, popes could win momentary political victories over kings and could achieve an uneasy equilibrium between royal and clerical authority. By the later thirteenth century the balance was already tipping in favor of monarchs such as Edward I of England and Philip the Fair of France. The trend accelerated during the late Middle Ages until, by 1500, the papacy had become far weaker as an international force and the monarchies stronger. "Nationhood," by any strict definition, had not yet come, but papal authority over the churches of the various kingdoms was becoming tenuous. The princely electors of Germany had long before denied the papacy any role in imperial elections or coronations, and papal influence in the appointment of French, English, and Spanish prelates had ebbed. More important still, the late Middle Ages witnessed a collapse of papal spiritual prestige and a widening chasm between Christian piety and the organized Church.

Mystics and Reformers

Christianity did not decline during this period; it merely became less ecclesiastical. The powerful movement of lay piety, which had been drifting away from papal leadership all through the High Middle Ages, now became increasingly hostile to ecclesiastical wealth and privilege, increasingly individualistic, and increasingly mystical. The wave of mysticism that swept across late-medieval Europe was not, for the most part, openly heretical. But by stressing the spiritual relationship between the individual and God, the mystics tended to deemphasize the role of the ordained clergy and the sacraments as channels of divine grace. Although they believed in the efficacy of the Holy

Eucharist and could express their devotion to it in the most moving terms, they also dwelled on the indescribable ecstasy of a mystical union with God, for which no clerical hierarchy, no popes, and no sacraments were needed.

Mysticism had always been an element in Christian devotional life and was well known to the High Middle Ages. During the twelfth century and especially in the thirteenth, the most celebrated mystical visionaries were women. As the authority of the clergy increased with the development of canon law and the growth of the Church bureaucracy, religious women—who were denied the priestly commission to preach and consecrate the Eucharist—found an alternative and more immediate source of divine authorization in their mystical union with Christ. The divine revelations of the twelfth-century abbess Hildegard of Bingen (d. 1179) impressed St. Bernard of Clairvaux so deeply that he addressed her as a "prophetess of God"; as a direct source of divine knowledge, Hildegard was consulted by theologians on thorny points of doctrine and by popes and emperors on questions of high politics. At the thirteenth-century abbey of Helfta in Saxony, Gertrude of Helfta (d. 1301/2) and other nuns had visions of a Christ who was at once regal and lovingly approachable; their writings express what has aptly been called "a poised, self-confident, lyrical female mysticism."

The nuns of Helfta may themselves have been influenced by the mystical writings of pious laywomen known as "Beguines"—whose loosely organized groups grew to considerable numbers during the thirteenth and early fourteenth centuries in the towns of Germany and the Netherlands. The Beguines sought to follow St. Francis's example of loving service to others in imitation of Christ—a kind of evangelism that was denied to the strictly cloistered female Franciscans, the Poor Clares (see p. 203). Living by no papally sanctioned religious rule and taking no lifetime vows, the Beguines were alternately praised and condemned by ecclesiastical authorities, but they continued to flourish into the late Middle Ages, representing a kind of mystical lay piety that grew increasingly significant in the fourteenth and fifteenth centuries.

The goal of imitating Christ gave rise in many thirteenth-century Beguine communities to powerful mystical experiences, expressed in vernacular prose and poetry of great immediacy and intensity. The Beguine Mechthild of Magdeburg (d. c. 1282), whose *Flowing Light of Divinity* is a vivid and deeply personal description of her experiences of divine union, ended her days as a nun of Helfta and was probably a source of inspiration for the outpouring of mystical writings there. And Mechthild, along with other Beguine mystics, may well have influenced the thinking of the great mystical theorist Meister Eckhart.

Writing in the early fourteenth century, the Dominican Meister Eckhart (d. 1327) taught that humanity's true goal is utter separation from the world of the senses and absorption into the Divine Unknown. Eckhart had many followers, and as the fourteenth century progressed, other mystical communities emerged. St. Catherine of Siena (d. 1380), another Dominican mystic, attracted disciples of both sexes by her single-minded devotion to repentance and social reform as expressions of an all-consuming love of God. And around

1375 the highly influential "Brethren of the Common Life" was founded by the Flemish lay preacher Gerard Groot, a student of one of Eckhart's disciples. The Brethren of the Common Life devoted themselves to simple lives of preaching, teaching, and charitable works. Their popularity in fifteenth-century northern Europe approached that of the Franciscans two centuries before, but like the Beguines the Brethren took no lifetime vows. Their schools were among Europe's finest and produced some of the leading mystics, humanists, and reformers of the fifteenth and sixteenth centuries. Erasmus and Luther were both products of the Brethren's schools, as was Thomas à Kempis (d. 1471), whose *Imitation of Christ* stands as the supreme literary expression of late-medieval mysticism.* The *Imitation of Christ* typifies the mystical outlook in its emphasis on adoration over speculation, inner spiritual purity over external "good works," and direct experience of God over the sacramental avenues to divine grace. The *Imitation* remained well within the bounds of Catholic orthodoxy, yet it contained ideas that had great appeal to the sixteenth-century Protestant reformers. The emphasis on individual piety, common to all the mystics, tended to erode the medieval idea of a Christian commonwealth by viewing the Church as a multitude of individual souls, each reaching out alone toward God.

This element of Christian individualism was carried at times to the point of heresy. John Wycliffe (d. 1384), a professor at Oxford, anticipated the later Protestants by placing the authority of Scripture over the pronouncements of popes and councils. Extending the implications of contemporary mysticism to their limit, Wycliffe stressed the individual's inner spiritual journey toward God, questioned the real presence of Christ in the Holy Eucharist, deemphasized the entire sacramental system, and spoke out strongly against ecclesiastical wealth. This last protest had been implicit in the thirteenth-century Franciscan movement, although St. Francis had shown his devotion to apostolic poverty by living it rather than forcing it on others. The compromises of later Franciscanism on the matter of property had given rise to a zealous splinter group—the "Spiritual Franciscans"—whose insistence on universal ecclesiastical poverty had made them anticlerical and antipapal. John XXII, the shrewd Avignonese "financier pope," had seen fit in 1323 to denounce their doctrine of apostolic poverty as heretical. And Wycliffe, more than a half century later, was stripped of his professorship and convicted of heresy. Owing to his powerful friends at court, and to the unpopularity of the papacy in fourteenth-century England, Wycliffe was permitted to die peacefully, but his followers, the Lollards, were hunted down ruthlessly (a parliamentary act of 1401 was entitled "The Statute on the Burning of Heretics"). By the early fifteenth century the Lollard threat had been contained, but the seeds of religious revolt were planted and continued to germinate.

*Although most scholars attribute *The Imitation of Christ* to Thomas à Kempis, the attribution is not certain.

English Lollardy represented an extreme expression of a growing discontent with the official Church. Wycliffe's doctrines spread to faraway Bohemia, where they were taken up by the reformer John Hus. The Hussites used Wycliffe's anticlericalism as a weapon in the struggle for Czech independence from German political and cultural influence. John Hus was burned at the stake at the Council of Constance in 1415, but his followers survived into the Reformation era as a dissident national group. Both Wycliffe and Hus represented, in their opposition to the organized international Church, a reconciliation of personal religious faith with the idea of national sovereignty. If Christianity was to be an individual affair, then the political claims of popes and prelates were meritless, and secular rulers might govern without ecclesiastical interference. Thus the radical thrust of late medieval Christianity, by its very anticlericalism, tended to support the growing concept of secular sovereignty. Ardent religious spirits such as John Hus—and Joan of Arc, burned as a heretic in 1431—could fuse Christian mysticism with the beginnings of patriotism.

POPES AND COUNCILS

The reformers, implicitly or explicitly, rejected the pope as the chief link connecting God and the Christian community. And the late-medieval papacy was vulnerable to their attacks. Early in the fourteenth century, as we have seen, the papacy had moved to Avignon on the Rhône River, just outside the domain of the French monarchy. There a series of able French popes ruled from 1309 to 1376. The Avignon popes were subservient to the French crown only on occasion; for the most part they were capable of strong, independent action. But their very location suggested to France's enemies that they were no longer an impartial international force. Attempts were made to return the papacy to Rome, but they were foiled by the violent factionalism of the Holy City. Meanwhile, the Avignon popes carried the thirteenth-century trend toward administrative and fiscal efficiency to its ultimate degree. The large, well-tuned bureaucracy of papal Avignon provided revenues and personnel sufficient to make the papacy an even stronger international power than before. Pope John XXII (1316–1334), a man of austere life and administrative genius, launched a thoroughgoing reform of the papal fiscal system that increased revenues significantly by attacking the longstanding custom of rakeoffs at every level between the taxpayer and the papal treasury. But the administrative machinery failed to inspire mystics and reformers, and France's neighbors resented the taxation and interference of what many mistakenly regarded as a tool of the French crown. Thus, while the papacy was growing wealthier and more efficient, its spiritual capital was diminishing.

At length, Pope Gregory XI responded to growing public pressure—and the urging of St. Catherine of Siena—by moving the Holy See back to Rome in 1376. Chagrined by the turbulent conditions he encountered there, Gregory made plans to return to France but died in 1378 before he could carry them out. Pressured by a Roman mob, the cardinals—most of them homesick Frenchmen—elected an Italian to the papal throne. The new pope, Urban VI, had previously been a colorless functionary in the ecclesiastical bureaucracy. Now, to everyone's surprise, he became a zealous reformer and began taking steps to reduce the cardinals' revenues and influence. The French cardinals fled Rome, canceled their previous election on the grounds of mob intimidation, and elected a French pope who returned with them to Avignon. Back in Rome, Urban VI appointed new cardinals, and for the next thirty-seven years the Church was torn by the "Great Schism." When the rival popes died, their cardinals elected rival successors. Excommunications were hurled to and fro between Rome and Avignon, and the states of Europe chose sides according to their interests. France and its allies supported Avignon, England and the Holy Roman Empire backed Rome, and the Italian states shifted from one side to the other as it suited their purposes. Papal prestige was falling in ruin, yet in the face of age-long papal claims to absolute spiritual authority, there seemed no power on earth that could arbitrate between two rival popes.

As the Great Schism dragged on, increasing numbers of Christians became convinced that the only solution was the convening of a general church council. Both popes argued that councils were inferior to them and could not judge them, and Christians were perplexed as to who, if not the popes, had the authority to summon a council. At length some of the cardinals themselves, in both camps, called a council to meet in Pisa. There, in 1409, a group of 500 prelates deposed both popes and elected a new one. Since neither pope recognized the conciliar depositions, the effect of the Council of Pisa was to transform a two-way schism into a three-way schism. The situation was not only scandalous but ludicrous. Finally the Holy Roman emperor arranged for the summoning of great churchmen from all across Europe to the Council of Constance (1415–1418). Here at last the schism ended. Two popes were deposed, the third resigned, and the Church was reunited by the election of a conciliar pope, Martin V (1417–1431).

To many thoughtful Christians the healing of the Great Schism was not enough. The papacy stood discredited, and it was argued that future popes should be guided by general councils meeting regularly and automatically. The role of councils and assemblies was familiar enough to contemporary secular governments. Why shouldn't the Church, too, be governed "constitutionally"? Such views were being urged by political philosophers such as Marsilius of Padua in the fourteenth century and Nicholas of Cusa in the fifteenth, and they were widely accepted among the prelates at Constance. That these delegates were essentially conservative is suggested by their decision to burn the religious rebel John Hus, who came to Constance with an imperial promise of safe conduct. Yet the Council of Constance made a genuine effort to reform the constitution of the Church along conciliar lines. The delegates affirmed, against papal objection, the ultimate authority of councils in matters of doctrine and reform, and they decreed that thenceforth general councils would convene at regular intervals.

These broad principles, together with a number of specific reforms voted by the Council of Constance, met with firm opposition from Pope Martin V and his successors, who insisted on absolute papal supremacy. The popes reluctantly summoned a council in 1423 and another in 1431, but worked to make them ineffective. The last of the important medieval councils, the Council of Basel (1431–1449), drifted gradually into open schism with the papacy and petered out ingloriously. By then Europe's enthusiasm for conciliarism was waning; the conciliar movement died, and a single pope ruled unopposed once more in Rome.

The men who sat on the papal throne between the dissolution of Basel (1449) and the beginning of the Protestant Reformation (1517) were radically different from their high-medieval predecessors. Abandoning much of their former jurisdiction over the international Church, they devoted themselves to the beguiling culture and bitter local politics of Renaissance Italy. By now most popes were Italian, and so they would remain on into the future. Struggling to strengthen their hold on the Papal States, maneuvering through the shifting sands of Italian diplomacy, they conceded to northern monarchs an extensive degree of control over Church and clergy in return for a formal recognition of papal authority and an agreed division of Church revenues between pope and king.

The fifteenth century ended with the pontificate of the Borgia pope, Alexander VI (1492–1503), whose scandalous behavior and bastard offspring were sufficient even to raise eyebrows in high-Renaissance Italy. Alexander's pontificate is a caricature of all that ailed the papacy at the end of the Middle Ages. Devoting himself to the advancement of his own family, he gave full support to the unprincipled military and diplomatic activities of his son, Caesar, who used assassination, treachery, and force to carve out a great Borgia state in central Italy.

As the Borgia pontificate vividly illustrates, the papacy by 1500 had ceased to be an international spiritual power. Fourteen years after Alexander VI's death, the Protestant Reformation exploded, and the tremendous popular response to Luther's rebellion bespeaks the failure of the late-medieval popes. Europeans were by no means prepared to abandon Christianity, but they were willing, in large numbers, to desert tarnished Rome.

THE WESTERN MONARCHIES

The late-medieval trend from international Catholicism toward secular sovereignty found forceful expression in Marsilius of Padua's important treatise, the *Defensor Pacis* (1324). Here the dilemma of conflicting sovereign jurisdictions, secular and ecclesiastical, was resolved uncompromisingly in favor of the state. The Church, Marsilius argued, should be stripped of political authority, and the state should wield sovereign power over all its subjects, lay and clerical alike. Thus the Church, united in faith, would be divided politically into numerous state churches obedient to their secular rulers and not to the pope. In its glorification of the sovereign state, the *Defensor Pacis* foreshadowed the evolution of late-medieval and early-modern politics.

It was only after 1450, however, that the Western monarchies were able to assert their authority with any consistency over the nobility. During the period from the early-fourteenth to the mid-fifteenth century, the high-medieval trend toward royal centralization seemed to have reversed itself. The major Iberian powers—Aragon, Castile, and Portugal—were tormented by sporadic internal upheavals and made no progress toward reducing Granada, the remaining Islamic enclave in the peninsula. For most of the period, England and France were involved in the Hundred Years' War (1337–1453), which drove England to the brink of bankruptcy and ravaged the French countryside and population.

England

The English Parliament developed significantly during these years. In the course of the fourteenth century, Parliament changed from a body that met occasionally to a permanent institution and split into Lords and Commons. The House of Commons, consisting of representative townsmen and shire knights, bargained with a monarchy hard pressed by the expenses of the Hundred Years' War. Commons traded its fiscal support for important political concessions, and by the century's end it had gained the privilege of approving or disapproving all taxation not sanctioned by custom. With control of the royal purse strings, Commons exerted increasing influence on legislation.

Chronology of Late-Medieval England and France

England	France
1307–1327: Reign of Edward II	1328–1589: Valois Dynasty
1327–1377: Reign of Edward III	1328–1350: Reign of Philip VI
1337–1453: Hundred Years' War	1337–1453: Hundred Years' War
1346: Battle of Crécy	1346: Battle of Crécy
1348–1349: Black Death	1348–1349: Black Death
	1350–1364: Reign of John, "the Good"
1356: Battle of Poitiers	1356: Battle of Poitiers
	1357: The Great Ordinance
	1358: Jacquerie Rebellion
1377–1399: Reign of Richard II	1364–1380: Reign of Charles V
1381: Peasants' Revolt	
1413–1422: Reign of Henry V	1380–1422: Reign of Charles VI, "the Mad"
1415: Battle of Agincourt	1415: Battle of Agincourt
1455–1485: Wars of the Roses	1422–1461: Reign of Charles VII
1461–1483: Reign of Edward IV	1429–1431: Career of Joan of Arc
1485–1509: Reign of Henry VII; beginning of Tudor Dynasty	1461–1483: Reign of Louis XI

Adopting the motto, "redress before supply," it refused to pass financial grants until the king had approved its petitions, and in the end the king almost always acquiesced.

Yet the late-medieval House of Commons was by no means the independent voice of a rising middle class. By and large, it was controlled by the force or manipulation of powerful aristocrats. Elections could be rigged; representatives could be bribed or intimidated. And although Parliament deposed two English kings in the fourteenth century—Edward II in 1327 and Richard II in 1399—in both instances it was simply ratifying the results of aristocratic power struggles. It is significant that such parliamentary ratification should seem necessary, but one must not conclude that Parliament had yet become a free agent. Symbolically, it represented the will of the English community; actually, it remained sensitive to royal and aristocratic forces and tended to affirm decisions already made in castles or on battlefields.

The Hundred Years' War, which proved such a stimulus to the growth of parliamentary privileges, also constituted a serious drain on English wealth and lives. Beginning in 1337, the war dragged on fitfully for 116 years with periods of savage warfare alternating with prolonged periods of truce. Broadly speaking, the conflict was a continuation of the Anglo-French rivalry that dated from the Norman Conquest. Since 1066, when William the Conqueror joined England to Normandy, English kings had ruled portions of France and had battled French kings on numerous occasions. In 1204 the Capetian crown had won the extensive northern French territories of the Angevin empire, but the English kings retained a tenuous lordship over Gascony in the southwest. The English Gascon claim, cemented by a brisk commerce in Bordeaux wine and English cloth, gave rise to an expensive but inconclusive war (1294–1303) between Philip the Fair of France and Edward I of England. Competing English and French claims to jurisdiction in Gascony constituted one of several causes for the resumption of hostilities in 1337.

Another cause of the Hundred Years' War was the Anglo-French diplomatic struggle for control of Flanders. The kings of France had long claimed supreme lordship over the Flemish, whereas England and Flanders had become tightly linked by a profitable wool trade. Tension mounted when in 1328 the last Capetian king of France died without sons, throwing the royal succession into dispute. The French crown was claimed by King Edward III of England (1327–1377), whose mother was a daughter of King Philip the Fair. But Edward's claim was contested by Philip of Valois, son of Philip the Fair's younger brother. The French nobility, arguing unhistorically that the right to inherit cannot pass through a woman, raised Philip of Valois to the throne. As King Philip VI (1328–1350), he became the first of a long line of Valois kings who ruled France until 1589. Edward III accepted the decision initially, but in 1337, when other reasons prompted him to take up arms, he revived his claim and titled himself king of France and England.

None of these causes can be considered decisive, and war might yet have been avoided. But Edward III and Philip VI were both chivalrous, high-spirited

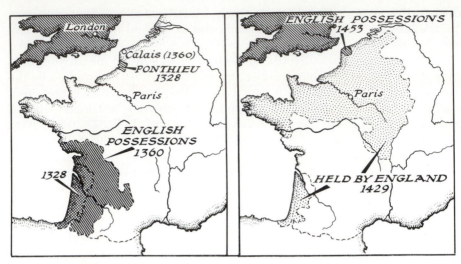

France in the Hundred Years' War

romantics who delighted in heroic clashes of arms. And the nobles of both sides were infected by similar attitudes. The French lost most of their ardor when English longbowmen won smashing victories at Crécy (1346) and Poitiers (1356). The English revered Edward III so long as English arms were victorious, but they deposed his successor, Richard II (1377–1399), who preferred reducing the power of his nobles to fighting the French. King Henry V (1413–1422) revived hostilities and gained the adulation of his English subjects by winning a momentous victory over the French at Agincourt in 1415. But Henry V's early death, and the subsequent military triumphs of the French visionary Joan of Arc* turned the tide of war against the English. By 1453, when the long struggle ended at last, England had lost all of France except the port of Calais on the English Channel. The age-long process of Anglo-French disentanglement was completed, and Joan of Arc's vision was realized: the Valois Charles VII ruled France unopposed.

The Hundred Years' War had been over for scarcely two years when England entered an era of civil strife between the rival houses of York and Lancaster. The Wars of the Roses, which raged off and on between 1455 and 1485, were the medieval English nobility's last hurrah. Nobles and commoners alike grew tired of endless bloodshed and longed for firm royal governance. They achieved it, to a degree, in the reign of the Yorkist Edward IV (1461–1483). Hostilities resumed during the brief, troubled reign of Richard III (1483–1485), whose alleged murder of two young princes in the Tower of London has generated heated controversy down to the present day (one occasionally sees American students wearing Richard III T-shirts). But with

*See pp. 309, 316–317.

Richard III's death in battle, strong monarchy came permanently to England with the accession of the first Tudor King, Henry VII (1485–1509). Both Edward IV and Henry VII sought peace, a full treasury, and effective government, and by the late fifteenth century these goals were coming within reach. The economy was reviving, many of the more warlike nobles had perished in the Wars of the Roses, and the English were more than willing to exchange military turmoil for obedience and peace. All that was needed now was strong royal leadership, and that was supplied in full measure by the willful, determined Tudors.

France

The Hundred Years' War was a far greater trial to France than to England. All the fighting took place on French soil, and mercenary companies continually pillaged the French countryside, even when they were not engaged in actual warfare. King John the Good (1350–1364)—a very bad king indeed—was powerless to cope with the English or bring order to a demoralized, plague-ridden land. In 1356, a decade after the French military debacle at Crécy and eight years after the onset of the Black Death, France was stunned by a crushing defeat at Poitiers. French nobles fell in great numbers, and King John himself was taken prisoner by the English.

The Estates General, meeting in Paris under the leadership of a Parisian cloth merchant named Etienne Marcel, momentarily assumed the reins of government. In 1357 they forced King John's son, the young Dauphin* Charles, to issue a radical constitutional statute known as the "Great Ordinance." This statute embodied the demands of the bourgeois-dominated Estates General to join with the monarchy in the governance of France. The Estates General were thenceforth to meet on regular occasions and to supervise the royal finances, courts, and administration through a small standing committee. The Dauphin Charles, deeply hostile to this infringement of royal authority, submitted for a time and then fled Paris to gather royalist support in the countryside.

By 1358 the horrors of plague, depression, and mercenary marauders had goaded the French peasantry into open revolt. The "Jacquerie"—as the rebellious peasants were called—lacked coherent goals and effective leaders, but they managed for two memorable weeks to terrorize portions of the northern French countryside. On one occasion they are reported to have forced an aristocratic wife to eat her roasted husband, after which they raped and murdered her. But the aristocracy and urban elites quickly crushed the uprising with a savagery worthy of the rebels themselves. The Jacquerie rebellion of 1358 evoked a longing for law and order and a return to the ways of old. This conservative backlash resulted in a surge of royalism that doomed Etienne Marcel's constitutional movement in Paris.

*Crown prince.

Marcel himself was murdered in midsummer 1358, and the Dauphin Charles returned to the city in triumph.

The Great Ordinance of 1357 became a dead letter after Marcel's fall, and in later centuries the Estates General met less and less frequently. The Dauphin Charles, who became the able King Charles V (1364–1380), instituted new tax measures that largely freed the monarchy from its financial dependence on assemblies and made it potentially the richest in Europe. The Estates General, unlike the English Parliament, failed to become an integral part of the government, and French kings reverted more and more to their high-medieval practice of dealing with their subjects through local assemblies. There were "Parlements" in France—outgrowths of the central and regional courts—but their functions remained judicial; they did not deliberate on the granting of taxes, and they did not legislate. French national cohesion continued to lag behind that of England, because France was much larger, more populous, and more culturally diverse. During the late Middle Ages its great dukes still ruled whole provinces with little interference from Paris. In the absence of an articulate national parliament, the only voice that could claim to speak for all the French people was the voice of their king.

Charles V succeeded in turning the tide of war by avoiding pitched battles. His armies harassed the English unceasingly and forced them, little by little, to draw back. By Charles's death the French monarchy was recovering. The English, reduced to small outposts around Bordeaux and Calais, virtually abandoned the war for a generation.

But Charles V was succeeded by the incompetent Charles VI (1380–1422)—"Charles the Mad"—who grew from a weak child into an unstable adult, periodically insane. His reign was marked by a bloody rivalry between the houses of Burgundy and Orléans. The duke of Orléans was Charles the Mad's brother, the duke of Burgundy his uncle. In Capetian times, such powerful fief-holding members of the royal family had usually cooperated with the king, but now, with a madman on the throne, Burgundy and Orléans struggled for control of the kingdom. In the course of the fifteenth century, the Orléanist faction became identified with the cause of the Valois monarchy, and Burgundy evolved into a powerful independent state between France and Germany.

With France ravaged once again by murder and civil strife, King Henry V of England resumed the Hundred Years' War and, in 1415, won his overwhelming victory at Agincourt. At this the Burgundians joined forces with the English, and Charles the Mad was forced to make Henry V his heir. But both kings died in 1422, and while Charles the Mad's son, Charles VII (1422–1461), carried on a half-hearted resistance, the Burgundians and English divided northern France between them and prepared to crush the remaining power of the Valois monarchy.

At the nadir of his fortunes, Charles VII, as yet uncrowned, accepted in desperation the military services of the peasant visionary Joan of Arc. Joan's victory at Orléans, her insistence on Charles's coronation in Reims Cathedral, and her capture and death at the stake in 1431 have become legendary. The spirit that she kindled raised French hopes, and in the two decades following her death Charles VII's armies went from victory to victory. The conquest of France had always been beyond English resources, and English successes in the Hundred Years' War had been largely a product of poor French leadership and paralyzing internal division. Now, as the war drew at last to a close, Charles VII could devote himself to the rebuilding of the royal government. He was supported in his task by secure tax revenues, a standing army, and the steady growth of the royal administrative machinery.

Centralization was carried much further by Louis XI (1461–1483), known as "the Spider King" because of the political webs that he wove so dextrously to entrap his enemies. Son and heir of Charles VII (whom he despised), Louis XI removed his rivals by clandestine murders, public beheadings, and various other dirty tricks. He also took important steps to stimulate the French economy—establishing new fairs to attract foreign merchants and their money, encouraging industries, and reducing internal tariffs. Siphoning off much of the resulting wealth with higher taxes, Louis XI more than doubled the royal revenues. To his delight, the Burgundian threat dissolved in 1477 when the last duke of Burgundy died fighting Louis' Swiss allies. The Spider King thereupon confiscated the entire duchy. Plotting his way through a labyrinth of shifting alliances and loyalties, he advanced significantly toward the goals of French unification and Valois absolutism.

By 1500 the French monarchy was ruling its subjects through a central administration of professional bureaucrats drawn from both the nobility and the middle class. The kings of France had largely won the loyalty of the nobility—as wise monarchs always had—by appointing nobles to high positions in the court, the royal administration, and the army. The towns were flourishing once again; the English were gone for good; and French soldiers were carrying the dynastic claims of the Valois kings into foreign lands.

The Iberian Peninsula: Spain and Portugal

The course of Iberian history in the late Middle Ages runs parallel to that of England and France: generations of internal turmoil gave way in the later fifteenth century to political coherence and royal consolidation. As the high-medieval reconquest of Muslim principalities rolled to a stop around 1270, the Iberian Peninsula contained three strong Christian kingdoms—Castile, Aragon, and Portugal—along with Muslim Granada in the extreme south. Of the major kingdoms, Castile was the largest and Aragon the most urbanized. During the thirteenth and fourteenth centuries, Aragonese kings conquered the Mediterranean islands of Majorca, Minorca, Sardinia, and Sicily, and Aragonese merchants began moving into international commerce.

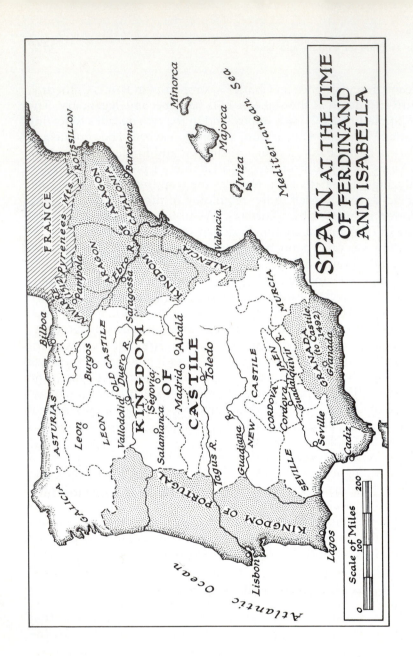

SPAIN AT THE TIME OF FERDINAND AND ISABELLA

FRANCE

Minorca

Majorca

Iviza

Mediterranean Sea

Pyrenees Mts.

ROUSSILLON

Barcelona

NAVARRE (1512)

Pampeluna

ARAGON

Ebro R.

CATALONIA

KINGDOM OF ARAGON

Valencia

KINGDOM OF VALENCIA

Bilboa

Burgos

OLD CASTILE

Saragossa

Duero R.

Alcalá

Madrid

Asturias

Leon

LEON

Valladolid

Segovia

Salamanca

KINGDOM OF CASTILE

Toledo

Tagus R.

NEW CASTILE

MURCIA

CORDOVA

Cordova

JAEN

Guadalquivir R.

GRANADA (to 1492)

Granada

GALICIA

Guadiana R.

KINGDOM OF PORTUGAL

SEVILLE

Seville

Cadiz

Lisbon

Lagos

Atlantic Ocean

Scale of Miles

0   100   200

Aragon and Castile were both plagued by civil turbulence during the late Middle Ages. The Aragonese monarchy strove with only limited success to placate the nobility and townspeople by granting significant concessions to the "Cortes," the regional representative assemblies. A prolonged revolt by the mercantile class in the Aragonese province of Catalonia was put down in 1472 only with the greatest difficulty. Castile, in the meantime, was torn by constant aristocratic uprisings and disputed royal successions. Peace and strong government came within reach at last when Ferdinand of Aragon married Isabella of Castile in 1469. Isabella inherited her throne in 1474; Ferdinand inherited his in 1479. And thereafter—despite the continuation of regional Cortes, tribunals, and customs—an efficient central administration governed the two realms and eventually transformed them into the Kingdom of Spain.

In 1492 the new kingdom completed the *Reconquista* by conquering Muslim Granada. Working tirelessly to enforce obedience, unity, and orthodoxy, the Spanish monarchy presented its Muslim and Jewish subjects with the choice of conversion or banishment, and the consequent Jewish exodus drained the kingdom of valuable mercantile and intellectual talent. The Spanish Inquisition became a tool of the state, and as an instrument of both political and doctrinal conformity, it brought the crown not only religious unity but lucrative revenues as well. The nobility was persuaded that its best interests lay in supporting the monarchy rather than opposing it, and regional separatism ebbed. With unity established and with the immense wealth of the New World soon to be pouring in, Spain in 1500 was entering a period of rich cultural expression and international power.

The wealth of Spain and Portugal in the sixteenth century resulted from their strategic location at the extreme west of Europe, facing the Atlantic. Important advances in shipbuilding and navigation opened the way for long ocean voyages, and by 1500 European captains had traversed the Atlantic and Indian Oceans. The conquest of these seas brought Spain a New World empire and the wealth of the Incas and Aztecs. It brought Portugal a direct sea route to India and a vast commercial empire in the Far East. And it provided Europeans with a piece of information that would enable them to transform the world. The voyages of discovery made it clear, for the first time in human history, that the oceans of the earth were linked into a single, vast body of water that would carry seaworthy ships to any coast on the face of the globe.

The earliest Atlantic explorations—apart from the remarkable voyages of the Vikings—were pioneered by Italian seafarers who could draw on their experience in Mediterranean commerce. In the early fourteenth century, Venetian galley fleets were making yearly expeditions through the Straits of Gibraltar to England and Flanders, and Genoese merchants were trading with the Canary Islands. By the mid-fourteenth century European ships had established commercial links with the Madeiras and Azores. Within the next century all these island groups, and the Cape Verde Islands as well, passed into Spanish or Portuguese hands, but the ships of the Iberian monarchies continued to depend often on the skill of Italian captains and crews. It was the Genoese captain Columbus who brought the Spanish monarchy its claim to the New World.

Missionary zeal, curiosity, and greed were the mixed motives of these maritime ventures. In the long run, greed was the primary consideration of both the sponsoring monarchies and the captains and private merchants, who stood to make their fortunes from successful voyages. But the great patron of Portuguese West-African exploration, Prince Henry the Navigator (1394–1460), seems to have been driven as much by the hope of Christian evangelism as by the desire to expand trade, acquire gold and slaves, and discover unknown lands. From his court at Sagres, he sent ships westward to the Atlantic islands and southward down the African coast to capture Moroccan fortresses and plant new trading colonies. At Sagres itself, Prince Henry collected an invaluable store of geographical and navigational data for the instruction of his captains. The Portuguese West-African voyages continued intermittently after Prince Henry's death and reached their climax in 1497–1499 when Vasco da Gama rounded the Cape of Good Hope and reached India. The substantial profit realized by da Gama's voyage demonstrated emphatically the commercial potentialities of this new, direct route to the Orient. The old trade routes were short-circuited, and the Ottoman Empire and Renaissance Italy both underwent a gradual commercial decline. The future lay with the rising Atlantic monarchies.

Germany and Italy

Late-medieval Germany and Italy suffered from much the same sort of regional particularism that afflicted England, France, and the Iberian Peninsula, but the late fifteenth century brought no corresponding trend toward centralization. Both lands passed into the modern era divided internally and incapable of competing with the Western monarchies. The weak, elective Holy Roman Empire that emerged in Germany from the papal-imperial struggles of the High Middle Ages was given formal sanction in the Golden Bull of 1356. The bull made no mention of any papal role in the imperial appointment or coronation, but left the choice of succession to the majority vote of seven great German princes. These "electors" were the archbishops of Mainz, Trier, and Cologne, the count palatine of the Rhine, the duke of Saxony, the margrave of Brandenburg, and the king of Bohemia. The electoral states themselves remained relatively stable, as did other large German principalities such as the Hapsburg duchy of Austria, but the Empire itself became powerless. Germany in 1500 was a Chinese puzzle of more than a hundred principalities—fiefs, ecclesiastical city-states, free cities, counties, and duchies—their boundaries shifting periodically through war, marriage, and inheritance. Imperial authority in Italian politics was as dead as papal authority in imperial elections. Germany and Italy were disengaged at last, but both continued to suffer the prolonged consequences of their former entanglement.

ITALY
c.1490

SWISS CONFEDERATION

Tyrol   Carinthia
Trent
SAVOY   Milan
Turin   Carniola
        Verona
MILAN   Padua
MANTUA   Venice
Genoa
GENOA   MODENA FERRARA
        Bologna
Lucca
Pisa   Florence
        FLORENCE   Urbino
        Siena   The Marches
        SIENA
        Umbria
        PAPAL
        STATES
        Rome

Adriatic   Sea

VENETIAN REPUBLIC

Dalmatia

Naples
KINGDOM

Otranto

OF THE

Palermo

TWO SICILIES

Scale of Miles
0   100   200

Through the domination of small states by larger ones, the political crazy-quilt of late-medieval Italy had evolved by the fifteenth century into a delicate power balance between five dominant political units: the Kingdom of Naples, the Papal States, and the three northern city-states of Florence, Milan, and Venice (which coexisted with a number of weaker city-states). Naples was ruled first by a French dynasty, and later by Aragon. Central Italy remained subject to a tenuous papal control, compromised by the particularism of local aristocrats and the political turbulence of Rome itself. Milan, and later Florence, ceased to be republics and fell under the rule of self-made despots. Throughout this period, Venice remained a republic dominated by a narrow commercial oligarchy.

The despots, ruling without the sanction of royal anointment or legitimate succession, governed more by their wits and by the realities of power than by traditions or customs. They have often been regarded as symbols of the "new Renaissance man," but in fact their opportunism was a quality well known to the northern monarchs, and their ruthlessness would have surprised neither William the Conqueror nor Philip the Fair. Yet the very insecurity of their positions and the fragile equilibrium of the five major Italian powers gave rise to a considerable refinement of traditional diplomatic practices. Ambassadors, skilled at compliments and espionage, were exchanged on a regular basis, and emerging from the tendency of two or three weaker states to combine against a stronger one came the shifting alliances known as the "balance of power" principle.

The Italian power balance was upset in 1494 when a powerful French army invaded the peninsula. For generations thereafter Italy was a battleground for French-Spanish rivalries, and the techniques and concepts of Italian Renaissance diplomacy passed across the Alps to affect the relations of the northern kingdoms. The modern tendency to ignore moral limitations and ecclesiastical mediation—to base diplomacy on a calculated balance of force—was growing throughout late-medieval Europe. But it reached fruition first in Renaissance Italy.

EASTERN EUROPE

Most of the Eastern European kingdoms were as unsuccessful as Germany and Italy in achieving political cohesion. Poland, Lithuania, and Hungary (as well as the Scandinavian states to the north) were all afflicted by aristocratic turbulence and dynastic quarrels. The Teutonic Knights were humbled by Slavic armies and

Chronology of Late-Medieval Eastern Europe

1237–1242:	Mongols invade Eastern Europe
1354:	Ottoman Turks invade Balkans
1377–1434:	Jagiello rules Lithuania
1386:	Union of Poland and Lithuania under Jagiello
1410:	Poland-Lithuania defeats Teutonic Knights at Tannenberg
1444:	Ottomans defeat Christians at Varna
1453:	Ottomans conquer Constantinople
1480:	Czar Ivan III the Great discontinues Mongol tribute

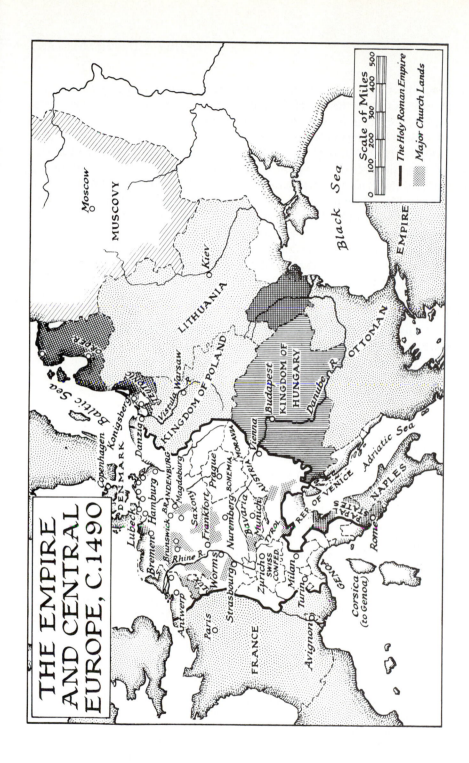

THE EMPIRE AND CENTRAL EUROPE, C.1490

Scale of Miles
0 100 200 300 400 500

The Holy Roman Empire
Major Church Lands

Moscow
MUSCOVY

Black Sea

Kiev

LITHUANIA

EMPIRE

ORDER

Baltic Sea

Copenhagen
Königsberg
Danzig
DENMARK
Vistula Warsaw
KINGDOM OF POLAND

Budapest
KINGDOM OF HUNGARY
Danube R.

OTTOMAN

Lübeck
Bremen Hamburg
Brunswick BRANDENBURG
Magdeburg
Saxony
Frankfort Prague
BOHEMIA
MORAVIA
AUSTRIA
Vienna

Adriatic Sea
REP. OF VENICE

PAPAL STATES

NAPLES

Rhine R.
Worms
Strasbourg
Nuremberg
Bavaria Munich TYROL
Zürich SWISS CONFED.
Milan
Turin
GENOA
Rome

Antwerp
Paris

FRANCE

Avignon

Corsica
(to Genoa)

internal rebellions, and most of the Balkan Peninsula was overwhelmed by the Ottoman Turks. Only the Russians and Ottomans were able to build strong states, and both, by 1500, were uncompromisingly autocratic.

Poland had become a Catholic-Christian kingdom around A.D. 1000, but throughout the High Middle Ages it had been paralyzed by aristocratic factions and disputed successions. In 1386 it united with rapidly expanding Lithuania, and the Polish-Lithuanian state became the largest political unit in Europe. It was also, very possibly, the worst governed. Under the Lithuanian warrior-prince Jagiello (1377–1434), who converted from paganism to Catholicism when he accepted the Polish crown, the dual state humbled the Teutonic Knights at the decisive battle of Tannenberg (1410). But even under Jagiello, Poland-Lithuania had no real central government; its nobles would cooperate with their ruler only against the hated Germans, and even then only momentarily. Stretching all the way from the Black Sea to the Baltic, incorporating many of the former lands of the Teutonic Order and most of the old state of Kievan Russia, Poland-Lithuania lacked the skilled administrators and political institutions necessary to govern its vast territories. Its nobles were virtually all-powerful, and its peasantry was slipping toward serfdom. Its political impotence guaranteed that no strong state would emerge between Germany and Russia during Europe's early modern centuries.

Russia and the Mongols

Russia had acquired its religion from Constantinople rather than the West, and Byzantine civilization was a potent force in the development of Russian culture. But Russia's development was also shaped—and slowed for several generations—by the Mongol invasions.

Led by the conqueror Ghengis Khan (c. 1160–1227), Mongol horsemen from the steppes of Central Asia had swept outward in all directions, terrorizing enemy armies and often slaughtering the entire populations of captured cities. After subduing neighboring tribal states, the Mongols extended their power across Korea and northern China and westward into Russia and Persia. After a pause following Ghengis Khan's death in 1227, when the leaders of the farflung Mongol armies returned home to parcel out his vast dominions among themselves, Mongol expansion resumed. For a brief time the Mongols threatened high-medieval Western Christendom, striking deep into the Catholic kingdoms of Hungary and Poland in 1241–1242 and routing all opposition. Then, after halting to consolidate their gains, the Mongol generals were again called homeward in 1246 to redivide the empire on the death of the Great Khan Ogodai, Ghengis Khan's son and successor. Never again would they move against Central Europe, but they retained their grip on Russia for more than two centuries.

During the era of Mongol domination, the princes of Christian Russia were permitted a good measure of autonomy but were subjected to heavy tribute payments. The "Grand Princes" of Moscow managed to turn the system to their advantage by collaborating with their Mongol overlords and winning the backing of the Orthodox Church. They were appointed sole collectors of the Mongol tribute, and on occasion they helped the Mongols crush the rebellions of other Russian princes, extending their own power and influence in the process. Moscow became the central archbishopric of Russian Orthodox Christianity, and when the Turks took Constantinople in 1453, Moscow, the "Third Rome," claimed spiritual sovereignty over the Orthodox Slavic world.

At first the Muscovite princes strengthened their position with the full backing of the Mongols. But toward the end of the fourteenth century Moscow began taking the lead in anti-Mongol resistance. At last, in 1480, Ivan III, the Great, Grand Prince of Moscow and Czar (Caesar) of the Russians, repudiated Mongol authority altogether and abolished the tribute.

The Muscovite princes enjoyed a certain measure of popular support in their struggle against the Mongols and in their battles against the Roman Catholic Lithuanians, but their rule was autocratic to a degree worthy of Byzantine emperors and Mongol khans. Nascent republicanism in city-states such as Novgorod was crushed with the expansion of Muscovite authority. The grand princes were despots, inspired politically by Central Asia rather than by the West. Their state had no local or national assemblies and no articulate middle class. Russia was eventually to acquire the material and organizational attributes of a great power, but the centuries during which it had been isolated from the rest of Europe could not be made up overnight.

The Ottoman Empire

By the fourteenth century the Mongol westward expansion had ceased, and the great outside threat to Eastern Europe now came from the Ottoman Turks pressing into the Balkans from Asia Minor. These nomads, propelled from their Central Asian homeland by the Mongols, had come into Asia Minor first as mercenaries, then as conquerors. Adopting the Islamic faith, the Ottomans subjected the greater part of Asia Minor to their rule and intermarried with the local population. In 1354, bypassing the diminutive Byzantine Empire, they invaded Europe. During the latter half of the fourteenth century, they crushed Serbia and Bulgaria and extended their dominion over most of the Balkan Peninsula. And in 1444, at the decisive battle of Varna, they decimated an anti-Turkish crusading army and consolidated their hold on southeastern Europe. After the great Ottoman victory at Varna, the storming of Constantinople in 1453 was little more than a postscript. Yet all Europe recognized that the sultan Mohammed II, in conquering the unconquerable city, had ended an era. It was a sign of the changing times that Mohammed II shattered the walls of Constantinople with artillery.

The Ottoman Empire endured until the twentieth century. As the Republic of Turkey it endures still. Like the princes of Moscow, the Ottoman

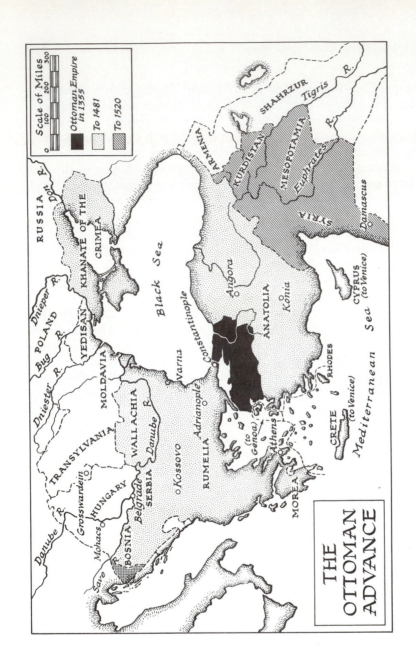

Scale of Miles
0 100 200 300

Ottoman Empire in 1355
To 1481
To 1520

RUSSIA

Don R.

Dnieper R.

Bug R.

Dniester R.

POLAND

YEDISAN

KHANATE OF THE CRIMEA

MOLDAVIA

TRANSYLVANIA

Grosswardein

HUNGARY

Danube R.

Mohacs

Save R.

BOSNIA

Belgrade

SERBIA

Danube R.

WALLACHIA

Kossovo

RUMELIA

Adrianople

Varna

Constantinople

Black Sea

ARMENIA

SHAHRZUR

Tigris R.

KURDISTAN

MESOPOTAMIA

Euphrates R.

SYRIA

Damascus

Angora

ANATOLIA

Konia

CYPRUS (to Venice)

RHODES

CRETE (to Venice)

Mediterranean Sea

Athens

MOREA

(to Genoa)

THE OTTOMAN ADVANCE

326

sultans were autocrats. Slaves served in their administration and fought in their armies alongside mounted noblemen of the Ottoman landed aristocracy. And while the sultans were living in splendor on the Golden Horn, overlooking the Bosporus from the city built by Constantine and adorned by Justinian, their government was insulating southeastern Europe from the civilization of the West.

16

Death, Disorder, and Renaissance

ECONOMIC AND SOCIAL CHANGES

Towns and Commerce

The shift from boom to depression came gradually and unevenly to Western Europe. As early as the mid-thirteenth century prosperity was starting to ebb. And from the early fourteenth century through much of the fifteenth, a number of related trends—shrinking population, contracting markets, an end to the long process of land reclamation, and a creeping mood of pessimism and retrenchment—resulted in a general economic slump and a deepening of social antagonisms. These trends were far from universal, and historians disagree sharply on their magnitude and impact. Still, as has been recently observed, "few (aside from Chaucer scholars) will maintain that the 1300s were the heyday of medieval civilization."

Economic decline was less marked in northern Italy than elsewhere, and various localities north of the Alps, profiting from favorable commercial situations or technological advances, became more prosperous than before. At a time when many English towns were declining, Coventry and certain others grew wealthy from the rise of woolen-cloth production. The Flemish town of Bruges remained throughout most of the late Middle Ages a bustling center of commerce on the northern seas. Florence, with its large textile industry and its international banking, was to become the focal point of Italian Renaissance culture. In Florence and elsewhere, enterprising individuals and families grew wealthy from the profits of international commerce and banking. The Bardi, Peruzzi, and Medici were the great Florentine banking families, and they had their counterparts north of the Alps in such figures as Jacques Coeur of Bourges, financier of the fifteenth-century French monarchy, and the Fuggers of Augsburg, bankers for the Holy Roman emperors. But such great financiers as these were exceedingly insecure in the turbulent years of the late Middle Ages. The Bardi and Peruzzi houses collapsed in the mid-

328

fourteenth century, and Jacques Coeur was ruined by his royal debtor, King Charles VII. Some fortunes continued to grow, but the total assets of late-medieval bankers fell considerably below those of their predecessors.

By the early fourteenth century Europe was clearly suffering from over-population. Northern European agriculture—typified by the manor and the heavy plow—had expanded to the limits of its technological capability, and newly cleared lands tended by now to be only marginally productive. Further population growth could be sustained only by a lowering of the peasantry's standard of living—either by subdividing peasants' holdings into smaller and smaller plots or by expanding cultivation into new and less fertile areas. When bad weather produced a series of poor harvests, grain prices would soar and food stocks dwindle alarmingly. As a result, the years 1315–1317 witnessed mass starvation across a broad area of northern Europe, and England was further afflicted by a devastating cattle disease from 1319 to 1321 and also a widespread crop failure in the latter year. The records of the English village of Halesowen, which may well be typical of many villages, indicate a population drop of some 15 percent as a result of these calamities.

Thus even before the onset of the Black Death in the mid-fourteenth century, Europe's population was leveling off and perhaps beginning to decline. The growing shortage of good land, and a long-range shift to a colder, rainier climate, brought adverse agrarian conditions that discouraged large families and depressed the birth rate. The fundamental trends of demographic and economic decline were not initiated by the plague, but they were enormously aggravated by it.

The Onset of the Black Death

The Black Death appears to have been a combination of two related diseases: *bubonic plague,* which is carried by black rats and spread by the fleas the rats carry and infect, and *pneumonic plague,* which results when a person with a respiratory infection contracts bubonic plague, and is spread by direct contagion. Bubonic plague came first, arriving from the East during the winter of 1347–1348 aboard rat-infested merchant ships and spreading swiftly among a population whose resistance may have been weakened by malnutrition. It was quickly followed by pneumonic plague. In these two forms, the Black Death was spread by contacts both between human and flea and between human and human. The swiftness of its spread can perhaps be explained by the lively European trade in (rat-infested) grain.

From the Mediterranean ports, the plague advanced across Europe with terrifying speed during the years 1348 and 1349. The death toll cannot be determined with any precision. The best estimate would be that about one-third of Europe's population perished. In many crowded towns the mortality rate exceeded 50 percent, whereas an isolated rural area might suffer much less. Consequently, the most enterprising and best-trained Europeans were hit hardest. Few urban families could have been spared altogether.

Europe was stunned by the onset of the plague. Fourteenth-century medicine was at a loss to explain the process of infection, while the unsanitary conditions of the towns encouraged its spread. One observer spoke of ships floating aimlessly on the Mediterranean with dead crews. Many people fled their towns. Others abandoned themselves to religious frenzy or debauchery. Some remained faithfully at their posts, hoping for divine protection. An inhabitant of Siena provides this description:

> Father abandoned child; wife, husband; one brother, another. For this illness seemed to strike through the breath and the sight. And so they died. And nobody could be found to bury the dead for money or for friendship....And in many places in Siena huge pits were dug and piled deep with great heaps of the dead....And I buried my five children with my own hands and many others did likewise. And there were many corpses about the city who were so sparsely covered with earth that dogs dragged them out and devoured their bodies.

At papal Avignon great religious processions were organized:

> Among them many of both sexes were barefoot; some were in sack cloth, some covered with ashes, wailing as they walked, tearing their hair, and lashing themselves with whips until they were bloody.

Social and Economic Effects of the Black Death

By the end of 1349 the Black Death had run its course, leaving its survivors traumatized and grief-stricken but determined to rebuild their lives. There is evidence of unusually high numbers of marriages and births in the years just following, as the people of Europe tried to preserve family lines and repopulate deserted lands and villages.

But in 1361–1362 the plague returned, striking especially hard at young people born since 1348–1349. This "children's plague" was only the first of a long series of revisitations: the plague returned in 1369, 1374–1375, 1379, 1390, 1407, and periodically throughout the fifteenth and sixteenth centuries and well into the seventeenth. Although none of these subsequent plagues resulted in deaths on the scale of 1348–1349, the seemingly endless recurrences tended to keep people in a state of anxiety about their lives and the lives of their families. And the population of Europe, having dropped drastically in the wake of the plague's first onset, appears to have continued its decline for the next 100 or 150 years. The population began rising again only toward the end of the fifteenth century. In 1500 it was still a great deal lower than it had been in 1300.

The grief brought about by the plague cannot be measured, but we can observe its more tangible effects: great numbers of deserted villages; unoccupied and dilapidated districts within city walls; the halving of the population of the Paris region between 1348 and 1444; the temporary decline of the European wool market; the severe shortage of labor.

Effects on the Countryside With grim efficiency, the Black Death provided a sudden, radical solution to the problem of agrarian overpopulation. There was now an abundance of arable land and an extreme shortage of cultivators.

The services of the plague's peasant survivors were thus much in demand, and their economic condition improved markedly. The plague-induced labor shortage resulted in a sudden upward trend in the wages of landless agrarian workers, and peasants could obtain land at much lower rents than before. Some enterprising peasants, profiting from the decline in land values, accumulated numerous estates, hired laborers to farm them, and prospered considerably in the process. Landlords, in the meantime, responded to the rising wage levels by attempting to hold down wages artificially, either by collective conspiracy or by legislation. In England, for example, the Statute of Laborers of 1351, and similar legislation that followed, was aimed at freezing wages in the wake of the plague. But such measures enjoyed little success; aristocratic landholders, in their competition for peasant labor, were often prepared to pay "black market" wages well in excess of the statutory levels.

The rising wages brought about by the labor shortage, and a decline in the price of grain resulting from the population drop, caught landlords between two blades of what has been called a "price scissors": as the expenses of farming rose and profits declined, landlords throughout much of northwestern Europe ceased the age-long process of cultivating their demesne fields directly and rented them out to peasants instead. The high-medieval pattern of manorial lordship over a dependent peasantry was thus disintegrating. Serfs were ascending to the status of tenant farmers, no longer subject to their lord's manorial court and no longer required to labor part-time on his fields. The decline of the old manorial regime occurred gradually and not without sporadic violence, but by 1500 its demise was evident.

Many peasants profited from these new conditions, but others found themselves dispossessed when their landlords, instead of renting out their demesnes, converted them to the production of more profitable luxury goods such as wool, meat, wine, and beer (from barley and hops). The plague and its revisitations resulted in a highly unpredictable economy with commercial booms and busts and violent price disruptions. It diminished the numbers of consumers—particularly townspeople, who throughout the High Middle Ages had constituted an ever-growing market for agrarian products. And while in much of northwestern Europe the labor shortage prompted lords to free their serfs, so as to induce them not to abandon their fields for better opportunities elsewhere, landlords in eastern Germany and Poland tended to tighten the bonds of serfdom and to exact peasant labor services more rigorously than ever. By 1500 these landlords were beginning to establish the large-scale grain-producing estates worked by serfs that would typify the Prussian and Polish agrarian economies of subsequent centuries.

Effects on the Towns Although the towns and cities of Western Europe declined sharply in population, they recovered from the impact of the Black

Death more quickly than the countryside, with its long-deserted villages and great patches of unworked, overgrown fields. Urban populations tended to be distinctly lower around 1500 than they had been around 1300 or 1348, but in the less populous world of fifteenth-century Europe, cities were becoming relatively more prominent than in the generations preceding the plague.

The postplague generations witnessed a considerable migration from the countryside into the towns and cities. But many of the newcomers were unable to find jobs and drifted into the growing mass of urban unemployed. The gap between the rich and the poor appears to have been widening, as privileged urban elites did everything possible to retain their positions. They closed ranks: guilds guarded their monopolies, and heredity became the chief avenue to the status of guild master. To retain their share of declining markets, guilds struggled with one another, with the district nobility, and with the increasingly restive urban proletariat—its sense of grievance growing as its upward mobility diminished. Florence, ravaged by the Black Death and burdened by years of inconclusive warfare, was terrorized by a workers' rebellion in 1378. And many towns were torn by the conflicts of rival aristocratic families and their factions. In general, however, the rich mercantile families retained their privileged economic status in the face of lower-class pressure by sharing their political authority with great magnates or kings or, in Italy, by relinquishing it to despots.

Violence afflicted both the cities and the countryside during the latter half of the fourteenth century. In the generation following the French Jacquerie of 1358, similar popular uprisings occurred in Germany, France, Spain, the Netherlands, and England. The English Peasants' Revolt of 1381, an effort to cast aside the last vestiges of serfdom, was a confused and bloody affair during which the severed head of the archbishop of Canterbury was carried around London on a stick. Although quickly suppressed, like the other uprisings, the English Peasants' Revolt bore witness to a society in crisis.

MILITARY CHANGES

Nevertheless, the ruling classes of European society managed to survive the late-medieval crisis. The landed aristocracy, forced by the "price scissors" to relinquish most of its demesnes and its lordship over serfs, developed its practice of chivalry to a point of unparalleled refinement and splendor: shining armor, elaborate tournaments, chivalric brotherhoods, and vividly colored banners bearing the coats of arms of individual noble families. But the dominance of mounted knights in warfare was challenged in late-medieval times by the growing use of well-drilled infantry, longbows, crossbows, and cannon. Gunpowder, invented in eleventh-century China, was in military use in Europe by the 1320s, and artillery became an increasingly important factor in the warfare of the later fourteenth and fifteenth centuries. But the landed nobility remained a warrior elite, and mounted knights retained much of their former military importance. The cavalry charge would continue to be an important military tactic for centuries to come.

Monarchies had employed small permanent forces of salaried knights ever since the eleventh century, but by 1500 such forces were much more numerous than before and included large numbers of trained footsoldiers. King Louis XI of France devoted some of his new tax revenues to maintaining a standing army of cavalry and infantry numbering some 20,000 or 25,000 men, which he could increase to several times that size in military emergencies. Standing armies would become a great deal larger during the next several centuries, but already they were beginning to assume some of the characteristics of an early modern military organization—such as standardized collective training of both infantry and cavalry, footsoldiers marching in step, and a greater use of uniforms. Cannons became an increasingly important factor in warfare, forcing a drastic shift in defensive architecture from turreted castles to lower-lying fortresses with much thicker walls, and the fifteenth century witnessed the development of smaller firearms for the use of individual gunners.

There was no decisive break between "medieval" and "modern" warfare: high-medieval military forces had often received regular wages; they had included archers, footsoldiers, and siege engineers as well as knights. European armies gradually increased, generation after generation, in size and technological sophistication. By 1500, as a consequence, the monarchs of Western Europe controlled military establishments of unprecedented size, expense, and destructive potential.

Economic Recovery

The consolidation of royal authority in late-fifteenth-century Western Europe coincided with a general economic upturn following the long recession. Europe's population in 1500 was lower than in 1300, but it was increasing again. Commerce had been reviving since about 1460, and towns were growing once more. Technological progress had never ceased, and now water-driven fulling mills were speeding wool production, while water-driven pumps were draining mines. With advances in mining technology, Europe was increasing its supply of silver and the various metals essential to its rising industries: iron, copper, alum, and tin. The development of artillery and movable-type printing depended not merely on the inventive idea but also on many generations of progress in the metallurgical arts. And advances in ship design and navigation lay behind the Atlantic voyages that would soon bring a torrent of wealth into Western Europe. By 1500 the long economic crisis had passed. Europe had entered on an era of economic growth and world expansion that would far outstrip its earlier surge in the High Middle Ages.

CULTURAL CHANGE

Growth and Decay

Printing and gunpowder were the two most spectacular technological innovations of the late Middle Ages. Gunpowder came first, and by the fifteenth century it was being used with some effect in the Hundred Years' War, the Turkish conquests, and, indeed, most of the military engagements of Europe. Printing from movable type was developed midway through the fifteenth century, and although its effect on European culture was immense, the full impact was not felt until after 1500. Even among the "new men" of the Italian Renaissance there were those who regarded printed books as vulgar imitations of handwritten originals. This fact should warn us against viewing late-medieval Europe—and even Renaissance Italy—exclusively in terms of new beginnings. There was, to be sure, a strong sense of the new and "modern" among many creative Europeans of the period, but there was also a perpetuation of medieval ways, styles, and habits of thought. Often one encounters a sense of loss over the fading of medieval ideals and institutions, a conviction that civilization was declining. The Renaissance humanist Aeneas Sylvius—later Pope Pius II (d. 1464)—could look at the Turkish threat and the strife among Christian states and conclude that nothing good was in prospect. The generation living after 1500, aware of the voyages of exploration and of the growing prosperity and political consolidation, might well be more hopeful of the future, but between about 1300 and 1500 a gloom hung over much of Europe.

Beneath the gloom one finds a sense of nervous unrest, a violent emotionalism that lent dramatic intensity to late-medieval works of art. The thirteenth-century ideal of balanced serenity lost its appeal in this age of crisis and recession. The practice of self-flagellation (whipping) acquired wide popularity, and the "Dance of Death" became a favorite artistic theme. Fear of witches began spreading through Europe from about 1300 and evolved after 1450 into a widespread witch-hunting craze that lasted far into the seventeenth century.*

The drift away from the relative confidence and order of high-medieval culture expressed itself in countless ways—in the intensifying conflict between class and class, in the architectural shift from high-Gothic symmetry to flamboyant decoration, in the divorce between knightly function and chivalric display, in the evolution from Christian commonwealth to territorial states, and in the disintegration of St. Thomas Aquinas's fusion of faith and reason. The medieval search for a rational cosmic order had reached its climax in Aquinas's hierarchical ordering and reconciliation of matter and spirit, body and soul, logic and revelation. The abandonment of the search is nowhere more evident than in the attacks of fourteenth-century philosophers on the Thomist system.

---

*Although the witch-craze began in the closing decades of the late Middle Ages, the notion that witch hunts are "medieval" is a modern superstition. Witch-hunting reached its height during the Renaissance and Reformation eras, at which time, as one student aptly put it, "Witches didn't have things too good. They were totally scapegoated."

Late-Medieval Thought

St. Thomas's *Summa Theologica,* like the high-Gothic cathedral, unifies religious aspiration and logical order on the basis of an omnipotent God who is both loving and rational. The fourteenth-century attack on this reconciliation was founded on two related propositions: (1) To ascribe rationality to God is to limit his omnipotence by the finite rules of human logic; thus, the Thomist God of reason gave way to a God of will, and the high-medieval notion of a logical divine order was eroded. (2) Human reason, therefore, can tell us nothing of God; logic and Christian belief inhabit two separate, sealed worlds.

The first steps toward this concept of a willful, incomprehensible God were taken by the Oxford Franciscan Duns Scotus (d. 1308), who produced a detailed critique of St. Thomas's theory of knowledge. Duns Scotus did not reject the possibility of elucidating revealed truth through reason, but he was more cautious in his use of logic than Aquinas had been. Whereas St. Thomas is called "The Angelic Doctor," Duns Scotus is called "The Subtle Doctor," and the extreme complexity of his thought prompted people in subsequent generations to describe anyone who bothered to follow Duns' arguments as a "dunce." The nickname is unfair, for Duns Scotus is an important and original figure in the development of late Scholasticism. Yet one is tempted to draw a parallel between the intricacies of his intellectual system and the decorative elaborations of late-Gothic churches. A Christian rationalist of the most thoroughgoing kind, he nevertheless made the first move toward dismantling the Thomist synthesis and withdrawing reason from the realm of theology.

Another Oxford Franciscan, William of Ockham (d. 1349), attacked the Thomist synthesis on all fronts. Ockham argued that God and Christian doctrine, utterly undemonstrable, must be accepted on faith alone, and that human reason must be limited to the realm of observable phenomena. In this unpredictable world of an unfathomable Creator, one can reason only about things that one can see or directly experience. Ockham's radical empiricism ruled out all metaphysical speculations, all rational arguments from an observable diversity of things to an underlying unity of things. And out of this great divorce of reason and faith came two characteristic expressions of late-medieval thought: the scientific manipulation of material facts and pietistic mysticism untouched by logic. In Ockham and many of his followers, one finds empiricism and mysticism side by side. For since the two worlds never touched, they were in no way contradictory. An intelligent Christian could keep one foot in each of them.

Ockham's philosophy thus served as an appropriate foundation for both late-medieval mysticism and late-medieval science. Some mystics, indeed, regarded themselves as empiricists. For the empiricist is a person who accepts only those things that are directly experienced, and the mystic, abandoning the effort to *understand* God, strove to *experience* him. Science, on the other hand, was now freed of its theological underpinnings and could proceed on its own. Nicholas Oresme, a teacher at the University of Paris in the fourteenth century, attacked the Aristotelian theory of motion and proposed a rotating earth as a possible explanation for the apparent daily movement of the sun and stars across the sky.

Oresme's theories probably owed more to thirteenth-century scientists such as Robert Grosseteste than to Ockham, but his willingness to tinker with traditional explanations of the physical structure of God's universe is characteristic of an age in which scientific speculation was being severed from revealed truth.

Many late-medieval philosophers rejected Ockham's criticism and remained Thomists. But owing to the very comprehensiveness of Aquinas's achievement, his successors were reduced to detailed elaboration or minor repair work. Faced with a choice between the tedious niggling of late Thomism and the drastic limitations imposed by Ockham on the scope of philosophical inquiry, many of Europe's finest minds shunned philosophy altogether for the more exciting fields of science, mathematics, and classical learning. When the philosopher John Gerson (d. 1429), chancellor of the University of Paris, spoke out in his lectures against "vain curiosity in the matter of faith," the disintegration of the faith-reason synthesis was clearly evident.

The fifteenth century witnessed a revival of Platonism and Neoplatonism in Renaissance Italy and in the north as well. The two leading philosophers of the Italian Renaissance, Marsilio Ficino (d. 1499) and Pico della Mirandola (d. 1494), were both Platonists. They were able to draw from an extensive body of Plato's writings that had been unknown to the high-medieval West, yet neither Ficino nor Pico was a first-echelon figure in the history of Western thought. Neither possessed the acumen of the best high-medieval philosophers, and neither approached the profundity of their great contemporary north of the Alps, Nicholas of Cusa (d. 1464).

Educated by the mystical Brethren of the Common Life, Nicholas of Cusa became first a conciliarist and later an ardent papist. He agreed, up to a point, with Ockham's view that human reason is limited to the disconnected phenomena of the physical universe. But he insisted that the contradictions and diversity of the material world were reconciled and unified in an unknowable God. Nicholas of Cusa regarded God as beyond rational apprehension—approachable only through a mystical process that he termed "learned ignorance." Like Aquinas, he believed in an underlying universal order, but like Ockham, he denied that any such order could be grasped by human reason. Yet his concept of an unknowable God was derived from a tradition far older than Ockhamism. It was rooted in the late-Roman Neoplatonism of the pagan Plotinus* and his Christian followers, a tradition that had run as an undercurrent through the entire Middle Ages. Like the older Neoplatonists, Nicholas of Cusa conceived of the universe as a ceaseless creative unfolding of the infinite God. But going far beyond his Neoplatonic predecessors, he reasoned that a universe emanating from an infinite deity cannot be limited by human concepts of space and time. In short, God's created universe was potentially infinite.

In his emphasis on mysticism and the limitation of human reason, Nicholas of Cusa was in tune with his age. In his synthetic vision of an ordered cosmos he echoed the thirteenth century. And in his bold conception of an infinite universe he anticipated modern philosophy and astronomy.

*See pp. 12, 95–96.

Arts and Letters

The change from high-medieval order to late-medieval diversity is clearly evident in the field of art. The high-Gothic balance between upward aspiration
and harmonic proportion—between the vertical and horizontal—was shifting
in the cathedrals of the later thirteenth century toward an ever-greater emphasis on verticality. Formerly, elaborate capitals and horizontal decorative
lines had balanced the soaring piers and pointed arches of the Gothic cathedrals, creating a sense of tense equilibrium between heaven and earth. But
during the late Middle Ages, capitals disappeared and horizontal lines became discontinuous, leaving little to relieve the dramatic upward thrust from
floor to vaulting. Late medieval churches achieved a fluid, uncompromising
verticality, a sense of heavenly aspiration that bordered on the mystical.

High Gothic interior: Nave of Amiens Cathedral, begun 1220,
showing the capitals and decorated stringcourse.

By about the mid-thirteenth century, the basic structural potentialities of the Gothic style had been fully exploited. Windows were as large as they could possibly be, vaultings could be raised no higher without structural disaster, and flying buttresses were used with maximum efficiency. The fundamental Gothic idea of a skeletal stone framework with walls of colored glass had been embodied in churches of incomparable nobility and beauty. During the late Middle Ages, buildings changed in appearance as tastes changed, but the originality of post-thirteenth-century Gothic architects was inhibited by their devotion to a style that had already achieved complete structural development. Accordingly, the innovations of late-Gothic architecture consisted chiefly of new and more elaborate decoration, with the result that a number of late-medieval churches are, to some

Late Gothic interior: Choir of Saint-Etienne at Beauvais, 1506–c. 1550, showing the absence of capitals, inconspicuous and interrupted stringcourse, and elaborate vaulting.

Flamboyant Gothic exterior: Saint-Maclou, Rouen (1437–1517).

modern tastes, overdecorated sculptural jungles. To other tastes, their decorative exuberance is a delight—akin to that of the Victorian buildings that are presently being restored all across the Western world.

Unrestrained verticality and unrestrained decorative elaboration were the architectural hallmarks of the late Middle Ages, and both reflected a shift away from rational unity and balance. Like Ockham's universe, the fourteenth- and fifteenth-century church became a fascinating miscellany of separate elements. Thus the "flamboyant Gothic" style emerged in late-medieval France, while English churches were evolving from the "decorated Gothic" of the fourteenth century to the "perpendicular Gothic" of the fifteenth and sixteenth, with its

Perpendicular Gothic interior: Chapel of Henry VII, Westminster
Abbey, London (early sixteenth century).

lacelike fan vaulting, its sculptural profusion, and its sweeping vertical lines.
In the course of the sixteenth century, Gothic architecture, having reached its
decorative as well as its structural limits, gave way throughout northern
Europe to the classical Greco-Roman style that had been revived and developed in fifteenth-century Italy and flowed north with the spread of Renaissance humanism.

Sculpture and painting, like architecture and thought, evolved during the
late Middle Ages toward multiformity. The serene, idealized humanism of

High Gothic sculpture: *Le Beau Dieu,* west portal of Amiens Cathedral (thirteenth century).

Late-medieval sculpture: *Three Mourners* from the tomb of Philip the Bold of Burgundy, by Claus Sluter and Claus de Werve (early fifteenth century).

thirteenth-century sculpture gave way to heightened emotionalism and an emphasis on individual peculiarities. Painting north of the Alps reached a pinnacle in the mirrorlike realism of the Flemish school. Painters such as Jan van Eyck (d. 1440), pioneering in the use of oil paints, excelled in reproducing the natural world with a devotion to detail that was all but photographic. Critics of the style have observed that detail seems to compromise the unity of the total composition, but in a world viewed through Ockham's eyes, such realism is a virtue. It was Italy, again, that developed a new style of painting and sculpture, based on the classical canon of naturalism subordinated to a unifying idea. And the Italian Renaissance style of painting, like Renaissance architecture, streamed northward in the sixteenth century to bring a new vision to trans-Alpine artists.

Late-Medieval Literature

Literature flourished in the late Middle Ages, and not simply in the form of treatises on mysticism. Christine de Pisan (d. *c.* 1434), Europe's first consciously feminist author, made adept use of the French vernacular in writing prose and poetry on an astonishing diversity of topics and in many literary forms: lyric poems expressing her abiding love for her late husband, who left her a widow at twenty-five; an autobiography; a book of moral advice for women and a companion volume for men; a verse history running from the Creation to her own time; a study of great women of history; and her deservedly celebrated treatise *The Letter to the God of Love*, in which she very effec-

The Madonna of the Chancellor Rolin, by Jan van Eyck (Flemish School, *c.* 1432).

tively rebuts the antifeminist diatribes embedded in Jean de Meun's conclusion of the *Romance of the Rose* (see p. 264). *The Letter to the God of Love* was of ground-breaking importance—the first clear instance in European history of a woman writing, as a woman, against the slanders that women had so long endured. The treatise gave rise to a heated debate between Jean de Meun's sympathizers and Christine de Pisan's admirers—of whom there were many. None, however, could match the eloquence of Christine herself as she responded to age-old allegations of the wickedness of women:

They murder no one, nor wound, nor harm,
Nor betray men, nor pursue nor seize them,
Nor houses set afire, nor disinherit men,
Nor poison them, nor steal their gold or silver;
They do not cheat men of their lands,
Nor make false contracts, nor destroy
Kingdoms, duchies, empires.

A number of late-medieval writers turned to graphic realism. England's Geoffrey Chaucer (d. 1400), in his *Canterbury Tales*, combines rare psychological insight with a descriptive skill worthy of the Flemish painters and late-Gothic stone carvers. *The Canterbury Tales,* one of the foremost literary works of the Middle Ages, presents a series of stories told by a group of men and women on a pilgrimage to the shrine of St. Thomas Becket at Canterbury Cathedral. We have already encountered one of Chaucer's Canterbury pilgrims, the oft-married Wife of Bath, who put an end to her husband's reading from the book of wicked wives. Chaucer describes another of the pilgrims, a corrupt friar, in these words:

Highly beloved and intimate was he
With country folk wherever he might be,
And worthy city women with possessions;
For he was qualified to hear confessions,
Or so he said, with more than priestly scope;
He had a special license from the pope.
Sweetly he heard his penitents at shrift
With pleasant absolution, for a gift.

François Villon (d. 1463), a brawling Parisian vagabond, expressed in his poems an anguished, sometimes brutal realism that vividly reflects the late-medieval mood of insecurity and plague:

Death makes one shudder and turn pale,
Pinches his nose, distends his veins,
Swells out his throat, his members fail,
Tendons and nerves grow hard with strains.

To Villon, writing in a society of sharp class distinctions, death was the great democrat:

I know this well, that rich and poor,
Fools, sages, laymen, friars in cowl,
Large-hearted lords and each mean boor,

Little and great and fair and foul,
Ladies in lace, who smile or scowl,
From whatsoever stock they stem,
Hatted or hooded, prone to prowl,
Death seizes every one of them.

Italian Renaissance Classicism

These northern moods and movements stood in sharp contrast to the growing, self-confident classicism of Renaissance Italy. Here the late-medieval economic depression was less severe and less prolonged; Italian merchants continued their domination of Mediterranean trade and extended their commercial activities into the Black Sea, returning to their homeland with wealth and plague. Although incessant interurban warfare made conditions just as insecure as in the North, the civic spirit of the independent north-Italian communes encouraged innovation and novel forms of expression. Italy had never been entirely at ease with Gothic architecture, and the triumphs of high-medieval culture were more characteristically French than Italian. England and France had enjoyed relative peace during much of the thirteenth century, whereas Italy had been battered by papal-imperial wars. Italy, in short, had less reason to be nostalgic about its high-medieval past, and the coming of the Renaissance was not so much the advent of a new epoch in European history as a reassertion of Italian culture over French.

The word "renaissance" means "rebirth." And the conception of Europe's rebirth in fifteenth-century Italy has long been a potent metaphor, conjuring up vague, simplistic images that haunt and mislead the half-educated even today. One imagines the birth of cities, of self-awareness, of reason, of individualism. But it cannot be supposed that the Italian Renaissance marked the rebirth of any of these things: they were characteristic ingredients of a civilization that had already been flourishing in Europe for some centuries (as this book has labored to demonstrate). What did occur in late-medieval Italy was a rebirth of a much more limited sort—a revival of Greco-Roman culture in a purer, more self-conscious form than before.

In an age of French arms and French culture, such as the thirteenth century had been, Italians could return in memory to the days when Rome ruled the world. Roman monuments and Roman sculpture were all around them, and when, in the fourteenth and fifteenth centuries, they abandoned the Gothic style and the intellectual habits of Paris theologians, it was to their indigenous classical heritage that they turned for inspiration. In sculpture, the calm spiritual nobility of stone saints gave way to a classical emphasis on the human body. The slender young Virgins of the High Middle Ages turned voluptuous. Architects, abandoning the Gothic spire and pointed arch, created buildings with domes and round arches and elegant classical facades. A number of the new, Humanistic scholars turned from the logic of Aristotle and Aquinas to the joys of Greco-Roman *belles lettres*. And painters, with few actual Classical models to follow, pioneered in techniques of linear and atmospheric perspective and imposed a Classical unity on their lifelike figures and landscapes.

Sistine Madonna, by Raphael (High Renaissance: early sixteenth century).

The concept of Renaissance "Humanism," like that of rebirth, is subject to serious misinterpretation. The Humanism of the Renaissance had to do neither with religious skepticism nor with democracy, but with an increased emphasis on the humanities—classical languages and literature, precise expression, historical scholarship, and the arts. The Renaissance revered the uncommon man, the man of keen intelligence, noble birth, and varied talents.

Women suffered a slump in status and social power as the previously overlapping spheres of public and private activity drew increasingly apart. Economic and political changes in Renaissance towns resulted in a gradual separation of home and workplace, and women came to be regarded more and more as domestic creatures whose work lacked the challenge and signif-

(Left) *The Golden Virgin,* from the south portal of Amiens Cathedral (thirteenth century). (Right) *David,* by Michelangelo (High Renaissance, Florence: completed 1504).

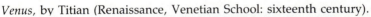

Venus, by Titian (Renaissance, Venetian School: sixteenth century).

Interior of S. Andrea at Mantua, by Alberti (Renaissance: fifteenth century).

icance of men's work. The Renaissance writer Castiglione thought that women should be well educated, but only so that they might be better company for men. As one historian has observed, "there was no renaissance for women—at least not during the Renaissance."*

While rebelling against the Middle Ages, the Renaissance retained much that was medieval. In 1492, while a worldly Borgia was acceding to the papacy and Columbus was discovering America, high-Renaissance Florence was passing under the influence of the austere Christian revivalist Savonarola. Renaissance Humanism was always an elitist phenomenon, restricted to urban nobilities and favored artists and leaving the Italian masses largely unchanged. Yet for all that, the Renaissance style represents a profound shift from the forms and assumptions of the Middle Ages. St. Thomas and his contemporaries had studied the Greek philosophers, but Renaissance Humanists looked back on Classical antiquity with a fresh perspective, seeing not a collection of ideas that might be used but a total culture that deserved to be revered and revived. It was this vision that underlay the new art and the new Classical learning of early modern Europe.

*Joan Kelly-Gadol, "Did Women Have a Renaissance?" in *Becoming Visible: Women in European History*, ed. Renate Bridenthal and Claudia Koonz (1977).

The Genesis of Modern Europe

One must not exaggerate the impact of the Renaissance on the development of modern civilization. The Renaissance contributed much to art and Classical studies; its scholars brought the same intellectual precision to the fields of history and philology that their medieval predecessors had applied to theology and law. The Renaissance witnessed major advances in diplomatic techniques but contributed little to constitutional or scientific development. Renaissance Humanists were no more interested in science than, say, a modern professor of English literature or Latin. Modern science grew out of the medieval universities. And modern legislatures—even if they meet in domed, round-arched buildings—are outgrowths of medieval representative assemblies. (The English Houses of Parliament are, appropriately, neo-Gothic in style.)

In the Europe of 1500, Italian Renaissance ideas were beginning to move across the Alps. But the promise of the future did not depend on the Renaissance alone. All across Europe commerce was thriving again and the population was growing. New inventions—gunpowder, the three-masted caravel, the water pump, the printing press—were changing the ways people lived. The papacy had degenerated into a local principality, but England, France, and Spain had achieved stable, centralized governments and were on the road toward nationhood. European ships had reached America and India, and the first cargo direct from the Orient had arrived in Portugal. The late-medieval era of crisis and retrenchment was clearly at an end, and the world lay open.

Suggested Readings

GENERAL

Robert Fossier, ed., *The Cambridge Illustrated History of the Middle Ages*, vol. 3, *1250–1520* (1986). The first of a richly illustrated three-volume series to be translated into English, this volume includes wide-ranging chapters by its distinguished editor and by other eminent French medievalists.

Daniel Waley, *Later Medieval Europe: From Saint Louis to Luther* (2nd ed., 1985). An excellent, relatively brief account of the late-medieval era (1250–1520) with a helpful concluding section on demography.

LATE-MEDIEVAL CHRISTIANITY AND THE CHURCH

Caroline Walker Bynum, *Jesus as Mother: Studies in the Spirituality of the High Middle Ages* (1982). Perceptive essays on the social history of spirituality, the discovery of the self, and mysticism among the nuns of Helfta.

C. M. D. Crowder, *Unity, Heresy, and Reform, 1378–1460: The Conciliar Response to the Great Schism* (1977). A brief, skillful introduction followed by translated excerpts from contemporary sources.

Richard Kieckhefer, *Unquiet Souls: Fourteenth-Century Saints and Their Religious Milieu* (1984). A learned, well-written examination of the lives and values of fourteenth-century visionaries and mystics, female and male, with three case studies.

Barbara Newman, *Sister of Wisdom: St. Hildegard's Theology of the Feminine* (1987). An important, subtle, deeply learned exploration of the theology of the great twelfth-century mystic Hildegard of Bingen.

Francis Oakley, *The Western Church in the Later Middle Ages* (1979). A sympathetic study that questions the notion of decline and stresses continuity with the past.

Edward Peters, *Inquisition* (1989). This thoughtful, comprehensive study examines both the history and the myth of the Inquisition down to the present day.

Yves Renouard, *The Avignon Papacy, 1305–1403*, trans. Denis Bethell (1970). A good general account emphasizing the economic and cultural vitality of the papal court at Avignon.

John A. F. Thompson, *Popes and Princes, 1417–1517: Politics and Polity in the Late Medieval Church* (1980). A good, concise summary and analysis of the waning authority of the papacy between the Council of Constance and the Reformation.

THE LATE-MEDIEVAL STATE

Christopher Allmand, *The Hundred Years War: England and France at War, c. 1300–c. 1450* (1988). Brief, current, and readable, this book is the best introduction to the subject.
William M. Bowsky, *A Medieval Italian Commune: Siena under the Nine, 1287–1355.* A prize winning work of scholarship, well-written and richly detailed, analyzing the cultural flowering and political stability of Siena under enlightened oligarchic rule.
Gene A. Brucker, *Renaissance Florence* (1969). A valuable study that makes clear the political and social tensions in a major Renaissance city.
F. R. H. Du Boulay, *Germany in the Later Middle Ages* (1983). A succinct, well-crafted synthesis of recent scholarship.
Bernard Guenée, *States and Rulers in Later Medieval Europe,* trans. Juliet Vale (1985). A study of major importance showing the parallel growth of centralized administrative institutions and a sense of national identity in the states of Western Christendom during the fourteenth and fifteenth centuries; translated from the 2nd French edition, 1981.
Charles J. Halperin, *Russia and the Golden Horde: The Mongol Impact on Medieval Russian History* (1985). The author convincingly argues that the Mongol impact has been overestimated.
David Herlihy, *Pisa in the Early Renaissance* (1958). A well-documented, thoughtful account of urban politics and society.
J. N. Hillgarth, *The Spanish Kingdoms, 1250–1516,* vol. 1, *The Precarious Balance, 1250–1410* (1976), and vol. 2, *The Castilian Hegemony, 1410–1516* (1978). A masterful account of late-medieval Spain with growing emphasis on Castile and Aragon.
Richard W. Kaeuper, *War, Justice, and Public Order: England and France in the Later Middle Ages* (1988). This important work of synthesis and reinterpretation explores the effects of war on the economy, social order and governance of the two realms.
Paul Murray Kendall, *Louis XI, the Universal Spider* (1971). A sensible biography that removes some of the stains from the reputation of the Spider King.
P. S. Lewis, *Later Medieval France: The Polity* (1968). Not a political narrative but a highly original study of government and social structure.
Garrett Mattingly, *Renaissance Diplomacy* (1955). A celebrated account of Italian diplomatic representation and dynastic politics.
David Nicholas, *The Domestic Life of a Medieval City: Women, Children, and the Family in Fourteenth-Century Ghent* (1985). A valuable, skillfully researched contribution to European family history, this work stresses the importance of the nuclear family and the simultaneous significance of larger bilateral kin groups.
———, *The Metamorphosis of a Medieval City: Ghent in the Age of the Arteveldes, 1302–1390* (1987). A worthy successor to the previous work.
Michael Prestwich, *The Three Edwards: War and State in England, 1272–1377* (1981). Succinct and authoritative; a masterful introductory account.

G. V. Scammell, *The World Encompassed: The First European Maritime Empires, c. 800–1650* (1981). This groundbreaking work stresses the medieval background—Norse, Germanic, and Italian—of the early modern voyages of exploration and the establishment of the Iberian, Dutch, French and English colonial empires.

Richard Vaughan, *Valois Burgundy* (1975). A short version, for students and general readers, of the author's earlier, four-volume history of late-medieval Burgundy.

Daniel Waley, *The Italian City Republics* (2nd ed., 1978). A lucid, well-illustrated discussion of the social and political milieu of the city states.

ECONOMIC AND SOCIAL HISTORY

T. S. R. Boase, *Death in the Middle Ages* (1972). A splendidly illustrated study of death and its effects on medieval culture with emphasis on late-medieval society.

R. H. Hilton, ed., *Peasants, Knights,and Heretics: Studies in Medieval English Social History* (1976). Fifteen innovative articles on aspects of English social and economic history in the High and late Middle Ages; not for beginners.

Emmanuel Le Roy Ladurie, *Montaillou: The Promised Land of Error* (1978). Translated from the French, this celebrated book provides, from detailed Inquisition records, a vivid and unique re-creation of Cathar and Catholic villagers and households in an isolated fourteenth-century village community in southwestern France.

Kate Mertes, *The English Noble Household, 1250–1600: Good Governance and Politic Rule* (1988). This important book constitutes the first serious study of one of the fundamental institutions of noble society.

Harry A. Miskimin, *The Economy of Early Renaissance Europe, 1300–1460* (1969). A brief, lucid, economically sophisticated account covering all of late-medieval Western Europe.

Raymond de Roover, *The Rise and Decline of the Medici Bank, 1397–1494* (1963). A valuable study that elucidates the policies and methods of this great financial institution in the context of both Florentine local politics and the fifteenth-century economy.

Philip Ziegler, *The Black Death* (1969). An attractively written summary addressed to the nonspecialist reader.

LATE-MEDIEVAL THOUGHT AND CULTURE

Johan Huizinga, *The Waning of the Middle Ages* (1924). Concentrating on France and the Netherlands, this classic work of cultural history stresses the fears and insecurities of the late-medieval world and the decadence of much of its culture, leaving one rather depressed.

George Kane, *Chaucer* (1984). A brief but illuminating biography.

Maurice Keen, *Chivalry* (1984). A comprehensive, fascinating study that endeavors to rid late medieval chivalry of its aura of decadence.

Gordon Leff, *The Dissolution of the Medieval Outlook* (1976). A brief, thoughtful essay on the gradual but far-reaching intellectual changes of fourteenth-century Europe.

Nicholas Mann, *Petrarch* (1984). A short, masterful intellectual biography analyzing the successive self-images that Petrarch projected in his writings.

Steven Ozment, *The Age of Reform, 1250–1550: An Intellectual and Religious History of Late-Medieval and Reformation Europe* (1980). A detailed study of the conflicts and interactions of religious ideologies from Thomas Aquinas to Calvin.

J. H. Plumb, ed., *Renaissance Profiles* (1965). Nine biographical sketches, each by a different scholar, of such Renaissance figures as Petrarch, Lorenzo de Medici, Leonardo da Vinci, and Pope Pius II.

Wim Swaan, *The Late Middle Ages: Art and Architecture from 1350 to the Advent of the Renaissance* (1977). A stylish, beautifully illustrated book that argues powerfully against artistic decline in late-medieval Europe.

Frank Tobin, *Meister Eckhart: Thought and Language* (1986). This study, the best on the subject in English, portrays Meister Eckhart as a rather eclectic Platonist.

Walter Ullmann, *Medieval Foundations of Renaissance Humanism* (1977). A forceful argument, to which many Renaissance historians have taken exception, that Renaissance humanism was in essence a secular political movement with roots extending back into the eleventh century.

SOURCES

Raymond B. Blakney, ed., *Meister Eckhart: A Modern Translation,* (1941).

Emilie Zum Brunn and Georgete Epiney-Burgard, eds., *Women Mystics in Medieval Europe* (1989). Brief, sensitive biographical sketches and excerpts from the writings of Hildegard of Bingen and four other female mystics of high- and late-medieval Europe.

Jean Froissart, *Chronicles.* Several editions. A contemporary bourgeois writer (d. 1410) treats the Hundred Years' War as a chivalric romance.

Douglas Gray, ed., *The Oxford Book of Late-Medieval Verse* (1985).

Thomas à Kempis, *The Imitation of Christ.* Many editions.

William Langland, *Piers the Ploughman,* trans. J. F. Goodridge (rev. ed., 1966). A profound allegorical poem of fourteenth-century England.

M. M. McLaughlin, *The Portable Renaissance Reader* (1953).

Theodore Morrison, ed., *The Portable Chaucer* (1949).

Elizabeth Alvilda Petroff, ed., *Medieval Women's Visionary Literature* (1986). An excellent anthology of contemporary literature that spans the entire medieval period but stresses its concluding centuries.

Christine de Pisan, *The Treasure of the City of Ladies, or The Book of the Three Virtues,* trans. and with an introduction by Sarah Lawson (1985).

APPENDIX 1

The Popes
of the Middle Ages*

Sylvester I, 314–335
Mark, 336
Julius I, 337–352
Liberius, 352–366
(Felix II, 355–365)
Damasus I, 366–384
Siricius, 384–399
Anastasius I, 399–401
Innocent I, 401–417
Zosimus, 417–418
Boniface I, 418–422
Celestine I, 422–432
Sixtus III, 432–440
Leo I, the Great, 440–461
Hilary, 461–468
Simplicius, 468–483
Felix III, 483–492
Gelasius I, 492–496
Anastasius II, 496–498
Symmachus, 498–514
Hormisdas, 514–523
John I, 523–526
Felix IV, 526–530
Boniface II, 530–532
John II, 533–535
Agapitus I, 535–536
Silverius, 536–537
Vigilius, 537–555
Pelagius I, 555–561
John III, 561–574
Benedict I, 575–579
Pelagius II, 579–590

Gregory I, 590–604
Sabinianus, 604–606
Boniface III, 607
Boniface IV, 608–615
Deusdedit, 615–618
Boniface V, 619–625
Honorius I, 625–638
Severinus, 640
John IV, 640–642
Theodore I, 642–649
Martin I, 649–655
Eugenius I, 654–657
Vitalian, 657–672
Adeodatus II, 672–676
Donus, 676–678
Agatho, 678–681
Leo II, 682–683
Benedict II, 684–685
John V, 685–686
Conon, 686–687
Sergius I, 687–701
John VI, 701–705
John VII, 705–707
Sisinnius, 708
Constantine, 708–715
Gregory II, 715–731
Gregory III, 731–741
Zacharias, 741–752
Stephen II, 752–757
Paul I, 757–767
Stephen III, 768–772
Adrian I, 772–795

*Antipopes are in parentheses.

Leo III, 795–816
Stephen IV, 816–817
Paschal I, 817–824
Eugenius II, 824–827
Valentine, 827
Gregory IV, 827–844
Sergius II, 844–847
Leo IV, 847–855
Benedict III, 855–858
Nicholas I, 858–867
Adrian II, 867–872
John VIII, 872–882
Marinus I, 882–884
Adrian III, 884–885
Stephen V, 885–891
Formosus, 891–896
Boniface VI, 896
Stephen VI, 896–897
Romanus, 897
Theodore II, 897
John IX, 898–900
Benedict IV, 900–903
Leo V, 903
(Christopher, 903–904)
Sergius III, 904–911
Anastasius III, 911–913
Lando, 913–914
John X, 914–928
Leo VI, 928
Stephen VII, 928–931
John XI, 931–935
Leo VII, 936–939
Stephen VIII, 939–942
Marinus II, 942–946
Agapitus II, 946–955
John XII, 955–964
Leo VIII, 963–965
Benedict V, 964–966
John XIII, 965–972
Benedict VI, 973–974
(Boniface VII, 974 and 984–985)
Benedict VII, 974–983
John XIV, 983–984
John XV, 985–996
Gregory V, 996–999
(John XVI, 997–998)
Sylvester II, 999–1003
John XVII, 1003

John XVIII, 1004–1009
Sergius IV, 1009–1012
Benedict VIII, 1012–1024
John XIX, 1024–1032
Benedict IX, 1032–1048
Sylvester III, 1045
Gregory VI, 1045–1046
Clement II, 1046–1047
Damasus II, 1048
Leo IX, 1049–1054
Victor II, 1055–1057
Stephen IX, 1057–1058
(Benedict X, 1058–1059)
Nicholas II, 1059–1061
Alexander II, 1061–1073
Gregory VII, 1073–1085
(Clement III, 1080 and 1084–1100)
Victor III, 1086–1087
Urban II, 1088–1099
Paschal II, 1099–1118
(Theodoric, 1100)
(Albert, 1102)
(Sylvester IV, 1105–1111)
Gelasius II, 1118–1119
(Gregory VIII, 1118–1121)
Calixtus II, 1119–1124
Honorius II, 1124–1130
Innocent II, 1130–1143
(Anacletus II, 1130–1138)
Celestine II, 1143–1144
Lucius II, 1144–1145
Eugenius III, 1145–1153
Anastasius IV, 1153–1154
Adrian IV, 1154–1159
Alexander III, 1159–1181
(Victor IV, 1159–1164)
(Paschal III, 1164–1168)
(Calixtus III, 1168–1178)
(Innocent III, 1179–1180)
Lucius III, 1181–1185
Urban III, 1185–1187
Gregory VIII, 1187
Clement III, 1187–1191
Celestine III, 1191–1198
Innocent III, 1198–1216
Honorius III, 1216–1227
Gregory IX, 1227–1241
Celestine IV, 1241

Innocent IV, 1243–1254
Alexander IV, 1254–1261
Urban IV, 1261–1264
Clement IV, 1265–1268
Gregory X, 1271–1276
Innocent V, 1276
Adrian V, 1276
John XXI, 1276–1277
Nicholas III, 1277–1280
Martin IV, 1281–1285
Honorius IV, 1285–1287
Nicholas IV, 1288–1292
Celestine V, 1294
Boniface VIII, 1294–1303
Benedict XI, 1303–1304
Clement V, 1305–1314
John XXII, 1316–1334
Benedict XII, 1334–1342
Clement VI, 1342–1352
Innocent VI, 1352–1362
Urban V, 1362–1370

Gregory XI, 1370–1378
Urban VI, 1378–1389
Clement VII, 1378–1394
Boniface IX, 1389–1404*
Benedict XIII, 1394–1423†
Innocent VII, 1404–1406*
Gregory XII, 1406–1415*
(Alexander V, 1409–1410)
(John XXIII, 1410–1415)
Martin V, 1417–1431
(Clement VIII, 1423–1429)
(Benedict XIV, 1425–1430?)
Eugenius IV, 1431–1447
(Felix V, 1439–1449)
Nicholas V, 1447–1455
Calixtus III, 1455–1458
Pius II, 1458–1464
Paul II, 1464–1471
Sixtus IV, 1471–1484
Innocent VIII, 1484–1492
Alexander VI, 1492–1503

*Popes at Rome.
†Pope at Avignon.

APPENDIX 2

The Early Carolingians

Pepin of Heristal (680–714)
Charles Martel (714–741)
Pepin the Short (741–768; King 751–768)

Charlemagne (768–814)
Louis the Pious (814–840)

The later Carolingians will be found under "Kings of Germany" and "Kings of France."

APPENDIX 3

Kings of Germany

Carolingians

Louis the German (840–876)
Charles the Fat (876–887; Emperor 884–887)
Arnulf (887–899)
Louis the Child (889–911)

Franconians and Saxons

Conrad of Franconia (911–919)
Henry the Fowler, duke of Saxony (919–936)
Otto I "the Great" (936–973; Emperor 962–973)
Otto II (973–983)
Otto III (983–1002)
Henry II (1002–1024)

Salians

Conrad II (1024–1039)
Henry III (1039–1056)

Henry IV (1056–1106)
Henry V (1106–1125)

Welfs

Lothar (1125–1137)

Hohenstaufen

Conrad III (1138–1152)
Frederick I "Barbarossa" (1152–1190)
Henry VI (1190–1197)
Frederick II (1215–1250)
Conrad IV (1250–1254)

Hapsburgs

Rudolf of Hapsburg (1273–1291)

APPENDIX 4

Kings of France

Carolingians

Charles the Bald (840–877; Emperor 875–877)
Louis the Stammerer (877–879)
Louis III (879–882)
Carloman (879–884)
Charles the Fat (Emperor 884–887, deposed)
   [Odo (not a Carolingian: 888–898)]*
Charles the Simple (898–922)
   [Robert I (King Odo's brother: 922–923)]*
   [Ralph (Robert I's son-in-law: 923–936)]*
Louis IV d'Outremere (936–954)
Lothar (954–986)
Louis V (986–987)

Capetians

Hugh Capet (987–996)
Robert II the Pious (996–1031)
Henry I (1031–1060)
Philip I (1060–1108)

Louis VI, "the Fat" (1108–1137)
Louis VII (1137–1180)
Philip II, "Augustus"
   (1180–1223)
Louis VIII (1223–1226)
Louis IX (1226–1270)
Philip III (1270–1285)
Philip IV, "the Fair" (1285–1314)
Louis X (1314–1316)
Philip V (1316–1322)
Charles IV (1322–1328)

Valois Kings

Philip VI (1328–1350)
John II, "the Good" (1350–1364)
Charles V (1364–1380)
Charles VI (1380–1422)
Charles VII (1422--1461)
Louis XI (1461–1483)
Charles VIII (1483–1498)

*Odo, Robert I, and Ralph (by marriage) are members of the family later known as the Capetians.

APPENDIX 5

Kings of England

The Anglo-Saxon Kings

Alfred (871–899)
Edward the Elder (899–924)
Athelstan (924–939)
Edmund (939–946)
Eadred (946–955)
Eadwig (955–959)
Edgar the Peaceable (959–975)
Edward the Martyr (975–978)
Ethelred the Unready (978–1016)
Edmund Ironside (1016)
Canute (1016–1035)
Harold Harefoot (1035–1040)
Harthacanute (1040–1042)
Edward the Confessor (1042–1066)
Harold Godwinson (1066)

The Norman Kings

William I (the Conqueror)
   (1066–1087)
William II (Rufus) (1087–1100)
Henry I (1100–1135)
Stephen (1135–1154)

The Angevin (Plantagenet) Kings

Henry II (1154–1189)
Richard I (Lion-Hearted) (1189–1199)
John (1199–1216)
Henry III (1216–1272)
Edward I (1272–1307)
Edward II (1307–1327)
Edward III (1327–1377)
Richard II (1377–1399)

The Lancastrian and Yorkist Kings

Henry IV (1399–1413)
Henry V (1413–1422)
Henry VI (1422–1461)
Edward IV (1461–1483)
Edward V (1483)
Richard III (1483–1485)

The First Tudor King

Henry VII (1485–1509)

Picture Credits

Alinari/Art Reference Bureau (pp. 37, 40, 176, 177, 201, 346 top right: Academia, Florence, 346 bottom: Uffuzi, 347)

Alinari/Art Resource (p. 18)

Anderson/Art Reference Bureau (p. 38)

Art Reference Bureau (p. 41)

Bayerische Staatsbibliothek München Clm 4452 fol. 24r (p. 123)

Cleveland Museum of Art: 40.128 Purchase from the J. H. Wade Fund, Bequest of Leonard C. Hanna, Jr. (p. 341 bottom)

Dresden Museum (p. 345)

Fox, Edward, *Atlas of European History,* Oxford Press (p. 50)

Giraudon/Art Resource (p. 134)

Heidelberg Universitatsbibliothek/Art Reference Bureau (p. 158)

Louvre: Cliche des Musées, Nationaux (p. 342)

Marburg/Art Reference Bureau (pp. 43, 75, 267, 268 top and bottom, 269, 270, 271, 339, 340, 341 top, 346 top left)

Marburg/Art Resource (pp. 62, 85, 91, 272, 273)

New York Public Library (p. 275)

Omirkon/Photo Researchers (p. 16)

Palais Synodale, Sens, France (p. 274)

Peters, Edward, *The World of the Middle Ages,* p. 263, reprinted by permission of Prentice-Hall, Inc., Englewood Cliffs, N. J. (p. 130)

Sandak, Inc. (p. 337)

Sandak, Inc./Courtesy of Professor Whitney S. Stoddard (p. 338)

C. Warren Hollister (pp. 116, 253)

Index